SLOCUM HOLLOW (NOW SCRANTON) IN 1840.

HISTORY

of the

LACKAWANNA VALLEY

WITH
ILLUSTRATIONS

― FIFTH EDITION ―
Revised and Enlarged

H. Hollister, M.D.

HERITAGE BOOKS
2011

HERITAGE BOOKS
AN IMPRINT OF HERITAGE BOOKS, INC.

Books, CDs, and more—Worldwide

For our listing of thousands of titles see our website
at
www.HeritageBooks.com

A Facsimile Reprint
Published 2011 by
HERITAGE BOOKS, INC.
Publishing Division
100 Railroad Ave. #104
Westminster, Maryland 21157

Entered according to Act of Congress, in the year 1869,
by H. Hollister, M.D.
In the Clerk's Office of the District Court of the United States,
for the Southern District of New York

Copyright © 1885 H. Hollister, M.D.

Index Copyright © 1998 Heritage Books, Inc.

— Publisher's Notice —
In reprints such as this, it is often not possible to remove blemishes from the original. We feel the contents of this book warrant its reissue despite these blemishes and hope you will agree and read it with pleasure.

International Standard Book Numbers
Paperbound: 978-1-55613-166-0
Clothbound: 978-0-7884-8617-3

PREFACE

TO THE FIRST EDITION.

In presenting to the public these " Contributions," it seems proper to state that the collection of the embodied facts was more the result of the love possessed by the writer for such incidents and history, than the hope of either a pecuniary reward, or a literary reputation.

Becoming familiar with a few features in the history of the Lackawanna Valley, the writer was induced, by the solicitations of his friends, to put them into a shape whereby their publication might possibly awaken an interest, or perhaps elicit new and more connected material from a region where nothing yet had been done in the way of gathering its local history.

From the absence of a proper and continued record—from indistinct and often conflicting memories—and from the death of all who were familiar with its earliest settlement, it is very probable that events narrated are sometimes given in an imperfect, and even in an inaccurate manner. It would not be surprising if such was the fact; but the reader must bear in mind that not only the personal, but the general history recorded here was written while the author was engaged in a large practice, and harassed by all the continual anxieties occurring in one of the most exhausting and thankless professions in the country.

While the author asks no indulgence from this circumstance, yet he apprehends that a practice of twelve years, with its too often accompanying annoyances—compelled to view human nature in every possible light, and encounter it in its most humiliating aspect—eminently fits him to bear the murmurs of those who suppose that a volume can be as easily *written* as *read*.

None of the Sketches are arranged in chronological order; many are necessarily brief, meager, and unsatisfactory, owing to the great dearth of material; while some, it is possible, do better justice to the subject.

It would have given pleasure to the writer, to have presented a genealogical view of the original families in the valley; but as this contemplated feature would necessarily have enlarged the volume beyond its intended limits, without adding much to its *general* interest, it was abandoned.

The obligations of the writer are due to all his friends, who have, by their liberal subscriptions to the volume, manifested such an interest in its welfare.

H. HOLLISTER.

Providence, Pa., 1857.

THE volume, of which a second edition is now published, has been so thoroughly modified and revised in its general outline, as to present the features of a different, and, I trust, a better work than the preceding one. Very many pages have been wholly obliterated; the remainder re-written and radically changed, while a number of pages of interesting historical matter—sought after from trustworthy records and testimony with an earnestness that possibly may deserve expressions of approbation and success—have been added thereunto.

In my former volume, I gave but a *general* recognition of the favors of my friends, who, in various ways, contributed toward its successful development. In this, I desire to return especial thanks to several persons whose manly sympathies and generous aid lay me under a grateful obligation and remembrance.

PREFACE.

For materials drawn from the Pennsylvania Archives and Colonial Records, and other authorities, appropriate acknowledgment appears in its proper place. In addition to these sources of information, fully noted and credited, I would return thanks to G. B. NICHOLSON, ESQ., for access to the Westmoreland Records; to B. H. THROOP, M. D., for valuable suggestions in regard to the volume; to SELDEN T. SCRANTON, of Oxford Furnace, N. J., for acts of friendship which characterize his desire to make every man's pathway blossom with the rose; to S. B. STURDEVANT, M. D., for favors which were given in so cheerful a manner as to greatly enhance their value; to the Rev. Dr. PECK, for the biographical sketch of the late Hon. GEORGE W. SCRANTON; to Hon. STEUBEN JENKINS, whose antiquarian knowledge promises to the world an invaluable *documentary* history of Gen. SULLIVAN's celebrated Wyoming expedition in 1770; to STEPHEN ROGERS and D. YARINGTON, for papers concerning the settlement of Carbondale; to N. ORR & Co., of New York, and EUGENE FRANK, of Wilkes Barre, for their skillful execution of the cuts adorning the work, and to HARPER & BROTHERS, for the sale and use of electrotypes, illustrating scenes in the Lackawanna Valley.

The author of the following pages, who was not born upon the banks of the Lackawanna, but was nurtured among her mountains, would do injustice to his own feelings did he not gratefully acknowledge the kind, yet undeserved, encomiums of the editorial fraternity, and the favorable reception the community gave his "Contributions" in 1857. May he not indulge in the hope that the young valley is not now less athletic and friendly than then?

H. HOLLISTER.

Providence, Pa., 1869.

LIST OF ILLUSTRATIONS.

	PAGE
SLOCUM HOLLOW IN 1840,	FRONTISPIECE.
CAMPBELL'S LEDGE,	26
INDIAN MAP OF CAPOUSE,	31
BALD MOUNT,	65
IRA TRIPP,	125
MONOCASY ISLAND,	169
BLOODY ROCK,	170
JOHN B. SMITH,	209
NAY-AUG FALLS,	212
THE OLD SLOCUM HOUSE,	219
WM. HENRY,	225
SELDEN T. SCRANTON,	241
JOSEPH H. SCRANTON,	245
B. H. THROOP, M. D.,	249
SCRANTON IN 1860,	261
FIRST BAPTIST CHURCH IN CARBONDALE,	299
FIRST LOCOMOTIVE RUN IN AMERICA,	354
THOS. DICKSON,	361
DELAWARE WATER GAP,	389
HON. JOHN BRISBIN,	391
HON. GEORGE W. SCRANTON,	405

	PAGE
Henry Roberts, M. D.,	411
H. Hollister,	418
L. A. Watres,	445
Dr. Silas B. Robinson,	459
Lewis Pughe,	467
The Riot in Scranton,	475
Archbald in 1844,	491
Wm. Merrifield,	495
E. Merrifield,	515

CONTENTS.

INDIAN HISTORY OF WYOMING.
Traditions regarding a great tyrant on the Susquehanna in 602—The Five Nations controlling the war-paths in the valley in 1640—The extent of their sachemship—The Monseys stroll along the Lackawanna about 1700—Teedyuscung and his Delaware tribe ordered to Wyoming—Visit of Count Zinzendorf to Wyoming—Dr. Gill's account of his visit—Journey of Conrad Weiser to "Woyamock" in 1754—"Spies" reported here—The Delaware Indian Village of *Asserughney*, near Campbell's Ledge—*Adjouqua*—A fort to be built at *Adjouqua* (mouth of the Lackawanna) at the request of the Six Nations in 1756—Interesting scrap of history.................17–29

INDIAN VILLAGE OF CAPOOSE.
Capoose, a contemporary of Teedyuscung, sells his lands in New Jersey, migrates to the Lackawanna and makes his "smoke" upon its bank—Is visited in 1742 by Count Zinzendorf—Hunting and planting grounds at Capoose—Alienation of the Delaware and Monsey tribes after Braddock's defeat—Gnaddenhutten burned, and Broadhead's plantation on the Delaware laid waste—Indian Congress held in Easton, in October, 1758—Log-houses built at Wyoming for Teedyuscung, by Gov. Penn—Major Parson's description of the Great Sachem while he was "brightening the chain of friendship" at Easton at this time 29–39

LACKAWANNA RIVER AND VALLEY.
Iroquois and Delaware diversity of names, now corrupted into *Lackawanna*—Beauty of the stream and valley—The union of the Lackawanna with the Susquehanna portrayed by the late Mrs. Sigourney...................40–43

WAS WYOMING ONCE A VAST LAKE?
The Kittatinny Mountain now serrated with gaps, forming a dam for the reception of the waters of the Chemung, Chenango, Delaware, and Susquehanna—Ridges *crossing* the great rivers—Interesting views of the celebrated C. F. Volney, Schoolcraft, and Professor Beck—A singular large rock at Pittston out of place—Opinion of the late Hon. Charles Miner and Judge Packer—*Débris* of ocean-life upon the Pocono 2,000 feet above tide water—Probable ancient course of the Susquehanna—Veins of coal obliterated by the agency of water favor the theory—Notches in the Moosic range near Scranton..43–49

WAR-PATHS.
From Asserughney Village to Capoose—One trail leads to the Delaware—The other diverges to Oquago (now Windsor, N. Y.).................49–50

INDIAN SPRING UPON THE MOOSIC MOUNTAIN.
Whites killed by its side in 1778..50–51

CONTENTS.

INDIAN RELICS AND FORTIFICATIONS.
Along the Susquehanna—At the mouth of the Lackawanna—Upon the Moosic—Mound opened at Capoose in 1795—Another found in Covington in 1833, containing vast deposits—Former neglect of scientific men in gathering and preserving Indian implements.................................51–59

INDIAN APPLE-TREE.
Orchard at the wigwams of Capoose a century ago—A single tree still seen by the roadside, bringing forth its fruit............................59–61

BEACON FIRES.
Traces of ancient signal fire-places upon the higher points of the Moosic Mountain, used by the red men at the time of their occupancy of the Lackawanna Forest...61–63

SILVER MINE ON THE LACKAWANNA.
The whites charged by the Indians with carrying off silver ore from Wyoming in canoes, in 1766—Interesting revelation of an old Oneida chief—Three *salt springs*, and three mines, respectively of *silver*, *gold*, and *lead*, reported by him to be located within the boundaries of Wyoming..63–64

GOLD MINE.
Bald Mount—A gold mine supposed to be located at its base—Singular report of a captive concerning it...................................64–67

SALT SPRINGS.
Their location..67–68

LEAD MINE.
Tuscarora Creek—An item of its local history—A reminiscence of Gen. Sullivan's march up the Susquehanna into the Indian empire in 1779....68–70

GENERAL HISTORY.
Wyoming, in its general signification, embracing not only the entire Lackawanna Valley, but all the territory within Provincial limits purchased by the Yankees—Reports of these lands reaching Connecticut, lead to the formation of the *Susquehanna Company* in 1753—Men who were sent out to explore Wyoming are tracked and watched by the Proprietary Government of Pennsylvania—Beauty of the inland settlement—Incipient strife for its possession—Its primary purchase of the Indians in 1754 by the Susquehanna Company and the Delaware Company—Pennsylvania, chagrined at the success of Yankee diplomacy, attempts to intimidate people from New England—Men and women to be shipped to Philadelphia, "men to be imprisoned or compelled to enlist in the Indian War on the Ohio "—Cayuga Indians also threaten the Yankees with savage greeting if they settle at Wyoming—The Moravians fraternize with the Indians at Wyalusing—Preaching at "Waioming and Leck-a-we-ke" (Lackawack) in 1755—Reward offered for Indian scalps—Cochecton settled—Charles Tomson and Christian Frederick Post visit Wyoming and "Lee-haughhunt" in 1758, by order of Governor Penn—Backsinosa with 100 warriors at Lee-haugh-hunt—Country visited and described in 1758 by two Indian interpreters, Moses Titamy and Isaac Hill—Teedyuscung complains of the Yankees along the Delaware—Settlement inaugurated in Wyoming

CONTENTS. 11

PAGE

in 1762—Teedyuscung again complains to the Governor, who makes fair promises—Fruits of the interview—Murder or expulsion of every white person from Wyoming in 1763—Evident complicity of Pennsylvania officials in the massacre—Atrocious butchery of friendly Indians at Lancaster by the whites—John Anderson opens a store at Wyoming in 1766—Original grant of lands to Connecticut and to Wm. Penn—Trenton Decree 70–105

GENERAL HISTORY (CONTINUED).

Purchase of Wyoming lands by Pennsylvania in 1768—Preparations of the Susquehanna Company to make a permanent settlement upon their purchase—Occupancy of the territory by Pennsylvanians—Block-house erected at the mouth of the "Lamawanack" in 1769—Settlers taken prisoners—Names of persons in Pittston "fit for mischief" in 1769–1772—The Lackawanna paths guarded by Pennymites to prevent the Yankees from escaping capture—Westmoreland Records, where are they?—Clearings extended up the Lackawanna—Settler's rights voted—Zebulon Marcy's cabin—Flints and cartridges carried to Wyoming by the Pennymites to tranquilize the "wrangling" inhabitants—Providence settled—General expulsion of the Yankees from the valley by Pennsylvania soldiers..105–121

ISAAC TRIPP.

Emigrates to Wyoming, where he plays a prominent part in its history—Taken prisoner at Capoose—Ira Tripp...............................121–130

WESTMORELAND.

Officially recognized by Connecticut as a portion of its Colony..........130–132

WALLENPAUPACK SETTLEMENT.

Within the jurisdiction of Westmoreland—Its history—Fort erected—Alarm of the inhabitants—They flee from the savages....................132–134

JAMES LEGGETT.

Civilization slowly carried up the Lackawanna—Vote of Congress regarding Wyoming difficulties..134–137

FIRST WAGON ROAD FROM PITTSTON TO THE DELAWARE.

Three shillings per day given men for working upon the road—Importance of the thoroughfare..137–139

MILITARY ORGANIZATION.

Rigid discipline essential to the existence of the young settlement—The inhabitants compelled to train every *fourteen* days—Ear-marks for cattle running at large...139–141

RELIGION, MORALITY AND STILL-HOUSES

First church erected in the central portion of the valley—Bundling—Indians forbidden to have whisky because of the murderous agitation it caused in the forest—Yet still-houses are encouraged by the whites—Eight still or beer houses in Providence in 1798—Recreation of the inhabitants—A committee meet in Wilkes Barre "*at six a Clock in ye forenoon*" to consider the province of "Lickquor"—Causes of its commercial importance....141–148

CONTENTS.

MILLS UPON THE LACKAWANNA 148-149

DR. JOSEPH SPRAUGE.
The first physician in the Lackawanna Valley—"Granny Sprauge' 150-151

DR. WILLIAM HOOKER SMITH—OLD FORGE.
Great surgeon in Gen. Sullivan's Expedition—First purchase of *stone-coal* recorded in Luzerne County, in 1791—Old Forge as described by the late Hon. Charles Miner in a letter to the writer 151-154

THE SIGNAL TREE 154-155

THE WYOMING MASSACRE.
Its cause, character, and consequences—Interesting version of events transpiring immediately before the battle, by a witness still living—But a single habitation left standing in the entire Lackawanna Valley—General Sullivan's Expedition in 1779—"Dried scalps of women and children" found in the wigwams by Col. Hartley—Proposition made to hunt the Indians with horses and *dogs*—Extraordinary adventure and escape 155-171

GENERAL HISTORY—(RESUMED).
Connecticut and Pennsylvania renew the struggle for Wyoming with increased bitterness—The Lackawanna people, turned out of their houses by armed bands urged on by land-jobbers, are treated "excessively cruel"—Every New England emigrant carried to prison and fed on bread and water—Liberated, they return and defy the Pennymites—A bold project of Col. Ethan Allen, John Franklin, and other shrewd Yankees to form a new State out of Wyoming, annihilated by the simple formation of Luzerne County in 1786—The various compromising laws give tranquillity to the settlement 177-186

PROVIDENCE TOWNSHIP AND VILLAGE.
Their general history—Rich lands of Capoose reluctantly vacated by their tawny occupants—Exeter, Providence, and the country north, made into one election district in 1774—Indian apple-tree at Capoose designated as "Ye Town Sign-post"—Meeting of settlers under its branches in 1775, to draw for lots in Putnam Township (now Tunkhannock)—Taxables of Providence Township for the year 1796—Dr. Silas B. Robinson—The "great blow" of 1834 186-205

DUNMORE.
Causes which led to its settlement and expansion—Source of its prosperity—John B. Smith 206-211

HISTORY OF SCRANTON.
The first log-structure erected in Deep Hollow (Scranton)—Philip Abbott gives expression to the necessities of the farmers at Capoose by the erection of a grist-mill upon Roaring Brook in 1788—Unique character of the mill—First bridge across the Lackawanna in 1796—Hyde Park cleared and settled—Dolphs—Dr. Joseph Davis—The Slocums acquire the property and inaugurate *iron-works*—Still-houses and general prosperity around Capoose—The old landmark of Slocum Hollow—Post-office established—Providential escape of Mr. Slocum, in 1808, from a frightful death—The

obliteration of the forge and still in 1826, temporarily suspends the life of Slocum Hollow—Four prominent gentlemen early agitating the interests of the valley—William and Maurice Wurts, Henry W. Drinker, and Wm. Meredith—Their plan to resuscitate the Hollow—A brighter aspect struggling its way into the settlement—Primary impulse toward a village in Scranton, given by the Drinker railroad project—Wm. Henry—Acquisition of the Slocum Hollow property by Messrs. Scrantons, Grant, and Mattes—Inauspicious attempt to start a furnace in Scranton in 1841—Dark period in the history of the iron-works, 1842-3—Joseph H. and E. C. Scranton—Sketch of the different churches in Scranton, from 1841 to the present time, with the names of the pastors—Unfaltering energy of Col. Scranton—Nail factory built below the falls of Nay-aug—Village of Harrison laid out in the woods—Selden T. Scranton—Failure to get a post-office re-established—The year 1846 auspicious in the history of Scranton—Bankruptcy only averted by the Trail—Lively times in the township—Dr. Throop builds a cottage near the swamp—Organization of the iron company—Difficulty of reaching a market for iron—Post-office again established in Scrantonia—Conception of a *locomotive road* westward, by Colonel Scranton—Wyoming House and hotels—Thrift of Scranton—Its newspapers—Description of the iron-works—List of physicians who have lived and practiced their profession within the city limits of Scranton—Its lawyers—Its industrial enterprises—Founderies—Machine-shops—Capouse Works—Sash and blind factory—Stove manufactories—Dickson Manufacturing Company..................................211–268

BLAKELEY.

Its name and general history—Second church in the valley built within its limits...269–273

YANKEE WAY OF PULLING A TOOTH........... 274

THOMAS SMITH....................... 275

SETTLEMENT OF ABINGTON.

The former danger and wildness of Leggett's Gap—Names of settlers...275–282

THE GREAT HUNTER, ELIAS SCOTT.

His encounter with a bear—Great destruction of rattlesnakes..........282–284

"DRINKER'S BEECH"—(*Now Covington*).

Its earliest history—25,000 acres of land purchased by Mr. Drinker in 1788, upon the Pocono—Ascending the narrow Lehigh in a batteau to its upper waters—Names of the first settlers—Drinker's Turnpike............284–288

SETTLEMENT OF JEFFERSON.

Its border traversed by the Yankees—Asa Cobb—A wolf killed by Mrs. Cobb with a pitchfork—Imaginary shire town and county...........288–291

CHASED BY A PANTHER.

Perils of the forest thirty years ago................................291–293

DUNNING.

Pleasant Valley—Barney's Ledge—Hon. A. B. Dunning..............293–295

CONTENTS.

CARBONDALE.

Ragged Islands—Capt. Geo. Rix—The "big flats" chopped and logged off—Unique attire of a woodman—Christopher E. Wilbur—1802-1814—Explorations by Maurice and Wm. Wurts—Dundaff laid out by Mr. Conyngham in 1822—Coal-mine opened—A village emerging from the Carbondale glen—First frame-house erected—Sled-loads of coal drawn twenty miles to the Paupack...295-300

LACKAWANNA VALLEY IN 1804.

Elder John Miller—A general retrospective glance of its inhabitants and its appearance as given by him—Zephaniah Knapp—Development of the valley...300-310

FORMATION OF TOWNSHIPS; PRIMITIVE MINISTERS.

Rev. Jacob Johnson, the first minister in Wyoming—Curious letter—Rev. Wm. Bishop—Hyde Park log church—Habits of the people..........310-314

PROPRIETORS' SCHOOL FUND AND PRIMITIVE SCHOOLS. 314-316

PATHS AND ROADS.

Journey from Connecticut to Pittston in 1793—Little Meadows—Visited in 1793 by Bishop Asbury...317-322

THE RISE OF METHODISM IN THE VALLEY.

Anning Owen—Two distinctive impulses given its development—Rev. Dr. Geo. Peck—Methodist ministers...322-326

SMELLING HELL....................326-328

FORMATION OF ANTHRACITE COAL.

Its vegetable character...328-329

ORGANIC REMAINS FOUND IN THE COAL STRATA.

Their abundance in the Lackawanna Valley.......................329-331

MINERALS AND MINING...............331-332

COAL LANDS FIFTY YEARS AGO.

Worthlessness of *stone*-coal in Slocum Hollow fifty years ago...........332-333

THE DISCOVERY AND INTRODUCTION INTO USE OF ANTHRACITE COAL.

General prejudice against its use—Difficulty of *giving* coal away, and the danger of attempting to *sell* it—Hon. Charles Miner—Jacob Cist—Triumphs of stone-coal—Used up the Lackawanna as a fuel in 1812—Details of interest...333-343

WILLIAM AND MAURICE WURTS.

Their explorations in the coal-fields of the Lackawanna—A trivial incident favors Wm. Wurts in purchasing the wild lands where Carbondale now stands—Hon. Paul S. Preston—First load of coal ever drawn from the Lackawanna shipwrecked in the turbid waters of Jones's Creek—New York and the Lackawanna Valley linked together by the social genius of canal, railroad, and river—Delaware and Hudson Canal Company—The first locomotive-engine in America runs a short distance from Honesdale, in 1828—Achievements of this great company—Thos. Dickson................343-363

CONTENTS.

FALLING IN OF THE CARBONDALE MINES.
Appalling tomb—One mile of slate and rock between the miners and the outer world...................363–367

EARLIEST MAIL ROUTE THROUGH THE VALLEY.
Letter carried to Teedyuscung in 1762......................367–369

THE PENNSYLVANIA COAL COMPANY.
The entrance of this gravity coal-road into the valley vehemently opposed by intriguing men—Its final success...........................369–372

FROM PITTSTON TO HAWLEY.
Fine views from Cobb Mountain—Local history—Cobb's Gap.........372–379

DELAWARE, LACKAWANNA, AND WESTERN RAILROAD.
Historical summary of the Susquehanna and Delaware Canal and Railroad Company—The Leggett's Gap Railroad; now merged into the Delaware, Lackawanna, and Western Railroad—A brief detail of the early struggles of energetic men to connect the Lackawanna with the Delaware—Henry W. Drinker, William Henry, Col. Geo. W. Scranton, John Brisbin, Samuel Sloan...379–393

LACKAWANNA AND BLOOMSBURG RAILROAD.
Crossing Wyoming battle-grounds—Wyoming scenery—Jas. Archibald...393–396

SKETCH OF THE EARLY HISTORY OF THE LEHIGH AND SUSQUEHANNA RAILROAD.
Indian civilizers at Gnaddenhutten (now Weissport) in 1746—Casual discovery of anthracite near Mauch Chunk, gives foetal life to the Lehigh Coal and Navigation Company, and tames the wild waters of the Lehigh—Slackwater navigation—The jealous interest of Wyoming, represented by Hon. Andrew Beaumont, inimical to the Lehigh Coal and Navigation Company—Jealousies allayed and harmony promoted by the company agreeing to build a gravity railroad over the mountain from White Haven to Wilkes Barre—Appalling flood upon the Lehigh in 1862—Locomotives descend from the mount into Wyoming—Grandeur of the mountain view—John Leisenring—John P. Ilsley...........................396–403

HON. GEORGE W. SCRANTON.
A sketch of his life, and an estimate of his moral character, by Rev. Dr. Peck..403–410

LEHIGH VALLEY RAILROAD.
The high ridge separating the Lehigh from the Lackawanna, receives another diadem of iron—Hon. Asa Packer—The commercial greatness and importance of this thoroughfare, fraternizing with the Delaware, Lehigh, and upper Susquehanna.....................................410–417

CONTENTS.

APPENDIX.

I.

Indian relic controversy—Wyoming fair 419–442

II.

The Lackawanna Valley fifty years ago and now 443
The churches of Scranton 444
Our school system 448
Health of the valley 449
Our charities—The Lackawanna and Moses Taylor Hospitals 449
Deaf and Dumb Institution 450
Home of the Friendless 451
Board of Trade 452
Our water 452
The lakes of the county 453
Precipices 453
Building development 454
Fire department 455
Mayors and the judiciary 455
Our physicians 458
The Delaware and Hudson Canal Company 458
Coal waste and coal-breakers 462
Henry Roberts, M.D 465
Hon. Lewis Pughe 466
The strikes 470
The Thirteenth Regiment 477
An industrial point 479
The industries of Scranton—The Dickson Manufacturing Company 480
Scranton Brass- and File-Works 484
Scranton City Foundry 484
Planing-mills—Providence 485
Scranton Stove-Works 485
Green Ridge 486
Scranton Glass Company 487
Green Ridge Iron-Works 487
Up the valley—Carbondale 488
Soldiers' Monument—Van Bergen & Co.'s Works 489
Jermyn—Jermyn Coffin- and Casket-Works—Moosic Powder-Works ... 490
Archbald in 1844 491
Knitting-Factory 492
Winton 492
Peckville 493
Olyphant 493
Price—Dickson City 494
The inception of Lackawanna County 497
Laying of the Corner-Stone 501
Speech of Alfred Hand 502
General History, by E. Merrifield 507
The Banquet: Gentlemen present—Speeches of Judge Woodward, Judge Jessup, Colonel Boies, J. F. Connolly, A. B. Dunning, W. W. Scranton, J. E. Barrett, E. P. Kingsbury, T. H. Dale, R. H. McKune, F. J. Fitzsimmons, Chas. Scranton, J. J. Albright, John Jermyn, Isaac C. Price 511–547
The Scranton Poor-House 548

HISTORY OF THE LACKAWANNA VALLEY.

INDIAN HISTORY.

THE Indian's side of history can never be written, because traditions running back through centuries, and cherished only by the red man whom they concerned, perished with the race that knew them. We shall read of homes reddened by the tomahawk or charred by the fagot, but not of the wrongs urging the wild man to defend the spot where his wigwam stood. When the plain cabins of the Dutch first rose on the banks of the Hudson, all the Indians "on the Connecticut, Hudson, Delaware, and Susquehanna rivers, were in subjugation to the Five Nations,"[1] whose capital near the placid waters of the Onondaga Lakes, lay but a day's walk or two from the head-springs of the Lackawanna.

In 1827, Cusick published traditions of the Tuscaroras running from "twenty-five hundred winters before Columbus's discovery of America" down to the days of Mahomet. "About the time of Mahomet's career in 602, a great Tyrant arose on the *Kaunaseh*, now Susquehanna River, who waged war with the surrounding nations, from which it appears that while in Africa, Europe, and Asia revolution succeeded revolution, empires rose on the ruins of empires, that in America the same scenes were acting on as great a scale—cultivated regions, populous cities and towns, were reduced to a wilderness, as in the other countries."[2]

---

[1] Smith's History of New York.   [2] American Antiquities, sec. ed., p. 349.

The Mohawks, asserting sovereignty over the proud Pequots and Narragansetts, numbering many hundred warriors, and exacting tribute from all the New England tribes as late as the sixteenth century, claimed the wilderness from the Connecticut to Wyoming. Massasoit, the ever warm friend of the Pilgrims, and his son Philip, afterward celebrated as King Philip, had frequent conflicts with this haughty, powerful tribe. The Dutch gave them the name of *Maquos*.[1] The French, between whom war was almost perpetual, called them Iroquois.[2]

When Captain John Smith was carried prisoner to the castle of Powhatan, in 1607, he learned that the "Sasque-sah-ha-noughs" (Susquehanna Indians), living upon the river by this name, "are a Gyant like people and are thus atyred," giving in his work a graphic illustration of a chief "atyred" in all the gorgeous style of the wild man.

The Confederation known as the Six Nations, formed by the union of Mohawks, Senecas, Onondagos, Oneidas, Cayugas, and the Tuscaroras, was not only formidable in the number of its warriors, but so democratic in the character of its organization, and so terrible in the exercise of its power, that few new settlements, made along the frontier, acquired either growth or age without harm or apprehension. Its power was absolute and unquestioned; its government a limited monarchy. This was vested in a Great Sachem or Chief, directed by a Council of Braves and aged warriors noted for wisdom and bravery. Its ever-burning *Council Fire* blazed from the plains of

---

[1] This word, derived from *moho*, signifies to eat.—Roger Williams. Or Mohawks signifies cannibals or *man-eaters*, among other tribes of Indians.—Trumbull, U. S., pp. 1–4; Hutchinson, vol. i., p. 405. This tribe was situated along the Mohawk, and from it took its name, and was one of the powerful Five Nations who in 1713 were joined by the Tuskaroras, a large tribe from North Carolina, and thence known by the name of Six Nations.—Williamson's North Carolina, vol. i., p. 202. Hon. De Witt Clinton, in N. Y. Hist. Soc. Col., vol. ii., p. 48, says that the Tuskaroras joined the other nations in 1712.

[2] N. Y. Hist. Col., vol. ii., p. 44.

Oh-na-qu-go, while the edicts and wishes of the assembled sachems, carried to Manhattan's shore by runners, were known and respected even in the far-off region of the magnolia and palmetto. With a dialect whose strange intonations bewildered the ear of the white man, and whose tongue, destitute of labials, was so diverse and corrupted from the parent language, that many of the tribes living on the same stream could only converse through an interpreter;[1] with neither books nor charts, with no history but the wigwam's lore, no guide but the moon's gray twilight, no valley was sunk too far away in the mountains, no stream stretched its tranquil length through grounds too remote from the war-path to escape the notice of men clad in skins, who occupied and gave them a name.

Charles Miner, in his really unequaled and charming *History of Wyoming*, remarks, with truth, that, "in unraveling the tangled web of Indian history, we found ourselves in the outset extremely embarrassed, especially when reading the pages of Heckewelder and other writers of the United Brethren. The removal of tribes or parts of tribes to the valley; their remaining a brief period and then emigrating to some other place, without any apparent motive founded in personal convenience, consistency, or wisdom, perplexed us exceedingly, as we doubt not it has others."

The forest between the Hudson and Lake Huron constituted the sachemship of the Iroquois, or Five Nations, whose "smokes" ascended from the mountains of Vermont to the head-waters of the Delaware, Susquehanna, and the Ohio. The number of their warriors in 1660 was estimated by Chalmers to have been twenty-two hundred, while Bancroft puts the figure at ten thousand. Their language, spoken by the Pequods, the Narragansetts, the Mohawks, and Delawares, was the mother-tongue that

[1] Jefferson.

welcomed the Pilgrims[1] and plead for Smith on the Chickahominy, through the fervid lips of Pocahontas. Between the Delaware and the Susquehanna, in the narrow, green plateau of the Lackawanna, dwelt a division of the Lenni-Lenape—the Minsi or Monsey clan, which, like the tribes at Wyoming, stripped of their glory by the Iroquois, melted away into other tribes strolling through the wilderness as conquerors. The Senecas and Oneidas, two of the rudest, most vindictive, as well as energetic members of the confederated Nations, took the most prominent part in the affairs of Wyoming. Their villages were strung around the lesser lakes feeding Ontario, while their seat of government was located at Onondaga, now Syracuse.

"The Onondagos," writes Miner, "were eminent as counselors, distinguished for eloquence, perhaps revered, like the tribe of Levi, as the priesthood of the confederacy, to whose care was committed the keeping or kindling the *sacred fire* around which their most solemn deliberations were held." After the Senecas and Oneidas, whose camp-fires gave a savage cheer to Wyoming as early as 1640,[2] had removed to the land of the Iroquois, feebler tribes, which had lost favor with the civil sachems or the great war chiefs, were concentrated in this lovely region under the immediate eye and reach of royal prerogative.

Thus came the Shawnees from southern everglades, whose names are yet affixed to the lower portion of Wyoming Valley, and thus the Nanticokes, in 1748, came from the *Chesakawon* on the Chesapeake, and found shelter on the Susquehanna until their removal to Onondaga in 1755. The Delawares, of whom Teedyuscung was long the leading sachem, playing an important part in the history of Wyoming, taunted as women and treated as vassals, were *ordered* by the Six Nations, in the most imperious manner, into this valley in 1742.

[1] Bancroft. [2] Miner.

At a great Council held at Philadelphia, July 12, 1742, where over two hundred warriors were assembled to *talk* with the Governor of Pennsylvania, in regard to the transgressions of the Delawares, who had sold lands on the river Delaware fifty years before, and who had refused to remove from the same, Canassategoe addressed them thus :—

"Cousins, you ought to be taken by the hair of your head and shak'd severely till you recover your senses and become sober. Our Brother Onas'[1] case is very just and plain and his Intentions to preserve friendship; on the other Hand your Cause is bad, your Heart far from being upright, and you are maliciously bent to break the Chain of friendship with our Brother Onas. But how came you to take upon you to Sell Land at all? We conquered You, we made Women of you; you know you are Women, and can no more sell Land than Women. You have been furnished with Cloaths and Meat and Drink by the Goods paid you for it, and now You want it again like Children as you are. Did you ever tell Us that you had sold this Land in the Dark? did we ever receive any Part, even the Value of a Pipe Shank, from you for it? You have told Us a Blind Story that you sent a Messenger to Us to inform Us of the Sale, but he never came amongst Us, nor we never heard any thing about it. This is acting in the Dark, and very different from the Conduct our Six Nations observe in their Sales of Land. On such Occasions they give Publick Notice and invite all the Indians of their united Nations, and give them a share of the Presents they receive for their Lands. This is the behaviour of the wise United Nations, but we find you are none of our Blood. You Act a dishonest part not only in this but in other Matters. Your Ears are ever Open to Slanderous Reports about our

---

[1] Penn received from the Indians the name of ONAS—*i. e.*, quill or pen, from the fact that he governed by these instead of guns.

Brethren. For all these we charge *You to remove instantly.* We don't give you the liberty to think about it. You are Women; take the Advice of a Wise Man and remove immediately. You may return to the other side of the Delaware where you came from, but we don't know whether Considering how you have demean'd yourselves, you will be permitted to live there, or whether you have not swallowed that Land down your Throats as well as the Land on this side. We, therefore, Assign you two Places to go to—either to *Wyomin* or *Shamokin.* You may go to either of these Places, and then we shall have you more under our Eye, and shall see how You behave. Don't deliberate, but remove away and take this Belt of Wampum."[1]

This peremptory command, given in such a haughty and offensive manner, admitting of no evasion or appeal, was obeyed by the Delawares, who at once repaired to the Wyoming hunting-grounds. "Such," says Chapman, "was the origin of the Indian town of Wyoming. Soon after the arrival of the Delawares, and during the same season (the summer of 1742), a distinguished foreigner, Count Zinzendorf, of Saxony, arrived in the Valley on a religious mission to the Indians. This nobleman is believed to have been the first white person that ever visited Wyoming. He was the reviver of the ancient church of the United Brethren, and had given protection in his dominions to the persecuted Protestants who had emigrated from Moravia, thence taking the name of *Moravians*, and who, two years before, had made their first settlement in Pennsylvania.

"Upon his arrival in America, Count Zinzendorf manifested a great anxiety to have the Gospel preached to the Indians; and although he had heard much of the ferocity of the Shawanese, formed a resolution to visit them. With this view he repaired to *Tulpehocken*, the residence

---

[1] Col. Rec., vol. iv., pp. 579-80.

of Conrad Weiser, a celebrated interpreter and Indian agent for the Government, whom he wished to engage in the cause, and to accompany him to the Shawanese town.

"Weiser was too much occupied in business to go immediately to Wyoming, but he furnished the Count with letters to a missionary of the name of Mack, and the latter, accompanied by his wife, who could speak the Indian language, proceeded immediately with Zinzendorf on the projected mission.

"The Shawanese appeared to be alarmed on the arrival of the strangers, who pitched their tents on the banks of the river a little below the town, and a council of the chiefs having assembled, the declared purpose of Zinzendorf was deliberately considered. To these unlettered children of the wilderness, it appeared altogether improbable that a stranger should have braved the dangers of a boisterous ocean, three thousand miles broad, for the sole purpose of instructing them in the means of obtaining happiness *after death*, and that, too, without requiring any compensation for his trouble and expense; and as they had observed the anxiety of the white people to purchase land of the Indians, they naturally concluded that the real object of Zinzendorf was either to procure from them the lands at Wyoming for his own use, to search for hidden treasures, or to examine the country with a view to future conquests. It was accordingly resolved to assassinate him, and to do it privately, lest the knowledge of the transaction should produce a war with the English, who were settling the country below the mountains.

"Zinzendorf was alone in his tent, seated upon a bundle of dry weeds, which composed his bed, and engaged in writing, when the assassins approached to execute their bloody commission. It was night, and the cool air of September had rendered a small fire necessary to his comfort and convenience. A curtain formed of a blanket and hung upon pins, was the only guard to the entrance of his tent.

"The heat of his fire had aroused a large rattlesnake which lay in the weeds not far from it ; and the reptile, to enjoy it more effectually, crawled slowly into the tent, and passed over one of his legs undiscovered. Without, all was still and quiet, except the gentle murmur of the river at the rapids about a mile below. At this moment the Indians softly approached the door of his tent, and slightly removed the curtain, contemplated the venerable man, too deeply engaged in the subject of his thoughts to notice either their approach, or the snake which lay extended before him. At a sight like this, even the heart of a savage shrunk from the idea of committing so horrid an act, and quitting the spot, they hastily returned to the town, and informed their companions that the *Great Spirit* protected the white man, for they had found him with no door but a blanket, and had seen a large rattlesnake crawl over his legs without attempting to injure him. This circumstance, together with the arrival soon afterward of Conrad Weiser, procured Zinzendorf the friendship and confidence of the Indians, and probably contributed essentially toward inducing many of them, at a subsequent period, to embrace the Christian religion.

"The Count having spent twenty days at Wyoming returned to Bethlehem, a town then building by his Christian brethren on the north bank of the Lehigh, about eleven miles from its junction with the Delaware."[1]

In the recently published life of Count Zinzendorf, by Dr. Gill, of London, this visit, as well as the character of the Indians at Wyoming, are thus described. "The Count as missionary to give these Indians a practicable insight into the religion he came to teach, by simply lead-

---

[1] Miner's Wyoming, p. 39.

ing a Christian life amongst them, and when favorable impressions had thus been made and inquiry was excited, he preached the leading truths of the gospel, taking care, not to put more things into their heads than their hearts could lay hold of. His mode of approaching them was carefully adapted to their distinctive peculiarities; his last tour, in the autumn of 1742, after crossing the primeval forest, he pitched his tent a short distance from 'Wayomick' the capital of the Shawanos, and remained there three weeks, observing the habits of the people, and conversing with them, so as to make himself familiar with their ideas, before he proceeded more directly with the special object of his mission. He found this tribe to be one of the most corrupt and most opposed to the truth. They soon concerted violent measures to get rid of him, and would have killed him and his companions, but that his interpreter, in whose absence the murder was to have been committed, returned unexpectedly and discovered the plot. Such was the form in which these poor savages manifested their hatred to a man whose motives they could not comprehend, and whom they looked upon as an intruder."

When Conrad Weiser, a celebrated Indian interpreter, visited Wyoming in 1754, he reported that he found but three Indian towns between Shamokin and Wyoming— Os-ko-ha-ny, Nis-ki-beck-on (Nescopeck), and Woyamock.[1] He also reported that the Indians on the Susquehanna had seen some of the New England men that came "as spies to Woyamock last fall, and they saw them making draughts of the land and rivers."[2] The Delawares had built "Woyamock, and twelve miles higher up the river a town called Asserughney, where about twenty Indian Delawares, all *violently against* the *English*"[3] were found at this time.

This village stood between the bold precipice, famed

[1] Col. Rec., vol. vi., p. 35. [2] Ibid. [3] Ibid, p. 66.

the world over as *Campbell's Ledge*, and the mouth of the Lackawanna, on the eastern bank of the Susque-

CAMPBELL'S LEDGE.

hanna.[1] This, like all their villages, was small, as hunt-

[1] Tachneckdorus, a friendly Delaware chief, informed the Governor of Pennsyl-

ing and fishing were the main sources of supporting the population, naturally averse to labor. This high ledge, affording an uninterrupted look-out over the valley below, was used by the Indians not only thus to guard their wigwams, nestled along the river, but to kindle their *beacon-fires* at the evening or midnight hour, as they were wont to be kindled on the Scottish highlands in the days of Wallace and Bruce, to show those who watched the portentous flame the presence of danger, or signal the movements of an enemy.

While *Asserughney* was the Indian name of the town, *Adjouqua* was applied to the lower portion of the Lackawanna Valley. This castle, or encampment, was the upper one of the Delawares in Wyoming. It was a point of importance because of its favorable location for trading purposes. The great war-path from the inland lakes of New York to Wyoming and the South, and the trail down the Lackawanna from the Minisink homes on the Delaware, passed through it. Fur-parties, and dusky chiefs, with their captives, alike followed the solitude of its passage through these true Indian lands.

Capoose village, up the shallow Lackawanna, eight miles from Asserughney, was built a few years previous to this, and occupied by the Monseys, who, like the more numerous Delawares, paid tribute to the Tartars of the western world at Onondaga. These villages were constructed in primitive fashion, from green bark, boughs, and weeds. As the war-paths passed through them, they

---

vania in February, 1756, "that *Neshcopeckon* is deserted upon a rumor that prevailed among them of your coming up with a large number of men to cut them off, and they, the Delawares, fled to Assarockney and higher up, having there a big hill on one side and the Sasquehannah on the other side of the present town." Colonial Records, vol. vii., p. 52. The number of warriors at Asserughney was estimated at two hundred.

In an old map of the country of the Six Nations, made by Guy Johnson in 1771, and found in the Documentary History of New York, vol. iv., p. 1091, a stream is put down in the place of the Lackawanna as *Mac-ha-pon-da* creek. Whether it had reference to Meshoppen or Lackawanna is difficult to determine from the map; probably the former.

were alike threatened by nomadic tribes, espousing the interests of the English or the French. This led the Six Nations, in June, 1756, to depute *Og-ha-gha-disha*, a chief of the Iroquois, living on the north branch of the Susquehanna, to ask the Provincial Council of Pennsylvania to build a fort at the mouth of the Lackawanna. At a Conference held at the camp at Armstrong's, June 10, 1756, between Col. William Claphan and Og-ha-gha-disha, the chief thus addressed the colonel:—

"My Brother: The Iroquois have sent me as a representative of the whole nation to treat with you (producing a belt of wampum), and will ratify all my contracts. Brother: they agreed to your building a fort at Shamokin, but are desirous that you should also build a fort three days' journey in a canoe higher up the North Branch in their country, at a place called *Adjouquay*, and this belt of wampum is to clear the road to that place. Brother: If you agree to my proposal in behalf of my nation, I will return and immediately collect our whole force to be employed in protecting your people while you are building a fort in our country at Adjouquay, where there is a good situation and fine soil at the entrance of a *deep creek* on a level plain five miles extending, and *clear of woods*. Adjouqua is fourteen miles above Wioming,[1] and old women may carry a heavy pack of skins from thence to the Minisink and return to Adjouqua in two nights. My Brother: The Land is troubled, and you may justly apprehend danger, but if you grant our request we will be together, and if any danger happens to you, we will share it with you. My Brother (laying down a belt of wampum folded in the middle):

---

[1] No allusion has ever been made to Adjouquay by Wyoming historians. Assarughney and Adjouquay are both spoken of by different Indians as being ten, twelve, and fourteen miles above Wyoming. This apparent discrepancy arose, not from the fact that miles were measured by *walks*, but that Wyoming was located either at the Delaware, Shawnees, or Nanticoke towns, all crouched along the river *below* the present location of Wilkes Barre.

this describes your path to Shamokin ; unfolding the belt and extending it to its full length, this is your road to Adjouquay."[1] Governor Morris thanked the chief for his kind speech, and in his reply said : " Brother : I am desired to build another fort fourteen miles above Wioming, at a place called Adjouquay. I have agreed to this request, and am taking measures to do it out hand, about which I shall want to consult you."[2]

A line of forts, some twenty miles apart, stretched along the frontier from the Potomac to the Delaware in 1756-58. Stroudsburg, the pretty shire town of the county of Monroe, although taking its name from Colonel Jacob Stroud, who commanded Fort Penn at this point during the Revolutionary war, received a definite step toward a settlement from the presence of one of the most eastern of these outposts, erected in 1757—Fort Hamilton.

INDIAN VILLAGE OF CAPOOSE.—TEEDYUSCUNG.

The low, rich bottom on the western border of the Lackawanna, between Providence and Scranton, was known to the earliest explorers as " Capoose Meadow"— a name probably given to perpetuate the memory of a civil chief, *Capoose*, excelling in the art of agriculture and peace. The Monseys, or a prominent branch of that tribe, left the Minisink and diffused through the Lackawanna Valley, as early as any authentic history comes down to the white man from the Lenni-Lenapes. As this village was visited in 1742 by Count Zinzendorf, who named the county Saint Anthony's Wilderness,[3] its date and occupancy must have been considerably anterior to this. This tribe, rudely gashing the margin of the Lackawanna for the reception of maize as early as 1700, appears originally to have been an off-shoot of the Delawares. Their history

---

[1] Col. Rec., vol. vii., pp. 157-8.   [2] Ibid., p. 159.
[3] Evens' Map of 1747, in Ebling's History of Pennsylvania.

and habits are so assimilated as to indicate a common origin. Both spoke the Algonquin language of the Iroquois—a language abounding in vowels and fertile in dialect—obeyed laws emanating from the same source, and both are intimately associated in colonial and provincial history. The Monseys, like every tribe, scattered along the Susquehanna and its branches, acknowledged the supremacy of the Onondaga head, and were so nomadic in their habits, that the Pennsylvania archives often refer to Monsey warriors from Wickalousin (Wyalusing), Chokonot (Cochecton), and from many other places along the rivers of the Province. When the Delawares moved to Ohio, the Monseys accompanied them, and ultimately dissolved into that conquered nation. Vast tracts of land was claimed by the Monseys and Delawares, who jointly occupied New Jersey, the Schuylkill Basin, and the rich valley of the Delaware in 1646.[1] January 30, 1743, *Capoose* gave to Moses Totomy, a Delaware of some local influence, power of attorney[2] to sell these lands to the whites, or transact any other business with the Government relating to lands claimed by him. The greater portion of these domains were thus sold by Capoose to Governor Penn in October, 1758. Thus the upper border of Adjourquay, exquisite in the beauty of woods veined with springs and creeks, whose waters ran to the sea unruffled save by rock or deer, rich in game and fish, easy of conquest, was selected by Capoose for his home after the English began to encroach upon forest-lands east of the Hudson. The hunting-grounds of Capoose extended down the Lackawanna and Nay-aug, and up the river to its very head-waters. The Scranton race-course is within the ancient border of Capoose; the Diamond mines open upon its western border.

Their burial-place, long since smoothed down by the plow, lay on the high bank of the Lackawanna, a quarter

---

[1] Bancroft.   [2] Pennsylvania Archives, 1758, p. 341.

of a mile above their town, where vast quantities of relics have been found heretofore by the antiquarian. Although the whole valley was familiar with the tawny cabin dwell-

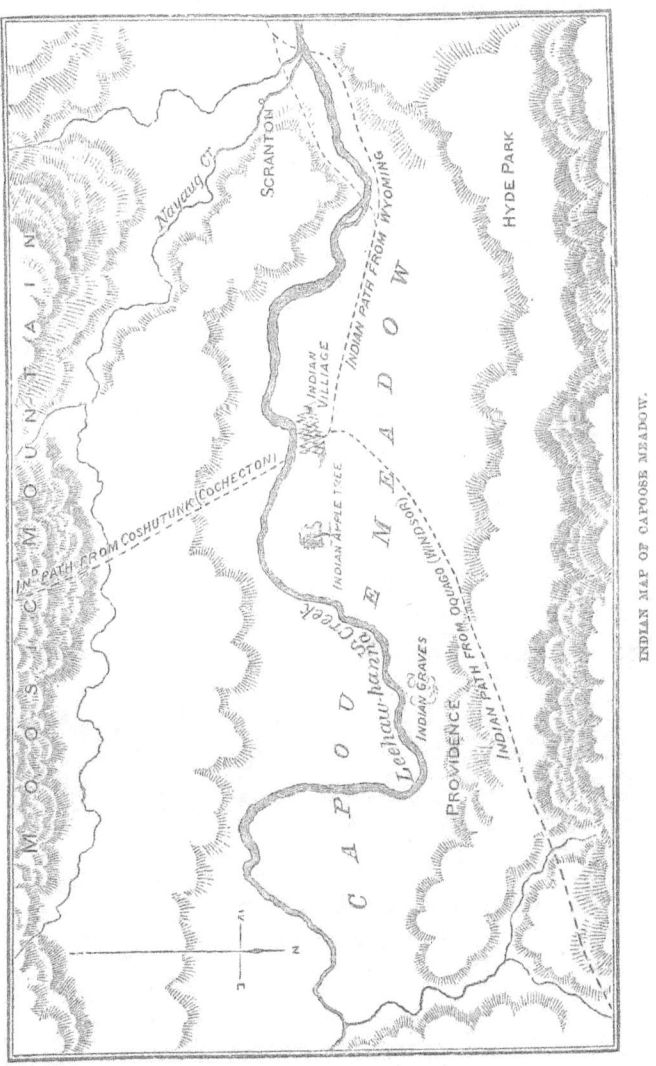

ers, long before the blankness of their lives were marked by the intrusion of the pale-face, ignorant even of the topography of the country, this clearing or meadow of

Capoose, was the main one found in the valley by the pioneer, where the wigwam stood on a cultivated spot. And even here, as the men were too lazy to plant the corn, or secure the scanty harvest, the labor fell upon the more submissive squaws. The Indian artisans were skilled in the art of manufacturing, from flint and stone, implements for agriculture and the chase, elegant arrow-heads and spear points; the rude pebble, and sometimes the rarer silex were shaped into pipes and ornaments of symbolic meaning, while bowls were fashioned from dried clay with an ingenuity never equaled by the white man within the stone period. While their war-path ran along under the sycamore and vine fringing the bank of the Lackawanna, the waters of the stream, sometimes wild in its uprisings, opened a favorite highway for their canoes descending with the silent warriors to the plains of Wyoming.

In accordance with the usual habit practiced by the Indians, of annually burning over their hunting-grounds with a view of destroying the smaller trees in the way of securing game, there was remaining, when the whites appeared, little underbrush to interfere in the chase around Capoose, now known as Tripp's Flats. The forest around it was stocked with game. The pheasant whirred from the brake in conscious security, the duck rode in the stream as if it were its own, the rabbit squatted in the laurel in drowsy attitude, the moose and elk stood among the pines or thundered through them like the tread of cavalry; the deer browsed daintly upon the juicy leaf, while the Moosic slope, unshorn of its foliage, offered to the panther and bear but little shield from the quick poised arrow of the woodsman. The beaver, muskrat, and otter, enlivened the stream in whose waters fish swam in schools. Perch, pike, and even shad, filled the Lackawanna, while every joyous brook from the mountain was spotted with trout. Hooks, constructed with singular ingenuity from bone, or nets woven from the inner bark of trees, or even the stone-tipped spear, which they threw with admirable adroitness at a distance of thirty feet, while the fish were moving rapidly, never failed to supply the wigwam with food.

Capoose himself was a contemporary of Teedyuscung of the Delawares, but so diverse in character and temperament, that while the latter was ambitious for distinction, and prominent in council gatherings, where he jointly looked after the interests of the Monseys and his own tribe, Capoose, undecked with the emblems of war, lived in amity with the whites, encouraged the culture of the soil, and left behind him a name untarnished with either blood or carnage.

Long after the occupancy of this region by Capoose, the Moravians indented a settlement in the Province above the Blue Mountain. On the wild waters of the Mahanoy, where it joins the Lehigh, eighteen miles above Bethlehem, these Indian civilizers encamped in 1743. "Except the erection of the fort," says Miner, "this was the first settlement in a northeast direction in Pennsylvania, above the Kittatinny Ridge or Blue Mountain." This was about forty miles from Wyoming, and the only road intervening was the narrow path of the warrior.

Easton, the shire-town of Northampton County, admirably located for agricultural purposes or traffic with the men who patrolled the forest, laid out for a village in 1750, and Lower Smithfield, on the Delaware, above the present village of Stroudsburg, had but a few clearings opened in 1751, occupied by Charles Broadhead, Samuel Dupue, John McMichael, John Carmeckle, John Anderson, James Tidd, Job Bakehorn, and Henry Dysert. These were held under proprietory auspices. No attempt had yet been made to settle Wyoming or Lackawanna. The hunter and trapper coveting furs, more bold than the emigrant, unwilling to risk his life for a doubtful home, had ventured hither, but the French and Indian wars of this period arrested explorations, and sent alarm into every inland settlement within the Province.

Braddock's defeat in 1755, disastrous especially to western Pennsylvania, illuminated the whole frontier with burning cabins. The French, promising large rewards for scalps to those they assured should again be reinstated upon lands already sold the English, readily won over the red-men, of whom thirty were reported at Wyoming, November 9, 1755, and "much larger bodies up the river and branches."[1]

The Indians, never slumbering, but ever ready to sway to and fro, as success alternated with either party, indulging in the hope that the English might be expelled from their former plains, entered into an alliance with the French with extraordinary zeal and readiness. Gnaddenhutten was burned in 1755 by "a band of Indians coming *from* Wyoming,"[2] and the plantations of Mr. Broadhead, some twenty-five or thirty miles from Bethlehem, of Frederick Heath on *Pocho Pochto* Creek, and Mr. Calvers, McMichael's, and "houses and families thereabouts were attacked by the Indians at daylight and burnt down by them."[3] Mr. Broadhead estimated the number of warriors at two hundred. This attack upon the settlement was marked by the same atrocity characterizing much of the border warfare.[4] As all the Susquehanna and Lackawanna Indians except the Monseys were disposed for peace in the spring of 1757,[5] Mr. Miner concludes that the Oneidas and Senekas from the lakes formed the war party. Hostilities had been suspended against the Delawares living "on the *east side* of the northeast branch of the Susquehanna,"[6] when they were complained of as being the most troublesome, and of whom Conrad Weiser reported in December, 1755, as being alienated from the English and living at Schantowano (Wayomack) in a town called Nescopeckon.

Had not the Wyoming Indians caught the war spirit

---

[1] Col. Rec., vol. vi., p. 752.   [2] Christian Library.   [3] Col. Rec., vol. vi, p. 752.
[4] Ibid., p. 759.   [5] Ibid., p. 506.   [6] Pennsylvania Archives, 1748–1756, p. 668.

at the war-dance, there certainly would have been no necessity for *desiring* peace on one side, or the suspension of hostilities on the other. Instead of being the above-named tribes alone, it is probable that the Delawares, exasperated by the sale of Wyoming lands to Connecticut people, or the Monseys, not yet desiring peace, issuing from the wigwams of Capoose, were jointly guilty of this murderous breach of good faith toward the United Brethren.

In 1757, Teedyuscung, the proud, jealous head of the Delawares, requested the Governor of Pennsylvania to so fix and define his land around his village on the Susquehanna that "his children can never sell or yours ever buy them," and to remain so forever. He also asked the Proprietary Government to assist him in building houses at Wyoming before corn-planting time. Ten log houses, "twenty feet by fourteen in the clear, and one twenty-four by sixteen, of squared logs, and dovetailed,"[1] were built for him in 1758. To check or crush the ambitious projects of New England men about forming a colony at Wyoming, influenced their erection by Pennsylvania quite as much as any especial regard for the Delaware sachem.[2] One of the masons was killed and scalped by six hostile Indians while engaged at this labor.

A treaty of peace was held at Easton, November 8, 1756, with great pomp and ceremony, when the conflicting interests of either party were long *talked* over and harmoniously adjusted amid the clattering of tongues and the smoke of the calumet. To cripple the French, against whom the English had formally proclaimed war in 1756, or rather to render the treaty of any practical value, the Iroquois, proud of their strength, never wielded in vain, and conscious of the wrongs of their fathers, they were impatient to redress, had first to be reconciled and consulted. "The influence of Sir William Johnson," says

---

[1] Pa. Arch., 1758, p. 8. [2] Col. Rec., 1754, p. 60.

Miner, "agent of Indian affairs, was invoked to bring the Six Nations to a new Congress. Neither presents nor promises were spared, and in October, 1758, there was opened at Easton, one of the most imposing assemblages ever beheld in Pennsylvania. Chiefs from the Six Nations were there, namely, Mohawks, Oneidas, Onondagas, Cayugas, Senecas, and Tuscaroras. There were also present embassadors from the tributary tribes of Minisinks, Mohicans, Wapingers, and Shawanese. Both the Governors of Pennsylvania and New Jersey attended; with Sir William Johnson and George Crogan, Esq., sub Indian agent, a deputation from the Provincial Assembly at New Jersey, and a large concourse of eminent citizens from Philadelphia and the neighboring counties. Teedyuscung on the way to the conference having fallen in company with the chief who had commanded the expedition against the Gnadenhutten and Fort Allen, high words arose between them, when the king raised his tomahawk and laid the chief dead at his feet. From this moment, though vengeance might slumber, he was a doomed man, a sacrifice alike to policy and revenge. At the Congress Teedyuscung, eloquent and of imposing address, took at first a decided lead in the debates." But one of the chiefs of the Six Nations, says Chapman, "on the other side, expressed in strong language his resentment against the British colonists, who had killed and imprisoned one of his tribe, and he, as well as other chiefs of those nations, took great umbrage at the importance assumed by Teedyuscung, whom, as one of the Delawares, they considered in some degree subject to their authority. Teedyuscung, however, supported the high station which he held, with dignity and firmness, and the different Indian tribes at length became reconciled to each other. The conference having continued eighteen days, and all causes of misunderstanding between the English and Indians being removed, a general treaty of peace was concluded on the twenty-sixth day of October. At this treaty the boundaries of the different purchases made from the Indians were more particularly described, and they received an additional compensation for their lands, consisting of knives, hats, caps, looking-glasses, tobacco-boxes, shears, gun-locks, combs, clothes, shoes, stockings, blankets, and several suits of laced clothes for their chieftains, and when the business of the treaty was completed, the stores of rum were opened and distributed to the Indians, who soon exhibited a scene of brutal intoxication."

Although for many years afterward, the tomahawk hung over the Lackawanna and Susquehanna settlements like a shadow over the mountain, the decline of the Indian empire in America can be dated from the last-mentioned treaty, while the power of the hitherto victorious French, then marching through the forest with General Forbes to attack Fort Du Quesne, was so suddenly shaken by the desertion of their allies, as to result in their defeat in this expedition, and their final overthrow in Northern America.

During this year, many of the Delawares and Monseys, and most of the Shawanese removed from the valley westward.

When Teedyuscung visited Easton, in July, 1756, Major Parsons was requested to keep a written memoranda of the general behavior and conversation of the king, from which it would seem that the high position assumed and maintained by him in Council, was hardly compatible or consistent with his ordinary life. "The king and his wild company were perpetually drunk, very much on Gascoon, and at times abusive to the inhabitants, for they all spoke English more or less. The king was full of himself, saying frequently, that which side soever *he* took must stand, and the other fall; repeating it with insolence, that he came from the French, who had pressed him much to join them against the English, that now he was in the middle between the French and English, quite disengaged from both sides, and whether he joined with the English or French, he would publish it aloud to the world, that all nations might know it. That he was born among the English, somewhere near Trenton, and is near fifty years old. He is a lusty, raw-boned man, haughty, and very desirous of respect and command ; he can drink three quarts or a gallon of rum a day, without being drunk ; he was the man that persuaded the Delawares to go over to the French, and then attack our frontiers, and he, and those with him, have been concerned in the mischief done to the inhabitants of Northampton County. Some of the Indians said, that between forty or fifty of their people came to Drahoga, from one of the lakes, about the time they set out, in order to fall upon our inhabitants, and addressed Teedyuscung to head them, but he told them he was going to the Governor of Pennsylvania to treat with him concerning a peace, which the Mohocks had advised him to do, and therefore he ordered them to sit still till he came back again to them. The towns people observed that the shirts which the Indian women had on were made of Dutch table-cloths, which it is supposed they took from the people they murdered on our frontiers. The king, in one of his conversations, said, that only two hundred French, and about eighty Indians were at the lake, where most of the English are, and that he could bring the most or all of them off. The Governor invited Teedyuscung and the Indians to dine with him, but, before dinner, the king, with some of them, came to the Governor, and made the Governor four speeches, giving four strings of wampum, after the Indian manner : one to brush thorns from the Governor's legs, another to rub the dust out of his eyes to help him see clearly, another to open his ears and the fourth to clear his throat that he might speak plainly. Teedyuscung claimed to be king of ten nations. Being asked what ten nations, he answered, the united Six Nations : Mohocks, Onondagoes, Oneidas, Senecas, Cyugas, and Tuscaroras ;

and four others, Delawares, Shawanees, Mohickons, and Munsies, who would all ratify what he should do. He carried the Belt of Peace with him, and whoever would, might take hold of it. But as to them that refused, the rest would all join together and fall upon them.

"All the Indians, in short, would do as he would have them, as he was the great man. The Governor used the same four ceremonies to Teedyuscung, accompanied with four strings of wampum, after which the Governor and Indians went to dinner, escorted by a detachment of the First Battalion of the Pennsylvania Regiment."[1] Conrad Weiser, the interpreter, was first introduced to Teedyuscung at this time, who, after watching his movements a single day, reported to the Council "that the king and the principal Indians being all yesterday under the force of liquor, he had not been favored with so good an opportunity as he could have wished of making himself acquainted with their history, but, in the main, he believed Teedyuscung was well inclined; he talked in high terms of his own merit, but expressed himself a friend to this Province."[2] Teedyuscung, at this council, was alleged to have been the instigator of the Indian outrages upon the whites in 1755, by sending large belts of wampum to various tribes on the war-path; but the shrewd informer or negotiator, with a view of personal advantage and emolument, informed Governor Morris that, as Teedyuscung had brought on the war, he was the only person that could effect a peaceful solution of all Indian affairs. To do this, "Teedyuscung must have a belt of wampum at least five or six feet long and twelve rows broad; and besides the belt, he must have twelve strings to send to the several chiefs, to confirm the words that he sends."[3]

[1] Pa. Arch., 1756, pp. 724–6. [2] Ibid., 1756, p. 727. [3] Ibid., 1748–'56, p. 730.

LACKAWANNA RIVER AND VALLEY.

The Indians, ever having an extraordinary appreciation of the beauties of nature, have given to their rivers and lakes, their mountains and valleys, names really rich and expressive. The transposition, however, of many of these names from one language to another, has so corrupted and changed their primitive expression, that much of their beauty is partially lost or wholly destroyed.

In the Algonquin or Iroquois vernacular, the valley was called *Ad-jou-quay*;[1] in the harsher dialect of the Delawares, where no adjectives were known, spoken by all intervening clans, from the Minisinks, on the Delaware, to Shamokin, it was known as *Lee-ha-ugh-hunt*[2] or Lee-haw-hanna, pronounced Lr-hr-hr-nr (Lar-har-har-nar), the letter *a* either being silent, or in the Indian guttural having the sound of *r*. In succeeding years, the modifications and construction of the word became so great as to become at length a matter of provincialism.

Although in 1759 the stream was designated as *Lee-ha-ugh-hunt* by the Monseys and Delawares living upon its banks, who complained of the intrusion of the whites at its mouth, the original map of Westmoreland (Wyoming), showing the Connecticut surveys in 1761, records it as *Lack-aw-na*. In 1762 the stream was known as *Lec-ha-wa-nock*;[3] in 1771 as *Lam-aw-wa-nak*;[4] in 1772 as Lock-o-worna;[5] in 1774, Lackawanna and Lock-a-warna;[6] in 1778 as *Lac*-u-wanack;[7] in 1790 as *Lak-u-wanuk*;[8] in 1791 as *Lackawanny*. From 1791 down to about 1837-'8, it was recognized both in private and official parlance as *Lack-a-wannock*. "Wannock" lopped off by gradual

---

[1] Col. Rec., vol. vii., p. 157.
[2] Pa. Arch., 1759, p. 421.
[3] Col. Rec., vol. ix., p. 7.
[4] Pa. Arch., 1771, p. 392.
[5] Westmoreland Records.
[6] Ibid.
[7] British Articles of Capitulation of three forts at Lacuwanack, July 4, 1778.
[8] Luzerne County Court Records, 1790.

habit at this time, became obsolete, and *wanna* took its place, thus adopting, as far as the idioms of language would permit, the original name as transmitted to us from Teedyuscung. Lackawanna is a corruption of the Indian " Lee-ha-ugh-hunt," or " Lee-haw-hanna ;" *Lee-haw*, or *Lee-ha*, the prefix, signifies *the forks* or point of intersection; *hanna*, as in Susquehanna, Toly-hanna, Toppa-hannock, Rappa-hannock, Tunk-hannock and Tunk-hanna, implies, in Indian language, a stream of water. Hence the name, *Lar-har-har-nar*, or Lackawanna, the meeting of two streams—a name highly poetic and sweet sounding.

The valley of the Lackawanna, picturesque and salubrious to a delightful degree, watered by a stream from which it derived its name, lies about one hundred and thirty-eight miles northwest of New York in a direct line. It is about thirty-five miles in length, runs south and southeast, and in its general topographical configuration is nothing more or less than a continuation, or rather extension, of the northern right arm of the classic and celebrated Valley of Wyoming cut in twain by Campbell's Ledge. The most northerly deposit of stone or anthracite coal found in America, enriches its entire border from the head of the Lackawanna, among the grand old beech and maples, down to its very mouth. The valley is, in fact, a gem carved out of a mountain of coal. Rimmed on either side by the coal and iron-clad *Moosic*,[1] beautiful in its midwinter or summer foliage, wrapping its jewels in harmonious beds, it reposes like a rough cradle or canoe, tapering off at its upper extremity in a narrow unimportant intervale. A few miles above Carbondale, the valley, already narrowed before, is more successfully interrupted by a succession of bowlders or hills, facetiously termed " Hog's Back," from their sharp, bris-

[1] This mountain, a low ramification of the great Appalachian chain, takes its name from the *Moose* inhabiting it at the time of the earliest explorations by the whites.

tling appearance. Now and then the mountain cleft for a trout brook, elbows against the stream, giving its waters, too swift and shallow for navigable purposes, graceful and gradual fall.

The Lackawanna River rises principally in Susquehanna County, but one considerable branch emerges from the same marshy region in Wayne that sends out the Starucca, Lackawaxen, and Equinunk to join the Delaware, which, after many counter and diverse movements for a distance of at least fifty miles, pours its gentle volume into the Susquehanna at Pittston. Along its banks, shorn of the fairest portion of timber by the lumberman, the landscape is singularly fine, with slope, field, and village, while the stream itself offers to the eye every variety of smooth water, pool, and rapids. Here its margin, rock-bound and abrupt, is carved from the low-browed cliff, and there the alluvial meadow or cornfield ready for the husbandman, attests the luxurious character of the soil.

Along the central and lower portion, coal of the finest quality is found in profusion, interstratified in many places with iron-ore of the most desirable and productive character.

The confluence of the Lackawanna and Susquehanna is described in the following beautiful lines by the late Mrs. Sigourney :—

THE SUSQUEHANNA.

ON ITS JUNCTION WITH THE LACKAWANNA.

BY MRS. SIGOURNEY.

Rush on, glad stream, in thy power and pride
To claim the hand of thy promised bride,
For she hastes from the realms of the darkened mine,
To mingle her murmured vows with thine:
Ye have met, ye have met, and your shores prolong
The liquid tone of your nuptial song.

Methinks ye wed as the white man's son
And the child of the Indian King have done.
I saw the bride as she strove in vain
To cleanse her brow from the carbon stain;
But she brings thee a dowry so rich and true
That thy love must not shrink from the tawny hue.

Her birth was rude in a mountain cell,
And her infant freaks there are none to tell;
Yet the path of her beauty was wild and free.
And in dell and forest she hid from thee;
But the day of her fond caprice is o'er,
And she seeks to part from thy breast no more.

Pass on, in the joy of thy blended tide,
Through the land where the blessed Miquon died.
No red-man's blood with its guilty stain,
Hath cried unto God from that broad domain;
With the seeds of peace they have sown the soil,
Bring a harvest of wealth for their hour of toil.

On, on, through the vale where the brave ones sleep,
Where the waving foliage is rich and deep.
I have stood on the mountain and roamed through the glen,
To the beautiful homes of the Western men;
Yet naught in that region of glory could see
So fair as the vale of Wyoming to me.

WAS WYOMING ONCE A VAST LAKE?

The Kittatinny, or Blue Ridge, which skirts along Pennsylvania and Virginia, is probably one of the most even ranges in the world. At its base it rarely exceeds a mile, while its summit, covered with perpetual foliage, preserves an uniformity of height that distinguishes it from all other mountains stretched across the country.

At some period in the world's history, this ridge doubtless was the margin of a vast lake into which ran the waters of the Chemung, Chenango, Delaware, and the Susquehanna, and over mountain, moor, and valley, rolled one common wave. Evidence of this is written upon rock and mountain around us, while the earth from the hill-side mine, disdains to conceal its share of the water spoils. The vast quantity of petrified shells, alluvials, and strata of shale and clay and organic remains, found along the Delaware, Lackawanna, and Susquehanna, and many other valleys, and the character of these rivers, all running in a transverse or *cross* direction, have been compelled to wash out by slow and triumphant progress, or rupture the obstructing heights to find their way to the sea, suggests the inquiry, Were they not once the bottoms of immense lakes? And did not the finny tribes, the huge serpent, and the whale, sport in these inland salt waters in times of yore?

No one can carefully examine the strata of the mountains of the United States, especially, the Alleghanies or Blue Ridge, or even glance at the map, without finding a fact existing in no other part of the world, that all their principal ridges *cross* the great as well as the lesser rivers, instead of running parallel with them. The Delaware, Susquehanna, Potomac, and Shenandoah, all issue from the steep mountains of the Blue Ridge.

One of the most distinguished authors and eminent naturalists, C. F. Volney, who visited Harper's Ferry in 1796, and who gave the subject great attention and research, believed that "the chain of the Blue Ridge in its entire state, completely denied the Potomac a passage onward, and that then all the waters of the upper part of the river, having no issue, formed several considerable lakes, which spread themselves between the Blue Ridge and the chain at Kittatinny, not only to the Susquehanna and Schuylkill, but *beyond* the Schuylkill, and even to the Delaware. It is obvious that the lakes flowing off must have changed the whole face of the lower country. Several branches having at once or in succession, given a passage to the streams of water now called James, Potomac, Susquehanna, Schuylkill, and Delaware, their general and common reservoir was divided into as many distinct lakes, separated by the risings of the ground that exceeded this level. Each of these lakes had its particular drain, and this drain being at length worn down to the lowest level, the land was left completely uncovered. This must have occurred earlier with the James, Susquehanna, and Delaware, because their basins are more elevated, and it must have happened more recently with the Potomac, for the opposite reason, its basin being the deepest of all."

How far the Delaware then extended the reflux of its waters toward the east, he could not ascertain ; " however, it appears its basin was bounded by the ridge that accompanies its left bank ; and which is the apparent continuation of the Blue Ridge and North Mountain. It is probable that its basin has always been separate from that of the Hudson, as it is certain that the Hudson has always had a distinct basin, the limit and mound of which is above West Point, at a place called the Highlands."[1]

Schoolcraft and Professor Beck, and other eminent writers, also subscribe to this theory. The basin of the Lackawanna, viewed from the summit of the mountain back of Scranton, or from one of the more elevated points farther up the valley, exhibits the internal appearance and form of a lake so plainly, that the idea of the ancient existence of one here is indubitably forced upon the observer. Other circumstances tend to confirm this impression, as the heaps of detached rock strewn below many of the gorges, especially at the Delaware Water Gap, where the waters were held back until the great embankment gave way before the weight of the vast body of water above, or by attrition, convulsion, or glacier action, and brought down all that stratum of earth and mud which now gives such agricultural strength and value to the shores of the lower Delaware.

A few yards above the bridge, across the Susquehanna at Pittston, can be seen a large rock of many thousand

---

[1] American Antiquities, pp. 352–373.

tons in weight, of which Mr. Charles Miner thus writes: "Standing on the bank of the river, a little below the mouth of the Lackawanna, and looking northward, it appears as if by some power little short of omnipotent, the solid rock[1] had been cloven down near a thousand feet to open a passage for the water. Being on the river-bank twelve years ago, with the able and lamented Mr. Packer, then chairman of the senatorial committee, to view the coal region of Luzerne, he pointed to a huge mass of broken and contorted rock, evidently out of place, which now lies at Pittston Ferry, between the canal and river, and expressed the decided and not improbable opinion, that in the convulsion of nature which separated the mountain above us, this mass must have been torn away and borne by the rushing flood to its present resting-place. Twenty miles below, where the Susquehanna takes leave of the plains, the mountains are equally lofty and precipitous. In many places the rocks distinctly exhibit the abrasions of water many feet above the highest pitch to which the river has ever been known to rise, going to show, that at some very remote period, this had been a lake, and indicating that there had been a chain of lakes probably along the whole line of the stream. Banks of sand-hills, covered with rounded stone, manifestly worn smooth by attrition, similar stones being found wherever wells are sunk, tend to confirm the opinion. The soil is chiefly alluvial, and the whole depth and surface, so far as examined, show great changes by the violent action of water."[2]

The existence of this lake or lakes, made by the intervening hills, explains the appearance of the several stages or flats observed along the Wyoming plains and the Lackawanna, and even at Cobb's Gap, where the roaring brook flees from the Pocono, as if the water once had a greater volume than now, or was higher at one period

---

[1] Campbell's Ledge.   [2] Miner's History of Wyoming, p. 12.

than at another, and by some means was drained off in such a manner that the receding wave made a new mark of embankment, indicating the original height of the shore of these lakes and rivers.

On the very summit of the Pocono[1] Mountain, about twenty miles east of the Lackawanna, lies a broad marsh, elevated many hundred feet above the Delaware Water Gap, 1,969 feet above tide-water, covered in a few places, as can be seen from the passing cars, with a deep strata of sand, similar to that found on the sea-shore, which, in spite of the drainage of the water around it by these great breaks in the mountain, has maintained its sedentary and original position, while the subsiding waters hollowed out the valleys and formed cascades of beauty, which marked and enlivened the wild landscape long after the Noachian deluge.

Mr. Schoolcraft, well known to the reading public as one of the most accurate and entertaining writers and explorers in American antiquities, corroborates this theory, and asks the question, "May we not suppose that the great northern lakes are the remains of such an ocean?"[2] If not so, they were probably the mere remnant of a great inland sea.

The weight of the accumulated waters, coming from the north, assisted perhaps by volcanic agency, possibly made the various gaps in the mountains, and as the liberated waters took up the line of march to the sea, the whole geological features of the lower country acknowledged the power of the watery plowshare. Whether this abyss boiled with a heat far beyond the temperature of white-hot iron, from the immense furnaces below over the seams of liquid coal, or at what period this watery or eruptive

---

[1] *Pocono* is the name given by the white people to the mountain dividing the Delaware from the Susquehanna, after the Indian name of the stream that flows from it, called by them *Poco-hanne*, which signifies a stream issuing from a mountain. "Hanne" means flowing water; *Tunk-hanne*, the smallest among other streams in the same locality. *Tope-hanne* (Tolyhaunah), alder creek or stream, &c.

[2] American Antiquities, p. 367.

conquest transpired, lies so far beyond the earliest times of any written or traditional history, that no explanation or data is known other than that found written upon the terraced rock along the sides and bottoms of these ancient mountain lakes.

Contemporary with these phenomena, or in more pre-Adamic times, it is evident that the topographical character of the Lackawanna Valley was essentially changed. The geological conformation of the country along the stream; the character, form, and direction of the Alleghany range thrown across southern New York; its mean altitude near the Great Bend of the Susquehanna River being but little if any greater than at Tioga Point; the comparative freshness and shape, as well as the confusion of all the strata of earth, stone, and coal, along the Lackawanna, with the general appearance of the country traversed by the Susquehanna and Lackawanna, afford abundant evidence of the correctness of this conclusion.

Instead of breaking off so abruptly from its apparent course at this point, and cautiously feeling its way far along the border of the mountains, until it reached Tioga Point, and then carrying its current through a passage ruptured through successive ridges, until, with all its beauty and boldness, it opened into the slackened waters of Wyoming, it probably struck boldly down into a channel now closed by some great upheaval or disturbance in the geological world, and sought the valley where now the Lackawanna mingles with the waters of the Susquehanna.

Trace up the Susquehanna, step by step, to the Highlands of New York, or down through its narrow passage to Wyoming, and not a single vein or spar of coal is visible; go up to the Lackawanna, modest in its volume, to the indicated point, and more than midway from the mouth of the stream, coal deposits, grand in their character and exhaustless in their creation, everywhere appear; all of which confirms the theory, that, whatever local causes or convulsions once effected the mineralogical features of the valley, the wave of the ocean, or the waters of a much larger stream than the Lackawanna once occupied its place.

No less than five veins of coal have been washed away from the eastern side of the Lackawanna, a mile above Scranton, by the propelling flood of olden time, and their crushed and blackened deposition found in the alluvial banks below. The city of Scranton, or the old village proper, embracing the sand banks, stands upon such a singular deposit.

Very many of our mountain notches appear like volcanic outlets. The evidence of subterranean or oceanic volcanic fires exists to-day in the ocean, and now and in a moment's clamor, make food of coasts and cities. Their existence explain why the carboniferous and even the granitic strata of rock are inclined to the horizon in angles of forty-five degrees and upward in so many of the mountain ranges throughout the coal basins of Pennsylvania, and which is so especially noticed and delineated in the huge ledge of rocks thus sloping in distinct lamination or layers in the well-known notch of the mountain between Providence and Abington, about two miles northwest of Scranton, called "Leggett's Gap."

WAR-PATHS.

One of the three long-trodden paths of the warrior leading out of Wyoming, led eastward to Coshutunk (Cochecton), a small Indian settlement upon the shore of the upper Delaware. Leaving the valley at *Asserughney* village, standing at the mouth of the stream, it followed the *eastern* bank of the Lackawanna up to Springbrook, Stafford Meadow, and Nayaug or Roaring Brook, crossing the last two named ones a short distance below the present location of Scranton, and passed into the Indian town of Capoose. Here one path led off to Oquago, New

York (now Windsor), about forty miles distant, through Leggett's Gap and the Abingtonian wilderness, while the other, diverging from Capoose in an easterly direction, plunged boldly into the forest, passing along where Dunmore now stands, up the mountain slope to its very summit. This foot-path crossed the Moosic range near the residence of the late John Cobb, Esq., and thence through Little Meadows, in Salem, and the low Wallenpaupack country beyond. This trail seldom ran *through* the gaps, but it generally, like many of their war-paths, kept the higher ground, or where the woods were less dense, because the warriors, agile and quick-sighted on the march, preferred climbing *over* a considerable elevation, to the labor of cutting a trail through more level ground, or deep wooded ravines, with their stone hatchets; besides this, overlooking points were chosen invariably, so that upon entering or leaving a valley, they could better discover the approach or presence of an enemy. Of this narrow trail, worn to the depth of several inches in many places on the mountains where roots and rocks offered no resistance to passing moccasins, few indeed, are the remaining traces where the warrior and the war-song enlivened the way but a little over a century ago. Near the mountain spring, however, this old Indian path for several hundred yards to the east of it, was so deeply indented as to show its depth and general outline even to-day.

The *first* rude wagon-road cut out and opened from the Hudson River to Wyoming Valley, for the pack-horse or wheels, followed this track the greater portion of the way, because of its being the most direct route from Connecticut to the backwoods of Lackawanna and Wyoming, then called Westmoreland by the Yankees, who began to people it.

INDIAN SPRING.

Almost upon the very summit of the Moosic Mountain, between the valley and Cobb's settlement, by the side of this old trail, bubbles from the earth a large spring, called the "Indian Spring." No matter how parched the lips of mother-earth—how shrunken the volume of streams elsewhere, this spring, indifferent to drought or flood, in summer or winter, is ever filled to its brim with cold pure water.

Away from the world's hot pulse ; hemmed in by the pine whose waving tops give partial entrance to the noonday sun, and once gave shelter to rovers of the wilderness strolling from tribe to tribe with friendly or avenging tomahawk, and lifting its fountain as it does almost from the very top of a high vertical ledge, running nearly a mile before it opens into Cobb's Gap, this spring from its peculiar location, has much to render it attractive and romantic to the visitor. It forms one of the lesser tributaries of Roaring Brook, from whence Scranton is supplied with water.

In July, 1788, two persons were killed at this point. Fleeing from Wyoming Valley resounding with the exultant shout of the tories and their red auxiliaries, and the faint cries of the captives reserved for ransom or torture, they bent over, thirsty and exhausted, for the invigorating draught. They never rose from their knees. The hatchet of the savage, intently watching the victims, flew from the ambush ; the stony knife dripped through their scalps, and the wolves at night made long and loud their carnival over the unresisting dead.

A large red rock rims one side of this spring, whose crimson color tradition imputes to the blood of the victims thus immolated.

INDIAN RELICS AND FORTIFICATIONS.

No evidence is found of Indian forts along the Lackawanna, although there existed one or more a few miles below its mouth, one of which is thus described by Chapman in his History of Wyoming :—

"In the valley of Wyoming, there exist some remains of Indian fortifications, which appear to have been constructed by a race of people very different in their habits from those who occupied the place when first discovered by the whites. Most of these ruins have been so much obliterated by the operations of agriculture, that their forms can not now be distinctly ascertained. That which remains the most entire was examined by the writer during the summer of 1817, and its dimensions carefully ascertained; although, from frequent plowing, its form had become almost destroyed. It is situated in the township of Kington, upon a level plain on the north side of Toby's Creek, about one hundred and fifty feet from its bank, and about a half mile from its confluence with the Susquehanna. It is of an oval or elliptical form, having its longest diameter from the northwest to the southeast, at right-angles to the creek, three hundred and thirty-seven feet, and its shortest diameter from the northeast to the southwest, two hundred and seventy-two feet. On the southwest side, appears to have been a gateway about twelve feet wide, opening toward the great eddy of the river, into which the creek falls. From present appearances, it consisted, probably, of only one mound or rampart, which, in height and thickness, appears to have been the same on all sides, and was constructed of earth; the plain on which it stands, not abounding in stone.

"On the outside of the rampart is an intrenchment or ditch, formed, probably, by removing the earth of which it is composed, and which appears never to have been walled. The creek, on which it stands, is bounded by a high steep bank on that side, and at ordinary times is sufficiently deep to admit canoes to ascend from the river to the fortification. When the first settlers came to Wyoming, this plain was covered with its native forest, consisting principally of oak and yellow pine; and the trees which grew in the rampart and in the intrenchment, are said to have been as large as those in any other part of the valley; one large oak, particularly, upon being cut down, was ascertained to be seven hundred years old. The Indians had no traditions concerning these fortifications, neither did they appear to have any knowledge of the purposes for which they were constructed. They were, perhaps, erected about the same time with those upon the waters of the Ohio, and probably by a similar people, and for similar purposes."

Another fortification existed on Jacob's Plains, or the upper flats in Wilkes Barre. Its situation is the highest part of the low grounds, so that, only in extraordinary floods, is the spot covered with water."[1] This fort seems to have been of about the same in form, shape, and size, to that described by Chapman, and in its interior, near the southern line, the ancient people all concur in stating that there existed a well.[2]

At the confluence of the Lackawanna with the Susquehanna, Indian graves and remains of wigwam life were found in great abundance sixty years ago. Skeletons exhumed by the waters of the spring freshets, lay in such numbers along the banks of the rivers, and so familiar had they become to the thoughtless passer, that boys were often seen with a thigh-bone in each hand drumming Yankee Doodle upon the whitened skulls, thus found upon the plain around them. Some of these were doubtless the remains of the warriors who fell in the battles of the valley, as bullets corroded and white, and sometimes broken arrow-heads, were found wedged in the bones, indicating the precise manner of their death.

Others, crumbling the moment they were uncovered, or only furnishing a dark and peculiar deposit, bore evidence of greater age in their burial. Bowls and pots of the capacity of a gallon or more, ingeniously cut from soap-stone, and ornamented with rich designs of beauty to the Indian's eye, were often found preserved with the

---

[1] Miner's History. [2] Ibid.

remains. As none of this soap-stone is found nearer this place than Maryland or New Hampshire, it would seem to indicate the migratory as well as the commercial character of the tribe once possessing them. Hard, highly polished, and handsomely dressed stones, five or six inches in length, fitted for the hand, and used, probably, for skinning deer and other animals, hatchets, beads, and the silent calumet, here and there intermingled with the remains.

On the brink of the western range of the Moosic, in Leggett's Gap, between Providence and Abington, an Indian grave was found in a very singular manner a number of years ago. A quick-footed deer, fleeing from his pursuer, leaped upon the end of a gun-barrel projecting from the ground, and brought it to the hunter's view. A little excavation exposed a large quantity of silica or flint stones worked into arrow and spear heads, a stone tomahawk, a French gun-barrel, an iron hoe, and some human bones, much decayed. The skeleton lay on its right side, with the knees drawn up, the head reclining toward the east, while immediately over reposed the implements and weapons of the deceased. The hoe and the gun, both much corroded, were probably obtained from the French, while their burial with the warrior upon this rugged spur of the mountain would indicate the time of their deposit as a period of peace. In his lap were found the arrows, made from one to two inches in length. Nearly a hundred small snail-shells, all fitted for stringing, and which had probably been used for belts or beads, lay immediately under the arrows. There was also a pipe, made from dark stone, one end of it being shaped for a stopple, and could be used for a whistle to gather the tribe from afar down the ravine, and the other for a scoop or spoon. This singular contrivance, if not used for a whistle, probably achieved great usefulness in porridge or broth. A small quantity of mineral, resembling black-lead, intended, doubtless, for medicine, had also been deposited in this isolated grave, beside the departed hunter.

A portion of these, and a vast quantity of other interesting relics of the red-man, in a fine state of preservation, are now in the possession of the writer, open and free to all who choose to visit them.

Upon the western bank of the Lackawanna, in the upper portion of Capoose Meadow, in Providence, opposite the residence of the late Dr. Silas B. Robinson, slopes off a gentle mound, where, in 1795, a number of Indian graves were discovered and exhumed by a party of settlers in search of antiquarian spoils. As one of the mounds seemed to have been prepared with especial attention, and contained, with the bones of the warrior, a great quantity of the implements of the deceased, it was supposed, erroneously no doubt, to have been the grave of the chieftain Capoose. These graves, few in number, perhaps pointed to the last of the group of Monsey warriors who had offered incense and sacrifice to the Great Spirit at Capoose. The strings of wampum and their war instruments—for which this mound was disturbed—bore them company as they lay piled over with the gray sand of the meadow, and were protected and comforted on their long journey by these rude, yet cherished, amulets. These graves, endowed with no utterance but that of uncertain tradition, have been so obliterated by the operations of agriculture that little or no trace of them now appears to the unpracticed eye.

Arrows, stone vessels, tomahawks and knives, stone mortars and their accompanying pestles for pounding corn into *nas-ump*, or samp, and other curious relics of Indian times, are occasionally found in the valley, and although time has robbed them of much of their original beauty and usefulness, they have not lost, nor never can lose, their savage interest.

To the antiquarian, however, nothing could provoke more inquiry and interest than the remains of an ancient Indian mound or encampment, found in Covington, Luzerne County, near the line of the Delaware, Lackawanna, and Western Railway, which to all appearances were as old as those existing in Wyoming Valley. These remains were discovered in 1833 by Mr. Welch, then a draughtsman in the Land Office at Washington, while he was hunting along Bell-meadow Brook, a small tributary of the Lehigh, on the Pocono. The accidental discovery of a piece of pottery among the loose pebbles on the bank of the brook, so different in its character to any thing he had ever seen before, naturally awakened his curiosity, and led to the subsequent excavation of a vast quantity of sharp and flinty arrow and spear heads, a large stone hatchet, bowls of immense capacity, fashioned and baked from sand and clay. These bowls were indented upon their sides with deep finger prints, and some were tastily ornamented with characters original and unique.

The late Richard Drinker, Esq., of Scranton, a gentleman eminent in his day for genial philosophy and social abilities, to whom the writer was indebted for the above facts, was present at the time of their discovery, and described the pottery thus found as being enormous in quantity. An elegant short pipe, belonging probably to a squaw, was also found immediately under the tomahawk, in so perfect a state of preservation that it was to all appearances, as fit for the consumption of their favorite weed as when first fashioned into shape. A huge pile of elk bones and teeth were also found, but the bones crumbled to dust the moment they were exposed to the touch or air. Underneath them all, lay the remains of a great camp-fire, which was probably hurriedly deserted, and as hurriedly smothered with sand and stone to the depth of twelve or fourteen inches. Ashes, coals, and half-burned brands, one of which still bore the marks of a hatchet distinctly upon it, were spread over a surface of at least fifteen feet.

The most singular article exhumed, was a number of flat, delicately smoothed stone, somewhat resembling a carpenter's whetstone in shape and size, each one bored with two or three small circular holes near the extremity or the center. Whether these had been drilled and used for weaving fish-nets from wood or hemp, constructing belts of wampum, or for other mechanical or ornamental purposes, is a matter of inquiry or conjecture.

Trees of Norway girth have grown upon the edge of this brook since this camp-fire went out forever, and almost upon these remains, one immense hemlock, green in its foliage, has defied the storms of centuries as it stands like a Roman sentinel of old, over this ancient sepulcher of the forgotten savage.

The absence of iron and copper utensils among the *debris*, furnished abundant proof that these relics had been deposited by the red-men in the stone period, long before their knowledge of the European race, but *why* they were thus left isolated from their war-paths, or the purpose or the cause of their smothered fire, the learned antiquarian can only conjecture.

The beaver, caught more for its furs than its *castoreum*—now a considerable medicinal agent—once held their court in a low marsh or meadow adjoining this camp, from which the Indians evidently obtained sand for their pottery.

In fact the Lackawanna, and the wilder waters of the *Le-hr* (Lehigh), were inhabited by the beaver at the time of the first settlement of the valley by the whites. Across these streams, especially the upper Lehigh, they built their "beaver dams" upon the most scientific principles of the engineering art, living upon ash, birch, poplars and the softer wood, of which they were particularly fond.[1] In the deepest part of the pond they built their houses, resembling somewhat the wigwam of the Indian, with a floor of saplings, sloping toward the water like an inclined plane. Here, secure in their moated castle, they

---

[1] There are many places along all the streams of the country, originally stripped of all their growth by the industrious and engineering beaver.

slept with their tails under water, ascending the floor with the rise of the stream. Rafting, when the rivers were swollen, destroyed their dams, and drove the beaver to creeks more quiet and remote. In 1826 there came from Canada an old trapper in search of the coveted furs, who caught with his traps all of these industrious animals but a single one lingering along the Lehigh and the Lackawanna; this lonely beaver by sharpened instinct, defied the trapper's cunning for a year or two, when, wandering down the swifter waters of the Alanomink in search of his lost companions, he was killed near Stroudsburg.

Is it not a little curious that with all the romantic ancient history of the Wyoming and Lackawanna valleys, so little attention until recently has been given toward gathering and preserving the various Indian implements once used in peace or in war? The writer has a passion for the *old*—not the old hills covered with forests, through whose hoary locks centuries have rustled unnumbered and unsung—but the lingering relics of a race, the bravest the world ever knew, which convey at once to the mind the ideal, the strife, the passions, the achievements, and the glory of another day and another race. These links and landmarks of remote antiquity; the rarer implements of copper sometimes found in their ancient graves; the rude inscriptions which mark the first impulses of the wild-men toward letters or written legend; the stone battle-ax or tomahawk once flung or brandished by the brave exulting over his fallen foe; the knife whose scalping edge gleamed alike over the victim in the cradle or the field; the keen edged arrow twanged upon its fatal mission, or the calumet cherished afar for its silent and subduing power, once smoked around the forest encampment—all are so associated with by-gone times, that as the plow now and then up-turns some little memento of the warrior's life, it astonishes the antiquarian to learn, that, aside from the really valuable and magnificent collection of Hon. Steuben Jenkins of Wyoming, and those possessed by the writer, so few of these memorials have been treasured up in the valley to-day. Such a group of Indian relics, embracing every variety able to illustrate the life, religion, and character of the former occupants of the country, long before the aggressions and repeated wrongs of the white man had become a great national reproach, and had turned the simple savage into a western heathen, compelled to fight for a standing-place, or starve with plenty around him and yet beyond his reach, could not fail to be invaluable as years rendered their possession difficult or quite impossible.[1]

Whatever might have been the former character of Indian warfare in the earliest history of Wyoming, or however much the infant settlements throughout the country may have suffered from the fagot and the knife—when the cries of helpless womanhood and the innocence of childhood plead alike in vain—it is established by indubitable evidence of government officials,[2] and elsewhere, that in the more recent wars the Indians have *not* been the aggressors. We know, by living testimony, that they have been crowded, inch by inch, southward and westward by the constant incursions and shameful encroachments of the Caucasian race, until, from being a great, proud, and powerful nation, respected for their virtues and feared for their strength, extending immense influence over the Western world, they have been reduced to a mere handful of lurking warriors, rendered desperate by maltreatment and impoverished by misfortune.

INDIAN APPLE-TREE.

In a description of New Netherland (New York), published at Amsterdam, in 1671, the appearance of the New Netherlanders (Indians of the Island of New York), are thus described, and will answer every description of the

---

[1] See Appendix. [2] See Mr. Bogy's Report on Indian Affairs.

Lackawanna Indians:—"This people is divided into divers nations, all well-shaped and strong, having pitch-black and lank hair, as coarse as a horse's tail, broad shoulders, small waist, brown eyes, and snow-white teeth; they are of a sallow color, abstemious in food and drink. Water satisfies their thirst; high and low make use of Indian corn and beans, flesh meat and fish, prepared all alike. The crushed corn is daily boiled to a pap, called by them *sappaen*. They observe no set time for meals. Whenever hunger demands, the time for eating arrives. Beaver's tails are considered the most savory delicacy. Whilst hunting, they live some days on roasted corn, carried about the person in a little bag. A little corn in water swells to a large mass. Henry Hudson relates that he entered the river *Montaines* in the latitude of forty degrees, and there went ashore. The Indians made strange gambols with dancing and singing; carried arrows, the points of which consisted of sharp stones, fastened to the wood with pitch; they slept under the blue sky, on little mats of platted leaves of trees; suck strong tobacco; are friendly, but very thievish. Hudson sailed up thirty miles higher, went into a canoe with an old Indian, a chief over forty men and seventeen women, who conducted him ashore. They all abode in one house well built of the bark of oak-trees."[1]

The domestic habits of the Monsey tribe, when not engaged in warfare, were extremely simple and lazy. Patches of open land or "Indian clearings" early were found in the valley, where onions, cantaloupes, beans, and corn, and their favorite weed, *tobacco*, were half cultivated by the obedient squaw.

On the low strip of land lying upon either side of the street railroad, midway between Scranton and Providence, and near the cottage built some years since by Dr. Throop, now known as the "Atlantic Garden," there

---

[1] Documentary History of New York, vol. iv., p. 124.

was found by the first white explorers into the valley, a permanent camp-place which had, to all appearances, long been used for tillage and a dwelling-place. Within this ancient clearing the passer can hardly fail to observe an apple-tree standing on the east side of the road, cragged and venerable, even if some of its limbs betoken the approach of age or the presence of neglect. Its precise location can be seen upon the Indian map of Capoose Meadow. This is the Indian apple-tree, of great age, thirteen and a half feet in circumference, and possibly was planted by the friendly hand of Capoose, more than a century ago. By arms selfish and rude, this old tree, which deserves a protecting fence to honor its memory, was bereft of its mates many years ago, because their wide-spread branches threw too much shade upon the inclosing meadow! A few sprigs of grass probably repaid for the destroying act. This single tree now stands alone as a relic of primitive husbandry at Capoose, affording in the summer months, by its green foliage, as ample shade to the lolling ox or idle boy as it once gave to the squaw or her lord when he skimmed along the *La-ha-ha-na* in his own canoe. In one of the apple-trees thus cut down, in 1804, were counted one hundred and fifty concentric circles or yearly growths, thus dating the tree back to a time long before the reports of the trapper or the story of the Indians came out of the valley to the whites. Seventy years ago a large wild-plum orchard, standing in a swale adjoining this clearing, hung with millions of the juicy fruit, while the grape, with almost tropical luxuriance, purpled the intermingling tree-tops. The vines, none of which now remain, as well as the apple-trees, were no doubt the result of Indian culture.

BEACON-FIRES AND INDIAN LEGEND.

Every gorge or up-shooting point in the range diversifying the valley is enriched with its tradition and story. In the Indian wars, the Moosic or Cobb Mountain, affording as it did an admirable view of the entire valley, and a wide scope of country toward the Wallenpaupack and Delaware, was long used by the forest men for the location of their beacon fires. Campbell's Ledge, from its sharp altitude, so located as to overlook both valleys as far as inhabited by them, was held in corresponding importance from this fact.

So well were these evening lights understood by them, that the warriors could be collected to any given point with rare speed and certainty. Should any thing on their part demand hasty action, fire after fire would spring up with wonderful rapidity on every height and plateau, at intervals of a few miles, upon the mountain-tops; and as they successively gleamed their lurid light to the sky, they conveyed a meaning to the savage mind well known as if their native guttural had told it in the valley. Once lighted, these beacon-fires, around which the warriors danced and sang in their wild joy, or prepared meals after the march of the day, could be seen for a great distance. No language was more silent or expressive to the inhabitant of the forest; none awoke greater danger to the pioneer than their appearance.

No matter how sudden or swift the pursuit, when the fireplace was reached the red chieftains had vanished, leaving nothing behind them but expiring brands. Along many of the higher peaks of the mountain, generally upon the eastern border of the Lackawanna, can yet be seen faint traces of these ancient beacons. Huge, gray stones, partially cracked by the heat of the fire whose location it marked, have been visited by the writer, upon an eminence distinguished at Spring Brook, near the residence of our hospitable and humorous friend, Edward Dolph. This peak is one of the prominent ones, where this primitive manner of telegraphing carried dismay or hope to many a watching woodsman down in the valley. These places faced the valley, and this one, unlike the others visited, appears not to have been disturbed in its solitude since the brand of the sachem expired a century ago.

Few portions of country afford a broader scope for legendary research than that along the Susquehanna and Lackawanna. Here, immured in the forest, marked only by paths and streams, and surrounded by every element of simplicity and beauty, the river clans smoked the peace-pipe or danced the war-dance, with whoops and halloos, and went forth with paint and sharpened weapon to gather the scalps of the spoilers of their threshold.

SILVER MINE ON THE LACKAWANNA.

Of the value of precious metals the Indians knew little or nothing until taught it by the whites, and then, learning to their dismay how fatal to their narrowing hunting-grounds were the aggressions of the expanding settlements, they practiced every possible caution in concealing all knowledge of mines and minerals in every portion of the wilderness. The Indian who, in thoughtless or drunken mood, betrayed the secret of their location, paid the penalty of his guilt by sudden death or lingering torture. Yet about one hundred years ago the whites learned by treachery, and lost by misfortune, knowledge of a *silver mine* located about two miles up the Lackawanna from its mouth.

In 1766 the Six Nations complained to the Proprietary Government at Philadelphia of white persons who had dug into a silver mine, twelve miles above the Delaware town of *Wy-wa-mick*, and carried away in canoes three loads of ore. An Indian trader named Anderson, who had brought a few goods up the river, was suspected of being the transgressor.

John Teal, a German, who died some years ago at an advanced age, threw some additional light upon the location of this hidden silver mine. He had lived long enough with the wild tribes to understand their dialect, and enjoy the confidence of an aged chief of the Oneidas, residing in western New York, who had assisted to efface every outward and visible evidence of the existence of this mine. When the chieftain saw that his days were few, he called his friend Teal to his wigwam, to intrust him with secrets of no longer consequence to the Indian. He informed him that there were *three salt* springs, one *silver*, one *gold*, and one *lead* mine in the vicinity of Wyoming, and all used by them while in possession of the country. The silver mine, long known to the scattered tribes, was on the northeast side of the Lackawanna, above a high ledge or mountain, half an hour's walk from the River Susquehanna, twelve miles above Wyoming. After the first Wyoming massacre, in 1763, the dwellers in wigwams, hoping to retain occupancy forever of the rich plains, coveted by triple parties, used this mine to their advantage; but when the intruders again made their appearance in such formidable numbers as to annihilate the long-cherished hope, the mine was so artfully concealed from the whites that none yet have found the spot yielding the precious metal.

Traditions, treasured up by old settlers half a century ago, tell of an excavation in the bank of the Lackawanna, between Old Forge and the Barnum farm, similar to that described in the Pennsylvania Archives of 1766.

That a silver mine was known and worked by the aborigines in this vicinity, is unquestionably proved by the fact that official complaint was made by them of the depredations of Anderson, but its precise location remains at present in great doubt.

GOLD MINE.

The chief described the gold mine as being under a ledge of rocks, a few miles above Wyoming Valley, at a point where a rock of the height of an Indian covered a spring.

Five miles westward from Scranton, in a direct line, on the western side of the mountain forming the boundary between the townships of Providence and Newton, rises a long ledge of rock known as *Bald Mount*, which, from its altitude, offers, when the day is clear, so wide a view of field, forest, and lake, that, in spite of the steep, zigzag way of approaching it, has become, during the summer hours, a popular resort for parties loving the romance

TOP OF BALD MOUNT.

of mountain life. At its very base lies the village of Milwaukie, watered by a stream turned to good mill account before it enters the Susquehanna, five miles below. Eight or ten villages can be seen from the mount, which, shorn of its larger trees by the force of the wind sometimes sweeping over it with great fury, is left comparatively bald, and thus given it a name. One large rock, prominent in position, is perforated with numerous holes of the capacity of from a quart to a gallon, as shown by the preceding illustration of Bald Mount. These were probably used by the Indian women for pounding their corn into samp. The large number of stone pestles found near it many years ago favor this theory.

Under this precipice can be seen one large conglomerate rock, evidently removed some distance down the mountain by the natives to conceal the real origin of the spring. In the removal of this rock the trees, bent at the time, grew up with a very perceptible inclination toward it. From beneath its honest features emerges a spring, surpassed in the purity of its waters by no other in the world, where many metallurgists and others have supposed the gold mine was located. Explorations hitherto made upon every side of Bald Mount have failed to satisfy expectations naturally awakened by these traditions.

In 1778, a young man who had been captured by the savages in Wyoming Valley, was carried to the top of a mountain where the Wilkes Barre settlement could be seen in the distance. Here they built their camp-fire. A transaction took place at this time which, from its novel character, excited the surprise and ever afterward impressed the mind of the young, unharmed captive. A venerable chief, to whom the young man owed his safety, and subsequently his release, removed a large flat stone covering the spring. The waters of this were so conveyed by a subterranean conduit, constructed for the purpose, as to deceive the men strolling through the wilderness in regard to the real source of the spring. At its mouth a roll of bark, forming a spout, was placed in such a manner as to direct the current into a handkerchief held under it by two of the Indians. For some moments the chief, reverently attended by the warriors, arrayed with bow and arrow, and forming a circle around him, stirred up the spring with a conscious knowledge of its gainful results. After an hour had elapsed, every stone previously disturbed was restored to its former condition; earth and leaves were left as if never touched, and no one, without ocular knowledge, would suspect the existence of a water-course. The handkerchief, covered with yellow sediment, was now lifted from the spout. The glittering product thus gathered by the chief was placed in a stone vessel with great care. After the fire was extinguished, and certain incantations performed with ceremonial exactness, the Indians left the spot in charge of the wild rock surrounding it, and resumed their march toward their land of maize among the lakes.

Six days' walk led the party to Kingston, New York, where the treasures of the mountain, thus artfully obtained, were exchanged with the whites, for such articles as want or caprice suggested to the occupants of the forest.

In after years the returned hero often related the incident to his family and friends, some of whom thoroughly traversed every portion of Bald Mount and Campbell's Ledge without discovering the secret channel or the golden spring.

SALT SPRINGS.

The three salt springs were respectively located, one at Martin's Creek, one in the mountain gap between Providence and Abington, the other on the *Nay-aug*, about five miles from the junction of this stream with the Lackawanna at Capoose. The last-named one, manipulated by the Indians to come out of the bed of the brook, was considered by the wild tribes as the richest, as it yielded the largest quantity of salt with the least labor. When a knowledge of this spring first came to the white man, deer came hither in herds. Sometimes there were hundreds in a drove around these salt licks; and it was rare during the spring or summer months not to find the buck or fawn cropping the wild grass growing luxuriantly around these briny places. In the upper part of Leggett's Gap, in the mountain west of Providence, there was a salt spring strongly impregnated with saline properties. When the white adventurer first sought the valley for his home, and found no luxury but steak from the bear or haunch from the deer, and heard no voice but that issuing from the throat of the rifle, the waters of this spring were often sought to obtain the scarce and necessary salt. The warriors' path from Oquago salt spring to Capoose passed by its waters. Much of the salt for the earliest settlers of the Lackawanna and Wyoming valleys was granulated here.

Mr. Blackman, who was taken captive from Wyoming, relates of the Indians, that when salt became scarce, they went up the Lackawanna and returned the next day, loaded with the desired article, which was sometimes *warm*. From a knowledge of this spring, advantage was early taken by the hunter and trapper, for in such numbers deer frequented this fountain to lap its waters, that they easily and often fell a trophy to the woodsman's gun.

A hunter of seventy winters tells the writer that, in his younger days, deer were so tame in the vicinity of this spring, that he has killed and dressed during his lifetime one hundred and forty-seven deer at this place alone!

That the natives frequented this place for the purpose of killing deer and curing venison, is satisfactorily proven by the quantity of warlike and domestic Indian relics found immediately around it at an early day.

LEAD MINE.

Tuscarora Creek, a wild, clear, rapid stream, retaining its original Indian name, and lying between Meshoppen and Wyalusing, puts into the east side of the Susquehanna, about thirty miles above the Lackawanna. Half a mile from its mouth, under a cliff leaning gloomily over a sharp bend of the stream, where the rocks go down into the waters here deeper than at any other point, a *lead* mine was worked by the Indians for making bullets, after they had been taught the use of the rifle by the English and the French. The Oneida chief informed Mr. Teal, that not only were the Wyoming Indians supplied with lead from this Tuscarora mine, but the French, while in harmony with the Iroquois, drew largely upon it.

The Indian, in his wild dream of future hope, imposed silence so effectually upon the rock along the Tuscarora, that although several companies have exhausted large sums of money in attempting to discover the lost mine, no knowledge of its location is had other than that coming from Indian tradition.

Tuscarora Creek has a scrap of history of its own. The great war-path from Tioga down to Wyoming, crossed the mouth of this stream. It was in the certified township of Braintrim and county of Westmoreland. In 1779, Gen. Sullivan, with his army, crossed the Tuscarora at this point. When his rear-guard had reached the south bank, where a large mountain, covered with oak, with little or no underbrush intervening to obstruct the view for a great distance, comes down to the very stream, a body of savages were seen stealing down its side for the purpose of securing a few prisoners. Familiar with the mode of Indian warfare, the guards leaped behind the trees, affording them partial shelter. The Indians, more skilled in the art and advantage of woodside encounter, as quickly betook themselves to the oak, which concealed even their presence, when the skirmish began.

Soldiers fell, wounded or dead, without knowing from what particular quarter bullets issued. At length Mr. Eleazer Carey, who saw his fellow-soldiers fall one after another, simultaneously with the crack of the rifle near by where he was standing, espied the dusky form of a warrior cautiously peering out from behind a tree not fifty yards from where he was standing, with his well-aimed gun in his hand, bring down a soldier at each discharge of his weapon. After the Indian had reloaded, Carey, who had resolved to kill him if possible when he should attempt to shoot again, watched with intense solicitude the warrior's rifle as it was again brought beside the tree. No sooner had the slight projecting cheek and eye of the Indian come out so as to be discerned by Carey, when the avenging bullet was sent forthwith into his brain. He gave one high leap, uttered one deep yell, and fell to rise no more. The Indians ran, caught up his body, and fled into the forest.

So much for mines and springs, which some day may possibly have more interest than that given them by rumors and vague recollections of tradition.

GENERAL HISTORY.

The *earliest* history of the Lackawanna Valley is so interwoven with that of Wyoming, that, to present a faithful picture of one, material must be largely drawn upon the other. In fact, while *Wyoming* in its limited signification now gives a name to a valley unsurpassed for the beauty of its scenery or the romance of its history, it was formerly used in a more enlarged sense to designate *all* the country purchased by the New England men of the Indians in 1754, lying in what is now known as Luzerne, Wyoming, Susquehanna, and Wayne counties. Thus the inhabitants of Providence, Salem, and Huntington, all comparatively remote from Wyoming Valley, were designated as "Wyoming Settlers,"[1] and came under the disputed jurisdiction of Connecticut.

In 1752, the cabin of no white man had broken the Wyoming forest. After a casual reconnoissance along its eastern border by the hunter, made with indefinite knowledge of the character of the plain occupied by Teedyuscung and *Backsinosa*, a Monsey chief at Capoose, and

[1] Miner.

reported with glowing exaggeration to adventurous men living in Hartford desiring to develop the western portion of their possessions, "a number of persons, principally inhabitants of Connecticut, formed themselves into a company for the purpose of purchasing the Susquehanna lands of the Indians, and forming a settlement at Wyoming. This association was called the "*Susquehanna Company*, and during the same year, 1753, they sent out commissioners to explore the contemplated territory, and to establish a friendly intercourse with such Indian tribes as should be found in possession of it."[1] These facts, carried to Philadelphia by Indian scouts and interpreters, alarmed the Proprietary Government of Pennsylvania, which also claimed this wild tract yet unlocked by any Indian treaty, grant, or title to *any* party. Daniel Broadhead and William Parsons, two justices of the peace in Lower Smithfield Township, Northampton County, on the war-path from Connecticut to Wyoming, were instructed by Pennsylvania to watch all persons and parties going hither either to explore or begin a settlement.

In fact no inland point within the province was watched with greater solicitude or devotion through many years of strange vicissitude than was Wyoming. The deep, broad Susquehanna coming down through the magnificent highlands and mountains from the wood-rimmed lakes of New York, carrying its flood sometimes rudely over its banks where the cabin-dwellers roamed in no doubtful security, gave to a valley naturally beautiful all the needed charms to captivate the Indian or allure the eye of the white man. Alive with moose, bear, and deer, fluttering with the wild turkey or the more gentle quail, the woods expanded into forest far extending in every direction of the compass, while water-fowl, and fish of every hue and variety—especially the shad—animated the river and all its winding tributaries.

[1] Chapman, p. 51.

Its possession was a prize as earnestly sought after by one party as it was sternly resisted by the other. Although no actual settlement had been instituted here by the New England people, yet it did not prevent the provincial authorities of Pennsylvania from exhibiting extraordinary vigilance and exertion to prevent even a purchase or survey of a valley so rich in agricultural prospects. James Hamilton, "Governor of Pennsylvania under the Proprietaries, having been informed of the intentions of the Susquehanna Company, considered it proper that immediate measures should be taken to defeat those intentions, and to purchase the land for the use of the Proprietaries of Pennsylvania,"[1] as the Attorney-General of Pennsylvania, to whom it had been referred, had decided "*that this tract of land* (Wyoming) *had not yet been purchased* of the Six Nations (Indians), but has hitherto been reserved, and is now used by them for their hunting-grounds."[2] Sir William Johnson, his Majesty's Indian agent for the colony, residing at Albany, in a letter dated March 20, 1754, was informed of the contemplated purchase, and requested to see "that nothing may be done with the Indians by the Connecticut agents, or any other in their behalf, to the injury of the Proprietaries of this Province."[3]

It should be understood by the general reader, that all lands claimed by the English in America were sold or *granted* to one or more persons with an understanding that the right, or rather the *necessity* still existed of repurchasing the same territory of the Indian tribes having ownership, before it could safely be occupied by the whites. Thus a portion of the land granted to William Penn by King Charles II., March 11, 1681, was repurchased by him of the native tribes in a manner so explicit and satisfactory to them that ever afterward his inter-

---

[1] Chapman, p. 52. [2] Opinion, French Francis, March 18, 1754.
[3] Pennsylvania Archives, 1754.

course with all the aborigines was marked by a constant and unvarying friendship unknown in modern times. To thus purchase Wyoming lands,[1] as well as to conciliate the good-will of the Indians, already excited by the bloody drama alternately played by the English or the French, "orders were received from England directing the colonies to hold a general treaty with the Indians at Albany in 1754, and to form, if possible, such an alliance with them as would insure their friendship and the safety of his Majesty's possessions in America."[2] By runners and messengers, young, swift, and ambitious, the wish of his Majesty's Government was announced to the various tribes interested and remote, and all assembled at Fort Stanwix (now Rome), in July, 1754.

As there was no known *printed* copy of any charter in America,[3] the real boundaries of the royal grant was understood by few or none, yet the authorities of Pennsylvania, believing at this time that Wyoming was within her territorial limits, anticipated and resisted the efforts of the Connecticut people, or the Yankees as they were termed, by every art of diplomacy and every mode of warfare.

John and Richard Penn, Isaac Norris, and Benjamin Franklin, were appointed by Pennsylvania as Commissioners to represent the interests of the Province, and true to their instructions from Governor Hamilton, these eminent gentlemen held *private* conferences with the Six Nations, with a view of securing Wyoming lands, in which they failed.

July 11, 1754, for a consideration of two thousand pounds, New York currency, the "chiefs, sachems, and heads of the Five Nations of Indians, called the Iroquois, and the native proprietors of a large tract of land on, about, and adjacent to the River Susquehannah, and

---

[1] When Wyoming is spoken of in relation to lands, Adjouqua or Lackawanna Valley is of course included within its meaning.
[2] Chapman, p. 51.   [3] Trumbull.

being within the limits and bounds of the charter, and grant of his late Majesty, King Charles 2nd, to the Colonys of Connecticutt," sold to the *Susquehanna Company* Wyoming lands bounded as follows: "Beginning from the one and fortieth degree of north latitude, at *ten miles east of the river* to the end of the forty-second or beginning of the forty-third degree of north latitude, and so to extend west two degrees of longitude one hundred and twenty miles, and from thence south to the beginning of the forty-second degree, and from thence east to the aforementioned boundrie, which is ten miles east of Suskahanna River, together with all and every the mines, minerals, or ore, &c."[1] All the territory lying between this line *ten miles east of the Susquehanna* and the Delaware River, was purchased by the *Delaware Company*, so that the lands of the Lackawanna Valley were embraced respectively in the purchases of the two companies. The townships of Pittson, Lackawanna, Providence, Newton, and a portion of Abington, were thus embraced within the Susquehanna purchase; while Covington, Springbrook, Madison, Jefferson, Scott, and Blakeley, with their vast array of thrifty villages, and the neighboring counties of Wayne and Pike, Susquehanna, and a portion of Monroe, were alike included by the Delaware Indian purchase.

The Proprietary Government, astonished and chagrined at a purchase it failed by the ingenious persuasions of her ablest representatives to thwart, began to suggest measures of practical severity to rid the valley of the Yankee intruders, should they venture upon their new purchase. It was not enough that the wolf crouched along the pathway to Wyoming, or that the savage, homeless and enraged, crossed the westward path where the French and Indian wars had strewn the dead to appall the adventurer.

---

[1] See Pa. Arch., 1748–1756, pp. 147–158, for original copy of deed, with names of purchasers.

Early in February, 1754, a few months previous to this sale, Wm. Parsons, of Lower Smithfield, notified Governor Hamilton that "some of his near neighbors had accompanied three gentleman-like men to Wyomink, who produced a writing under a large seal, empowering them to treat and agree with such persons as were disposed to take any of these lands of them."[1] He also informed the Governor "that it may be the means of occasioning very great disorder and disturbances in the back parts of the province." Persons living in Lower Smithfield Township, near Stroudsburg, holding lands under the Proprietary direction and authority, looked so favorably on the proposed settlement of Wyoming lands, that Daniel Broadhead, Esq., then prominent in the history of Northampton County, as the *name* is yet in that section of country, wrote to Governor Hamilton, February 24, 1754, that "there has been and is, great disquietude amongst the people of these parts, occasioned by some New England gentlemen, to such a degree that they are all, or the majority of them, going to quit or sell their lands for trifles, and to my certain knowledge, many of them have advanced money on such occasions, in order that they might secure rights from the New England Proprietaries, which right I suppose is intended to be on Sasquehannah at a place called Wyomink."[2]

The Provincial Council of Pennsylvania recommended Governor Hamilton to write to the Governor of Connecticut, "to stop the departure of their people on a dangerous enterprise as this," and "forthwith dispatch Conrad Weiser to the Six Nations and those at Wyoming, to put them upon their guard against those proceedings."[3] Governor Fitch replied that he "knew nothing of any thing being done by the Government to countenance such a proceeding as you intimate, and

---

[1] Col. Rec., vol. v., p. 736. [2] Ibid., p. 757. [3] Ibid., p. 758.

as I conclude, is going on among some of our people."
Mr. Armstrong reported to the Government, "that the people of Connecticut are most earnestly and seriously determined to make a settlement on the Susquehanna, within the latitude of the province, relying on the words of their grants, which extend to the *South Sea*, provided that they can succeed in a purchase of these lands from the Six Nations, which they are now attempting by the means of Colonel Johnson and Mr. Lydias of Albany, having subscribed a thousand pieces of eight for that purpose, each giving four dollars for what they call a Right."[1]

Under date of December 2, 1754, five months after the successful negotiations for Wyoming, James Alexander wrote to Governor Morris that he believed that "more vigorous measures will be wanting to nip this affair in the bud, than writing to governors and magistrates, or employing a few rangers, as I before proposed. I question if less will do, than a superior number to the Connecticut men, women, and children, that come, and *bring them to Philadelphia;* the women and children to ship off to Governor Fitch, *the men to imprison till bailed* or *list for Ohio*,[2] *this done twice* or *thrice* will terrify others from coming; and one or two thousand pounds laid now out in this service, may save scores of thousands that it may afterwards cost. I doubt not, Connecticut will amuse and give good words till a great number be settled, and then bid defiance."[4]

Every movement in Hartford, where the interests of these two companies were discussed publicly and freely, was watched by persons employed by Pennsylvania to do so, who, in December, 1754, reported the prospects and development of the organization to Governor

---

[1] Col. Rec., vol. v., pp. 773–4.

[2] A very *humane* way to dispose of peaceful settlers, to have them enlist in the French and Indian war on the Ohio!

[3] Col. Rec., vol. vi., p. 267.

Morris, thus: "There was a great meeting about a fortnight ago in Hartford, of the people concerned in the design'd. The original shares are six hundred. The scheme stood thus. They made a purse, each man paying four dollars towards the purchase, &c., but since that they have [been] obliged to pay five more, so that the original shares of the purchase 'tis nine dollars a man. These sharers engaged to go themselves, or to procure one to go in their stead to the Sasquehannah, and there to make a settlement, build a building, clear so much land, &c., on their respective lots in a given time. The grand emigration does not propose to go forth till all be quietly settled, but in the mean time, 'tis said there will be some individuals going."[1]

In spite of *talks* and treaties, Wyoming, full of natives reluctant to yield possession of their plain to the spoiler of their heritage, remained unpeopled and untouched by the whites. Even some of the Cayuga Indians, seduced into French interests, inimical to the English, hearing that "a lot of people from New England had formed themselves into a body to settle the lands on Susquehanna, and especially *Sea-hau-towano* (Wyoming) threatened, if they done so, to *first kill all their creatures*, and then if they did not desist, they themselves would all be killed, without distinction, let the consequences be what it would."[2] This threat of "Tachnechdorus, the chief of Smamockin, of the Cayiuker," was carried into execution at Wyoming a few years later, when the first settlement here was destroyed, the emigrants shot and scalped by the same band that murdered Teedyuscung in his Susquehanna wigwam.

The colony of Connecticut, aware of the extent of their original grant, and conscious of the integrity of the Indian purchase of Wyoming by the Susquehanna Com-

---

[1] Col. Rec., vol. vi., pp. 267-8.
[2] Pennsylvania Archives, 1748-1756, pp. 259-60.

pany, gave consent to establish a settlement here. In the summer of 1755 the company "sent out a number of persons to Wyoming, accompanied by their surveyors and agents, to commence a settlement. On their arrival, they found the Indians in a state of war with the English colonies; and the news of the defeat of General Braddock having been received at Wyoming, produced such an animating effect upon the Nanticoke tribe of Indians, that the members of the new colony would probably have been retained as prisoners had it not been for the interference of some of the principal chieftains of the Delaware Indians, and particularly of Tedeuscund, who retained their attachment to their Christian brethren of the Moravian church, and their friendship in some degree for the English. The members of the colony, consequently, returned to Connecticut, and the attempt to form a settlement at Wyoming was abandoned until a more favorable opportunity."[1]

The efforts of the Moravian missionaries from Gnadenhütten and Bethlehem, to introduce Christian influences along the foliage of the Indian forest, were not altogethe in vain. At *Machwihilusing* (Wyalusing)[2] a settlement had been made by these zealous and determined German brethren, under the pastorship of the Rev. David Zeisberger, which flourished through all the intermediate Indian wars and massacres up until 1770, when, as the territory occupied by them had been sold to the Connecticut people, the Moravians removed to Ohio, to whither the Delawares had preceded them. Living on the great canoe-route and war-path from Onondaga to Wyoming, these heroic missionaries, who had sacrificed every social comfort for the stern incidents of border life, with no ambition but the good and welfare of the race they sought to elevate, were left unharmed by the warriors desolating the country around them.

[1] Chapman, p. 65. [2] Heckewelder.

The Colonial Records give an account of a council held July 11, 1760, with a large number of Minisinks, Nanticokes, and Delawares, "from an Indian town called *Michalloasen* or *Wighalooscon*, about fifty or sixty miles above Wyomink, on the Susquehannah,"[1] but while it was visited by these missionaries, previous to this it was not chosen by them for a permanent abode until May 9, 1765. "Having fixed on a convenient spot for a settlement, they immediately began to erect a town, which, when completed, consisted of thirteen Indian huts, and upward of forty houses built of wood, in the European manner, besides a dwelling for the missionaries. In the middle of the street, which was eighty feet broad, stood a large and neat chapel. The adjoining lands were laid out into neat gardens; and between the town and the river, about two hundred and fifty acres were divided into regular plantations of Indian corn. The burying-ground was situated at some distance back of the buildings. Each family had its own boat. To this place they gave the name of Friedenshuetten (Huts of Peace). This new settlement soon assumed a very flourishing appearance."[2]

The Wyalusing Indians exhibited toward the whites with whom they came in contact a conciliatory and Christian disposition. At a council held at the State House in Philadelphia, September 17, 1763, John Curtis spoke for the Wyalusing Indians as follows:—

"Brothers:—After the treaty, two years ago, as the Indians were returning home, a Delaware was killed. As soon as the news reached the Indian country, some of his relations were so exasperated, that four of them immediately set off and came down with an intention to kill some of the white folks. On their way they called at Wighalousin and stopt there. When they informed us of their design, the Indians of Wighalousin, men, women, and children, did all in their power to dissuade them from it,

---

[1] Col. Rec., vol. viii., p. 484.   [2] Christian Library.

and joined in a collection of wampum[1] and delivered it to them to pacify them, on which they returned home."[2]

Nor was the Lackawanna part of Wyoming without its spiritual advisers as early as October 26, 1755. At the request of the friendly Indians living on the Susquehanna and *Lee-kaugh-hunt* (Lackawanna), the Moravian missionaries of Bethlehem visited Wyoming at this time (to use the Indian's own phrase), "to speak words to them of their God and Creator as often as they desire it."[3]

They remained six days at "*Waioming*, the Shawanese town, and at *Leckaweke*, the Minising town." They preached twice at *Leckaweke*,[4] where they found the natives enjoying their yearly thanksgiving harvest-feast with song and dance, interpolating their songs with an occasional yell or war-whoop, secure in their corn-fields and "well affected towards the English,"[5] to whom they gave every outward assurance of friendship. Twenty-eight days after this, Gnadenhutten was devastated, and no white settlement in Pennsylvania, above Bethlehem, escaped wholly from the uplifted tomahawk. The Indian town of Nescopicken (Nescopick), one day's journey from Wyoming, became the head-quarters of the French and Indians.[6] Not a single white person lived in either of the valleys of Wyoming or Lackawanna. The Indians, won over by the shrewdness of the French, bent on conquest and carnage, went even below the Blue Mountains to the Tulpehocking, within thirty miles of Philadel-

---

[1] *Wampum* or Wampon, called also Wampampeag; a kind of money in use among the Indians. It was a kind of bead made of shells of the great conch, muscle, &c., and curiously wrought and polished, with a hole through them. They were of different colors, as black, blue, red and white, and purple; the last of which were wrought by the Five Nations. Six of the white, and three of the black or blue passed for a penny.—Trumbull's U. S., vol. i., p. 23. In 1667, Wampon was made a tender by law for the payment of debts, "not exceeding 40 shillings, at 8 white or 4 black for a penny; this was repealed in 1671."—Douglas, vol. i., p. 437.

[2] Pa. Arch., 1760.   [3] Ibid., 1755, p. 492.
[4] Either Assarughney, Capoose, or an Indian town at the Lackawack.
[5] Pa. Arch., 1755, pp. 459-60   [6] Ibid., 1756, p. 558

phia, unresisted. Along the Delaware, from Easton to Broadhead's, the country was absolutely deserted. Broadhead's place was attacked, and bravely defended by the courageous inmates. In fact, Lower Smithfield, where Broadhead's clearing was located, was so constantly threatened by the arrowed warriors, that Benjamin Franklin, in July, 1756, ordered a company of foot to be raised "of fifty able men to protect the inhabitants while they thresh out and secure their corn," and scout from time to time for one month, and "for pay, to receive six dollars per month, and one dollar extra for use of gun and blanket." The men were notified that if they should kill any Indians while thus ranging, "forty dollars will be allowed and paid by the Government *for each scalp of an Indian* so killed."[1] This is the first recorded instance where a premium was offered for scalps in the vicinity of Wyoming.[2] No fortunes, however, where made by scalp gatherers.

After Braddock's memorable defeat in July, 1755, the whole frontier of Pennsylvania was left so destitute of protection, that several friendly Indian chiefs of the Susquehanna tribes visited Philadelphia, and urged upon the Government the importance of building such places of defense, which if they failed to do all the tribes now peaceably inclined, would raise the hatchet as auxiliaries of the exultant French. This prudent advice, however, was not taken until after the Lehigh village of Gnadenhutten had been obliterated by the torch, when a chain of simple forts or block-houses were erected along the Susquehanna and Delaware. It is impossible at the present day, to ascertain the exact location of these forts. "Those west-ward of the Sasquehana," the Pennsylvania Archives inform us, "are about twenty miles asunder, and those between Sasquehana and Delaware about

---

[1] Pa. Arch., 1756, p. 516.
[2] As early as 1689, in the beginning of King Philip's war, one hundred pounds was offered for Indian scalps by New England officials.

ten." The fort at Shamokin was built in July, 1755, from logs huge and hewn. Fort Allen, at Gnadenhutten, was built in January, 1756. The fort at Wyoming and the one asked for at Adjonquay by the Iroquois chiefs were erected the same year.[1] These forts were strongly built, stockaded, and of ample capacity to accommodate the sparsely settled places around them in any exigency. From twenty to fifty men were stationed in these protecting outposts, until after the treaty of 1758 fulfilled the expectations of peace, when many of them were abandoned. The warriors at Tioga and Wyoming and Lackawanna were estimated at this time at seven hundred, fifty of whom were Monseys, at Capoose.

Cushietunck (Cochecton), on the upper Delaware, was settled by the Delaware Company in 1757, which place, in spite of colonial feuds, or Pennymite resistance, prospered in its aspirations and development. Cochecton, like Wyoming, was claimed by Pennsylvania as "lying in the upper part of Northampton County, opposite the Jersey Station Point," and the same vexatious measures employed in one place were also used in the other to expel the New England comers.

A mere glimpse of this section of country as it appeared to Charles Tomson, and Christian Frederic Post, who journeyed toward Wyoming and Lee-haw-hanna in 1758, by order of the Governor of Pennsylvania, and at the request of the Indians, is interesting in an historical light, as reflecting the shadows of one hundred and ten years ago. These Indian civilizers left Philadelphia, June 7, 1758, and in two days reached Fort Allen, on the Lehigh, where they engaged Moses Tetamy and Isaac Still, and three other Indians, to accompany them.

"On Sunday morning we set forward pretty early, and by 12 o'clock reached the Nescopekun Mountain, within fourteen or fifteen miles of Wyoming. Here we met nine

---

[1] Pa. Arch., 1748–1756.

Indians traveling down to Bethlehem. They had left Wyoming the day before, and had been six days from Chenango, a Town of the Nanticokes on Susquehanna, about half way between Owegey and Ossewingo. There was one Nanticoke, one Monsey Captain, one Delaware, four Mawhiccons, and two Squaws. Upon meeting them, we stopped and inquired the news, and from several questions asked, we learned that Teedyuscung was well and at Wyoming, that all was quiet among the Nanticokes, that their principal men were at the Council at Onondaga, which was not yet broke up; that Backsinosa was at *Lee-haugh-hunt* (Lackawanna), but that he was preparing to go somewhere, he said to his own Country. Being informed of our going to Wyoming with good news to all the Indians, they told us that they thought it was by no means safe for us to proceed; that strange Indians were thick in the woods about Wyoming; that a party was seen but four days ago whose Language none of the Delawares there understood, nor did they know of what Nation they were. This alarmed our Indians, they pressed us to turn back with this Company, and make all haste for Fort Allen, and two of them would go and invite Teedyuscung to come to us there. This we objected to, on account of losing time, so we proposed to go forward to the Wyoming Hills, and there wait till two of our Company went forward and informed Teedyuscung of our coming, and know of him whether it would be safe to go to the Town. The Indians we met thought it dangerous to proceed any farther, as they had seen fresh Tracks crossing the Path in two or three places between this and Wyoming, and at one place not half a mile from where we then were. Upon this it was proposed and agreed upon, to go back to the east side of the Hills, and there lodge to-night, till two of our Indians went and invited Teedyuscung to come to us. Next day Teedyuscung came to us."[1] After a long talk and dinner with

[1] Pa. Arch., 1758, pp. 412-22.

Teedyuscung and other chiefs, from the valley, they were made familiar with all the news, rumors, and complaints of the Indians, and sent back, as Teedyuscung assured them that it was absolutely unsafe for them to venture farther. They also reported that "Backsinosa, with about one hundred men, lives yet at Lee-haugh-hunt"[1] (Lackawanna), at Assarughney, a place of so much importance that a friendly Indian who passed there a few days previous, "saw four Canoes made of bark, and two Floats there hid in the bushes,"[2] which he learned had just been used by a party coming from Broadhead's, by the way of Lee-haugh-hunt and Capoose.

After the purchase of Wyoming lands in 1754 by the Connecticut Susquehanna Company, Pennsylvania awakened to the importance of cultivating more intimate relations with the Indians. Teedyuscung was informed by the Provincial Council, that "*his* continuance at Wioming is of great service."[3] The natives being too lazy or too little skilled in agricultural affairs to supply their wigwams with vegetable food, brought it in canoes from Fort Augusta, sixty miles below, thus often exhausting the supply around Sunbury and Northumberland. In May, 1755, the Indians on the Susquehanna were reported starving because of the scarcity of deer.[4] To obviate this, as well as to carry out the policy instituted by Pennsylvania, "fifty or sixty Carpenters, Masons, and Laborers, were sent to Wyoming to build and plant for the Indians. After a very fatiguing march they arrived at Wyoming on the 22d May, 1758, and put the hands to work the next day. As the Battoes did not arrive from Fort Augusta at the time appointed, we were brought to very short allowance in provisions, &c. For several days we had no bread at all, which created no little uneasiness among the men. We kept working until the 27th, when Joseph

---

[1] Pa. Arch., 1758, p. 421.
[2] Col. Rec., vol. viii., p. 127.
[3] Ibid., p. 138.
[4] Pa. Arch., 1758, p. 310.

Croker, one of our masons, was killed and scalped by six of the enemy Indians; this misfortune made our men uneasy. The next day, the Battoes arrived with provisions, which enabled us to carry on the work and finish ten houses. We also plowed some ground for them to plant in, and split some rails to fence it; after which they thought it proper to let us know that it was late in the season, and the grass grown very high, so that the ground when plowed was not fit for planting but in a few places, such as old Towns and the like, we might return until a more favorable time, which we complied with on Friday, the 2d June, and got safe Tuesday evening following."[1]

On the same day that this party returned to Fort Augusta, Moses Tetamy and Isaac Still, both Indian interpreters, left Philadelphia to visit the Monseys at Minisinks, for the Government. The fourth day's journey by the way of the warriors' path over the Lehigh Mountain, brought them to Wyoming, where they were welcomed and treated with great consideration as public messengers. After staying all night at Wyoming, they left early in the morning on horseback, and at night "came to *Tenkghanake* (Tunkhannock), about as far above Wyoming as from Wyoming to Fort Allen. This is an old Town, nobody lives there, but over the river we saw some Minisink Indians, Hunters, who called to us, and when we went over treated us kindly, and gave us some Bear meat and venison. The road from Wyoming to Tenghanaoke, is broken and hilly."[2]

The Western Indians held a great council over the Ohio in June, 1760. Frederic Post and John Hays attempted to accompany Teedyuscung thither, but the two interpreters were denied passage through the Seneca country. A description of their journey through Wyoming, as given in the words of their journal, can not fail to interest very many:—

"Saturday, May 10.—Heassie wether: Sett off from

---

[1] Col. Rec., vol. viii., pp. 134–5.   [2] Pa. Arch., 1756, p. 509.

fort Allen at Eight o'Clock, and traveled till it was Late through a vast Desert; Lodged in the Woods.

"Sunday, 11th.—Sett to the way Early and Arived at Wioming in the Evening, where we were Informed that Teedyuscung was Set off on his Journey this Morning, but they sent for him Imediately on our Coming.

"Monday, 12th.—Teedyuscung Came home About Eleven o'Clock, and we had several Conferences with him this Day.

"Tuesday, 13th.—Wrought at Makeing Belts and Strings of our Wampum, was used very Kindly, and talked of Going Next Day.

"Wed'y, 14th.—Very Rainy Wether, so that we Could not set out, So we followed our old Business of Belt making.

"Thursday, 15th.—Wether the Same; Made Belts.

"Friday, 16th.—Designed Going, but Teedyuscung would not Go until he had a field of Corn planted first, and we all asisted him and planted it this Day.

"Satturday, 17th.—Set of Early and traveled smartly, Crossed a Large Creek about one o'Clock, called *Ah-la-hon-ie* (Lackawanna?), and so followed Our Course up the East Side of the Sisquhana River till Night, and Set up our tents in an Old Indian Town called *Quelootama*, Being fourteen in Number in all.

"Sunday, 18th.—Wet Weather, Nevertheless we traveled Smartly Cross a very Large Creek called *Wash-coking* (Meshoppen), Lodged on the Banks of Sisquhana, and had a very Wet Night of it.

"Monday, 19th.—Set off Early, tho wet, and Arived at a town called *Qui-ha-loo-sing* (Wyalusing), the Govenours Name Wampoonham, a very Religious Civilized man in his own way, and Shewd us a great Deal of Kindness, and we held a Conference with him this Evening, and when over, Mr. Post Gave us a Sermon, at their Request.

"Tuesday, 20th.—They Called us to Council, and

seemed to be very friendly, and Delivered to Teedyuscung three prisoners By a string and promised to bring them Soon down; this town is Situated on Sisquhana, East side, about twenty Houses full of People, Very Good Land, and Good Indian Buildings, all New; had Sermon this Evining again.

"Wednsday, 21st.—They told us there was another prisnor in this town, but the man that had hir would not Consent to Give hir Up yet, but if he Did not he Should Leave their town; We Set off about Eleven o'Clock, and Crossed Qui-ha-loo-sing Creek about a mile above the town; We traveled Through Swamps, Rocks, and Mountains about 15 Miles, then came to the River, and took up Lodging on the Bank."

Thursday and Friday they visited Diohaga, Snake Hole, and Asinsan. At the last-named place "the Indians Began to Sacrifice to their God, and Spent the Day in a very Odd manner, Howling and Danceing, Raveling Like Wolves, and Painted frightfull as Divels.

"Monday, 26th.—The Indians, Haveing Got Rum, Got Drunk, all in General, Except some old men; and Teedyuscung Behaved well on this Occasion, for when his Sone brought in the Kegg of Rum, he would not taste it; we were very much Abused and Scolded by the Indians, and *thretened Often to Rost us.* They Bid us Welcome to this town, but if we came any farther they would Rost us in the fire.

"There was a great Sacrifice of a hogg, which gathered a Great Number of them together, and after their Sacrificial Rites were over, they Encouraged us to Go on, But we Could not See it Clear, for the old father Mingo always Sent us word not Go, but that Teedyuscung and his Indians Might Go, but that we should not Go, nor any White man Should pas through their Country."

After visiting various Indian towns, witnessing deer sacrifices, and holding councils with the Delawares, Wonamies, and Monseys, they concluded to return home, as the old Indian "agreement was that no white man Should pas throw their Country, for fear of Spyes to see their Land."

The fertile meadows now extending at certain intervals along the river from Binghamton to Tunkhannock, they describe as "an Ordinary Country, Nothing but Mountains and Rocks and pine timber, save the Small Low lands the Indians plants their Corn on.".

On the ninth day of the homeward journey, interlined by many vexations and delays, and lodging in the woods, where "the Knates Bit so hard," they approached Wyoming. "About Eleven o'Clock we came to a narrow pass where the horses, with Hight of the River, was obliged to Swime a considerable way, and had to all get in the Canoo, then took our horses again and had to Swim another Large Creek and Climbe many a hill, but at Lenth we Got to Weoming, thank God.

"Saturday, 28th.—Set of from Weoming and traveled Over the Mountains, and Lodged in the Woods, and had very wet Weather," &c., &c.[1]

In April, 1761, before the snow-drifts had melted from the cold gorges of the mountain, the route had been surveyed by a party which "marked trees for twenty miles from the Delaware in the way toward Susquehannah, and laid out lots for a town at a place called *Leighwackson*, or Lackervak, about eight miles westward from Casheitunck."[2] Teedyuscung himself visited Philadelphia during this month, to express to the Governor his uneasiness about this settlement, which he reported was so unsafe for his pale brother "that they (the Connecticut men) kept continual watch for fear the Indians would shoot them."[3]

In August, 1762, the adventurous spirit of New England emigration began to move toward Wyoming with greater success than ever before. A few miles below the village

---

[1] Pa. Arch., 1760, pp. 735–41. [2] Col. Rec., vol. viii., p. 614. [3] Ibid., p. 595.

of Assarughney, and a mile or two above the Indian town at Wyoming, runs into the Susquehanna a short, sluggish creek, celebrated afar by the name of *Mill Creek*.

Two hundred persons from the colony of Connecticut began a settlement on the shaded margin of this stream at this time. "They found the valley covered with woods, except a few acres in the immediate vicinity of the Shawanese and Wyoming towns, which had been improved by the Indians in the cultivation of their corn, and which was still in part occupied by them."[1] A few acres of land was cleared and sown with wheat and rye, after which the emigrants concealed their agricultural implements in the ground and returned to Connecticut to winter, returning in the spring.

Teedyuscung, jealous of his plains yielding with the simple tillage of the squaws, again visited Philadelphia, Nov. 19, 1762, and sought a private interview with the Governor, to complain of the settlement upon *Lec-hawanock* Creek. The Governor desired Teedyuscung to speak nothing but the honest truth, which he promised to do, and then addressed him as follows :—"Brother: You may remember that some time ago I told you that I should be obliged to remove from Wyomink on account of the New England people, and I now acquaint you that soon after I returned to Wyomink from Lancaster, there came 150 of those people, furnished with all sorts of Tools, as well for building as Husbandry, and declared that they had bought those Lands from the Six Nations, and would set tle them, and were actually going to build themselves Houses, and settle upon a creek called *Leckawanock*, about seven or eight miles above Wyomink. I threatened them hard, and declared I would carry them to the Governor at Philadelphia; and when they heard me threaten them in this manner, they said they would go away and consult their own Governor; for if they were carried to

---

[1] Chapman.

Philadelphia, they might be detained there Seven Years, and they said further, that since the Indians were uneasy at this purchase, if they would *give them back* the money it had cost them, which was *one or two Bushels of Dollars*, they *would give them their Lands again*. Ten days after these were gone, there came other fourteen men, and made us the same speeches, declaring that they expected above three thousand would come and settle the Wyomink Lands in the Spring, and they had with them a Saw and Saw-Mill Tools, proposing to go directly and build a Saw-Mill about a mile above where I live, but upon my threatening those in the same manner I did the former Company, they went away, and, as I was told, buried their tools somewhere in the Woods. These people desired me to assist them in surveying the Lands, and told me they would reward me handsomely for my trouble, but I refused to have any thing to do with them. Brother: Six days after these were gone there came eight other white men and a mulatto, and said the very same things to me that the others had said, and immediately I got together my Council, and as soon as we had finished our Consultations, I told these people that I actually would confine them and carry them to Philadelphia and deliver them to the Governor there, upon which they went away, saying they would go to their own Governor, and come again with great numbers in the Spring. Some of these people stole my Horse that I bought at Easton, but they gave me another Horse and five pounds in money, in satisfaction for my Horse. Brother: Tho' I threatened these people hard, that I would confine them and carry them down to you, yet I did not mean actually to do it, remembering that you charged me not to strike any White Man, tho' they should come, but to send you the earliest notice of their coming that was in my power. Brother: Before I got up to Wyomink from Lancaster, there had come a great Body of these New England People with intent actually to settle the Land, but the Six Nations passing by at that time from Lancaster, sent to let them know that they should not be permitted to settle any of these Lands, and on their expressing great resentment against them, and threatening them if they persisted, they went away. This I was told by Thomas King, who was left behind at Wyomink by the Six Nations, to tell me that they intended to lay this whole matter before the great Council at Onondagoe, and that they would send for me and my Indians to come to Albany in the Spring, where they are to have a meeting with the New England people, and desired that I would be quiet till I should receive their Message, and then come to Albany. On this speech of Thomas King's we met together in Council, and agreed not to give him any promise to come to Albany, but to advise the Governor of Pennsylvania of this, and take his advice what to do, and if he will go with us and advise us to go, we will go in case we are sent for in the Spring. Brother: Surely as you have a General of the King's Armies here, he might hinder these people from coming and disturbing us in our possessions. Brother: About six days after I left Wyomink I received a Belt, which was brought me by the Indian man Compass; it came first to Nutimus, and from him to me. By that Belt, Beaver desired that I and the Delawares, the Wapings, and Mohickons, settled at Wyomink, would remove thence and come and live at Allegheny. Brother: I have one thing more to say, and I shall have finished all I have to say at this time. Brother: You may remember that at the Treaty at Easton we were promised that a *Schoolmaster* and *Ministers* should be sent to instruct us in religion, and to teach us to read and write. As none have yet been provided for us, I desire to know what you intend to do in this matter. I have now done." [1]

The Governor, in reply, informed Teedyuscung, that as Wyoming lands had never yet been purchased from the

---

[1] Col. Rec., vol. ix., pp. 6-8.

Six Nations, he had sent a messenger to warn the Connecticut people away from Lechawanock Creek, who met them returning because of the rough manner spoken to by the Indians. After commending Teedyuscung for his fidelity and good behavior, the Governor said, "Brother: You know that your Uncles, the Six Nations, have kindled a fire for you at Wyomink, and desired you would stay there and watch, and give them notice if any White people should come to take away the Lands from them, and that you would not suffer them to do it. Be assured that this winter, *measures will be taken to prevent these troublesome people from coming to disturb you.* On these considerations I desire you to remain quiet where you are, and not move away, as you seem to have no inclinations to go away only on account of these New England disturbers. The times have been so unsettled, that there has been no opportunity of sending Ministers and Schoolmasters among you. Now there is a likelihood of a general peace being soon established, if you determine still to continue at Wyomink, I shall consider of this matter and send you an answer at a proper time."[1]

The complaints of Teedyuscung, nor the threats of Lieutenant-Governor Hamilton, were hardly necessary, as the next year (1763) witnessed the murder of the king of the Delawares, in his simple cabin by the river side, and the flight or massacre of the defenseless yeomanry at Wyoming. When Teedyuscung sank the tomahawk into the skull of the offending Iroquois warrior on his way to Easton, in 1758, unavenged and apparently unnoticed at the time, he wrote his own death-warrant in the blood of the fallen chief. Indian revenge slumbers only to increase its intensity. Under the garb of friendship, he was visited at his village by some warriors of the Six Nations from the upper branches of the Susquehanna, plied boun-

---

[1] Col. Rec., vol. ix., p. 9.

tifully with liquor, of which he was passionately fond, and while thus inebriated in his wigwam, helpless, asleep, and alone, the celebrated and venerable chieftain perished in the flames, on the night of April 19, 1763. His own dwelling, and twenty others surrounding it, had been set on fire simultaneously, by these emissaries from the Six Nations, who thus sought and found revenge upon the unforgotten and unresisting offender.

Some four months previous to this the Yankees had returned to the valley with their families, bringing along cattle, sheep, hogs, and grain sufficient to last them until the coming harvest. Traffic and fur-trading had sprung up with the surrounding tribes, with whom the most friendly and harmonious relations had hitherto supposed to have existed, when suddenly, on the afternoon of the fifteenth of October, while the farmers were hard at work in the field, unsuspicious of approaching danger, they were surrounded by "a party of Indians, who massacred about twenty persons,[1] took several prisoners, and having seized upon the live stock, drove it toward their town. Those who escaped, hastened to their dwellings, gave the alarm to the families of those who were killed, and the remainder of the colonists—men, women, and children—fled precipitately to the mountains, from whence they beheld the smoke arising from their late habitations, and the savages feasting on the remains of their little property. They had taken no provisions with them, except what they had hastily seized in their flight, and must pass through a wilderness sixty miles in extent before they could reach the Delaware River. They had left brothers, husbands, and sons to the mercy of the savages; they had no means of defense, in case they should

---

[1] The following persons were among the killed:—"Rev. Wm. Marsh, Thos. Marsh, Timothy Hollister, Timothy Hollister, Jr., Isaac Hollister, Nathan Terry, Wright Smith, Daniel Baldwin and wife, Isaac Wiggins, Zeruah Whitney. Mr. Shepherd, and a son of Daniel Baldwin, were taken prisoners."—*Annals of Luzerne.*

be attacked, and found themselves exposed to the cold winds of autumn without sufficient raiment. With these melancholy recollections and cheerless prospects did the fugitives commence a journey of two hundred and fifty miles on foot." [1]

Thus by one stroke, seldom surpassed in suddenness or atrocity, by the same savages that slew Teedyuscung and then attempted to fix the ignominious crime upon the New England men, having no knowledge of its inception or no part in its execution, every living white person was swept from Wyoming in an hour, and the valley again left in the sole occupancy of the Indian. Their removal or destruction at this time, if more vindictive and cruel, was *no more certain* than that vouchsafed them by the Provincial Government, had a few more days of quiet husbandry have been allowed them by the Indians. On the Tuesday before the first massacre, October 17, 1763, Major Clayton marched to Wyoming [2] to carry out the instructions of the Provincial Government, already anticipated by the firebrand and hatchet. He "met with no Indians, but found the New Englanders who had been killed and scalped a day or two before they got there. They buried the dead, nine men and one woman, who had been most cruelly butchered; the woman was roasted, and had two hinges in her hands, supposed to have been put in red hot, and several of the men had awls thrust into their eyes, and spears, arrows, pitchforks, &c., sticking in their bodies. *They burnt what houses the Indians had left*, and *destroyed a quantity of Indian corn*. The enemy's tracks were up the river toward Wighaloesing." [3]

On the 20th October, Governor Hamilton ordered Colonel James Bard to Wyoming as a commissioner, not to look after the warriors thus arrayed for murder and

---

[1] Chapman. [2] Pa. Arch., 1763, p. 125.
[3] See Letter from Paxton, Lancaster County, dated Oct. 23, 1763.

mischief, but "to require and command the Inhabitants, in His Majesty's Name, *forthwith* to desist from their said undertaking, and to depart and remove from thence," &c.[1]

It is hardly possible that news of the massacre carried by the slow canoe-route, or narrow foot-path, could have reached Philadelphia at this time, as no allusion is made to it until October 25, 1763, when the Rev. John Elder, of Paxton, captain of two Lancaster companies, wrote as follows to Governor Hamilton: "Sir, In a Lett'r I writ to your Hon'r the 17th Inst., I acquainted you that it then was impossible to suspend the Wyoming Expedition. The party is now returned, and I shall not trouble your Hon'r with *my account* of their proceedings, as Major Clayton informs me that he transmitted to you, from Fort Augusta, a particular journal of their transactions from their leaving Hunters till they returned to Augusta.[2] The mangled Carcases of these unhappy people presented to our Troops a melancholy Scene, which had been acted not above two days before their arrival ; and by the way the Savages came into the Town, it appears they were the same party that committed the Ravages in Northampton County, and as they set off from Wyoming up the same Branch of the River, towards Wihilusing, and from several other Circumstances, it's evident, that till that Branch is cleared of the enemy, the frontier settlem'ts will be in no safety."[3]

Nothing whatever was done by the authorities of Pennsylvania toward punishing, or even rebuking, the authors of this preconcerted destruction of life and property, made more atrocious by the fact that settlers living in Northampton County uttered no complaint, and interposed neither inquiry nor remonstrance at this or any other time.

---

[1] Col. Rec., vol. ix., p. 61.

[2] No such Report appears either in the Pennsylvania Archives or Records.

[3] Pennsylvania Archives, 1760–76, p. 127.

In fact so great and so apparent was this stoic indifference exhibited toward the welfare of a feeble but energetic colony, struggling alike with starvation and savage treachery, that Governor Amherst of New York wrote to Governor Hamilton that, "I can not help repeating my surprise at the infatuation of the people in your Province, who tamely look on while their brethren are butchered by the Savages, when, without doubt, it is in their power, by exerting a proper spirit, not only to protect the settlements, but to punish any Indians that are hardy enough to disturb them."[1]

While there seems to have been no complicity, either charged or suspected, between the provincial authorities of Pennsylvania and the disaffected portion of the Six Nations in regard to the annihilation of the young settlement at Wyoming, no one can peruse the Pennsylvania Archives or the Colonial Records of Pennsylvania, embracing as they do, the earliest written history of Wyoming, without reflections not flattering to the magnanimity either of the Province or the State.

In the earlier history of the valley, barbarities were sometimes practiced, both by the red and the white man, upon the weaker party. Conrad Weiser, after visiting Wyoming, in 1755, describes the capture of an Indian, who "begged his life, but (shocking to me) they shot him in the midst of them, scalped him, and threw his body into the river."[2] Two months after the Connecticut settlers were slaughtered and first expelled from Wyoming, the Conestogae Indians—the remains of a tribe of the Six Nations—were massacred in Lancaster by the whites. On the 14th of December, 1763, these Moravian Indians, who had lived under the faith of the Government for sixty years, were shot and clubbed in cold blood, and every indignity practiced upon the women and children, whose age and sex plead alike in vain to the avenging hand of

---

[1] Col. Rec., vol. ix., p. 62.   [2] Ibid., vol. vi., p. 763.

the Paxton men. "They surrounded the small village of Indian huts, and just at break of day broke in upon them all at once. Only three men, two women, and a young boy, were found at home. These poor, defenseless creatures were immediately fired upon, stabbed, and hatcheted to death! The good Shehaes, who was very old, having assisted at the second treaty held with Mr. Penn, in 1701, was, among the rest, cut to pieces in his bed! The Magistrates of Lancaster sent out and collected the remaining Indians, *promised them protection*, and put them in the work-house, a strong building, as a place of greatest safety. On the 27th of December, these cruel men, armed as before, broke open the door, and entered with the utmost fury in their countenances. When the fourteen poor wretches saw no possible *protection* nor escape, and being without the least weapon of defense, they divided their little families, and children clinging to their parents; they fell on their faces, protested their innocence, declared their love to the English, and that in their whole lives they had never done them injury; and in this position they all received the hatchet! Men, women, and children were every one inhumanly murdered in cold blood."[1]

This ferocious transaction, the authors of which, although well known in the community, ever remained unpunished, created among the Indian tribes throughout the country a profound sensation, and for months awakened no little solicitude in the head of the Government of Pennsylvania. Governor Penn, justly indignant, and conscious of the great wrong inflicted upon the Indians, whom the official men of the province had sworn to protect, fearing its deplorable effect upon the usually stoical but ever-vindictive savage, promptly and boldly denounced the guilty party as "villainous and murderous," and issued warrants for their arrest; and yet, al-

---

[1] See Prout's History of Pennsylvania, vol. i., pp. 326-8; also, Col. Rec., vol. ix., pp. 102-5, 107, 112-13, 121-3, 125, 127-9, 132, 137, 142, 170, 409.

though they were living within the county, they were never reprimanded, arrested, nor punished.

The property of these tomahawked natives, consisting of "three horses, two belts of wampum," a number of deeds, treaties, and documents, written on parchment, and signed by Wm. Penn, in 1701, and Logan and others, were subsequently returned to their relatives in the Indian country.

This wanton and wicked breach of faith on the part of citizens of Lancaster and Paxton, contributed to influence the Moravian Indians at Wyalusing and elsewhere along the Susquehanna to remove westward, and had very much to do henceforth toward inspiring a spirit of warfare and revenge along the border, as well as to palliate and excuse the treatment of *their* captives taken from the whites.

In a message to Gov. Penn from the Assembly, in Feb., 1768, a portion of these outrages are thus enumerated: "In the year 1763, the cruel Massacre of Twenty Indians, chiefly of the Six Nations, were perpetrated at Conestago and Lancaster. In the same year a Delaware Chief met with the same fate between Sherman's Valley and Juniata. In 1765, a Chief of the Six Nations was murdered near Bedford. In the year 1766, a principal warrior of the Delawares was killed between Red Stone creek and Cheat river; and three Delaware Chiefs were robbed and murdered near Fort Pitt, by two inhabitants of this Province. An Indian was lately murdered in Northampton County; besides the late barbarity committed by Frederic Stump and his servant on ten Indians at Middle Creek. And *not one of those murderers have been brought to punishment.*"[1] England and France having concluded a definite peace in 1763, hostilities ceased throughout the colonial settlements.

In September, 1766, an adventurous trader, named John

---

[1] Col. Rec., vol. ix., pp. 478–9.

Anderson, had a store of goods at Wyoming, for traffic with the red men, and was complained of by the Nanticoke, Conoys, and Mohickons, from the Council Fires at Chenango, in the following manner to John Penn:—
"Brother: As we came down from our Country we stopped at Wyoming, where we had a Mine in two places, and we discovered that some white People had been at work in the Mine, and had filled three Canoes with the Ore; and we saw their Tools with which they had dug it out of the ground, were they had made a hole at least forty feet long, and five or six feet deep. It happened, formerly, that some white People did now and then take only a small bit, and carried it away, but these People have been working at the Mine, and have filled their canoes. We desire you will tell us whether you know any thing of this matter, or if it be done by your Consent. We are informed that there is one John Anderson, a Trader, now living at Wyoming, and we suspect that either he or somebody employed by him has robbed our mine. This Man has a Store of Goods there, and it may happen, when the Indians see their Mine robbed, they will come and take away his Goods."[1]

Governor Penn replied that he knew nothing of the mine or Anderson, who had settled in the Indian country without his knowledge or wish. "But you know," addressing the chief, "that notwithstanding all our Care, as it is such a Distance, People may go there and we know nothing of it."[2] The knowledge of this silver mine perished with the race that knew it.

For six years, aside from the intrusion of these explorers and traders, Wyoming was left in its native solitude, and as the intervening years make no history for the valley then in dispute between Pennsylvania and Connecticut, a brief synopsis of the different charters and grants relating to the disputed territory claimed

---
[1] Col. Rec., vol. ix. pp. 329–30.   [2] Ibid., p. 332.

by the respective parties, and a mere outline of the claim and controversy arising from the same, will not only be expected by the intelligent reader, but it is indispensable to a proper appreciation of the history of the Lackawanna Valley, then within the contested limit. In fact, the *earliest* history of the valley, could not be complete nor understood without such a general exposition of grants and charters, running along down into the Connecticut claim, from the first grant of land in America, in 1606, by the English Government.

As early as 1606, King James of England, jealous of the ambitious French, advancing to traffic on the Indian shore of the western continent, divided that part of North America, lying between the 34th and 45th degrees of latitude, into two portions. The northern part he granted by patent to Thomas Hanham and others, who associated themselves for the purpose of opening a trade with the Indians for skins, furs, and tobacco. Forty noblemen, knights, and gentlemen were incorporated, March 3, 1620, by King James, into a company known as "*The Councils established at Plymouth, in the County of Devon, for the Planting, Ruling, and Governing of New England, in America,*"[1] to whom and their assigns were granted all "That part of America, lying and being in breadth from the forty degrees of the said Northerly latitude from the Equinoctial line, to forty-eight degrees of the said Northerly latitude, inclusively, and in length of and within all the breadth aforesaid, throughout the mainland from sea to sea," &c.[2] While the governing powers and privileges of this Plymouth corporation were being exercised in England, the laws and regulations of the body were to extend over *New* England, which thus derived its name from this grant. Originally embracing *all* of New England, portions of this vast territory were divided and subdivided, as to subsequently form the New England

---

[1] Trumbull.   [2] Ibid.

States. Each sale and division of property thus effected, had to be ratified by the legislative power in England to make it valid and binding.

A portion of the territory of the Plymouth Company was sold in 1628, and subsequently became the State of Massachusetts. Another portion, now forming the State of Connecticut, was transferred to the Earl of Warwick in 1630, who, in March, 1631, sold the same territory to Lord Gay and fifteen others. It embraced "all that part of New England, in America, which lies and extends itself from a river, there called Narragansett river, the space of forty leauges upon a straight line near the shore, towards the southwest, west and by south, or west as the coast lieth, towards Virginia, acounting three English miles to the leauge ; and, also, all and singular the lands and hereditaments whatsoever, lying and being within the lands aforesaid, north and south in latitude and breadth, and in length and longitude, *of and within all the breadth aforesaid, throughout the main lands there, from the western ocean to the south sea.*"[1]

By virtue of this royal grant, a small band of energetic men made the first settlement on the bank of the Connecticut River, in 1633. This last-named grant was sold in 1662 to the Free Planters of the Colony of Connecticut for 16,000 pounds sterling. King Charles the Second confirmed the charter to the Connecticut colony, of "all that part in our dominion in New England, in America, bounded on the East by Naragansett Bay, where the said river falleth into the Sea, and on the North by the line of the Massachusetts plantation, *on the South by the sea*, and in longitude as the line of the Massachusetts Colony running from East to West (that is to say) from the Naragansett Bay on the East, to the South sea on the West part."

These several instruments, taken as a whole, open a full view of the ancient territorial limits of Connecticut.[2]

---

[1] Trumbull.   [2] Chapman.

Forty leagues (120 miles) along the coast from Narragansett Bay toward Virginia, would terminate very nearly on the fortieth degree of north latitude, fixed as a boundary in the original grant to the Plymouth Company and would embrace the comparative little territory of both Wyoming and Lackawanna valleys.

The original charter of William Penn, which granted to him so many of the coal and iron-clad valleys and mountains of Pennsylvania, and which subsequently developed the Pennymite war in Wyoming, dates back to March 4, 1681. "Out of a commendable desire to enlarge our English Empire," &c., Charles the Second granted to William Penn, "all that tract or parte of land in America, with all the Islands therein conteyned, as the same is bounded on the East by the Delaware river from twelve miles distance, Northwarde of New Castle Towne unto the three and fortieth degree of Northern latitude, if the said River doth extend soe farre Northwards. But if the said River shall not extend soe farre Northward then by the said River soe farre as it doth extend, and from the head of the said River the Easterne bounds are to bee determined by a meridian line, to bee drawn from the head of the said River unto the three and fortieth degree, the said land to extend Westwards, five degrees in longitude, to bee computed from the Easterne Bounds, and the said lands to bee bounded on the North by the beginning of the three and fortieth degree of Northern latitude," &c.[1]

The opposing claims of Pennsylvania, as set forth by its agents, Messrs. Bradford, Read, Wilson, and Sargeant, before the Court of Commission assembled at Trenton, New Jersey, in November, 1782, to finally determine the controversy between Pennsylvania and Connecticut regarding Wyoming, will be found in ample detail in the Pennsylvania Archives, 1782-3. They claimed Wyoming

---

[1] See Col. Rec., vol. i., pp. 17-26, for copy of original charter.

by virtue of the royal purchase of Mr. Penn, who with succeeding proprietaries had negotiated with the Indians for the full and absolute right of pre-emption for all the lands in dispute. They also claimed "that the Northern bounds have always been deemed to extend to the end of the forty-second Degree, where the figures 428 are so marked on the map; the River Delaware being found to extend so far North and farther; the said River, pursuing the East or main Branch thereof, above the Forks at Easton, hath been ever deemed to be one Boundary of Pennsylvania from twelve miles above New Castle, on the said River," &c.[1]

The northern part of the territory granted to William Penn, spread over a part of the western lands before granted to the colony of Connecticut, equal to one degree of latitude through the whole breadth of said grant.

The collisions, running through thirteen years of crimson austerities between Pennsylvania and Connecticut for jurisdiction and right of soil in Wyoming, originated either in great want of knowledge of the topography of America by the English Government, or an unpardonable careless exercise of it in regard to this charter to William Penn, which thus interfered with and *overlapped* lands already sold to Connecticut. Of this interference, Mr. Penn had notice at the time of his taking out his patent for those lands.[2]

The Indian title to the wilderness overshadowing the Schuylkill and "*Lechhaiy Hills*" (Lehigh) had been extinguished as early as 1732; and the land about the mouth of the creek called *Lechawachsein* (Lackawaxen) was purchased of the Indians by the Provincial Government of Pennsylvania in October, 1756;[3] but Wyoming, more isolated in its sylvan solitude, had been reserved by the tribes controlling it, for hunting-grounds or a retreating place long after their intercourse began with the whites.

---

[1] See Pa. Arch., 1782, p. 701. [2] Ibid., p. 707. [3] Ibid., p. 722.

It was first sold by them, July 11, 1754, as before related, to the Connecticut Susquehanna Company.

It will be readily seen that the charter of Connecticut, embracing Wyoming, was given *nineteen years anterior* to that of Pennsylvania, possessed and settled by Connecticut with her strong and sturdy sons, and yet, after a deliberation of over five weeks in 1783, the adjusticating commissioners at Trenton, gave an opinion in the matter as follows, that astonished the citizens of both States with its brevity and its *bias* :—" We are unanimously of Opinion that the State of Connecticut has no Right to the Lands in Controversy. We are also unanimously of Opinion that the Jurisdiction and Pre-emption of all the Territory lying within the Charter Boundary of Pennsylvania, and now claimed by the State of Connecticut, do of Right belong to the State of Pennsylvania."[1] This decision, known as the "*Trenton Decree,*" from which there was no possible appeal or redress, while it decided the question of *jurisdiction* only, indicated the selfish and illiberal spirit that would and that did ultimately inspire a judicial opinion in regard to the right of soil already held by Connecticut by every essential condition giving validity to a title, viz.: grant from the king—purchase of the soil from the Indian owners, and actual occupancy of the same.

Generations have been born and buried since our hillsides and villages, now exulting and expanding in their thrift, knew no tranquillity but that given for an hour by the stronger wielded bayonet of one rival party or the other, struggling for mastery of the valley; and even while the Indian wars smote down a father or a son with no shroud but the gloom of the forest, and no grave but some friendly rock yet full of the farewell whispers of the dead; or even when the Revolution came with its burden borne cheerfully and valiantly even here, the Connecticut set-

---

[1] Pa. Arch., 1783, p. 732.

tlers had hardly a moment's respite from officious sheriffs, and their often brutal posses, sent out by Pennsylvania to annoy, imprison, or expel the naturally quiet people of Wyoming.

The Connecticut controversy and the Pennymite contention for Wyoming, which had all the grand features of an epic poem, has long ceased to occupy the public mind as it did prominently for a half a century, because less occasion for its existence was known after the *final* compromising law of 1799 established kind and harmonious relations between the contending parties ; but no one can peruse the able works of Peck, Miner, Chapman, or Pearce, or wade through the voluminous official papers of the State, giving such vast variety and abundance of *documentary* evidence pertaining to this matter, without feeling that the early emigrants from Connecticut who sought out and settled the lands of the Susquehanna and Delaware companies at Wyoming and Wallenpaupack in the best faith, were shamefully robbed and wronged by unprincipled persons acting by and with the authority of Pennsylvania. The bad spirit evinced by either party, as far as it relates to the history of the Lackawanna Valley, will be briefly noticed in a future page.

GENERAL HISTORY—CONTINUED.

To obviate trouble with a portion of the Indians rendered dissatisfied with the sale of Wyoming lands by the representations of the Penn interests inimical to the sale, the English Government, through its agents in America, held a treaty at Fort Stanwix, near Oneida Lake, in the fall of 1768, with the Six Nations ; at which time and place the most friendly assurances were given and received by both parties, and the lands on the Susquehanna were ceded to the English. At the same general treaty, some of the chiefs of the Six Nations, willing to sell their lands to as many parties and as many times as pay would be forthcoming, gave the Proprietaries of Pennsylvania a deed of Wyoming lands which had been sold *nineteen years previous* to the Susquehanna Company.

Immediately after the close of this Indian Congress, the Susquehanna Company held a meeting at Hartford, and voted to settle Wyoming at once. It was also "voted that forty Persons, upwards of the age of twenty-one years, Proprietors in said Purchase, proceed to take possession of said land by the first day of February next, and that two hundred more of the age aforesaid join the said forty as early in the Spring as may be."[1] For the purpose of encouraging the self-reliant men who were expected to encounter many a repelling wave as they went into this Indian land, the sum of two hundred pounds was appropriated to purchase "proper materials, sustenance, and Provisions for said forty." Five townships, each five miles square, were to be laid out for "the said forty and the said two hundred persons, reserving and appropriating three whole Rights or Shares in each Township *for the Public use of a Gospel Minister and Schools* in each of said Towns, and also reserving for the use of said Company all Beds, Mines, Iron Ore, and Coals."[2] John Jenkins, Isaac Tripp, Benj. Follett, Wm. Burk, and Benj. Shoemaker, were appointed a committee to exercise a general superintendence over the affairs of the forty settlers, and to lay out and prepare a road through the wilderness to Susquehanna River. Fifty pounds, Connecticut currency ($167), was voted this committee to build this, the first road opened from the East to Wyoming. This trail or public road followed the warriors' path, and, unbridged for swamps and streams sometimes formidable indeed, was simply widened for the saddled horse.

A road had been opened to Teedyuscung's village from

---

[1] Col. Rec., vol. ix., p. 570. [2] Ibid.

Shamokin in 1759. Wyoming, which lay in serene grandeur amid her mountain shades, had been watched by Governor Penn with an extraordinary appreciation of its importance and relations to his own Province. Not only this, but the fear of a new Colony or Province, distinct from that of Pennsylvania or Connecticut, and comparatively independent of either, to embrace Wyoming and Lackawanna valleys, Wallenpaupack, and Cochecton within its boundary, contributed much toward inspiring the unyielding opposition of Penn to any movement of men aiming to develop the backwoods of Wyoming. After the Proprietaries' purchase of these lands in November, 1768, Governor Penn proceeded forthwith to lease one hundred acres for seven years to Messrs. Ogden, Jenkins, and Stewart, ostensibly to establish an Indian trading post, but really to baffle the efforts of the Susquehanna Company to colonize and settle the territory, and to retain possession himself. "These lessees," says Chapman, "with several other adventurers, removed to Wyoming in January, 1769, and took possession of the improvements made by the Connecticut people, from which they had been driven by the Indians in 1763." The forty persons sent out by the Susquehanna Company from Hartford, arrived on the ground, February 8, 1769. "On their arrival at the place where they had built a log house in 1763, they found Captain Amos Ogden, an Indian Trader, and others with him, had entered into their s'd house. Our Settlers, not willing to use any force to regain the s'd house from him or them, set themselves to build a number of Log Houses, or rather Huts, for their shelter, and went quietly about their lawful business in the peace of God and the King."[1] The forty settlers at Mill Creek were taken prisoners by the Ogden party, carried to Easton jail, seventy miles away, promptly released on bail, and as promptly sought their Wyoming cabins.

[1] Pa. Arch., 1771, p. 404.

In the month of March following, being joined by some one hundred and fifty others from Connecticut and Lancaster County, Pennsylvania, who, finding their comrades at Mill Creek under bonds to appear at Easton Court during this month, stopped at the mouth of the Lackawanack, where they erected some rude log structures for dwellings and defense. When the first party of New England men were on their way to Wyoming in January, 1769, Thos. Bennett, of Goshen, New York, was induced to accompany the party hither. Immediately after the capture and partial dispersion of the settlers at Mill Creek, he went with some "New England men to a place called *Lamawanak*, and there built a Blockhouse,"[1] for the purpose of resisting the aggressions both of the Pennymites and the hostility of the surrounding Indians. After Bennett's arrest by the Pennsylvania authorities, he endeavored to exculpate himself from censure by affirming "that the only reason of his ever appearing in arms at the Fort was to keep Centry sometimes in his turn, when they were under apprehensions of being attacked by the Indians, a number of them being then there, who appeared very angry and painted, and threatening to roast a Hog in the Fort and have a dance ; and that the said Indians carried off a Hog."[2]

"Nothing," says Bancroft, "could restrain the Americans from peopling the wilderness. To be a freeholder was the ruling passion of the New England man. Marriages were early and fruitful. The sons as they grew up, skilled in the use of the ax and the rifle, would, one after another, move from the old homestead, and with a wife, a yoke of oxen, a cow, and a few husbandry tools, build a small hut in some new plantation, and by tasking every faculty of mind and body, win for themselves plenty and independence. Such were they who began to dwell among the untenanted forests that rose between the

---

[1] Pa. Arch., 1760–1776, p. 391.   [2] Ibid., 1771, p. 392.

Penobscot and the Sainte Croix, or in the New Hampshire grants, on each side of the Green Mountains, or in the exquisitely beautiful Valley of Wyoming, where, on the banks of the Susquehanna, the wide and rich meadows, shut in by walls of wooded mountains, attracted emigrants from Connecticut, though their claim of right under the charter of their native colony was in conflict with the territorial jurisdiction of the Proprietaries of Pennsylvania."[1]

Of the forty adventurers plunging into the forest thus disputed, to be greeted only with writs and arrests by the Pennymites, apprised of their coming by swift-footed couriers from the Delaware, none chose to stop and settle at *Capoose*, yet watched with bow and battle-ax. Hunters and trappers had achieved rare sport along its borders, trodden by game easily secured, but the emigrant, hopeful and heroic as he came from his home, passed by the wigwams, and went with the main body down to the mouth of the stream.

The names of the five original townships laid out here, were Wilkes Barre, Hanover, Plymouth, Kings-town, and Pitts-town; Providence, or "Sixth Town of ye Capoose Meadows," being laid out and added in 1770. *Lackawannock* was then applied to the country in the immediate vicinity of the mouth of the stream, embracing the village of Asserughney, occupied by the swarthy aborigines. It was in the new laid-out township of Pittstown, and as its banks were *clear of wood for five miles*, it promised economy of labor in cultivation, and was chosen for a settlement partly for this reason, and partly because of the unfriendly occupancy of the Mill Creek clearing, a few miles below it, by the Pennymites.

Although all persons from the "Colony of Connecticut attempting to settle upon a Large Tract of Land, within the Limits of this Province, lying at and *between* Wyoming, on

---

[1] Bancroft's History United States, vol. v., p. 165

the River Susquehanna, and Cushietunk, on the River Delaware," were notified at this time by Governor Penn, whose eye was sleepless upon the distant valley, to leave the settlements *forthwith*, the solitude of the Lackawanna, interrupted only by the low babbling of brooks, or the dull sounds from the Indian clearings, began to attract the emigrant, who came hither with all the industrious qualifications belonging to the New England character. In fact, civilization was never carried westward into the wilderness by a more gallant and deserving body of men, than those who formed the vanguard of this frontier settlement. Descending from the same stock of determined pioneers, that wrought out a colony amid the vales and hills of Connecticut, they entered with equal zeal into this new acquisition, hoping to achieve greater conquests with the plow and hard-swung ax, and, if need be, lay the foundation for a grand commonwealth, as other provinces had been laid out before.

In May, 1769, Charles Stewart, Esq., writes from "Manor of Stoke,"[1] that he had but twenty-four men to *oppose* the New England men, of whom, "one hundred and forty-six, chiefly on horseback, passed by our houses this afternoon (May 16, 1769), about three o'clock, and are now encamped on the East side of the River. From the view I had of those Gentry, in their procession by our Houses, they appear to be at least an equal number of them of *the very lowest class*, but are almost all armed and *fit for mischief*."[2]

Such was the language, and such the bitterness of the reception meted out to the new-comers from Paxton, entering the valley.

It was thus amidst king's writs, posses, and arrests, as will be seen, and all the exacting severities incident to

[1] In 1769, Wyoming was laid out into two vast manors by Pennsylvanna surveyors, viz.: "Manor of Stoke," embracing the east side of the Susquehanna, and "Manor of Sunbury," extending over the west side.

[2] C. Stewart's Letter, May, 1769.

the backwoodsman's life a century ago, that the Paxton boy forgot his fruitful intervale, and the Yankee forsook his stone-clad homestead in Connecticut, for the inhospitable plains of Wyoming.

Thirty-five of the persons thus described by Mr. Stewart, located near Pittston. Their names were:—

" Benj. Shoemaker,   William Leonard,   Azariah Dean,
John McDowell,   John Leonard,   John Wheat,
Samuel Weyburn,   Samuel Marvin,   John Wharburt,
John Lee,   —— Marvin,   Jacob Welch,
Joseph Lee,   Rheuben Hulburt,   Jabez Cook,
Thomas Bennett,   Samuel Clark,   Ebenezer Nultrip,
Benj. Follett,   John Gardner,   —— Chambers,
—— Cornstack,   John De Long,   —— Gore,
Daniel Hains,   John Smith, Esq., & his —— Babcock,
John McDowell, Jr.,   two sons, —— Smith   —— Wright."
Benj. Shoemaker, Jr.,   and —— Smith,
Asher Harrod,   Joseph Moss,

Although many of these men subsequently settled in the more central or lower townships, they at this time located on the belt of ground running in such exquisite beauty from Campbell's Ledge down to the outlet of the Lackawanna.

This so aroused the indignation of John Jenkins, Esq., sheriff of Northampton County, to whom was intrusted a general supervision of the Proprietaries' interest at Wyoming, that he assembled a posse to arrest or drive away the settlers into the cold hospitality of the woods. He "went to *Lacknawanak*, near Wyoming, on Susquehanna, in the County of Northampton, where the intruders had built their two houses, One of which was a Strong Log house built for Defense; that the said Intruders betook themselves to their said Houses, and declared they would not give up the Possession of the said Lands, but would maintain the same as their own, and put to Death any persons that attempted to dispossess them; that the said Justices, after long and fruitless expostulation, recorded the forcible Detainer, and this Deponent, by their

Orders, prepared to take the said Intruders, and received two Blows from some of them, but having forced into one of the houses, and taken those that were therein, the rest surrendered, and the whole thirty taken into Custody,"[1] and carried over the mountain to Easton jail, with the exception of those who escaped from the sheriff while on the way.[2]

This was in 1769. Having friends in Pennsylvania, they readily obtained bail, and immediately returned to Lacknawanak.

The summer of this year, now agitated and then pacified by the alternation of strength of the respective parties, left the Pennymites in the possession of the valley. During the year 1770 the intestine feud, from which the inhabitants had hoped to be exempt, resulted in the temporary expulsion of the Yankees. The following is "a list of Lackawany who drew in 1770,"[3] and were thus expelled:—

"Topez Williams, by   Silas Parks,
P. Williams,   Prime Alden."

In 1771 the following persons "drew lands in Lackawanny":—

"Jacob Anguish,   David Brown,   Ebenezer West,
Peter Daman,   Martin Weilson,   Samuel Stubbs, by
John Osborn,   Elipolet Stevens,   Austin Hunt,
John Depeiw,   Dan'l St. John,   Ebenezer Marcy, by
Levi Green,   Elizar Fillsbury,   Isaac Allen,
Peter Mathews,   Stephen Wilkox,   Caleb Bates, by
James Hesdale,   Richard Woodward,   Wm. Hopkins.
David Sanford, by   Sam'l Slaughter,
Jenks Corey,

In the Westmoreland Records, from whose musty pages the foregoing list of names is taken, is the following entry:—

[1] Pa. Arch., 1760-76, p. 343.
[2] See Miner's Wyoming; also Pa. Arch., 1763, pp. 401-8.
[3] Westmoreland Records.

"N. B. On the north side of Lackawan, drawd lots, 1772.

Jeremiah Blanchard,	Samuel Slater,	Joseph Fish,
Abram Harden,	John Corey,	Ebenezer Bachus.
Richard West,	Daniel Haller,	

"Lotts on the South side of the Lackawan river.

Johnathan Corey,	Stephen Harding,	Capt. Bates,
Ebenezer West,	Ebenezer Marcy,	David Brown,
David Sanford,	Augustin Hunt,	James Fledget."
Abraham Utter,		

Blood having been shed in the winter of 1771, and both parties having fresh accessions, the contest was renewed with redoubled violence. Men were raised by Captain Ogden "to reduce the *Rebells* at Wioming." In August, 1771, he "moved on to the Forks of Lahawanak and Wyoming paths."[1] He captured the fort by stratagem, sent the Yankees to Easton jail, plundered the cabins, devastated the ungathered crops, and intimidated and suppressed every sentiment friendly to the Connecticut people thus stigmatized as rebels.

In a spirit of vague Christianity he sent "a party of six men to lay on the Sheholey road from Wioming to Delaware, *to prevent expresses going that way to N. England*"[2] after relief.

Dr. Ledlie, under date of August 16, 1771, writes to Governor Hamilton, that "we were just sending off Flour by way of Lackawanack, and that we shall keep the *Shehole* and Minisink Paths Guarded to prevent more People, &c., coming to them." This Shehole path was the warriors' trail up the Lackawanna to Paupack and the Delaware.

When the Yankees again returned from jail, they made a temporary camp-place above Pittston. Here a spy, "named Jas. Bertrong, was taken prisoner by a party

---

[1] Letter, John Van Campen, August 16, 1771.

[2] Pennsylvania Archives, 1771, p. 429.

of Men at Lachnwanack," who reported that fifty or sixty men under Lazarus Stewart and Zebulon Butler, were then defying the authorities of Pennsylvania.

While this strife sacrificed much of the social relations, and retarded the industrious tendency of the settlement, it was not wholly fatal to its growth.

The immediate head or seat of the democratic colony, originally claimed and disputed for by the settlers at Kings-Town, was finally located in Wilkes Barre, where, in or around the fort, the people gathered at stated intervals and held council together; discussed its affairs generally, and settled abstract principles of public right and good relating to the interests of Wyoming, with a fairness and freedom that harmonized well with the liberal character of the settlers from Connecticut. The proceedings of these meetings, kept through all the years of peace and war, until Connecticut lost jurisdiction over Westmoreland, were recorded in a written book called the *Westmoreland Records*.[1]

Settlers were permitted "to make a pitch"[2] or settle in none of the up or down river territory only by the consent or vote of the inhabitants at these meetings; and even then only upon certain stipulated conditions.

"At a meeting of ye Inhabitants of ye townships at Wyoming, in Wilksbury, legally warned and held, Dec. 7, 1771, Capt. Zebulon Butler was chosen mod-

---

[1] These old records, which once occupied a musty coop in Wilkes Barre, *could not be found a few months ago*, when the writer sought for them through a clever and prominent official, are the most curious literary fragments of antiquity yet remaining amongst us. These meetings, which gave birth to these Records, were called "Ye meeting of ye proprietors," where all had an equal voice in the deliberations. A "moderator," and "clerk" were chosen at each meeting. This book recorded all deeds of land, &c., and was commenced in 1770, and terminated only with the expulsion of Connecticut jurisdiction at Wyoming, in 1782. We know of no other ancient manuscript, whose publication would link together and afford more insight into ancient times than the three or four volumes of Westmoreland Records, if *they can be exhumed*. The Historical Society of Wilkes Barre, if not able or disposed to print, ought to be their custodian.

[2] The homes or clearings of the settlers early took and long retained this name

erator for ye day," it was voted "that this Company is to take in Settlers on ye following Considerations: that those that take up a Settling Right in *Lockaworna*, shall pay to this Company Forty dollars, and those that take a Right in Wilksbury or Plymouth, shall pay Fifty Dollors; and those that take a Right in Kingstown, shall pay Sixty Dollors, all for ye use of this Company, etc."[1] A committee was also appointed to take bonds from those who should be admitted as settlers.

Lackawanna, or Lockaworna as then designated, being more remote from the main settlement, protected by blockhouses or forts, and from its very isolation, up in the narrow valley, more exposed to wild beasts and Indians, than either Wilkes Barre or Kingston, although enjoying the same federative government, was offered to persons whose courage overreached their means, upon terms apparently more advantageous and easy. Of the original number of two hundred and forty, who emigrated to Wyoming in 1769—all of whom were male—only thirty-five were located along the Lackawanna. In regard to these, who lived within reach of the block-house at Pittston, it was voted, April 25, 1772, by the Susquehanna Company, "that those 35 men that is now in ye township of Lockoworna, shall be entitled to all ye Companyes Right to sd. township."

With a view of imparting to the colony a healthy moral stamina, a committee of five persons were appointed at the same meeting, "to admit settlers into ye six mile township. But for no one of the committee to admit in settlers unless ye major part of said Committee be present to admit," and then to allow only "such as good, wholsom inhabitants" to settle.[2]

December 17, 1771, "this meeting is opened and held by adjournment, voted, that Joseph David Sanford, Barnabas Cary, Elezer Cary, jun., Arter French, John Fra-

---

[1] Westmoreland Records.   [2] Ibid.

zier, Timothy Reine, jun., Stephen Harden, and Caleb Bates, have each one a Settling Right in ye township."[1]

Not only had morality its defenders and advocates among the early settlers, but *industry* was considered such an essential qualification to the prosperity of the new settlement, that at a meeting of the inhabitants held in Wilkes Barre Fort, in December, 1771, it was voted "that Frank Phillips be admitted to Purchoys a settling Right in Lockaworna, Provided he puts an Able Bodyed man on sd. Right, and Due Duty Equal to ye Rest of ye Settlers."

April 29, 1772, voted "that Samuel Slougher is admitted in as a Settler, in Room of Mortin Nelson, in ye township of Lockoworna," and in January 13, 1772, voted "that David Carr is admitted in as a Settler in Lockaworna, and hes Given His Bond for Forty Dollors."

By the old roadside in Pittston township, on the right as you descend the valley, about three miles up from Pittston, could be seen a few years since the *debris* of a chimney of one of the earliest cabins of the white man erected in the valley in 1770. It was built by Zebulon Marcy, who emigrated from Connecticut in the spring of this year, in the twenty-sixth year of his age. He was brother of Ebenezer, who came into possession of this rustic dwelling some time afterward.

Choosing this spot for his residence, upon the warriors' path, from its inviting soil and convenient location, his hut, formed from logs in the stern simplicity of the times, subsequently became famous for its genial hospitality.

At the time of the Wyoming massacre, eight years after locating here, Ebenezer Marcy was engaged with his comrades below in the defense of Wyoming from the ravages of the merciless Indians, Tories, and British, when the news that the brave defenders had retreated before the pursuing and mongrel horde, flew through the settlement with astounding effect and rapidity. Hurriedly snatch-

---

[1] Westmoreland Records.

ing her children from the house, and securing a loaf of bread for the supperless fugitives, she fled from the valley on the evening of July 3, 1778, across the mountain to Stroudsburg, in company with all her neighbors thus left feeble and defenseless. "She was," says Miner, "taken in labor in the wilderness. Having no mode of conveyance, her sufferings were inexpressibly severe. She was able to drag her fainting footsteps but about two miles that day. The next day, being overtaken by a neighbor with a horse, she rode, and in a week's time was more than 100 miles with her infant from the place of its birth." The child born at this time, and subsequently married twice, died a short time since in Wyoming County.

Marcy himself was a man of some local prominence in his day, and was chosen the first constable of Pittston, in January, 1772.

Barnabas Carey, whose right to settle in the township was voted in 1771, pitched farther up the valley, where, from the fallen tree and the fresh-peeled bark, he fashioned a cabin to afford him protection from the storms and the wolves. This was the first one erected by the white man *above* the Falls of the Lackawanna, and the honor of the achievement belongs to Carey. The next year he sold his claim to "the eight meadow Lott in ye Township Lockaworna to Jeremiah Blanchard for thirteen pounds and four shillings."[1]

Constant Searles and John Phillips were among the Yankee emigrants who located in the valley in 1771. Frank Phillips, who was voted a settling right in "Lockaworna" in December, 1771, was the father of John, only fourteen years of age, and settled in the "gore," or wedged-like shape of land, lying between Pittston and Providence.

Six years later, Phillips's farm was sold to his son,

---

[1] Westmoreland Records, 1771.

John, for thirty pounds, current money. Among the five commissioners chosen to purchase land, whereon to erect the necessary public buildings, at the time of the formation of Luzerne County, in 1786, was John Phillips.

After the Trenton Decree authorized a re-survey of the prolonged disputed lands in the seventeen old certified townships, Pennsylvania sent to Wyoming "200 flints and 2 Boxes of cartridges," because the inhabitants were reported "wrangling."[1] At this time the Pennsylvania soldiers, excited and brutal with rum, and under the command of Captains Shrawder and Christie, began to lay open fields of grain for common pasturage, destroying every thing belonging to the Yankee settlers, while establishing the boundaries of Pennsylvania, regardless of those of Connecticut.

Phillips and his family were among those driven from their farms in 1784, in a manner so graphically described by Hon. Charles Miner in his History of Wyoming:—

"On the 13th and 14th of May the soldiers were sent forth, and at the point of the bayonet, with the most highhanded arrogance, dispossessed one hundred and fifty families; in many instances set fire to their dwellings, avowing the intention utterly to expel them from the country. Unable to make any effectual resistance, the people implored for leave to remove either up or down the river, as with their wives and children, in the state of the roads, it would be impossible to travel. A stern refusal met this seemingly reasonable request, and they were directed to take the Lackawaxen road, as leading most directly to Connecticut. But this way consisted of sixty miles of wilderness, with scarce a house; the roads were wholly neglected during the war, and they then begged leave to take the Easton or Stroudsburg route, where bridges spanned the larger streams, still swollen by recent rains. All importunities were vain, and the

---

[1] See Pennsylvania Archives, 1784.

people fled toward the Delaware, objects of destitution and pity that should have moved a heart of marble. About five hundred men, women, and children, with scarce provisions to sustain life, plodded their weary way, mostly on foot, the roads being impassable for wagons, mothers carrying their infants, and pregnant women literally wading the streams, the water reaching to their armpits, and at night slept on the naked earth, the heavens their canopy, and scarce clothes to cover them. A Mr. John Gardner and John Jenkins, both aged men and lame, sought their way on crutches. Little children, tired with traveling, crying to their mothers for bread, which they had not to give them, sunk from exhaustion into stillness and slumber, while the mothers could only shed tears of sorrow and compassion, till in sleep they forgot their griefs and cares. Several of the unfortunate sufferers died in the wilderness, others were taken sick from excessive fatigue, and expired soon after reaching the settlements. A widow, with a numerous family of children, whose husband had been slain in the war, endured inexpressible hardships. One child died, and she buried it as she could beneath a hemlock log, probably to be disinterred from its shallow covering, and be devoured by wolves."

A small mound, sheltered by a friendly hemlock, lies by the roadside in Wayne County, where the little one was buried.

"One shocking instance of suffering is related by a survivor of this scene of death; it is the case of a mother, whose infant having died, roasted it by piecemeal for the daily subsistence of her suffering children."[1]

Elisha Harding, who formed one of this party, says that "the first night we encamped at the Capouse, the second at Cobbs, the third at Little Meadows (Salem), cold, hungry, and drenched with rain—the poor women and

[1] Chapman.

children suffering much. The fourth night at Lackawaxen, fifth at Bloomington, sixth at Shehola, and seventh on the Delaware, where the people disbanded—some going up and some down the river."

Pennsylvania repudiated this ferocious conduct of the soldiers, and at once indignantly dismissed the respective companies engaged in proceedings so infamous.[1]

After the Compromising laws had pacified the valley, Phillips returned and took possession of his former farm.

Timothy Keys, Andrew Hickman, and Mr. Hocksy settled in Providence Township in 1771. Keys was chosen constable of Providence, June 30, 1772. Among the first five women coming to Wyoming was the wife of Hickman.

The Westmoreland Records inform us that "Augustine Hunt, one of ye Proprietors in ye Susquehanna Purchois has made a pitch of about one hundred and fifty acres of Land in Lockaworna township in 1772."

John Taylor, with no companions but his ax, his rifle, and his faithful dog, early made a pitch in Providence on the elevation below Hyde Park, affording such views of village and valley, and known throughout the valley as the "uncle Jo. Griffin farm." Mr. Taylor subsequently became a man of more than ordinary usefulness in the colony. He was a prominent member of a number of committees, which received their existence with the expansion of the settlement, and he took an active part in the social and political organizations of the day.

Pitts-town, which was named in honor of the distinguished advocate and defender of American interest, *Wm. Pitt*, as was Wilkes-Barre from the united names of two bold and eloquent champions of American rights in the British Parliament, was one of the original townships laid out by the *Proprietors* of the Susquehanna Company, and extended from Wilkes Barre to Providence.

[1] Miner.

Among the early families here, were the Browns, Bennetts, Benedicts, Blanchards, Careys, St. Johns, Marcys, Sawyers, and Silbeys. One of the Pittston forts being erected on the farm of Brown, was named in honor of him, and was at the time of the Wyoming massacre occupied by a small company of men commanded by Captain Blanchard.

This block-house was built in 1772. At a meeting of the proprietors and settlers held in Wilkes Barre, May 20, 1772, it was voted "that ye Proprietors Belonging to ye town of Pittston Have ye Liberty to Go into their town, and there to fortyfie and Keep in a Body Near together and Gourd by themselves until further notice from this Committee." [1]

Samuel Harden was chosen collector for Pittston, and Solomon Johnson "for ye town of Providence," in December, 1772.

Meadow lot, No. 13, in Lockawarna, was sold to Jeremiah Blanchard, in May, 1772, by Dr. Joseph Sprauge, one of the proprietors of the town, and the *first* physician who practiced medicine in the valley.

John Stevens was a proprietor in "ye township called ye Capouse Meadow." In May, 1772, he conveyed to John Youngs a settling right at Capouse Meadow, merely for the "consideration of ye Love, Good will and affections I Have & Do Bare towards my Loving Son in Law, John youngs, son to my wife Mary."[2]

Isaac Tripp.

At Capoose Meadow, where the rude bearing of Indian life had been modified by whites friendly in their intercourse and gaudy with their presents, acres of rich woodlands had been surveyed and purchased for a few shillings in Connecticut currency, but no one

---

[1] Westmoreland Records. [2] Ibid.

was willing to encounter its dangers or share attractions until Isaac Tripp, a man of five and thirty, built for himself a shelter among the pines in 1771.

Emigrating to the broader plains of Wyoming with the original pioneers of 1769, and, finding the block-house at Mill Creek in possession of the Pennymites, prepared, with a body of men commanded by Capt. Ogden, to dispute and enforce jurisdiction over the valley, Tripp and his companions, looking for no such chilly reception even amid the snows of winter, made preparations to recapture a prize of such vital importance to their existence as a part of a company or colony. "Isaak Tryp," was one of the Proprietors of the Susqehanna Company. He had seen some service in the French and Indian wars previous to this, while a few of his companions had been schooled in the raw exercises of the militia of Connecticut. All, however, who had adventured thus far into Wyoming, yet filled with the sullen redskins, were familiar with the use of the rifle, never failing in the hands of the woodsman, robust and self reliant, versed in the achievement of hook and line, and more skilled in securing the deer and tracking the bear, than in the more deceptive art of diplomatic cunning.

With all their conceptions, however, of military discipline learned in the warfare of border life or practiced in the parks of their native inland villages, they were now completely outwitted by the superior tact of the Ogden party secure in the occupancy of the block-house. Ogden, says Miner "having only *ten* men able to bear arms, one-fourth only of his invading foe, determined to have recourse to negotiation. A very polite and conciliatory note was addressed to the commander of the *forty*, an interview respectfully solicited, and a friendly conference asked on the subject of the respective titles. Ogden proved himself an accomplished angler. The bait was too tempting. Propose to a Yankee to talk over a matter especially which he has studied, and believes to be right, and you touch the most susceptible chord that vibrates in his heart. That they could out-talk the Pennymites, and convince them the Susquehanna title was good, not one of the forty doubted. Three of the chief men were deputed to argue the matter, viz.: Isaac Tripp and Benjamin Follet, two of the executive committee, accompanied by Mr. Vine Elderkin. No sooner were they within the block-house, than Sheriff Jenkins clapped a writ on their shoulders.—'Gentlemen, in the name of the Commonwealth of Pennsylvania, you are my prisoners!' 'Laugh when we must, be candid when we can.' The Yankees were decidedly outwitted. By common consent the prisoners were transported to Easton jail, guarded by Captain Ogden; but accompanied in no hostile manner, by the thirty-seven remnants of the forty."

Tripp was promptly liberated from jail by his friends, and returning again to the valley, was an efficient contributor to the public weal, and an intelligent actor in the long, embittered dispute between the Provincial authorities of Pennsylvania and those of the Colony of Connecticut for Wyoming, before its peaceful and final solution.

Upon the Westmoreland Records his name, or that of "Esq. Tripp," as he was familiarly called, often appears. At a meeting of the Susquehanna Company, held at Hartford, Ct., June 2, 1773, for the purpose of electing officers for the Westmoreland Colony, Gideon Baldwin, Timothy Keys, and Isaac Tripp, were chosen Directors or Proprietors of Providence.

The first recorded purchase of land in Providence by Tripp was made in 1774. This purchase embraced lands where stood the wigwams of Capoose, upon the flats subsequently known as "Tripp's Flats." As this old deed possesses some local interest it is inserted entire.

"To all People to whom these Presents shall come. Know ye that I Daniel Adams of west-moreland, in ye

County of Litchfield and Colony of Connecticutt, in New England, for and in Consideration of Ninety pounds Currant money, of Connecticutt, to me in hand, Paid. Before ye Ensealing hereof to my full satisfaction by Isooc Tripp, Esq., of ye same town, County, and Colony, aforesaid, ye Receipt whereof I am fully sattisfyed and contented and Do therefore freely, fully, and absolutely Give, Grant, Bargain, Sell, alienate, Convay, and Confirm unto him, ye said Isooc Trypp, His Hairs, Exec ors. Admin ors. and assighns, for Ever all and singular one Certain Lott of land, Lying and Being in ye township of Providence, Known by No. 14, Lying on the west side of Lockawarna River, and Butted and Bounded as follows: abuting East on sd. River; west on sd. town Line, North and South on Land Belonging to sd. Tripp, and Contains by Estimation 375 acres, be ye same more or Less, Reference being had to ye Survey of sd. town for ye more perticulerments. Bounds thereof to be and Remain unto him ye sd. Isooc tripp, and to his heirs, Execu—ors, or Admin—ors, or assigns for Ever free and clear from me, ye sd. Daniel Adams, or any Heirs, Execu—ors, or Admin—ors, or assigns, or any other Persons by from or under me or any part thereof, as witness, my hand this 7th Day of July, in ye year of our Lord, 1774, and in ye 14th year of his majosties Raign.

"Signed, sealed, and Delivered In Presence of

DANL. ADAMS.

"NATHAN. DENISON AND

"SAML. SLATER, JR.

"Received ye above Deed to Record July ye 8th, A. D. 1774, and Recorded By me.

"EZEKIEL PEIRCE, clerk."[1]

At the time that Tripp located upon the Indian clearing already awaiting culture, Providence was designated in the ancient records as the "sixth town of ye Capouse Meadows."

[1] Westmoreland Records, 1774.

IRA TRIPP

These once beautiful flats, now rooted into mines, and robbed of their natural beauty by tall coal work, with their accompanying culm or waste coal spread over many a fair acre, perpetuate the names of their first white occupants, and bring them down through generations into the hands of Ira Tripp, Esq., a gentleman of wealth, entitled to no little consideration for those frank, popular attainments and social qualifications which mark, in the public mind, the rulings of the hour.

The Scranton court-house, standing on the original farm of Ira Tripp, overlooks the ancient abode of Capoose, pointed out by a single tree.

Isaac Tripp, the grandson of Isaac Tripp, Sen., came into the valley in 1774, and chose this inviting spot for his residence.[1]

In October, 1773, Maj. Fitch Alden purchased of John Stevens, of Wilkes Barre "one Certain Lott of Land Lying in ye township of Providence, on ye North side of Lockaworna River; sd. Lott is known by Number two and Contains 370 acres." Fifteen pounds lawful currency was the price given—about $45.

Provisions were so scarce in all the settlements, from

---

[1] The following note, regarding Isaac Tripp, appears in the History of the Abington Baptist Association, a small volume, compiled a few years since by Rev. Edward L. Baily, A. M.: "This Isaac Tripp was in early life a resident at 'Capouse Meadows,' in the Lackawanna valley. In the eighteenth year of his age, and soon after the Wyoming massacre, he was taken captive by the Indians, and with others marched to Canada. On the way he experienced the most excruciating sufferings from the gnawings of hunger and cruel treatment of the savages, who bound his hands behind him and compelled him to run the gauntlet. At Niagara he met his cousin, Miss Frances Slocum, who was also a captive from the Wyoming valley. They planned their escape, but their intentions being discovered by their captors, they were separated, never more to meet on earth, and young Tripp was sold to the English and compelled to enter their service, in which he reluctantly continued until the close of the revolutionary war. He now returned to his early home and resumed the peaceful pursuits of the farm. He moved to Scott, Luzerne county, and finally settled in the Elkwoods, in Susquehanna county. His wife died in Clifford, May 10th, 1816, aged 67 years. He followed her to the grave April 15th, 1820, aged 60 years. The remains of both now repose in the burying ground near Clifford corners."

Wyoming to Capoose, in the winter of 1773, that a party of persons, among whom was John Carey, were sent to Stroudsburg to obtain them. The distance was fifty miles through the forest, where all the intervening streams, being unbridged, had to be crossed upon ice, or forded, or swam. The party went the entire journey on foot, and returned to their half-famished friends with the needed flour.

Neither Fitch, Youngs, nor Stevens made any improvement on their lands, still unchopped and unoccupied in 1773. Fitch sold his purchase in 1774 to John Alden for eighty pounds, New York currency. It must be borne in mind that, after the original survey of the Connecticut Indian Purchase of the Susquehanna Company, all the land thus embraced was laid out in shares and half shares, many of which lay for years beyond the sound of the ax-stroke, while others, more favorably located, were sold by the proprietors of each town for a trifle, and re-sold by the purchaser to any one having the courage to risk life or sacrifice any social relation among panthers, Indians, and wolves.

Isaac Tripp, the grandson of Isaac Tripp the elder, was "taken prisoner in 1778, and two young men by the name of Keys and Hocksey; the old gentleman they (the Indians) painted and dismissed, but hurried the others into the forest (now Abington) above Liggitt's Gap, on the warriors' path to Oquago. Resting one night, they rose the next morning, traveled about two miles, when they stopped at a little stream of water. The two young Indians then took Keys and Hocksey some distance from the path, and were absent half an hour, the old Indian looking anxiously the way they had gone. Presently the death-whoop was heard, and the Indians returned, brandishing bloody tomahawks and exhibiting the scalps of their victims. Tripp's hat was taken from his head, and his scalp examined twice, the savages speaking earnestly, when at length they told him to fear nothing—he should not be hurt; and carried him off prisoner."[1]

The Indians, finding Tripp disposed to yield gracefully to his new position without concern or restraint, painted his face with war-paint, as a protective measure against any warriors chancing to meet him, and sent him back to his home, at Capoose, where the next year he was shot by a party of savages from the lakes, while at work in the field, unconscious of danger.

In the spring of 1803 two skulls, white as snow, and some human bones, porous and weather-beaten by the storms of quarter of a century, were found in Abington, by Deacon Clark, upon the edge of a little brook passing through Clark's Green, and were at this time supposed to be, as they probably were, the remains of Tripp's tomahawked companions.

Isaac Tripp, Sen., was shot near Wilkes Barre Fort, in 1779, under the following circumstances: In the Revolutionary War, the British, for the purpose of inciting the savages to more murderous activity along the frontier and exposed settlements, offered large rewards for the scalps of Americans. As Tripp was a man of more than ordinary efficiency and prominence in the colony, the Indians were often asked by the British why he was not slain. The unvarying answer was that "Tripp was a good man." He was a Quaker in his religious notions, and in all his intercourse with the Indians his manner had been so kind and conciliatory, that when he fell into their hands as a prisoner the year previous, at Capoose, they dismissed him unharmed, and covered him with paint, as it was their custom to do with those they did not wish to harm.

Rendering himself inimical to the Tories by the energy with which he assailed them afterward in his efforts to protect the interests of the Wyoming Colony at Hartford, whither he had been sent to represent its grievances, a

---

[1] Miner's History, p. 240.

double reward was offered for his scalp, and, as he had forfeited their protection by the removal of the war-paint, and incurred their hostility by his loyal struggles for the life of the Republic, he was shot and scalped the first time he was seen.

WESTMORELAND.

Up until this time (1774) the Susquehanna Company, struggling against every element adverse to its existence, had hoped that Wyoming might, by special authority from the king, be erected into a separate colony of its own, but the remonstrances of the Proprietary Government, inflexible in its purpose to expel all power and people from the valley but its own, combined with the war-feeling everywhere generated and cherished throughout the American Colonies against the British Government, easily defeated a measure fraught with equal consequence to both of the contending parties.

Under these circumstances, Connecticut, not forgetting that, by virtue of its charter, its possessions extended indefinitely to the West—even to the Pacific—yielded to the appeals repeatedly coming over the mountain from Wyoming, to extend official and parental protection to the settlement, assailed from within and without, passed through its General Assembly, in January, 1774, the following act:—

"It is enacted that the Inhabitants dwelling within the Bounds of this Colony, on the West Side of the River Delaware, be, and they are hereby made and constituted a distinct Town, with like Powers and Priviledges as other Towns in this Colony by Law have, within the following Bounds and Limits, vizt: Bounded East by Delaware River, North by the North Line of this Colony, West by a North and South Line across the Colony at fifteen miles distance from a Place on Susquehanna River called Wyoming, and South by the South Line of the Colony, which Town is hereby annexed to the County of Litchfield, and shall be called by the name of Westmoreland : That Zebulon Butler and Nathan Denison, Esquires, Inhabitants of said Town, are appointed Justices of the Peace in and for the County of Litchfield ; That the former is authorized and directed to issue a Warrant, as soon as may be, to notify the Inhabitants of the said Town of Westmoreland in said County, to meet at such Time and Place as he shall appoint, within said Town, to choose officers, and to do any other Business proper to be done at said Meeting; and

"That the Governor of this Colony is authorized and desired to issue a Proclamation, forbidding any Person or Persons whatsoever taking up, entring on, or settling any of the Lands contained or included in the Charter of this Colony, lying Westward of the Province of New York, without Liberty first had and obtained from the General Assembly of this Colony.

"These Acts are made and passed by our Assembly, for the Protection and Government of the Inhabitants on the Lands mentioned, to preserve Peace and good Order among them, to prevent Hostilities, Animosities, and Contentions among the People there, to promote public Justice, to discourage Vice and Iniquity, and to put a Stop to Intruders entering on those Lands.

"I am, with great Truth and Regard, Sir,
"Your most Obedient,
"Humble Servant,
"JONᵀᴴ· TRUMBULL.
"Honorable JOHN PENN, Esquire."[1]

This act on the part of Connecticut gave a fresh impetus and marked out a new era for the inland settlements. Wyoming, thus ceasing to exist as a distinct republic,[2] acknowledged only the laws and jurisdiction of Connecticut. The inhabitants of the valleys, always favoring peace and good order, naturally expressed a hope that their grievances, hitherto vexatious and fatal to their thrift, might be

---

[1] Col. Rec., vol. x., pp. 151–2.   [2] Chapman.

lessened somewhat, if not entirely removed, by this affiliation. The Revolution, however, gave a different and more patriotic direction to the spirit of independence early inherited: else these intrepid sons, wielding alike the ax and the musket in either hand, would not have battled so long in vain for rights so stoutly upheld and denied them.

WALLENPAUPACK SETTLEMENT.

One of the most sluggish streams gathering its waters from the roof of the mountain dividing the Delaware and the Susquehanna, is the Wallenpaupack in Pike County, some thirty miles eastward of the Lackawanna, crossed by the solitary Indian path leading from the Delaware to Wyoming. Along this creek, the first permanent settlement began in 1774, and although miles of forest and mountain intervened, the earliest settlers, for many years, traveled over forty miles to Wilkes Barre, to election, court, and public meetings of great importance. "Some time between the years 1750 and 1760," says Hon. Warren J. Woodward, Esq., in Miner's History of Wyoming, "a family named Carter settled upon the Wallenpaupack Creek. This is supposed to have been the first white family that ever visited the neighborhood. The spot upon which the house was built is in view of the road leading from Sterling, in Wayne County, to the Milford and Owego turnpike, seven miles southwest from Wilsonville. The old Indian path, from Cochecton to Wyoming, crossed the Wallenpaupack about thirty rods below the house of the Carters. During the French and Indian war, which commenced in 1756, the members of the family were all murdered, and the house was burned by a tribe of Indians in the service of the French. When the emigrants from Connecticut arrived on the banks of the Wallenpaupack, the chimney of the house and a stone oven alone were standing.

"When the first Wyoming emigrants from Connecticut

reached the Wallenpaupack, the main body halted, and some pioneers were sent forward, in a westerly direction, to procure intelligence of the position of the country on the Susquehanna. The pioneers followed the Indian path before alluded to, leading from Cochecton in New York, across the Leckawaxen, to the point on the Wallenpaupack below the Carter house, where there was an 'Indian clearing,' and thence to the 'Indian clearings' on the Susquehanna. This path crossed 'Cobb's Mountain.' The pioneers attained the summit, from which the Susquehanna was in view, in the evening, and built up a large fire to indicate to the settlers the point to which they should direct their course. The next morning, the emigrants commenced their journey, building their road as they proceeded. That road, leaving the Sterling road before mentioned about a mile down the creek below the site of the Carter house, is the one which is now constantly traveled between Wilkes Barre and Milford. It is said to have been most judiciously located. The point on which the fire was built on Cobb's Mountain, was near the present residence of John Cobb, Esq., and is pointed out by the people residing on the Wallenpaupack to the present time.

"At some period, shortly before the Revolutionary War, a settlement was commenced at Milford, on the Delaware, now the capital of Pike County. The settlers were all Pennsylvanians. This was the only inhabited part of what now constitutes Wayne and Pike counties, except the Connecticut colony planted on the Wallenpaupack. The emigrants to the latter left Connecticut in 1774. Within a year after their arrival, two townships were erected under the names of Lackaway and Bozrah. The settlement extended four miles and a half along the creek. The farms still remain of the same size as originally fixed, and with two exceptions they still remain in the possession of the descendants of the settlers in 1774.

"One of the first labors of the settlers after their emigration, was the erection of a fort. This fort, which was probably somewhat primitive in its construction, was a field containing about an acre, surrounded by a trench, into which upright pieces of hewed timber were firmly fixed. The spot was selected from the circumstance of its containing a living spring. The fort was erected on the eastern side of the Sterling road, almost immediately opposite the point where the road leading through Salem, over Cobb's Mountain, and along the Lackawanna to the Wyoming settlements, called the 'Old Wyoming road,' branches off from the Sterling road. It is six miles southwest from the hamlet now marked on the maps as Wilsonville. Within the inclosed space was a block-house, also built of squared pieces of hewed timber, upon the top of which was a sentry-box, made bullet-proof. There was, besides, a guard-house, standing just east of the block-house. The defenses were so constructed that a rifle-ball fired from the high ground on the east into the fort, would strike the palisades on the opposite side above a man's head. After the rumors of the Indian troubles on the Susquehanna reached the Wallenpaupack, the settlers constantly spent the night in the fort. The spring, whose existence and situation governed the colonists in their selection of a stronghold, still bubbles by the way-side, and nothing but a pile of loose stones indicates to the traveler the formidable neighborhood to which it has been exposed "

JAMES LEGGETT.

The loose-tongued tributary of the Lackawanna coming with shout and foam through the deep notch in the mountain between Abington and Providence, two miles north of Scranton, known as "Leggett's Creek," derived its name from James Leggett who emigrated from " ye Province of New York," in 1775, and erected his rude bark cabin at the mouth of the creek, still bearing his name. In the original draught of the township of

Providence by the Connecticut Susquehanna Company the wild land where Leggett cleared, had been allotted to Abraham Stanton. This was in 1772. In 1773 he transferred his right to John Staples. By a vote of the Susquehanna Company, Staples's claim to this forest-covered part of the township, was declared forfeited because of some dereliction of duty. It was next granted to David Thayer in 1774. Like preceding owners, neither of whom had cut a tree or cleared a foot of land, he escaped from ownership without becoming either richer or poorer by selling this and several tracts of land along upper Capoose to James Leggett in June, 1775, who was the first white man to make a clearing *above* Providence Village.

A little distance above the grist-mill of the late Judson Clark, Esq., in Providence, Leggett cleared a small spot to show the fertility of the soil, where he built his cabin on the bank of the creek in 1775 ; but the exciting aspect of border life, often rendered appalling by the howl of the wolf, or the whoop of the red-man reluctant to depart from a valley he had loved and lost, contributed so little to charm the solitude of his domestic life, that he abandoned his stumpy new land and retired to White Plains, New York.

After the close of the Revolutionary struggle, in which he took an honorable part, he returned to his clearing in Providence, and erected upon this creek the first saw-mill clattering in this portion of the Lackawanna.

Benjamin Baily purchased a lot from Solomon Strong, below that of Leggett's, in 1775, selling it again the next year to Mr. Tripp "for a few furs and a flint gun."[1] In 1777, Mathew Dalson bought 375 acres of land on " ye Capous River so called," bounded on the north by "Lands belonging to one Loggit"[2] This purchase included lands now known as "Uncle Josh Griffin's farm."

---

[1] Westmoreland Records, 1777. [2] Ibid.

While the pioneers up the Lackawanna were thus one by one stretching the boundaries of the settlement with vigorous stroke and handspike, Wyoming, feverish with the sanguinary and intermitting character of the contest alternating now with success and then with the expulsion of one party or the other, received from the young, but giant American Congress, the following resolution, dated in Congress, Dec. 20, 1775:—

"Whereas, a Dispute Subsists between some of the Inhabitants of the Colony of Connecticut, Settled under the Claim of the Said Colony on the Lands near Wioming, on the Susquehannah River, and in the Delaware Country, and the Inhabitants Settled under the Claim of the proprietaries of Pennsylvania, which Dispute it is apprehended will, if not Suspended during the present Troubles in these Colonies, be productive of pernicious Consequences which may be very prejudicial to the common Interest of the united Colonies—therefore,

"Resolved, That is the Opinion of this Congress, and it is accordingly recommended that the contending parties immediately cease all Hostilities and avoid every Appearance of Force untill the Dispute can be legally decided : that all property taken and detained be restored to the original Owners, that no Interruption be given by either party to the free passing and repassing of persons behaving themselves peaceably through said disputed Territory, as well by land as Water, without Molestation, either of person or property; that all persons seized on and detained on Account of said Dispute, be dismissed, and permitted to go to their Respective Homes, and that all things being put in the Situation they were before the late unhappy Contest, they continue to behave themselves peaceably on their respective possessions and Improvements untill a legal Decison can be had on said Dispute, or this Congress shall take further Order thereon. And nothing herein done shall be construed in prejudice of the Claims of either party.

"December 21st.

"Ordered, that an authentic Copy of the Resolution passed yesterday, relative to the Dispute between the people of Connecticut and Pennsylvania be transmitted to the contending parties.

"Extract from the Minutes.
"CHAS. THOMSON, Sec^y."[1]

This resolution, by its temporary suspension of the authority of the land-jobbers of Pennsylvania, gave partial repose to Wyoming and Lackawanna even in the midst of war, while the inhabitants, long harassed by fratricidal warfare, hoped to witness gleams of approaching peace.

FIRST ROAD FROM PITTSTON TO THE DELAWARE.

During the year 1772, the first road from Pittston to the Delaware was made by the inhabitants. Previous to this, the Governor of Pennsylvania, at an official interview with Teedyuscung, in March, 1758, suggested to him the propriety of opening a great road from the head-waters of the Susquehanna down through Wyoming to Shamokin, to which the shrewd chief, from motives of interest, objected.[2]

The nearest point from the Westmoreland Colony to the settlement on the Delaware in the vicinity of Stroudsburg, was about forty miles. From this the valley was separated by a country whose general features partook strongly of the sternness of the times, while the wilderness from Capoose eastward, swarming with beasts and savages, had through it no other road than that built with difficulty by the first party of emigrants to Wyoming, in 1769.

This followed the warriors' trail, which was simply widened by the felling of large trees and the removal of a few troublesome stones for the passage of a wagon.

---

[1] Col. Records, 1775.   [2] Col. Rec., vol. viii., p. 55.

Paths through the forest, made by the Indian centuries before, and trodden by the race that greeted the Pilgrims from the Mayflower's deck, or trees marked by the hunter or ax-man scouting far away from his rocky homestead, furnished the only guidance along the forest profound in the depth and extent of its solitude.

This natural privation to every frontier settlement in the earlier history of the country—the absence of roads—and the necessity of better communication with the parent State, or the nearer villages toward the Hudson, induced the proprietors and settlers holding their meeting in Wilkes Barre, October 2, 1772, to vote "that Mr. Durkins of Kingstown, Mr. Carey of Lockaworna, Mr. Goss for Plymouth, Mr. Danl. Gore for wilkesbarre, Mr. william Stewart for Hannover, are appointed a comtee to Draw subscriptions & se what they Can Git sighned by ye adjourned meeting for ye making a Rode from Dilleware River to Pitts-town."

At the adjourned meeting, held October 5, 1772, it was "voted that Esq. Tryp, Mr. John Jenkins, Mr. Phillip Goss, Mr. John Durkins, Captain Bates, Mr. Daniel Gore, Mr. william Stewart are appointed Comtee-men to mark out ye Rode from Dilleware River to Pitts-town," etc.[1]

This committee were to act until the completion of the road. October 19, 1772, "voted that Esq. Tryp is appointed to oversee those persons that shall from time to time be sent out from ye severall towns to work on ye Road from Dilleware River to this & so that ye work be Done according to ye Directions of ye Com^{tee}, that was sent out to mark ye Road."[2]

This road, then considered no usual achievement, was commenced in November, 1772; every person owning a settling right in the valley, or on "ye East Branch of the Susquehanna River," from the Indian village of

---

[1] Westmoreland Records, 1772.   [2] Ibid

Capoose to the mouth of the stream, assisted toward its construction.

Wages paid then would hardly tempt the sluggard of to-day from his covert, for it was "voted, that those Persons that shall Go out to work on ye Rode from Dilleware River to ye westermost part of ye Great Swamp[1] Shall Have three sillings ye day Lawfull money for ye time they work to ye Exceptance of ye overseors; and from ye Great Swamp this way, Shall Have one shilling and sixpence pr. Day and no more."[2]

Isaac Tripp being appointed to oversee the work, was allowed "Five Shillings Lawfull money pr. Day." This rough, hilly road, quite if not *more* important in its consequence to the people of the inland settlement of that day than any other pike or railroad subsequently has been to the valley, was at length completed, and it is said to have been judiciously located.

MILITARY ORGANIZATION.

When this road was built, times were indeed perilous. Ninety-five years ago the settler fought against foes more savage and exasperated than the yellow panther or the bear. People in our day, familiar only with the smooth current of rural life, can hardly estimate the exposure and insecurity of that period. The pioneer, as he toiled on the plain or in the narrow clearing, kept closely at his side his sharpened knife and loaded musket, expecting every rustle of the leaf, every sound wafted by the gale springing up from the west, to announce the approach of the savage. And even when they slept within their lonely cabins, their arms stood freshly primed beside them awaiting the appearance of the foe.

In 1772, it was voted that each and *every* settler should provide himself with a flint-lock and ammunition, and

---

[1] This is now known as the "Shades of Death." [2] Westmoreland Records.

continue to guard around the threatened plantations until further notice.

In fact, the existence of all the settlements, *as Connecticut settlements*, on the Lackawanna or Susquehanna, became so doubtful at times, from the persistent assaults of the Pennymites, and the incursions of the savages, more stealthy yet less feared, that the settlers, occupied with thoughts of their common safety, met every *fourteen days* to practice military discipline and tactics.

At a meeting of the inhabitants and proprietors held March 22, 1773, it was voted "that the Comtee of Settlers be Desired to send to the several towns or to their Comtee Requiring them to Call all the Inhabitants in Each of ye said towns to meet on Thursday Next at five a Clock in ye afternoon on sd. Day in some Convenient place in sd. town, and that they then Chouse one Person in Each of sd. towns as an officer to muster them & so that all are oequipt according to Law with fire arms and ammunitions, & that they Chuse two Sergants & a Clerk, & that the sd. Chieff officer is Hereby Commanded & Directed to Call ye Inhabitants together once in 14 Days for ye future until this Company orders otherwise, & that in Case of an allarm or ye appearance of an Enemy, he is Directed to Call ye sd. Inhabitants together & stand for ye Defense of ye sd. towns & settlements without any further order."[1]

Order and discipline were not only observed in a military point of view, but were carried into every social, commercial, and domestic arrangement.

Thus by paying a trifle, settlers had voted to them an *ear mark* for cattle and sheep. The Records tell us that "Joseph Staples, his Ear mark a square Hole through ye Left Ear." "Job Tryp ye 2nd, His Ear mark—a smooth Cross of ye Left Ear, & a Half penne ye fore side of Each Ear." "William Raynold, his Ear mark a swallow's tail in ye left Ear & a Half Cross on ye Right Ear.

[1] Westmoreland Records.

"Entered April 28th, 1774, pr. me Ezekiel Pierce, Clerk."

John Phillip's ear mark was "a smooth cross of ye Right Ear & a Half penney ye fore side ye same."

Swine, too, had rigid laws imposed upon them.

A wandering one having intruded or broken into Mr. Rufus Lawrence's field of oats, "back in the woods," damaging thereby 15 bushels of oats, "August ye 23d, 1777, then ye above stray Hog was sold to ye Highest Bidder, & Simon Hodds was ye Highes Bidder, and Bid her of at

	D.		
		1	3 3
Constable fees for Posting the Hog		0	2 3
And travil to Kingstown District		0	1 3
Selling ye Hog		0	3 0
Clerk's Fees for Entiring, &c		0	1 0
		1	10 9 "

RELIGION, TEMPERANCE, AND STILL-HOUSES.

As there are no Colonial nor private records to be found of the early church movements in the Lackawanna Valley, even if any were made at the time, it is extremely difficult, if not quite impossible, to form any thing like a correct estimate of the moral and religious standard of the settlers at that day.

For religious purposes alone, the old Christian church standing in Hyde Park, was, with three exceptions, the first one erected in the valley. This was built in 1836. Some seven years previous to this, a church had been erected in Carbondale ; in 1832, one was erected in Blakeley ; in 1834, one was *raised* in Providence, and blown down the same year. The plain, substantial school-house or log-cabin, standing by the road-side, furnished hospitable places where meetings were held, without display or restraint, for very many years.

The French and Indian war, running from 1754 to 1763, impeded religious advancement throughout the entire Colonial dependencies, while the Indian troubles subsequent to that period, the Revolutionary struggle, as well as the intestinal warfare in Wyoming, all seem to have been alike fatal to morals and life.

"Bundling," that easy but wicked habit of our grandfathers, appears to have been wonderfully prevalent at an early date along the valley, as well as in many other portions of the country, and was not unfrequently attended with consequences that might naturally have been expected by a philosopher. Besides this, there is every reason to believe that the current morals of the day had the greatest liberty of standard, and that one prominent and almost universal characteristic of the people was the love of *whisky*, which was as terrible then as now. As early as 1757, it was found that giving an Indian half a gill of whisky, was attended with bad consequences.[1]

The sale of whisky to them was wholly stopped and forbidden by the authorities, in 1765, as it was perceived that much of the murderous agitation in the forest was caused by *rum*.[2]

At Capoose or Wyoming, Indians were not permitted to drink the inspiring "fire-water," as can be seen by a vote of "the Propriators and Settlers Belonging to ye Susquehannah Purchase Legolly warned and Held In Wilkesbarre, December 7th, 1772. Voted that Asa Stevens, Daniel Gore, and Abel Reine are appointed to Inspect into all ye Houses that Sell or Retail Strong Drink on forfiture of his or their Slettling Right or Rights, and also forfit ye whole of ye Remainder of their Liquor to this Company, and that ye Com^tee above are appointed to take care of ye Liquor Immediately."

The Yankee-like and agreeable provision of having the liquor forfeited, and the *immediate* care that was doubtless directed to it by those to whom it was intrusted, did not prevent its sale to the thirsty warriors, who were turbulent and dangerous when under its influence. Their

---

[1] Col. Rec., vol. viii., p. 11. [2] Ibid., vol. ix., p. 500.

squaws, during their drunken frolics, were often cruelly beaten, and sometimes badly wounded.

Measures still more stringent and severe were adopted by the inhabitants afterward to prevent access to it by the neighboring savages. It was "voted that no Person or Persons, settlers or forrinors Coming into this place shall at any time hereafter Sell or Give to any Indian or Indians any Spiritous Lickquors on ye *forfitures* of all such Lickors and ye *whole* of all their Goods and Chattels, Rights, and Effects that they Have on this Purchase; and also to be voted out of this Company, unless upon some extraordinary reason, as sickness, etc., without Liberty first had and obtained of ye Comtee of Settlers, or Leave from ye Com[tee] that is appointed to Into them affairs."[1]

In 1772 there was but *one* licensed house in the valley to sell spirituous liquor. This committee, composed of Avery, Tripp, and others, met in Wilkes Barre, in June, 1772, "*at six a Clock in ye forenoon*," where, in the simple language of the day, they resolved that, "Whereas there is and may be many Disorders Committed by ye Retailing of Spiritous Lichquor in Small Quanteties to ye Indian Natives, which Disorders to prevent it is now Voted, that there shall be but one Publick house to Retail Speriteous Lichquors in small Quonteties in Each of the first towns, and that Each Person for ye Purpose of Retailing, as aforesd. shall be appointed by the Comtee they Belong; and that they and each of them shall be under the Direction of sd. Comtee, by whom they are appointed, Not Repugnant to ye Laws of the Colony of Connecticutt, and that such Retailors that shall not Duly observe such Directions and Restrictions as they shall severally receive from sd. Comtee, shall on Complaint made to this Company, shall see Cause to Inflict, Not Exceeding his or their Settling Right, Regard being Had to ye Nature and agrevation of ye offence."[2]

---

[1] Westmoreland Records, 1772.   [2] Ibid.

At this time there was no *still-house* in the colony. An embargo was, for a short time, laid upon the transportation of grain. Dec. 18, 1772, it was voted at the town meeting, "that no Person or Persons Now Belonging to the Susquhannah Purchase, from the 18th Day of this present December, until ye first Day of May Next, shall sell to any person or Forrinor or Stranger any Indian Corn, Rye, or Wheat to Carry Down the River out of ye Limits of this Purchase."

In fact, the amount of grain then raised both in Wyoming and Lackawanna, was so scanty and limited, that within all the country now embraced by Luzerne County, no *half bushel* measure was required until 1772. It was then voted "that this Company shall at ye Cost & Charge of this Company as soon as may be, send out to ye Nearest County town in ye Coloney's, & Procure a Sealed Half Bushel & a peck measure & one Gallon pot, Quort pott, point pot, Half point & Gill measure, for a Standard and Rule for this Company to by soon as may, and also sutable weights as ye Law Providedes, etc."

Nothing, however, contributed so much toward establishing *still-houses* here than the absence of a market for the grain raised upon the lowlands in great abundance. Whisky had a commercial and an accepted importance, superior to the depreciated Continental currency, besides it had the virtue of always being ready and *practical* in its application. One gallon of whisky, being worth fifteen or twenty cents, was deemed equivalent to a bushel of rye. Wheat was carried in huge wagons to Easton, a distance of nearly seventy miles through the wilderness, and exchanged for large iron kettles for boiling maple sap into sugar. The journey generally took a week, and the wheat brought from seventy to eighty cents per bushel. The kettles were hired out to persons having maple woods; one pound of sugar per year being given for each gallon held by the rented vessel. The maple sugar, run into cakes of every conceivable variety and size, was worth *five cents* per pound, and was for a long time the only kind used in the settlement.

The isolated condition of the settlers, stern and somber in many respects, was not without its gleams of sunshine. When the wool was gathered from the sheep, or the well-dressed flax ready for the spindle, the young and blooming girls, according to the custom of the people, assembled at some point in the neighborhood, generally under the shade of some tree, with their "spinning-wheels;" where, in a single afternoon, knot after knot of yarn came from their nimble hands, which afterward was woven and whitened into sheets for the coming bride. Dressed in red-dyed fabrics, manufactured by their own tidy hands, they brought with their simple gear and glowing cheeks more pleasure, and gave more artless charms to the maiden not ashamed to toil in field or house, than all the daubs of to-day bestow upon the thoughtless wearer.

In the clear, crisp edge of an evening in autumn, came troops of boys from remote parts of the valley, on foot or on horseback, as was the custom to travel from place to place; if women rode, it was behind the man upon the horse's back. As the spinning or husking ceased, the enjoyments of the evening began. The supper-table was now spread by clean hands, with rye-bread, pumpkin-pies, "Jonny-cake," and dough-nuts, whisky, and rich milk, and when all were gathered around it, many were the good wishes and sweet words whispered behind a pile of dough-nuts or friendly bowl. Some boisterous games closed up the amusements of the evening, when in the soft light of an autumn moon, the "gals"—as all women at that day were called—wended their way slowly homeward with their beaus.

In accordance with the New England habit, Saturday night, if *any*, was observed instead of Sunday evening. With the sunset of Saturday night all labors closed until the following Sunday at sundown. The youth went to see his sweetheart on Saturday evening, as it then was considered the regular time for courting. As "many hands make light work" the older people often met for a "logging bee,"—a way of destroying logs, by rolling them in heaps and burning them; which was at one time the only mode of getting rid of some of the finest timber growing in a new country, before railroads, with their iron nets caught up the products of the forest from the spoiler's handspike.

The coarser grain being turned into the still-house, made whisky so cheap that no "husking," "raising," or "logging bee," nor any public business or social meetings of the inhabitants took place without this abundant product of the still.

The negative spirit of morality prevailing in all the settlements as early as 1773, not coming up to the rigid standard of New England proprietary, led the better class of inhabitants, at a meeting of the Proprietors held at Wilkes Barre, Feb'y 16, of this year, even in the midst of commotion, to appoint a committee composed of William Stewart, Isaac Tryp, Esq., and others "to draw a plan in order to suppress vise and immorality that abounds so much amongst us, and carry ye same before ye next meeting."[1]

Twenty-five years later, the *progressive* measures of public morals are recorded in the following curious deed of land, bearing date August 15, 1798, from Messrs. Baldwin and Faulkner to Joseph Fellows:—

"Know all Men by these Presents, that we Waterman Baldwin & Robert Faulkner, both of Pittstown in the County of Luzerne, in the State of Pennsylvania, being *desirous to promote the interest and general Welfare* of said Pittstown, and to encourage and enable Joseph Fellows of the said Town, County and State, To erect a Malt-house and Beer-house, *which we conceive will prove of general utility to our neighborhood*, as also in

---

[1] Westmoreland Records, 1773.

consideration of *Fifty cents* to each of us paid by the said Joseph Fellows to our full satisfaction, &c., sell to said Fellows a certain piece of land for the purposes just named."

In 1800, *eight* still or beer houses stood along the Lackawanna from its mouth to the upper border of Capoose, in prosperous operation, located as follows : Asa Dimock and Joseph Fellows, each had one never idle in Pittston ; Mr. Hubbuts, another in Lackawanna ; Benjamin and Ebenezer Slocum owned two in Slocum Hollow ; Captain John Vaughn and Mr. Stevens operated one in upper Providence (now Blakeley), while Stephen and Isaac Tripp each ran with vigor their separate stills upon Tripp's Flats; all distilling the cheap and surplus corn and rye into a beverage finding a ready market. Located as it were almost before every man's door, these institutions, looked upon with favor by the yeomanry of the valley, drew from the ripened grain the bewildering draught, used from the cradle to the grave. Children put to sleep by eating bread soaked in whisky and maple sirup, gave no trouble to mother or nurse, as they grew rapidly in stature and good-nature. And yet popular as was this beverage everywhere in Pennsylvania, striking the brightest intellects or narcotizing the feeblest conceptions, its adulteration was so well understood by Daniel Broadhead, commander of Fort Pitt in 1780, who, when officially informed that a requisition for 7,000 gallons of whisky had been made for the troops in the District of Westmoreland, indulged in the hope that " we shall yet be allowed some liquor which is fit to drink."[1]

If the morals of the community a century ago, took some romantic strolls to suit the taste or condition of the pioneers, they were in a great measure vindicated by the necessities which instituted them. But little gold or silver found its way into the settlement, bank bills were

[1] Pa. Arch., 1780, p. 641.

unknown, and as the Revolutionary Scrip, treasured by few, had but indifferent value, the commercial agency of whisky was recognized in all the laws of trade with the same uniformity and force that the Indians in their political economy acknowledged the currency of *zeawant* or wampum. Property changed hands, and many a settler acquired a peaceful title to wild domains by the exchange of a few gallons of whisky.

These still-houses were well patronized, and brought incipient fortunes to their possessors, because they were thus sustained by men who prized and practiced the largest latitude of liberty.

In 1788, the only person recommended to the Supreme Executive Council of Pennsylvania as suitable to keep a house of entertainment in Pittston, was Waterman Baldwin. The next year he was indicted for keeping a tippling-house, and fined five pounds. The next person in the Lackawanna Valley receiving a license from the Governor of Pennsylvania to open a *tavern*, in 1791, was Johnathan Davies.

SAW AND GRIST MILLS.

Logs rolled up in their rough state into a log-house, with every crevice chinked with mud, or bark peeled from the tree and shaped by the aid of young saplings into a wigwam-like cabin, rude and diminutive in outline, formed the only dwelling of the pioneer a century ago. Ash-trees ungracefully split by the beetle and wedge into thin layers, or the more readily prepared bark, afforded roofing, whose special purpose seemed to be to *let in* every unwelcome element, without regard to economy or comfort.

As the settlement expanded up the rich and narrow valley, the need of a saw and grist mill became so urgent, that in the summer of 1774, one of each was built by the township of Pittstown below "Ye Great Falls in the

Lackawanna River."[1] The same year, they were both purchased by Solomon Strong, and from him they passed into the hands of Garrit Brinkorkoof, July 6, 1775. They were the first mills erected on the bank of the Lackawanna. After doing good service to the settlement, both mills were destroyed, either by the spring freshets or the torch of the Tories and Indians, leaving in 1778 but a single dwelling unharmed along the entire Lackawanna—that of Ebenezer Marcy. The waterfall here was so admirably adapted to mill purposes, and the straight pine, green with its foliage, running from creek to mountain, seemed so easy of conquest, that Solomon Finn and Elephat L. Stevens were induced to build a saw-mill at this point in 1780. Down the steep bank, opposite the upper end of Everhart's Island in Pittston, half a mile above the depot of the L. & B. R. R., totter the walls of a fallen grist-mill, once standing upon the foundation of this old saw-mill. The song of its jarring saw, sent far up and down the wooded glen in olden times, long since has ceased to tell the story of its former usefulness and glory.

In 1798, Isaac Tripp and his son Stephen, built a small grist-mill on Leggitt's Creek, in Providence, but the dam, thrice built and thrice washed away, owing to defective construction, proving a failure, the mill was abandoned. The next grist-mill built upon this stream still farther up in the Notch, was erected in 1815 by Ephraim Leach.

A saw-mill was built upon the Lackawanna, in Blakeley Township in 1812, by Moses Vaughn; in 1814, Timothy Stevens, a mill-wright of some character, erected a grist-mill above this point; in 1816, Edmund Harford began another upon one of the fairest of the upper tributaries of the Wallenpaupack, in Wayne County, a few miles above the ancient Lackawa settlement.

[1] Westmoreland Records, 1774.

DR. JOSEPH SPRAUGE.

With the first party of adventurers coming into Wyoming, there came no physician, because the invigorating character of exercise and diet enjoyed by the pioneer, whose daily life, enlivened by the choir of falling trees or the advancing ax, knew the want of no medical representative, until Dr. Joseph Sprauge came from Hartford in 1771.

Of the yet uninhabited forest, called in the ancient records, "Ye Town of Lockaworna," whose upper boundaries extended nearly to the present village of Scranton, Dr. Sprauge was one of the original proprietors. To dispose of lots or pitches to the venturing woodsman, probably contributed more to bring him hither than any expectation of professional emoluments or advantage in a wilderness, making, in the hands of the Indian, a *materia medica* which no disease could gainsay or resist.

His first land sales were made in May, 1772.[1] For a period of thirteen years, with the exception of the summer of 1778, Dr. Sprauge lived near the Lackawanna, between Springbrook and Pittston, in happy seclusion, fishing, hunting, and farming, until, with the other Yankee settlers, he was driven from the valley, in 1784, by the Pennymites. He died in Connecticut the same year.

His widow, known throughout the settlement far and near, as "Granny Sprauge," returned to Wyoming in 1785, and lived in a small log-house then standing in Wilkes Barre, on the southwest corner of Main and Union streets. She was a worthy old lady, prompt, cheerful, successful, and, at this time, the sole *accoucheur* in all the wide domain now embraced by Luzerne and Wyoming counties. Although of great age, as late as 1810 her obstetrical practice surpassed that of any physician in this

---
[1] See Westmoreland Records, 1772.

portion of Pennsylvania. For attending a case of accouchement, no matter how distant the journey, how long or fatiguing the detention, this sturdy, faithful woman invariably charged *one dollar* for services rendered, although a larger fee was never turned away, if any one was able or rash enough to offer it.

DR. WILLIAM HOOKER SMITH AND OLD FORGE.

If the Lackawanna Valley owes its earliest explorations and settlement wholly to Moravian fugitives, who, to escape persecution, fled from the banks of the Neckar and the Elbe to the yet untroubled plateau above the Blue Mountains, in 1742, it owes to the memory of the late Dr. William Hooker Smith, whose mind first recognized and faintly developed its mineral treasures, its grateful acknowledgments.

He emigrated from "ye Province of New York,"[1] and located in the Wilkes Barre clearing in 1772, where he purchased land in 1774.

The Doctor's father was a Presbyterian clergyman living in the city of New York, and the *only* minister there of this denomination in 1732; and such was the feebleness of his congregation, that he preached one-third of his time at White Plains.[2]

As a surgeon and physician, his abilities were of such high order that he occupied a position in the colony, as gratifying to him as it was honorable to those enjoying his undoubted skill and experience. With the exception of Dr. Sprauge, Dr. Smith was the only physician in 1772 living between Cochecton and Sunbury, a distance of one hundred and fifty miles.

The formation of Luzerne County created positions of trust and honor, among which was the magisterial one; and although the doctor was a Yankee by birth, habit, and education, such confidence was reposed in his capacity

---

[1] Westmoreland Records, 17772.   [2] Hist. Col., N. Y.

and integrity, that he was chosen the first justice in the fifth district of the new county. His commission, signed by Benj. Franklin, then President of the Supreme Executive Council of Pennsylvania, bears date May 11, 1787.

In 1779, he marched with the troops under General Sullivan into the Indian country along the upper waters of the Susquehanna, and by his cheerfulness and example taught the soldiers to endure their hardships and fatigues, taking himself an earnest part in that memorable expedition which brought such relief to Wyoming and such glory to the American arms.

Nor did Congress, prompted by noble impulses, forget his services as acting surgeon in the army, when, in 1838, $2,400 was voted to his heirs.

That his mind, active, keen, and ready, looked beyond the ordinary conceptions of his day, is shown by his purchased right, in 1791, to dig iron ore and stone coal in Pittston, long before the character of coal as a heating agent was understood, and the same year that the hunter Gunther accidentally discovered "black-stones" on the broad, Bear Mountain nine miles from Mauch Chunk.

These purchases, attracting no other notice than general ridicule, were made in Exeter, Plymouth, Pittston, Providence, and Wilkes Barre, between 1791-8. The first was made July 1, 1791, of Mr. Scot, of Pittston, who, for the sum of five shillings, Pennsylvania money, sold "one half of any minerals, ore of iron, or other metal which he, the said Smith, or his heirs, or assighns, may discover on the hilly lands of the said John Scot by the red spring."[1]

Old Forge derived its name from Dr. Smith, who, after his return from Sullivan's expedition, located himself permanently here on the rocky edge of the Susquehanna, beside the sycamore and oak, where first in the valley the sound of the trip-hammer reverberated, or mingled with the hoarse babblings of its water. The forge was erected

[1] Luzerne County Records.

by Dr. Smith and James Sutton in the spring of 1789, for converting ore into iron. It stood immediately below the falls or rapids in the stream, about two miles above its mouth, and not far from the reputed location of the silver mine before spoken of. Before the erection of these iron-works none existed in Westmoreland except those in Newport, operating in 1777.

"My recollections of Pittston and Old Forge," wrote the late Hon. Charles Miner, in a letter to the writer, twelve years ago, "are all of the most cheerful character. I have, at the old tavern, on the bank of the river above the ferry, seen the son of Capt. Dethic Hewit, the gallant old fellow, who, in the battle, when told, 'See, Capt. Hewit, the left wing has given away, and the Indians are upon us; shall we retreat?' answered to his negro drummer, *Skittish Pomp*, 'No, I'll see them damned first,' and fell. His son was at the house, and sang with the spirit his father fought—

> "'So sweetly the horn
> Called me up in the morn,' &c., &c.

"But to the Forge.

"The heaps of charcoal and bog ore, half a dozen New Jersey firemen at the furnace! What life! What clatter! And then at the mansion, on the hill, might be seen the owner, Dr. Wm. Hooker Smith, now nearly superannuated, who, in his day, was the great physician of the valley during the war, and if, perchance, the day was fine, and his family on the parterre, you might see his daughters, unsurpassed in beauty and grace, whose every movement was harmony that would add a charm to the proudest city mansion."

The doctor was a plain, practical man, a firm adherent of the theory of medicine as taught and practiced by his sturdy ancestors a century ago. He was an unwavering phlebotomist. Armed with huge saddle-bags rattling with gallipots and vials and thirsty lance, he sallied forth on horseback over the rough country calling for his services, and many were the cures issuing from the unloosed vein. No matter what the nature or location of the disease, how strong or slight the assailing pain, *bleeding* promptly and largely, with a system of diet, drink, and rest, was enforced on the patient with an earnestness and success that gave him a wide-spread reputation as a physician.

The forge prospered for years—two fires and a single trip-hammer manufacturing a considerable amount of iron, which was floated down the Susquehanna in Durham boats and large canoes. The impure quality and small quantity of ore found and wrought into iron, with knowledge and machinery alike defective; the labor and expense of smelting the raw material into ready iron in less demand down the Susquehanna, where forges and furnaces began to blaze; the natural infirmities of age, as well as the rival forge of Slocum's, at Slocum Hollow, all ultimately disarmed Old Forge of its fire and trip-hammer.

After leaving his forge, he removed up the Susquehanna, near Tunkhannock, where, full of years, honor, and usefulness, he died in 1815, among his friends, at the good old age of 91.

THE SIGNAL TREE.

As the emigrant from Connecticut found himself, after a long journey, on one of the peaks of the Moosic Mountain, five miles northeast from Scranton, overlooking the fertile plain of Wyoming, twenty miles away, he could discover, by the naked eye, when the day was clear, looming up from the surrounding trees, covering the mountains northwest of Wyoming, a pine-tree, majestic in its height, its trunk shorn of its limbs almost to its very top, resembling, from the marked umbrel spread of its foliage, a great umbrella, with the handle largely disproportioned. This is the tree known as the *signal tree*. Over the deep foliage of trees surrounding, this one floats with an air of a monarch, catching, as the sun sinks away in the west, the latest glimpse of its rays. "Tuttle's Creek," famous for its Pennymite history and local interest, leads its sluggish way through Kingston, from which this grand pitch-pine is plainly visible. Tradition tells that at the time of the battle, an Indian was stationed in the top of the tree, so that when the defeat of the whites was announced by the louder peals of the war-whoop, he commenced to cut off the limbs of the tree, and as this could be seen many miles from every direction, parties of Indians were thus informed to watch the paths leading out of the valley and prevent the escape of the fugitives. This, however, is mere tradition. A more reasonable interpretation of the matter is this : Some years ago one of the knots of this tree was removed, and from the concentric rings or yearly growths indicated by them, the lopping of the limbs was dated back to 1762—the first year a settlement was commenced here by the whites—thus showing quite clearly that the tree had been trimmed previous to the massacre, and that it had been used by the emigrating parties from Connecticut as a *guiding* tree to the Wyoming lands, where a colony, with no roads but the warriors' pathway, and but little knowledge of a reliable character of the locality of the new country, crossed the frowning mountains, mostly on foot, and made a permanent residence in 1769.

Evidence of fracture, made by the ax or hatchet, a century ago, upon the limbs, has been so obliterated by intervening years, that the indifferent and unskilled observer looks in vain for the cause of the absent limbs.

THE WYOMING MASSACRE.

The summer of 1778, momentous in the history of the Lackawanna Valley, witnessed either the slaughter, capture, or flight of *every* white person within its border. There is no data to determine the exact population of the Lackawanna portion of the Wyoming possessions in 1774. Westmoreland, embracing all the settlements on the Susquehanna from Athens to Wyoming, and from Wallenpaupack to the mouth of the Lackawanna, had about 2,300 inhabitants at this time. Of this number, Wyoming, with its broad productive acres, had a large proportion, because of the greater protection of its sheltering block-houses. Seventy-five or about one hundred persons, probably enumerated the *whole* united population of the Lackawanna Valley at the commencement of the American Revolution. These shared in the deliberations and dangers of their brethren along the Susquehanna.

Although the people of Connecticut met at Hartford in September, 1774, to devise measures of resistance to British wrong, her young colony at Wyoming, just formed into the town of Westmoreland, absorbed with the Provincial conflict, now interrupted and then resumed, had done nothing in the way of building forts, or preparing for the bloodier wrestle for independence, until it had actually begun. At a town meeting, "legally warned and held in Westmoreland, Wilkes Barre district, Aug. 24th, 1776," it was unanimously voted that the people erect forts in Hanover, Plymouth, Wilkes Barre, and Pittston at once, at points deemed most judicious by the military committee, "without either fee or reward from ye town."[1]

This was done so generally, that before the battle on Abraham's Plains, July 3, 1778, there stood eight forts in Wyoming Valley, constructed principally of logs.

On the high bank of the river, nearly opposite Pittston, where a large spring of water emerges from the plain, there had settled a Tory named Wintermoot, who, after clearing sufficient land, erected a rude stockade or fort, known as Wintermoot's Fort. Although this simple fact

[1] Westmoreland Records.

afforded no evidence of Tory proclivities, its erection at this point, at this exciting period, justly aroused the suspicions of the loyal element in the neighborhood, and led to the erection of another a mile above Wintermoot's, where lived the acknowledged patriotic families of the Hardings and Jenkinses. It stood in the narrow defile in the mountain nearly opposite Campbell's Ledge, a mile above the mouth of the Lackawanna.

To meet some of the demands of war, Congress called upon Connecticut, in August, 1776, to raise two companies of eighty-four men each for the defense of Westmoreland. Wyoming promptly furnished them. No sooner, however, was the number complete, than Congress, itself in jeopardy, and yet unremitting in its efforts to raise troops, saw with concern the critical and greater needs of the country elsewhere. The American army, of about 14,000 men, under General Washington, had been driven from Long Island and New York by the British army, numbering 25,000. Forts Washington and Lee, on the Hudson, had fallen. With only 3,000 brave men, General Washington retreated to Newark, and was driven from camp to camp with his half-fed, ill-clothed, yet unswerving soldiers, crossing the Delaware as the victorious British approached Philadelphia. At this dark moment in the nation's history, Congress, which had hastily adjourned the same day from Philadelphia to Baltimore, hardly appreciating the perils menacing Wyoming, ordered the two companies raised for its defense to join the commander-in-chief "*with all possible expedition.*" This being done, Wyoming was left comparatively defenseless.

Events of vast importance began to develop in many parts of the country, and excite apprehension in the mind of the patriot. Burgoyne, with victorious troops, was sweeping down from the Canadian frontier, accompanied by his red and white skinned auxiliaries, ready for pillage or revenge. Ticonderoga had fallen into his hands, and while General Howe was crowding up victory after victory in New York and New Jersey, the Indians living along the upper branches of the Susquehanna and Chenango, restless and joyous with the hope held out by Brant and Butler of regaining their lost Wyoming, became unanimous and sanguinary allies. Parties of them were seen, here and there, emerging from the mountain forest into the valley, shedding no blood, destroying no property, but securing a captive at every possible opportunity. The whole settlement saw and felt the coming danger. Scouting parties of bold, experienced woodmen, were sent out daily from the valley to watch the three great war-paths radiating from it, while drillings or trainings were held every *fourteen* days, when the old and young, the feeble and the strong, drilled side by side in their country's service; expecting every bark of the watch-dog, or click of the rifle, to give note of the approach of the exasperated bands.

The colony, now (1778) nine years old, had, out of its total population of about 2,000 persons, 168 in the main army under General Washington, when the meditated attack on Wyoming came to the knowledge of the inhabitants. A large body of Indians and Tories had assembled at Niagara and at Tioga for this purpose; the Indians being under the command of the famous chief of mixed blood, named Brant, or *Gi-en-gwah-toh*.[1] The time of attack was probably suggested by the Tories expelled from Wyoming, wishing for the bloodiest revenge upon the settlement, known to be almost without soldiers or fire-arms.

From the lower Susquehanna, the Delaware, the far-off Lackawaxen, from the few low wigwams serving the wild men on the Lackawanna, the Indians were summoned by the Great Chieftain to *Oh-na-gua-ga*, to join the enterprise, while the Tories throughout Westmoreland simultaneously repaired to the enemy.

---

[1] "He who goes in the smoke."—*Col. Stone.*

Early in the spring of 1778, Congress had been apprised by General Schuyler of the threatened attack, but so engaged was this body in this all-absorbing struggle for national existence, that nothing was, or could be done for the safety of Wyoming until March 16, 1778, when it was resolved "that one full company of foot be raised" here for its defense. This really furnished no assistance, as the men were compelled "to find their arms, accoutrements, and blankets" from the exhausted resources of the interior.

Congress has been censured by the historian in no flattering terms, for not recalling to Wyoming the absent soldiers under Captains Durkee and Ransom; but it must be remembered that the remnant of Washington's army was retreating before the superior and exulting forces of the British, and had not its exhausted strength been invigorated sufficiently by re-enforcements to check and drive back the invaders, it is impossible to estimate the consequences to the country to-day. Independence would have been retarded, and possibly postponed forever.

In May, 1778, the first life was taken in Westmoreland, near Tunkhannock, by the Indians, who each day became more defiant and numerous. A day or two afterward, a scouting party of six persons were fired upon, a few miles farther down the river, by a body of savages lurking along the war-path; two whites were wounded, and one fatally, when, springing into their canoe, they escaped down the Susquehanna. Alarm spread throughout the entire settlement. Persons living along the Lackawanna at Capoose, apparently remote from danger reaching even the outer towns, either deserted their homes and sought protection in the forts, or fled to the parent State for greater security. The terror of the inhabitants, already wrought up to a fearful pitch, was still increased by an event simple in its character, yet tragic in its meaning.

"Two Indians, formerly residents of Wyoming, and acquainted with the people, came down with their squaws on a visit, professing warm friendship; but suspicions existed that they were spies, and directions were given that they should be carefully watched. An old companion of one of them, with more than Indian cunning, professing his attachment to the natives, gave his visitor drink after drink of his favorite rum, when in the confidence and the fullness of his maudlin heart, he avowed that his people were prepared to cut off the settlement; the attack to be made soon, and that they had come down to see and report how things were. The squaws were dismissed, but the two Indians were arrested and confined in Forty Fort." [1]

Men heard this intelligence with lips compressed and determined, and at once prepared to receive those with whom they were so soon to converse from the throat of the musket. Every instrument of death was examined and fitted for immediate use. Guns were repaired and fitted with new flints, bayonets were sharpened, bullets molded, powder made and distributed, and every man and boy able to shoulder a musket, fell into the ranks of a new militia company formed by Captain Dethic Hewit, or joined the *daily* train-bands, expecting the latest messenger to herald the approach of the invaders. Two deserters from the British army, one by the name of Pike, from Canada, and the other a sergeant named Boyd, from Boston, Miner relates, "were particularly useful in training the militia."

While these preparations were being made along the excited valley, beyond succor offered by Connecticut, and withheld by Pennsylvania, the Indians, Tories, and British, darkened the waters of the Susquehanna at Ta-hi-o-ga with a fleet of rafts, river-boats, and canoes, preparatory to a descent upon the "Large Plains."

In all the wide expanse of territory, within the limits of Westmoreland—about seventy miles square—there was

---

[1] Miner's History.

no larger field-piece than the old flint musket, with the exception of a single cannon at the Wilkes Barre Fort. This was a four-pounder, of no use, as no suitable balls were in the settlement, and had been brought into the colony merely for an alarm-gun in the Yankee and Pennymite war. The force of the Americans, without appropriate arms, discipline, or strength, amounted to about four hundred persons, to resist the attack of nearly four times their number.

The enemy, numbering about four hundred British provincials, six or seven hundred Seneca and Mohawk Indians, in paint and war-costume, familiar with every part of Wyoming, a large body of Tories gathered from afar, commanded by Colonel John Butler, a British officer, and accompanied by the notorious Brant, an Iroquois chief, left their rendezvous on Tioga River, descended the Susquehanna below the mouth of Bowman's Creek, near Tunkhannock, about twenty miles above the head of the Valley of Wyoming, where they landed on the west bank of the river. Here, in a deep, sharp curve in the river, they moored their boats, marching across a rugged spur of the mountain, thus shortening the distance a number of miles. On the 30th of June, just at the edge of the evening, they arrived on the western mountain, a little distance above the Tory fort of Wintermoot's. This fort, standing about one mile below Fort Jenkins, probably owed its inception to some ulterior design of the British and Tories, whom it served so well. From Fort Jenkins, eight persons having neither notice nor suspicion of the proximity of the enemy, had gone up the valley into Exeter to work upon their farms, a little distance from the fort, taking with them their trusty and ever-attending weapons of defense, with their agricultural utensils. While unsuspectingly engaged at their work, which they were about closing for the day, they were surrounded by a portion of the invading army, with a view of making them prisoners, so that the British Butler might learn the actual state and strength of the Wyoming people.

Surprised but not intimidated by the fearful odds against them, they chose to die by the bullet rather than risk the hatchet or the torturing scalping knife brandished before them. They fought for a short time, killing five of the enemy, three Tories and two Indians, when four of their own number fell, and were hacked into shreds by the exasperated savages; three were taken alive, while a single boy leaped into the river, and, aided by the gray twilight of evening, was enabled to escape, amid a hundred pursuing bullets. One of the slain was a son of the barbarous Queen Esther, who accompanied the expedition with her tribe, and whose cruelties at the *bloody rock*, inspired with greater atrocity from the recent loss of her offspring, forever connects her name with infamy.

Two Indians who were watching the mutilated remains of the dead, for the purpose of killing or capturing the friends who might seek the bodies at night, were shot by Zebulon Marcy, from the Lackawanna side of the river. For several years, Mr. Marcy was hunted and watched by a brother of one of the Indians swearing that he would have revenge.[1] Although Marcy's house was the only one left standing along the Lackawanna in 1778, from some unexplained Indian freak, he was never harmed by them.

Fort Jenkins, thus bereft of its protectors, capitulated the same evening to Captain Caldwell, while the united forces of Butler and Brant bivouacked at the friendly Tory quarters of Fort Wintermoot. No sooner did the dull report of musketry, echoing from under Campbell's Ledge down the valley, denote the presence of the foe, than the real critical position of the settlement at the mercy of the coming wave, was appreciated in all its

---

[1] Miner.

sternness. Men not accustomed to scour the woods for miles in the vicinity of their homes to discover Indian trails, and give warning to their neighbors and families of suspicious approach or retreat, would have shrunk from the fierce-coming struggle with dismay; but these self-reliant men left the scythe in the swath, the plow in the furrow, and, gathering up the weak and weeping ones, hurried them to Forty Fort. This fort stood on the west bank of the river, below Monockonock Island, and three miles above Wyoming Fort, where, in a short time, were collected the principal forces of Wyoming Valley, consisting of three hundred and sixty-eight men, very indifferently armed and equipped. On the Lackawanna side of the river, at Pittston, nearly opposite Wintermoot's, Fort Brown had been erected; this was garrisoned by the settlers from the lower portion of the Lackawanna and Pittston, numbering about forty men, under the command of Captain Blanchard. Another company was at Capoose.

By the aid of spies, full of stratagem and daring, continually reconnoitering the unharvested plains upon either side of the river, Col. John Butler learned how completely at his mercy was the entire valley, unless re-enforcements hoped for by the Connecticut people, and expected from the main army, should arrive and drive back his mongrel horde. Already were the two upper forts in his possession, with all the canoes and means of crossing the river, but not wishing to bring his Indians into the excitement of a general battle, where, becoming infuriated and ungovernable after a victory, scenes of torture and bloodshed might be enacted too revolting to witness, and yet too general and wide-spread to check, he sent one of the prisoners taken in Exeter to Col. Zebulon Butler, on the morning of the day of battle, accompanied by a Tory and an Indian, demanding the immediate surrender, not only of the fort he commanded, but of all others in the valley, with all the public property, as well as the militia company of Capt. Hewit, as prisoners of war. It can be said to his credit that he also suggested to the commander of Forty Fort the propriety of *destroying all intoxicating drinks*, provided these considerate terms were rejected; "for," said the British Butler, "drunken savages can't be controlled." The acceptance of these apparently exacting, but really liberal terms, was urged by some, in hopes that the tide of slaughter might be stayed; the majority opposed it, and the messenger was sent away with this decision.

A council of war was immediately held in the fort. While a few hoped that the absent military companies would arrive, and furnish re-enforcements able to offer battle and expel the enemy from Wyoming, if a few days intervened; others more rash and impulsive replied that the force concentrated in the fort could march out upon the plains, where the enemy were encamped, and, being familiar with the ground, could surprise and possibly capture them; that many of their homes already lit by the torch, their crops destroyed—that the murder of the Hardings at Fort Jenkins was but the prelude to the drama about to redden Wyoming, unless interrupted by prompt offensive measures, and that *they* were anxious and determined to fight. Unfortunately this counsel prevailed.

With the colonial development in Westmoreland had grown the love of *rum*.[1] So fixed, so general, in fact, had become this pernicious and unmanning habit—so essential was whisky regarded in its sanative and commercial aspect, that one of the first buildings of a *public* character erected in the colony, after a stockade or fort, was a still or brew house. The almost universal custom of drinking prevailed at this time to an alarming extent, not only throughout the Lackawanna and Wyoming settlements, but along the whole frontier of upper Pennsylvania.

[1] In 1783 the Pennsylvania troops stationed at Wyoming were supplied with "2¼ Gill of Liquor" to one pound of bread.—Pennsylvania Archives, 1783, p. 118.

"It being known that among the stores there was a quantity of whisky, Col. Butler desired it might be destroyed, for he feared if the Indians became intoxicated he could not restrain them. The barrels were rolled to the bank, the heads knocked in, and the liquor emptied into the river."[1]

The venerable and yet intelligent Mrs. Deborah Bedford, one of the last survivors of the Wyoming massacre, informed the writer in 1857 that, "in accordance with the request of Col. Butler, all the liquor in the fort was rolled out and emptied into the Susquehanna, *with the exception of a single barrel* of whisky, spared for medicinal purposes. The head of this was knocked in during the council of war;" and as "the debates are said to have been conducted with much warmth and animation,"[2] it is more than possible that the inspiring influence of this barrel contributed, to a certain extent, toward the result of the deliberations. "A hard fight was expected up the valley," continued the reliable lady, from whose young, anxious eye nothing escaped in the fort, "and as the drum and fife struck up an animating air, while the soldiers marched out the fort one by one, a gourd-shell, floating in the inviting beverage, was filled, and passed to each comrade, and drank."

Motives, alike natural and delicate, have hitherto suppressed evidence showing that if *some* of the soldiers, brave as they might have been, and were, had not "taken a little too much,"[3] their ideas of their own strength were singularly confused and exalted. However pleasant it might be to pass by this great error of the times—an error which rendered certain and merciless the fate of Wyoming —with the same studied silence and charity observed by others, justice to the living, uttering no censure, and to the dead, needing no defense, demands a *truthful* record.

---

[1] Miner's History of Wyoming, p. 232.
[2] Chapman's History of Wyoming, p. 122.   [3] Peck's Wyoming, pp. 364-5.

Col. George Dorrance, an officer whose prudent counsels to remain in the fort were disregarded, was taunted with cowardice because of his counter-advice against this death-march up the valley.

The forces of Brant and Col. John Butler were at Wintermoot's Fort, opposite Pittston. To silently reach this point, and, protected by the large pine-trees sheltering the plain, spring on the enemy unawares, was the plan finally adopted. The little band, on the afternoon of the 3d of July, numbering about 350 of the sturdiest remaining settlers, under the command of Colonel Zebulon Butler, left the fort amid the prayers of dear and devoted kindred. Old men, whose hands were tremulous and unsteady; young ones, unskilled in years—marched side by side to the place of conflict. So great the emergency at this time, so much to be won or lost by the coming battle, that none remained in the fort save women and children. Rapidly up along the west bank of the river, Col. Z. Butler cautiously led his forces within half a mile of Wintermoot's. Here he halted a few minutes, and sent forward two volunteers to reconnoiter the position and strength of the enemy; these were fired upon by the opposing scouts, who, like the main body of the British, were not only apprised by Indian runners of the departure of the Yankees from Forty Fort, but were prepared to give them a murderous welcome. As the Americans approached the British soldiers and painted savages, Wintermoot's Fort, which had served its intended mischievous purpose, was set on fire by the Tories for reasons unknown. The British colonel promptly formed his forces into line of battle; the Provincials and Tories being placed in front toward the river, while the morass at the right concealed vast numbers of the dusky warriors under Brant and the drunken Queen.

Among the tall pines unmelted from the plain, Colonel Zebulon Butler placed his men so as better to resist the first attack of the enemy, preparing to begin the strife.

Colonels Butler and Dorrance each urged the soldiers to meet the first shock with firmness, as their own lives and homes depended on the issue. Hardly had the words rang along the line, before the bullets of the enemy, pouring in from a thousand muskets, began to thin the ranks of the Connecticut party.

"About four in the afternoon the battle began; Col. Z. Butler ordered his men to fire, and at each discharge to advance a step. Along the whole line the discharges were rapid and steady. It was evident, on the more open ground the Yankees were doing most execution. As our men advanced, pouring in their platoon fires with great vivacity, the British line gave way, in spite of all their officers' efforts to prevent it. The Indian flanking party on our right, kept up from their hiding-places a galling fire. Lieut. Daniel Gore received a ball through the left arm. 'Captain Durkee,' said he, 'look sharp for the Indians in those bushes.' Captain D. stepped to the bank to look, preparatory to making a charge and dislodging them, when he fell. On the British Butler's right, his Indian warriors were sharply engaged. They seemed to be divided into six bands, for a yell would be raised at one end of the line, taken up, and carried through, six distinct bodies appearing at each time to repeat the cry. As the battle waxed warmer, that fearful yell was renewed again and again, with more and more spirit. It appeared to be at once their animating shout, and their signal of communication. As several fell near Col. Dorrance, one of his men gave way; 'Stand up to your work, sir,' said he, firmly but coolly, and the soldier resumed his place.

"For half an hour a hot fire had been given and sustained, when the vastly superior numbers of the enemy began to develop its power. The Indians had thrown into the swamp a large force, which now completely outflanked our left. It was impossible it should be otherwise: that wing was thrown into confusion. Col. Dennison gave orders that the company of Whittlesey should wheel back, so as to form an angle with the main line, and thus present his front instead of flank, to the enemy. The difficulty of performing evolutions, by the bravest militia, on the field, under a hot fire, is well known. On the attempt the savages rushed in with horrid yells. Some had mistaken the order to *fall back*, as one to *retreat*, and that word, that fatal word, ran along the line. Utter confusion now prevailed on the left. Seeing the disorder, and his own men beginning to give way, Col. Z. Butler threw himself between the fires of the opposing ranks, and rode up and down the line in the most reckless exposure.

"'Don't leave me, my children, and the victory is ours.' But it was too late."[1]

When it was seen that defeat had come, the confusion became general. Some fought bravely in the hopeless conflict, and fell upon the battle-ground bayonet-pierced; others fled in wild disorder down the valley toward Forty Fort or Wilkes Barre without their guns, pursued by Indians whose belts were soon reeking with warm scalps.

"A portion of the Indians' flanking party pushed forward in the rear of the Connecticut line, to cut off retreat from Forty Fort, and then pressed the retreating army toward the river. Monockasy Island affording the only hope of crossing, the stream of flight flowed in that direction through fields of grain."[2] The Tories, more vindictive and ferocious if possible than the red-men, hastened after the fugitives.

Mr. Carey and Judge Hollenback were standing side by side when the victorious forces of the enemy appeared in view; Carey ran with the speed of a deer, while Hollenback, throwing away his gun and stripping to the waist, followed him toward Wilkes Barre. Being thus divested of his clothing he was enabled to leave his weaker comrade in the rear, swam the river in safety, and

[1] Miner.   [2] Ibid.

was the first to tell the tale of defeat to the village of Wilkes Barre, then consisting of twenty-three houses. Carey fled to the river, where, under its deep-worn bank he found shelter, as he sank too exhausted to swim, still retaining his musket. He heard the quick footsteps of the fugitives, and as they were plunging in the water to reach Pittston Fort, saw the swift-sent tomahawk overtake many a neighbor struggling in the river in vain. Upon the bank below him, three soldiers were clubbed to death by the Tories. His own musket he grasped still more firmly, determined to sell his life as dearly as possible, if required; escaping detection, he swam the river at night and escaped.

MONOCASY ISLAND, FROM THE EAST BANK OF THE SUSQUEHANNA.

Of the cruelties practiced by the Tories and Indians after the battle, one instance will suffice to illustrate. A little below the battle-ground there lay, and still lies, in the divided waters of the Susquehanna, an island green with willows and wild grass, called "Monockonock Island." As the path down the valley swarmed with warriors, few of the fleeing settlers pursued it, but scattered through the fields. Others fled to this island for refuge. This was perceived by the Tories, ruthless in pursuit, who reaching the island deliberately wiped their guns dry to finish the murderous drama. "One of them, with his loaded gun, soon passed close by one of these men who lay concealed from his view, and was immediately recognized by him to be the brother of his companion who was concealed near him, but who being a Tory, had joined the enemy. He passed slowly along, carefully examining every covert, and directly perceived his brother in his place of concealment. He suddenly stopped and said, 'So it is you, is it?' His brother, finding that he was discovered, immediately came forward a few steps, and falling on his knees, begged him to spare his life, promising him to live with him and serve him, and even to be his slave as long as he lived, if he would only spare his life. '*All this is mighty good*,' replied the savage-hearted brother of the supplicating man, '*but you are a d—d rebel*,' and deliberately presenting his rifle, shot him dead on the spot."[1] The name of the fratricide Tory was John Pencil, and the miserable wretch, shunned by the Indians whom he accompanied to Canada, was afterward killed and devoured in the Canadian forest by wolves.[2] Such was the spirit of the Wyoming massacre, and such was the doom of the fratricide.

BLOODY ROCK.

After the pursuit of the fugitives had ceased, scenes of torture began. Opposite the mouth of the Lackawanna, and almost under the shadows of "Campbell's Ledge," a band of Indians, wild with exultation, had gathered their prisoners in a circle, stripped of their clothing, and with sharpened spears drove them into the flames of a large fire, amidst their agonizing cries and the yells of the infuriated savages. On the battle-ground, was cleft each scalp

---

[1] Chapman's History, pp. 12–78. [2] See Dr. Peck's Wyoming, pp. 37–15.

of the dying and the dead, before the bloody work was carried to "Bloody Rock." "This celebrated rock is situated east of a direct line between the monument and the site of Fort Wintermoot, on the brow of the high steep bank which is supposed to have been the ancient bank of the river. The rock is a bowlder, and it is a sort of conglomerate, principally composed of quartz."[1] It formerly rose some two feet above the earth but the constant attrition of the frequent visitor desiring a fragment of the interesting bowlder to carry away as a relic, has scalped or shorn it almost even with the ground. Around the rock, standing distinctly out on the plain, otherwise smooth and rockless, some eighteen of the prisoners who had been taken under the solemn promise of quarter, were collected and surrounded by a ring of warriors under the command of Queen Esther. In the battle she had led her column with more than Indian bravery, and now around the fatal ring was she to avenge the loss of her first-born, slain in the encounter with the settlers, at the head of the valley, a day or two before. Swinging the war-club or the merciless hatchet, she walked around the dusky ring, and, as suited her whim, dashed out the brains of the unresisting prisoners. Two only escaped by superhuman efforts. The bodies of fourteen or fifteen were afterward found around this rock, scalped and shockingly mangled. Nine more were found in a similar circle some distance above.[2] About 160 of the Connecticut people perished in the battle and massacre; 140 escaped. The surviving settlers fled toward the Delaware. Before them frowned the foodless forest, since known as the "*Shades of Death ;*" behind, save the low wail of the scattered fugitives, clambering up the mountain side by the light of their burning homes, all was silence and desolation. The forest-dwellers had cruelly revenged their wrongs; the Tory by

---

[1] Peck's Wyoming, p. 284.   [2] Miner.

his club and bayonet had surpassed the wild man in ferocious instinct—the British soldier, led hither by command, turned from the unsoldier-like scenes of the day and night with aversion, and all sank exhausted on the grounds of the old Indian empire for repose.

The Pittston forts surrendered to Colonel J. Butler early on the morning of the fourth, upon the following terms:—

"Articles of Capitulation for three Forts at Lacuwanack, 4th July, 1778. Art. 1st.—That the different Commanders of the said Forts do immediately deliver them up, with all the arms, ammunition, and stores, in the said forts." "2d.—Major Butler promises that the lives of the men, women, and children be preserved intire."[1]

These terms were honorably complied with, and not a person in Pittston was molested by the Indians; all the prisoners in the forts were marked with black war-paint, which exempted them from immediate harm. Forty Fort was surrendered the same day to Major John Butler.

Five days after the battle, Colonel Butler retired from Wyoming with his forces, so elated with his success that he reported to his government that he had "taken 227 scalps and only five prisoners," "taken eight palisades, (six) forts, and burned about *one thousand dwelling houses*, all their mills, etc.," having, "on our side one Indian, two Rangers killed, and eight prisoners wounded." "We have also killed and drove off about one thousand head of horned cattle, and sheep and swine in great numbers."[2]

After Butler had gone northward, a party of rangers and Indians whom he had sent, went "to the Delaware to destroy a small settlement there, and to bring off prisoners."[3] These, after remaining a few days at Wyoming for scalps and plunder, visited the Lackawanna Valley

---

[1] Copied from Her Majesty's State Paper Doc. in London. Miner.
[2] See Butler's Report. Peck's Wyoming, pp. 52–6. [3] Ibid.

on their way to the Paupack and Delaware. Wyoming, with the exception of a few houses around Wilkes Barre fort, was depopulated, and presented one dark picture of conflagration and waste. Up the Lackawanna, every house and barn, with the single exception of Marcy's, was burned to the ground, and every family that could escape fled on foot toward Stroudsburg for safety.

Six miles up the Lackawanna, a small stream called Key's or Kieser's Creek, emerges from a long line of willows, where the savages overtook and shot and scalped two men by the name of Leach and St. John, who were removing their families with ox-teams from the smoking valley below. "One of them," says Miner, "had a child in his arms, which, with strange inconsistency, the Indian took up and handed to the mother, all covered with the father's blood. Leaving the women in the wagon unhurt, they took the scalps of their husbands, and departed." At Capoose, Mr. Hickman, attending to his crops, unconscious of danger so near, was murdered by the same band, as were his wife and child. His log cabin was burned to the ground.

Isaac Tripp, a Mr. Hocksey and Keys were captured and carried from the Capoose into the forest of Abington at this time. Tripp, who had hitherto, in his intercourse with the Indians, shown them kindness, was painted and released, while his two companions were led out of the path, tomahawked, and left unburied in the woods near Clark's Green.

No white person was left alive in the entire valley in 1778, after the massacre, nor did any settlers venture to return to the Susquehanna or the Lackawanna to bury the dead or gather the crops, until some three months afterward.

In September, Colonel Hartley was sent up into the Indian country to chastise them, while the grain was being secured. He arrived at Wyalusing, September 28, with his men worn down, and his "Whiskey and Flour all gone."¹ "In lonely woods and groves we found the Haunts and Lurking Places of the Savage Murderers who had desolated our Frontier. We saw the Huts where they had *dressed and dried the scalps* of the helpless women & Children who had fell in their hands."²

In October, "Three persons were killed near Wyoming, and another was sent in with his life, *scalped to his Eyebrows* almost."³

No single massacre in America during the Revolution, awakened throughout the whole land a sensation so universal and profound as did this. General Washington, pained by the sanguinary blow struck at Wyoming, ordered General Sullivan, in 1779, to visit and lay waste the Indian country along the northwestern frontier, from whence much of its force had come. The expedition, however, being retarded for a time from various causes, and the numerous massacres being still unavenged, a proposition was made to the authorities of Pennsylvania, April, 1779, by William McClay, to hunt the Indians out of the Lackawanna and Wyoming valleys with horses and *dogs*. He says "that a single troop of Light Horse attended by dogs, would destroy more Indians than five thousand men stationed in forts along the Frontiers."⁴ This system of warfare, however, was never adopted here.

Gen. Sullivan proceeded to the very heart of the Indian empire around the lakes in July, 1779, and after burning *eighteen* of their villages,⁵ destroying a large number of warriors, and a vast quantity of corn, peach orchards, &c., returned to Wyoming, October 7, with the loss of only forty men.

"The army marched to Lackawanna, distant 9 miles from Wyoming. (Wilkes Barre.) This place contains two hundred acres of excellent level land, and beautifully

---

¹ Pa. Arch., 1778, p. 5.   Ibid.   ³ Ibid., p. 16.
⁴ Ibid., 1779, p. 357.   ⁵ See Pennsylvania Archives, 1779, p. 709.

situated, having a fine creek bordering on the east side of the river in front, and a large mountain in the rear, which forms this place a triangular form."[1]

The following account of an extraordinary adventure and escape of a messenger, coming from Sullivan's camp to Easton, illustrates how little pleasure there was in traveling then, even in the *rear* of his army:—

Sunday Morning.
                    Sullivan's Stores, 1st July, 1779.
S^r,

This will inform you of the most singular event that perhaps you ever met with.—One of my Expresses, (Viz^t,) James Cook on his return from Weyoming this day, about the middle of the afternoon, in the Swamp was fired upon by the Indians & Tories—he supposes between Thirty & Fifty Shot. One Shot went thro' his Canteen, one thro' his Saddle, one thro' his Hunting Shirt, one was shot into his Horse. Two Indians or Tories being yet before him, both discharged their Pieces at him, threw down their Firelocks with a determination to Tomahawk him—advanced within Eight Yards of him, at which Time he, with a Bravery peculiar to himself, fired upon them, killed one of them on the spot and wounded the other, notwithstanding he threw his Tomahawk at the Express, missed him, but cut the Horse very deep upon the Shoulder. He got hold of Cook, thought to get him from his Horse, tore his Shirt, which is stained much with the Indian's Blood; the Horse being fretted by his Wound raised upon his hind Feet, Trampled the Indian or Torie under him, who roared terribly, at which time Cook got clear; the other Indians on seeing him get off, raised the Whoop as if all Hell was broke loose. He supposes he rode the Horse afterwards near four Miles, but by the loss of Blood began to Stagger, when he alighted, took

---

[1] Report of Geo. Grant, Serg. Maj. to ye 3d Reg. of N. J., under Maj. Sullivan, in 1779.

off his Saddle & Letters, ran about a Mile on foot, where he fortunately found a stray Continental Horse, which he mounted & rode to this Place.

It is easy to account for his getting the Horse as there are numbers of them astray about the Swamp. Mr Cook's Firelock was loaded with a Bullet & Nine Buck shot, & the Indians being close together when he fired is the reason why the one might be killed and the other Wounded.

From a Perfect knowledge of the mans Sobriety, Integrity and Soldierism, no part of this need be doubted.

I am sir,

Your most ob^t Humble serv^t,

(Copy.)   ALEX'R PATTERSON.

Directed,—To His Excellency Joseph Reed, Esqr, Present.

Smarting under the chastisement given by General Sullivan, bands of Indians, which had returned, dexterous and wary, prowled around the cabin of the valley husbandman, and their tomahawks struck alike the laborer in the field and the child in the cradle; and yet, in spite of such adverse danger, besetting every hour with blighted hopes and ruined prospects, the settlement began to fill up with many of the former returning occupants.

In the fall of 1778, the region of Capoose, depopulated so completely of every white inhabitant, began to receive back some of the more resolute of its former denizens. A small portion of the fall crop, escaping destruction by mere accident or caprice, was thus secured, which, by the aid of bear-meat and venison, easily obtained, as every pioneer was a hunter, enabled them to pass through the winter with comparative comfort, unmolested by Tories or Indians. In March, however, 1779, the last predatory band, hoping for conquest, yet rejoicing in the ruin they had wrought, after attacking Wilkes Barre in vain, turned up the old Lackawanna to the settlement at Capoose. Isaac Tripp was shot in his own house on the flats, and three men, named Jones, Avery, and Lyons, were carried away in the forest, and never heard of afterward.

GENERAL HISTORY RESUMED.

Instead of the repose hoped for by the inhabitants of Wyoming at the close of the American Revolution, the temporarily suspended animosities between Pennsylvania and Connecticut, gathering strength by the intervention of the Great War, broke out afresh with all the venom and violence begotten by a dispute involving every impulse of passion and every consideration of selfishness.

Connecticut, through its General Assembly, "holden at Hartford, Oct. 9, 1783, asserted its undoubted and exclusive right of jurisdiction & Pre-emption to all the Lands lying West of the Western limits of the State of Pennsylvania, & East of the Mississippi River, and extending througout from the Latitude 41° to Latitude 42° 2 north, by virtue of the Charter granted by King Charles the second to the late Colony of Connecticut bearing date the 25 day of April, A. D. 1662,"[1] while it relinquished all claim to Wyoming after the unexpected decision of the Commissioners at Trenton.

Soon after the promulgation of the *Trenton Decree*, "two boxes of musket cartridges, and two hundred rifle-flints" were ordered to Wyoming with Northampton militia, to look after persons not readily acquiescing in a decision known to be adverse to every principle of common sense and equity. Because the inhabitants refused to be ground into ashes unmurmuringly, they were reported "wrangling" and full of a "Letegious Spirit."[2]

Toward the Lackawanna people, more defenseless and exposed, because fewer in number, proceedings were instituted by the Pennymites more tyrannical and oppress-

---

[1] See Pennsylvania Archives, 1783, p. 116.   [2] Ibid., pp. 47-9.

ive than elsewhere, simply from the fact that this weakness could offer no resistance. Families were turned forcibly out of their houses, regardless of age or sex; the sick and the feeble, the widow and the orphan, were alike thrust rudely from their sheltering homes, while fields of grain, and all personal property, were stolen or destroyed by a band of men armed with guns and clubs, in the interest of the Pennsylvania land-jobbers.[1]

The decision of the Trenton court, looked upon as a simple question of *jurisdiction* only, without affecting the *right of soil*, was accepted in good faith by the people generally. "We care not," said they in an address to the General Assembly, "under what State we live in, if we live protected and happy."

The land-jobbers, in their passion for self-aggrandizement and emolument, not content to allow an interpretation of this decision favorable to the settlers, yet so foreign to their own selfish purposes, urged troops upon Wyoming, upon the arrival of which "the inhabitants suffered little less than when abandoned to their most cruel and savage enemies. The unhappy husbandman saw his cattle driven away, his barns on fire, his children robbed of their bread, and his wife and daughters a prey to licentious soldiery."[2] Memorials and petitions, couched in respectful tone and language, sent repeatedly to the Assembly, met with open derision or contemptuous silence. It was well for Wyoming, feeble yet unshrinking, to stand alone in the war-path in time of massacre and bloodshed, and grapple with the blows otherwise aimed at the lower inland settlements of Pennsylvania, but not to enjoy even the desolation of wild-woods without insult and disfranchisement. "The inhabitants," says Chapman, "finding at length that the burden of their calamities was too great to be borne, began to resist the illegal proceed-

---

[1] Z. Butler's Petition to Congress, 1784.
[2] Chapman's History of Wyoming, p. 138.

ings of their new masters, and refused to comply with the decisions of the mock tribunals which had been established. Their resistance enraged the magistrates, and on the 12th of May (1784), the soldiers of the garrison were sent to disarm them, and under this pretense one hundred and fifty families were turned out of their dwellings, many of which were burnt, and all ages and sexes reduced to the same destitute condition. After being plundered of their little remaining property, they were driven from the valley and compelled to proceed on foot through the wilderness by way of the Lackawaxen to the Delaware, a distance of about eighty miles. During this journey the unhappy fugitives suffered all the miseries which human nature appears to be capable of enduring. Old men, whose children were slain in battle, widows with their infant children, and children without parents to protect them, were here companions in exile and sorrow, and wandering in a wilderness where famine and ravenous beasts continued daily to lessen the number of the sufferers. One shocking instance of suffering is related by a survivor of this scene of death ; it is the case of a mother whose infant having died, roasted it by piecemeal for the daily subsistence of her remaining children !"[1]

Elisha Harding, Esq., who was one of the exiles, says "it was a solemn scene ; parents, their children crying for hunger—aged men on crutches—all urged forward by an armed force at our heels. The first night we encamped at Capoose, the second at Cobb's, the third at Little Meadows so called, cold, hungry, and drenched with rain, the poor women and children suffering much."

In fact, the mutual hatred of each party, cherished from Capoose to Wyoming with every expression of bitterness, was so intense and general, and the settlers up the lesser valley shown so little clemency by the nomadic hordes of Pennymites sent up from Sunbury and elsewhere, that

---

[1] Chapman's History of Wyoming, p. 138.

even Brigadier-General Armstrong, afterward Secretary of War, harsh and covetous himself, reported to President Dickenson in October, 1784, that "the treatment of the Lackawany people has been *excessively cruel.*"[1] Voluntary evidence so explicit from such a quarter, needs no corroborative testimony to give it weight.

No person suspected of being a well-wisher of the Yankees, remained in the settlement unharmed and unmolested. Nor was the rude expulsion of the inhabitants, who, thus dragging themselves along, out of the valley, too weak and despairing to offer resistance, until they sank to the ground from hunger and exhaustion, to await the coarse instincts of their pursuers, more merciless than the savages' wild work six years before with brand and battle-ax.

Thus for the *fifth* and last time was every New England emigrant expelled from the Lackawanna within twelve years, to find a home in the vacant wilderness with their perishing children and wives, or journey on foot to the Delaware, beyond the reach of their pursuers, if not carried to Easton jail. No portion of the American frontier in the early history of the country so wantonly and perennially inflicted sorrows upon the peaceful adventurer as did the Lackawanna from 1763 to 1784.

While this ferocious conduct on the part of Pennsylvania soldiers was repudiated and condemned by the State, the authorities, chagrined at the indignation her rash and incompetent instruments had evoked throughout the confederation, it had the effect, indirectly, of creating the new county of Luzerne two years afterward.

After being released from jail, whither nearly all the male portion of the inhabitants had been driven, charged with no crime that could be sustained, and yet compelled to live on water and bread in a dismal prison,[2] they returned to their desolated homes after their release.

---

[1] Pennsylvania Archives, 1784, p. 688.   [2] Ibid., p. 614.

The farmers up the Lackawanna, far away from their native hills, thus irritated and interrupted in their labors by the Pennymites, and occupied wholly with thoughts of their wrongs, sent Mr. Benjamin Luce the following notice:—

"Lackawany, Oct. 8, 1784.
"Sir

We understand that you are obstinate and treat the Yankees ill; therefore this is to warn you in the name of the Connecticut Claimants to depart and leave the house of Richard Hollsted, in 12 hours in peace, or expect trouble. If we are obliged to send a party of men to do the business you must abide the consequences.

EBENEZER JOHNSTON,
WATERMAN BALDWIN."[1]

Thus passed the summer and winter of 1784. The spring of 1785 developed no healthier sentiment nor kindlier feelings.

One or two affidavits, taken from a large number of a similar character in the Pennsylvania Archives of 1785, serve to illustrate the spirit in which this struggle for Wyoming was carried on. In March of this year, a constable named Charles Manrow affirmed,

"That Gangs of the Connecticut Party are daylay gowing through the Wioming Settlements distressing, the few Families yet in the place who are attached to Government, by Robing, Plundering and Turning them out of Doors in a most naked and Distressed situation, that yesterday was a day set for all those People who had not actually been Throwed out of Doors by Violence, to be goan that they had Received the Last notice without Distress. That on the Twenty Second Instant, Six of them came to the Hous of this Deponant at about the sun Setting, and Turned his Family all out of Doors, Throwed his goods all out and Considerable part broke to pieces, Took his Grain,

[1] Pa. Arch., 1784, p. 679.

meet, salt, and many other things, that his Children had no Shoes, and little Cloathing, Thretning if they Return into the Hous, they would burn it down with them in it, when this deponant asked the officer of the party, what authority he had for such Conduct who Produced his Precept Signed Ebenezer Johnson their Col. or Commanding Officer."[1]

"*Daniel Swarts*, being duly sworn doth depose and say, that on the Twenty Second Instant a Gang of Twelve of the Connecticut Claimants came to the house of this Deponant with arms Thretning the Family so that his wife is in a situation, that her life is almost despaired of, ordering them Immediately out of Doors, That he has been Plundered of the most of his Effects so that his Family is almost naked, himself much beat and abused and halled out of Doors by the hare of his head."[2]

Upon the other hand, every usurpation aiming to obliterate Wyoming as a *Connecticut* colony—every scheme having for its object the destruction of the industrious element, which, amidst wars, massacres, expulsions, imprisonments, and every intolerant artifice, had brought blooming fields out of the wild acres from Nanticoke to Capoose, was tried in vain by the Pennsylvania land speculators. Diplomacy, the weapon of subtle men, pacified and accomplished in a short time, what all else had failed to do.

On the 25th of September, 1786, Luzerne County[3] was erected out of that part of Northumberland County extending from Nescopeck Falls to the northern boundary of the State. Within its area, it included all the Yankee or New England Colony west of New York, except a few settlers along the Delaware and Paupack. It comprised within its boundaries all of Susquehanna, Wyoming, Columbia, and Lycoming, the greater part of Bradford, and a fractional portion of Sullivan and Montour.

[1] Pa. Arch., 1785, p. 708.   [2] Ibid., p. 709.
[3] Named from the French minister, Chevalier de la Luzerne.—*Chapman.*

The year of 1786 marks an important era in upper Pennsylvania. The removal of Indian tribes, the peaceful solution of the Connecticut-Pennsylvania controversy, made many an upland clearing in the edge of the forest rejoice with the returning emigrant or new settler.

"Deep Hollow" (now Scranton) resounded with the stroke of the advancing ax;—the Lehigh and Lackawaxen were each explored by Pennsylvania to learn their navigable capacity,[1] while separating this territory into a new county, gave hope and impulse to many a brave heart shrinking from no danger, but longing for the unrestrained and uninterrupted quiet of rural life.

The formation of Luzerne County, while it tranquilized a contest unparalleled in reciprocal bitterness and pertinacity, also annihilated a bold project of a few of the more ambitious Yankee occupants of Wyoming, led by Col. John Franklin, John Jenkins, and Solomon Strong, of forming a new and independent State out of the 42d Degree of Latitude, through Pennsylvania and a portion of New York, with Wilkes Barre as the capital.

John Franklin, Solomon Strong, James Fin, a Baptist minister, John Jenkins, and Christopher Holbert conceived the scheme. The celebrated Col. Ethan Allen of Vermont, who was twice visited by Strong, and urged to throw the strength of his unbounded popularity into the movement, finally espoused the cause of the Connecticut claimants against Pennsylvania.[2] By the aid of Col. Allen, Vermont had been carved from the rough borders of New York in spite of remonstrance or force, and why could not an independent Republic be established at Wyoming in defiance of the wishes and power of a State, dishonoring its robes by harsh intercourse with a young border colony which had stood for years in blood for its defense, like a Roman sentinel on the outer wall? Six

---

[1] Col. Rec., vol. xv., p. 65.   [2] See Pa. Arch., 1783–6, pp. 761–4–6.

hundred men, mostly Yankees, were here, which with the invincible Green Mountain Boys, obtained by asking, and the Connecticut party from the West Branch of the Susquehanna, whither Mr. Fin had been sent to develop and strengthen the enterprise among the inhabitants, it was reasonably supposed that a body so formidable in numbers, commanded by a colonel so renowned and brave as he was known to be, having the right and possession of the valleys and all roads to and from them both by land and water, would be able not only to repel all opposing force, extinguish the claim and grasping avidity of Pennsylvania, but triumphantly assert and achieve independence. The appearance of Col. Allen at Wyoming at this time, clad in his Revolutionary regimentals, while the public mind down the Susquehanna and up the Lackawanna, favorably discussed the contemplated project, gave to it still greater importance.

The creation of the new county of Luzerne, which was originally intended merely as an instrument to defeat these wronged yet patriotic schemers—and *nothing more* —introduced elements and authority into the Lackawanna and Wyoming domain, which the quick, keen eye of Col. Allen saw it would be folly, if not treason, to oppose. The colonel soon afterward returned to Vermont. Aside from a collision necessarily renewed and long continued between the respective States concerned by fostering the design with arms, it is impossible for the broadest calculator to-day to estimate the consequences resulting to the country, especially to the Lackawanna and Wyoming portion of it, had the projected State, with the hero of Ticonderoga as its Governor, been wrought into being.

Col. Franklin, the offending front and acknowledged head of the Connecticut party, was afterward arrested, thrust into a Philadelphia prison, loaded with chains, and fed in the dark, damp cell upon bread and water; and yet after he was released, in October, 1787, upon his own parole,[1] he returned to the valley, and although, like all the settlers, adverse to the broad, bold usurpations of the Provincial speculators, who had been shamefully wronged, he smoked the pipe of peace, and sought with persistent steadiness and honesty to aid the operations of the various compromising laws.

The questions at issue, acquiring importance at the expense of the interests of the settlements, being no longer known, men of peaceful nature but public enterprise began to project highways in the county among which was a public road or turnpike, from the Delaware, near Stroudsburg, to the incipient village of Montrose, then in Luzerne. In March, 1788, five commissioners, consisting of Henry Drinker, Tench Coxe, John Nicholson, Mark Wilcox, and Tench Francis, were elected for this purpose.[2] The route, surveyed at the expense of the State, remained unbuilt for years. In May following, commissioners were appointed by Pennsylvania, to visit Luzerne County and examine the quantity and quality of land within the seventeen certified townships, for the purpose of enabling the House to fix upon a proper compensation to be paid the owners thereof. Two townships, viz.: Pittston and Providence, embraced all the domain settled in the Lackawanna Valley. The latter being five miles square, contained 16,000 acres and ran from the township of Lackawa, east of Cobb Mountain, to the Moosic elevation separating Exeter from Providence. Capoose, rich in agricultural resource and intrenched in the shade of pines, boundless and beautiful in their expansion, was the principal point, inhabited by three or four families.

A number of settlers in the Lackawanna had bought and paid both the Susquehanna Company and the State of Pennsylvania for their lands, but in order to restore harmony, and give full operation to the compromising

---

[1] Col. Rec., vol. xv., p. 304.   [2] Ibid., p. 425.

law, they surrendered their titles again to the State for a mere nominal consideration, and purchased their own lands again at the appraisement of the Commissioners appointed by the State.

Such land, according to its quality, was divided into four classes:—

"As soon as forty thousand acres should be so released to the State, and the Connecticut settlers, claiming land to the same amount, should bind themselves to submit to the determination of the Commissioners, then the law was to take effect; and the Pennsylvania claimants, who had so released their land, were to receive a compensation for the same from the State Treasury, at the rate of five dollars per acre for lands of the first class, three dollars for the second, one dollar and fifty cents for the third, and twenty-five cents for lands of the fourth class. The Connecticut settlers were also to receive patents from the State confirming their lands to them, upon condition of paying into the Treasury the sum of two dollars per acre for lands of the first class, one dollar and twenty cents for lands of the second class, fifty cents for lands of the third class, and eight and one-third cents for lands of the fourth class—the certificates issued by the Commissioners to regulate the settlement of accounts in both cases. Thus, while the State was selling her vacant lands to her other citizens at twenty-six cents an acre, she demanded of the Connecticut settlers a sum which, upon the supposition that there was the same quantity of land in each class, would average ninety-four cents an acre."[1]

PROVIDENCE TOWNSHIP AND VILLAGE.

The Lackawanna, from the two Indian villages of Capoose and Asserughney, was explored in 1753; it was laid out into two townships in 1770, viz., Pittstown and Providence—the first, named after the celebrated Pitt,

[1] Chapman, p. 169.

the British Commoner; the latter after Rhode Island's capital, as thirty of the Susquehanna Company, owning the wild lands, came from the "Colony of Rhod-island." Pittstown embraced the first five miles of the valley; Providence extended its boundaries still five miles farther up. Both townships unrolled an area of six thousand acres, divided into lots of 300 acres each, called *shares*. For greater convenience and availability, lots were sometimes subdivided into half lots or shares. Providence, originally surveyed five miles square, was the sixth township formed; was designated in the Westmoreland Records as "Ye 6th Town of Capoose," because Capoose, cleared of its timber, lay on the path which brought emigrating parties into the Monsey town, where they were fed on venison and fish, and kindly treated by the bow and oar's men inhabiting it. These Indians, roaming over the territory for twenty years after the original sale of the lands, were skilled in the use of the bow and tomahawk, which the French, by lavishing gifts with prodigality, adroitly turned upon the English in 1755–6. At the Indian Treaty, held at Easton in the fall of 1758, this tribe "brightened the Chain of Friendship and cleared the blood from the Council Seats" ever afterward.

Being some ten miles away from Pittstown block-house, settlers were less readily prepared to encounter the greater danger apparent in this township, than to labor in clearings more favorably located on the Susquehanna.

Timothy Keys and Solomon Hocksey, two young men from Connecticut, struck the first blow into the woods of the new township in 1771. With gun and ax they penetrated the willowed glen now known as Taylorsville, where they built their cabin by the side of the brook named from Mr. Keys. One vast park, filled with deer, stood between this creek and Capoose, marked by a single foot-path.

Capoose lands originally fell into the hands of Capt. John Howard, from the Susquehanna Company, a gentle man unacquainted with their precise location or their wonderful fitness for immediate culture. As there was no disposition to settle them, for the prudential reasons already named, he interested with him in the lands Christopher Avery and "Isooc Trypp of west-moreland in ye County of Litchfield & Colony of Connecticutt in New-England,"[1] both bold Yankees, seeking fortune in Wyoming as early as 1769. The latter, more fearless and determined than his fellows, could not overlook the garden, where orchard and vineyard, cared for no longer by the strolling braves, enraptured the eye with blossom and promise. Near the vacated wigwams he shaped his cabin in 1771, and, without clearing a foot of land, planted and raised a crop of corn, the first season, on the plantation deserted but a short time previous. Mr. Tripp being neither scalped nor endangered during the winter, others, reassured and emboldened by his good luck, sprinkled their cabins along the stream, giving an air of comfort to the wilderness, here and there eruptive with stump.

A lot "in ye Township of New-Providence, alious Capoose," surveyed to Col. Lodwick Ojidirk, passed into the hands of Johnathan Slocum, in 1771, "on account of Doeing ye Duty of a settler," for Ojidirk. This tract, containing 180 acres, was sold to James Bagley, April 29, 1778. Bagley's Ford, near the mouth of Leggett's Creek, took its name from this old resident.

Among the pioneers who purchased lots or shares of the Connecticut Susquehanna Company, in the township, between 1772–5, the Westmoreland Records mention John Dewit, Andrew Hickman, Fred. Curtis, Isaac Tripp, Jr., Solomon Johnson, Thos. Pukits, Benj. Baily, Mathew Dalson, Ebenezer Searles, James Leggett, Gideon Baldwin, John Stevens, Johnathan Slocum, Maj. Fitch, John Aldren, Christopher Avery, and Solomon Strong. Solomon Strong, identified in 1785–6 with Col. Ethan Allen,

---

[1] Westmoreland Records.

John Jenkins, and the brave John Franklin, in the attempted formation of a new, distinct State out of Westmoreland, like Fitch, Searles, Aldren, Stevens, and Ojidirk, had no interest in the township other than a speculative one; this was trifling, as Baily acquired his 300 acres of woodland from Strong, for a "few furs and a flint gun."[1]

Land was cheap, and, when purchased for a few shillings an acre, excavations in the great woods over it were only made by hard, patient labor, and, after the trees had paid reluctant homage to the ax, their removal and destruction gave infinite trouble and work. Instead of leaving the fallen timber to season for a year, and then, when favored by a long dry spell, apply the torch for a good burn, making "logging" barely necessary, the pioneer, pressed by the wants of his family, drew the green trees into log-heaps where they were roasted and burned into ashes. And even after the new land was thus prepared for the reception of seed, the corn, promising reward to the toiling husbandman, must be defended against the vigilant raccoon and squirrel, before the husking bee secured the crop in the garret, away from its nimble enemies.

The houses, beginning to gladden the waste places, had but a single story, were built from green logs up-rolled and chinked with mud, to protect the inmates from cold, and gave one-third of this space to huge stone chimneys. There was not in the entire township, in 1775, so strange a feature as three houses in a cluster, or two within sight of each other. Every farmer was his own carpenter, and thus every style of architecture became popular. Doors were made without boards; windows, without glass. The rich skin of the fawn easily obtained, or the bushy robe snatched from old bruin while visiting the barn-yard, brought comfort and ornament to the cabin, warmed in

[1] Westmoreland Records.

winter by piles of fire-wood, and illuminated at night with pine-knots everywhere abundant.

The township had neither physician nor lawyer for a long time afterward, nor does it appear that any physical or material interest suffered from their absence; for what tonic can equal hard work and coarse food in the field or forest, and what law compare with common honesty, blended with common sense?

No newspapers entered their cabins, for none were printed in the country; almanacs, selling for a shilling a-piece, supplied the settlement with the news of the year. Falling and burning the giant timber gave recreation to the settlement, disturbed by no breach of the social relations.

Nothing exhibits the New England character in a light more favorable and philanthropic, than the fixed organic rule of the proprietors of each township, of setting apart and reserving forever certain lots for gospel and school purposes before others were offered to the settler. In every township one lot of three hundred acres was thus reserved for the first minister of the gospel *in fee*—one for a parsonage—one for the support of a school; three were reserved as public lots, subject to the future disposition of the town. Nearly 2,000 acres of land were thus held in Providence Township. Paths cut through the woods —over hills instead of around them—were more bridle-ways than roads, while fallen trees or friendly ford-ways served for stream-crossing.

"The *town* of Westmoreland legally incorporated for civil purposes, was about seventy miles square, and could only be established by Supreme Legislative authority. Within this limit a number of townships of five or six miles square, were laid off by the Delaware and Susquehanna Companies, divided into lots, which were drawn for by Proprietors, or sold. These townships had power to make needful laws and bye-laws for their interior regulation, the establishment of roads, the care or disposal of vacant lots, and other matters entirely local. Of these, there already existed Wilkes Barre, Hanover, Plymouth, Kingston or the Forty, Exeter, Pittston, and Capouse or Providence ; more were from time to time added. A town meeting, therefore *now* when 'legally warned,' called together all the Freemen, in all the townships or settlements, from the Delaware to fifteen miles beyond the Susquehanna, and from the Lehigh north to Tioga Point."[1] At the first town meeting legally warned and held in Westmoreland, "at eight of the clock in ye forenoon, March ye 20th, 1774," for the purpose of choosing town officers, all this vast territory, sparsely occupied, was divided into eight separate districts. Wilkes Barre, Plymouth, Hanover, and Kingston, made four districts. Voted, "that Pittson be one district by ye name of Pittston district; and that Exeter, Providence, and all the lands west and north to ye town line, be one district, by ye name of ye North District ; and that Lackaway settlement and Blooming Grove, and Sheolah, to be one district, and to be called by ye name of ye Lackaway district ; and that Coshutunk, and all ye settlements on Delaware, be one district, and joined to ye other districts, and known by ye name of ye east district."[2] From the Lackawanna portion of the town, or "ye North District," Isaac Tripp, Esq., who declined serving, was chosen *Selectman* for the ensuing year, John Dewit of Capoose chosen of the *Surveyors of highways*, John Abbot, one of the *Fence-Viewers*, Gideon Baldwin, one of the *Listers*, Barnabas Cary and Timothy Keys, two of the *Grand Jurors*, and James Brown one of the *Tything* men. These persons, the old records informs us, were "all loyal subjects of His Gracious Majesty King George the Third."

August Hunt and Frederick Vanderlip, two residents of New Providence, were expelled from the township at

[1] Miner's Wyoming, p. 154. [2] Westmoreland Records, 1774.

this meeting, because they were men "that have, and now do so conduct themselves by spreading reports about ye town of Westmoreland, much to ye disturbance of ye good and wholsome inhabitants of this town, and by their taking up and holding land under ye pretention of ye title of Pennsylvania."[1] "Voted that Hunt be expelled this purchase, and he be, as soon as may be, removed out of ye town by ye committee at ye cost of this Company, in such way as ye Committee shall think proper."[2]

"Voted that ye Indian apple Tree, so called at Capoose, shall be ye Town Sign Post for ye town of New Providence."[3] Each township had a prominent tree as a Town Sign Post, which, in the absence of press, newspaper, or almanac, made a public point where all notices of a public character had to be affixed to be legal. Such tree notices, always written—for all the inhabitants could read and write—made a meeting *legally warned*. This apple-tree, venerable in its broad branches, as if arrayed in the foliage of its youth, planted more than a century and a half ago, yet blooms and bears its fruit by the road-side, between Providence and Scranton, a few hundred feet above the site of the ancient village of Capoose.

In the winter of 1775, there was a meeting of the settlers under this apple-tree, to dispose of land on the Susquehanna at the site of the present village of Tunkhannock, as can be seen by "a list of men's names that drew for lots in the township of Putnam (now Tunkhannock), in Susquehannah, Dec. 20th, 1775, at Providence."[4] Among persons thus drawing lots appear the names of Isaac and Job Tripp, William West, Paul Green, Job Green, Zebulon Marcy, and John Gardner.

An unsuccessful effort was made at this time to change the name of Providence for that of *Massassoit*, as is shown by the old surveys and maps preserved among the archives of the county. The few savages remaining in

---

[1] Westmoreland Records, 1774.   [2] Ibid.   [3] Ibid.   [4] Ibid., 1775.

the valley in 1776-7, as they could not preserve their neutrality despite the tempting offers of the Tories and British in 1778, left charred and crimson traces of their presence. Settlers fled to Stroudsburg with their affrighted loved ones, or removed temporarily to Wyoming, where the muttering of the savages hissed down through the forests from the upper lakes. Isaac Tripp, Timothy Keys, James Hocksey, and Andrew Hickman, with his wife and child, alone remained. These few, having dispute only with wolves, panthers, and bears, around the rich intervale of Capoose, living amicably with the hand preparing to strike, gave no thought of the danger of ambush or encounter with a foe until it came. And even when the Senecas, dancing the war song in prospective triumph, ready to sting with their arrows, poisoned and loaded, hastened from their wild parks into the flood of canoes moored for Wyoming, these settlers, conscious of no wrong done by themselves, cherished the hope that *their* frail cabins, isolated and remote, would be spared by the bands which had promised neutrality or friendship.

After the Wyoming massacre, it took but a few quick strokes of the hatchet to do the work of depopulating the entire Lackawanna Valley, leaving it a waste, where the camp fire again gleamed upon the roaming conquerors.

A few months after the massacre, the inhabitants returned to Wyoming to bury the dead and secure the remnant of the crops; but not until after Gen. Sullivan, in the summer of 1779, had carried fire and bullet through the Indian lodges along the upper Susquehanna, did the few former occupants of Providence lands venture back to the ashes on their farms, where their cabins once were standing. These few persons, influenced by the objective attitude of the Pennymites, were able to enlarge the range of agriculture in the township but little, if any.

In 1786, Isaac Tripp, 3d, emigrated from Rhode Island

with his son, Stephen, then ten years old. He brought with him at this time no other member of his family, and it was not until 1788 that his residence at Capoose became permanent.

Miner informs us that a company of soldiers were at Capoose at the time of the Wyoming massacre, but, as all the valuable papers having reference to the history of the township's affairs at this particular time were destroyed, it is impossible to tell the precise time they retired before the savages ascending the Lackawanna.

The pacification of the valleys in 1786-8, by measures long delayed, imparted new impulse to every interest by removing all barrier to agricultural progress and prosperity. Men began to enjoy a conscious security, denied them till now, which expanded into measures of public good.

The route for a public highway across Luzerne had been surveyed in 1778 by legislative authority, the commissioners of which reported "that Providence, situated favorably between two mountains, would be of vast importance to the road."[1] These facts being promulgated, had their influence with men willing to wrestle with the forest for slight reward and secure homes.

Aside from the structure at the mouth of Leggett's Brook, put up unframed by Mr. Leggett in 1775, to be abandoned soon afterward, the first house erected upon the site of the present village of Providence was a low double log affair, built in 1788 by Enoch Holmes. The single apple-tree, standing near the northeast corner of Oak and Main streets, marks the precise location of his cabin. Along the terraced slope of Providence, the heavier wood had been cleared away, either by Indian husbandmen or by whirlwinds, such as in later years disturbed the equanimity of the young village, thus rendering necessary but little intrusion upon the thickets to fit the land for

---

[1] Commissioners' Report, 1778, p. 10.

planting or pasturage. He remained here two years with his family, pounded his maize and prepared his hominy, subsisting upon venison, bear meat, and the varied products of his clearing, in peaceful solitude.

In the winter months he constructed brooms, baskets, and snow-shoes from the laminated ash and basswood, carrying them on foot to Wilkes Barre to exchange for the most needed commodities. With no capital but a large family, increasing with each succeeding year, he toiled upon his hill-side opening until 1790, when he removed north of Leggett's Creek.

Daniel Waderman, of Hamburg, Germany, was the second settler. While visiting London in 1775, he was seized by the British press-gang, and forced into unwilling service. He was present at the battle of Bunker Hill, followed the fortunes of the British until 1779, when he was taken prisoner on the Mohawk. Taking the oath of allegiance, he enlisted in the American service, and, by his faithful deportment as a soldier during the remainder of the war, proved himself an unquestioned patriot. Under the shadows of the bluff, deepened by foliage extending down to the edge of the Lackawanna, this scarred veteran, in 1790, brought forth his cabin. The house of Daniel Silkman now occupies its site. For a period of twenty-one years Mr. Waderman lived here in comparative thrift and contentment, acquiring, by frugality, means to purchase wilder lands farther up the valley, where he died in 1835.

Preserved Taylor, Coonrad Lutz, John Gifford, Constant Searles, John House, Jacob Lutz, Benjamin Pedrick, Solomon Bates, and the Athertons, settled in the township in 1790, while John Miller, afterward famous for ministerial achievements and other good works, unbosomed the uplands of Abington. During this year alterations were made in the township lines.[1]

While townships, as surveyed under Connecticut jurisdiction, retained the *name* originally given them, their *boundaries* were purposely extinguished, or so radically altered by Pennsylvania landholders as to lose in a great measure their former identity and relation.

In March, 1790, Providence township line, defined twenty years previous by Connecticut settlers, was obliterated by the Luzerne County Court, which divided the county into eleven townships, one of which, Lakawanak, extended over the Lackawanna Valley.

The people of the old upper township of Providence, or Capoose, readily acquiescing in arrangements inaugurated by Pennsylvania, were thus compelled to transact all business of a public nature at Pittston, some ten or twelve miles away from their homes.

The inhabitants asked for a restoration of Providence township, because "the Town of Providence," says their petition, "labor under great disadvantages by reason of being annexed to Lackawanna, that the inhabitants live remote from the place where the Town meets on public occasions, and that they have a very bad river to cross, which is impassible at some times." In 1792 the petition was granted.

The first bridge across the Lackawanna was built in 1796. Until this time there were three public fords across the stream above Pittston, viz.: Tripp's, Lutze's, and Baggley's. Along the stream, where the banks were low and the waters shallow, a place was selected for a fordway, which, in the absence of a horse or a tree, was crossed on foot alike by heroic women and men. The abrupt character of the bank of the stream at Providence village, and for quarter of a mile below it, allowed of no crossing in this manner, nor was the Lackawanna at this point spanned by a bridge until the Drinker Turnpike rendered one necessary in 1826.

The two-wheeled ox-cart, drawn at a snail's-pace, over roads filled with stones, obstructed by hills, served the purposes of the settlement during the summer months, while the cumbrous snow-shoe or the wooden sled, bent from the oak or beech, brought happiness to many a home. Oxen were generally used both for farming and traveling. In 1792 there were in Providence township but ten horses. twenty-eight oxen, and fifty-two cows.

The original Griffin in Providence was Stephen, who, in 1794 left Westchester County, N. Y., to battle with Pennsylvania forests. He located near Lutze's fordway. Thos. Griffin became a resident of the valley in 1811, James in 1812, and Joseph and Isaac in 1816. The far-seen hill, below Hyde Park, crowned on its western edge by a noble park reserved for deer, is known throughout the valley as "Uncle Joe Griffin's" place, where he lived for half a century. He filled the office of justice of the peace for many years. In 1839-40, conjoined with the late Hon. Chester Butler, he represented the interests of the county in the State Legislature with credit. With the exception of Isaac Tripp, Sen., sent to Connecticut from Westmoreland, in 1777, Jos. Griffin, Esq., was the first man thus honored by the people of the valley.

The taxables of Providence township, embracing the entire settlement from Rixe's Gap to Pittston, numbered in 1796 ninety persons, sixty-one only of whom resided within its boundaries, as will be seen by the following "Providence Assessment for the Year 1796."

"The Lenni-Lenape Tribe"

WANDA WISNEWSKI, Elizabeth, N. J.: Enclosed is the poem "The Wedding of Warinanco," by Cal. J. McCarthy, which was asked for by A. L. W. in your issue of April 26. There are twelve four-line stanzas, the first of which follows:

In sixteen hundred sixty-five
There lived the Lenni-Lenape tribe,
Along the Staten Island Sound,
Where all the sub-tribes could be found.

Names of Inhabitants.	No. Oxen.	Cows.	Horses.	Occupation or Profession.	Residence.	Tax.
Atherton, Corn's.		1		Farmer.	Providence.	.86
Atherton, John.		1	2	Farmer.	do	1.51
Atherton, Elezer.		1	1	do	do	1.29
Atwater, Benj.		1		do	do	1.26
Abbott, Philip.		1				.06
Alesworth, Wm.	2	2		Innkeeper.	do	2.65
Abbott, James.		1	2	do	do	4.69
Bishop, Wm.				Preacher of the Gospel.	do	1.00
Brown, James.		1		Tailor.	do	.16
Bagley, James.	2	1	2	Farmer.	do	3.34½
Brown, Benj.				do	do	.90
Bagley, Asher.		1		do	do	1.56
Bagley, Jesse.		1		do	do	.07
Butler, Zeb'm. heirs.					Wilkes Barre.	.75
Bidwell, David.						1.25
Benedict, Silas.						.06
Bates, Solomon.		1	1	Farmer.	Providence.	1.01
Corey, Phebe.	2	3		Spinster.	do	2.26
Cogwell, William.	2	2		Farmer.	do	.32
Cobb, Asa.	2	4				1.56½
Carey, John.	2			Farmer.	Providence.	1.20
Chamberlain, John.						.25
Clark, William.						.72½
Conner, James.						.65
Covel, Mathew.				Physician.	Wilkes Barre.	.35
Dolph, Aaron.	2	1		Farmer.	Providence.	.71
Dolph, Charles.		2		do	do	1.77
Dolph, Moses.				do	do	.70
Dolph, Johnathan.	4	3		do	do	1.99
Dean, Johnathan.				do	Rhode Island.	1.10
Goodridg, Wm.	2	1		do	Providence.	1.41
Gardner, Stephen.	2	2		do	do	2.55½
Gifford, John.	2	1		do	do	.24
Hoyt, Stephen.				do	do	.72
How, John.	1	2		do	do	1.14
How, John, Jr.		1	2			1.14
Hoyt, Ransford.						.33
Hardy, Wm.		1				.07½
Holmes, Enock.		1	1	do	do	1.26
Hall, Nathan.		1		do	do	.65
Hunter, John.					New York.	2.00
Halstead, John.		1		do	Providence.	.06
Halstead, Jonar.			1	do	do	.20
Hopkins, Ichibod.					Stockbridge.	1.33
Fellows. Joseph.				do	Providence.	.30
Howard, James.				do	Connecticut.	.60
Hibbert, Ebenezer.				do	Nantacook.	.40
Lutz, Coonrad.		3	1	do	Providence.	1.44
Lutz, John.			1	do	do	.16
Lamkins, John.		1		do	do	.62
Lewis, James.	4	3		do	do	2.27
Lutzs, Mich.	2			do	do	.50
Lutz, Jacob.		2	1	do	do	1.07
Lutzens, Nicholas.	2	1	1			3.03
Miller, Christopher.		1		do	do	.07
Miller, Samuel.				do	Pittston.	.30
MacDaniel, John.						1.05

Names of Inhabitants.	No. Oxen.	Cows.	Houses.	Occupation or Profession.	Residence.	Tax.
Mills, John...............			1	Farmer.	Pittston.	.77
Obedike, Lodwick........					Rhode Island.	.60
Park, Ebenezer..........	2	1		do	Providence.	1.69
Picket, Thomas..........	2			do	do	.25½
Pedrick, Ben.............	2			do	do	2.07½
Potter, David.............						.60
Ross, Wm................				do	Wilkes Barre	1.10
Ross, Timothy...........						.55
Ross, Nathan............						1.72½
Ralph, Johnathan........		1	1	do	Providence.	.11½
Rozel, John...............				do	New York.	3.00
Smith, Thomas...........	2	2		do	Providence.	1.62
Stephen, Timothy........		1		do	do	.66
Slaiter, Samuel...........						1.70
Simral, Wm..............		1	1	Farmer.	Providence.	.75
Scott, Daniel.............	1	1		do	do	.79
Searles, Constant.........		1	1	do	do	1.14
Sills, Shadrick............					Lonenburg.	1.10
Selah, Obediah...........						.60
Stanton, Wm.............	2	2	1	do	Providence.	.85
Taylor, Daniel............	2	4		do	do	1.71
Taylor, John..............	2	2		do	do	.88
Taylor, Preserved........	2	3	1	do	do	1.82
Taylor, Abraham.........		1		do	do	.56
Tripp, Isaac, Jr...........	2	2	1	do	do	.44½
Tripp, Amasey............				do	do	1.00
Tripp, Isaac..............	2	1	3	do	do	15.89
Wright, Thomas..........				Merchant.	Pittston.	2.12
Washburn, Elizabeth.....				Spinster.	Providence.	.45
Carey, Barnabas..........				Farmer.	do	.36
Tompkins, Ben...........			1	do	do	.89
Lewis, James.............						.10
Gaylor, ———............					Connecticut.	.60

Town Meetings were first held in Providence at the house of Stephen Tripp, in 1813. The entire vote of the township, then extending jurisdiction over the subsequent townships of Lackawanna, Covington, Jefferson, Blakeley, Greenfield, and Scott, numbered eighty-two, as follows:—

	Federal vote.......... 46	Democratic.......... 36
1814.	" " 47	" 36
1815.	" " 51	" 44
1828.	" " 55	" 55

As late as 1816, wild game thronged the thickets around Slocum Hollow. Benjamin Fellows, Esq., a hale old gentleman, informs the writer that he has often seen fifty turkeys in a flock feeding on the stubble in his father's field, in Hyde Park, while deer tramped over the plowed land like herds of sheep. In 1804, in company with other hunters, he killed both panthers and bears in the woods between Hyde Park and Slocum Hollow.

The general history of the township contains little of general interest. Roads were few and rugged, and the inhabitants, priding themselves in assiduous labor and frugality, lived and died contented. They enjoyed neither churches nor school-houses, for none had yet emerged from the clearings; were annoyed by few or only light taxes; and yet kindness and hospitality were so blended with their daily toil on farms rendered fertile by a good burn or unvaried cultivation, that the social relations of the residents of the township were rarely, if ever, disturbed by sectarian partiality or political asperities. The general health was good, with no prevailing sickness until 1805, when the typhus fever, or "the black tongue," as it was termed, carried its ravages into settlements just beginning to feel the impulse of prosperity, along the borders of the Susquehanna and the Lackawanna. Drs. Joseph Davis and Nathaniel Giddings, the latter of whom settled in Pittston in 1783, became the healing Elishas to many a needy household. H. C. L. Von Storch settled in Providence in 1807. A German by birth, he inherited the habits of industry and economy characterizing the people, which in a few years enabled him to unfold the field from the forest, and gather about him a competency.

The main portion of Providence village stands upon land which came into possession of James Griffin in the winter of 1812, who moved with his family into the solitary log-house vacated by Holmes. The labor of destroying the large trees upon the new land for the reception of seed not always rewarding the husbandman with the yield expected, owing to the occurrence of frost and the presence of wild animals, was so slow, that the settlement of the township, encouraged only by a lumber and agricultural interest, made tardy advancement. As late as 1816, *three* settlers only lived in the immediate vicinity of the Borough, Daniel Waderman, James and Thomas Griffin. The next year a clearing was commenced in the Notch by Levi Travis.

The land originally reserved in Providence exclusively for school purposes, owing to the prolonged Wyoming dispute and change of jurisdiction, lay idle. *Forty-eight* years elapse after the settlement of the valley before a *school-house* was erected within its limits. The first school-house, diminutive in proportion, but yet sufficient for the demand upon it, was built, a few rods below the Holmes house, in 1818. It is still standing by the road-side and used as a dwelling. Previous to this, schools were kept in private houses, and sometimes under the shade of a tree in summer, and some, if taught at all, were taught to read, write, and cipher by the fireside at home. In the upper portion of the village, near the terminus of the Peoples Street Railway, stands an old brown school-house, erected in 1834, known as the Heerman's or "Bell school-house." The bell giving the house its name, costing fifteen dollars, paid for by subscription, hung in the modest belfry for forty-five years, when it was transferred to the Graded School building. It was the first bell ever heard on the plains of the Lackawanna, and as its animating tones rang out on the air, and were borne by the breeze over hill and valley, it awakened a pride that was ever cherished by the older inhabitants until its sudden and vandalic removal a few years since. The bell is yet sound and sweet in its vibrations, and serves to call the unwilling urchin to school as in days of yore. A partisan spirit was introduced into the school, which so embittered the relations of the neighborhood as to result in the erection of a new school-house across the river in 1836 under Democratic auspices.

Dr. Silas B. Robinson came into the township in 1823, where he creditably practiced his profession nearly forty years. So long had he lived in the township, and so well was he known for his blunt manners, blameless life, and kind heart, even with all his pardonable eccentricities, that his presence was welcome everywhere, and his sudden death in 1860 widely lamented.

Nothing tended to give a vigorous direction to Providence toward a *village* more than the Philadelphia and Great Bend Turnpike. This highway, well known as the "Drinker Turnpike," promised as it passed through the village with a tri-weekly stage-coach and mail, to land passengers from the valley in Philadelphia after *two* days of unvarying jolting. This road, chartered in 1819, completed in 1826, was the first highway *through* Cobb's Gap. The Connecticut road, long traversed by the emigrant, casting a wishful look into the valley, passed *over* the rough summit of the mountain, here cut in twain by Roaring Brook. The Luzerne and Wayne County turnpike built this year, intersected Drinker's road at Providence.

As the village from these causes, and from its central position began to grow into importance, Slocum Hollow, shorn of its glory by the abandonment of its forge and stills, was judged by the Department at Washington as being too obscure a point for a post-office, as the receipts for the year 1827 averaged only $3.37½ per quarter. The office was removed the next year to its thriftier rival, Providence.

[1] The change that a third of a century brings our race, can be readily appreciated by a glance at "The list of Letters remaining in Providence Post Office, July 1, 1835" as copied from the *Northern Pennsylvanian*, a weekly paper printed in Carbondale, by Amzi Wilson. Of the persons thus addressed but a single one survives,—the venerable Zephaniah Knapp of Pittston.

Elezor H. Atherton,	Henry Pepper,	Amasa Cook,	Louisa Forest,
John Lurne,	Francis Mead,	David Patrick,	David S. Rice,
Hannah Van Stork,	John Morden,	Stephen Tripp,	Comer Phillips,
Barney Carey,	Wm. C. Green,	Alva Dana,	Robert C. Hury,
Aug. Jenks,	Thos. T. Atherton,	Selah Mead,	Phineas Carman,
Zephaniah Knapp,	John Bilson,	P. C. ———,	Samuel Waderman,
Maria Chase,	David Krotzer,	Samuel Stevens,	Isaac Searles,
Joseph Lance,	Michael Agnew,	Oliver Phillips,	W. Whitlock.
William G. Knapp,			

JOHN VAUGHN, Jr., P. M.

On what is now the southwest corner of Market and Main streets, Elisha S. Potter and Michael McKeal in 1828 inaugurated a country store upon the popular principle of universal credit, and they were so successful in establishing it, that some of their dues are yet outstanding. The late Elisha S. Potter, and our townsman Nathaniel Cottrill, looking forward to the future value of the idle acres surrounding "Razorville," as the village was long called, purchased fourteen acres of the Holmes tract in 1828, including the fine water privileges, for $285 per acre. Mr. Cottrill shortly afterward came into possession of the entire interest of Esq. Potter, and erected a grist-mill upon the premises. The village has been visited by three tornadoes since its settlement. The most fearful one, or the "great blow," swept away a great portion of the village on the 3d of July, 1834. During the afternoon of that day, which was one of unusual warmth, the thunder now and then breaking from the blackened sky, gave notice of the approaching storm. It came with the fury of a tropical whirlwind. A strong northwesterly current of air rushing down through Leggett's Gap, met the main body as it whirled from the more southern gap, contiguous to Leggett's, and concentrating at a point opposite the present residence of Mr. Cottrill, commenced its wild work. As it crossed the mountain, it swept down trees of huge growth in its progress, leaving a path strewn with the fallen forest.

At Providence seems to have been the funnel of the northwest current, which, as it arrived at the Lackawanna, was turned by that from the southwest to a northeast direction. Before dusk the gale attained its height, when the wind, accompanied with clouds of dust, blew through the streets, lifting roofs, houses, barns, fences, and even cattle in one instance, from the earth and dashing them to pieces in the terrible exultation of the elements.

Nearly every house here was either prostrated, disturbed, or destroyed in the course of a few seconds. A meeting-house, partly built, in the lower part of the village, was blown down and the frame carried a great distance. The house and store of N. Cottrill, standing opposite the tavern kept by him at this time, was raised from its foundation and partly turned around from the west to the northwest, and left in this angular position. The chimney, however, fell, covering up a cradle holding the babe of Mrs. Phinney, but being singularly protected by the shielding boards, the child, when found in about an hour afterward, was laughing and unharmed.

Some large square timber, lying in the vicinity, was hurled many rods: one large stick, ambitious as the battering ram of old, passed endwise entirely through the tavern-house, and was only arrested in its progress by coming into contact with the hill sloping just back of the dwelling, into which it plunged six or seven feet. In its journey—or *forcible entry*, as lawyers might term it— it passed through the bedroom of Mrs. Cottrill, immediately under her bed.

Gravel-stones were driven through panes of glass, leaving holes as smooth as a bullet or a diamond could make, while shingles and splinters, with the fleetness of the feathered arrow, were thrown into clapboards and other wooden obstructions, presenting a strange picture of the fantastic.

The office of the late Elisha S. Potter, Esq., standing in the lower part of the village, was caught up in the screw-like funnel of the whirlwind, and carried over one hundred feet, and fell completely inverted, smashing in the roof; it was left in its half-somerset position, standing on its bare plates. The venerable and esteemed old squire and Mr. Otis Severance, who were transacting business in the office at the time, kept it company during its *aerial* voyage, both escaping with less injury than fright.

The embankment of the old bridge across the Lackawanna, from its south abutment, was sided with large hewn timbers, remaining there for years, and well saturated with water. On the lower side these were taken entirely from their bed, and pitched quite two hundred feet into the adjacent meadow. An old aspiring fanning-mill, standing at the front door of the grist-mill, upon the ground, took flight in the whirlwind, and was carried in the door of the second story of the mill, without being broken by the power so rudely assailing.

Along the eastern side of the road leading to Carbondale, in places where the focus of the current dipped or reached the earth, all was wreck and disorder. Young hickory-trees left standing by the settlers for shade or other purposes, and apple-trees bending with the ripening apple, fell like weeds, and the remaining branches and roots, twisted, torn, and uprooted, revealed to the passer-by the strength of the blow.

At the present thriving and appropriately-named Capoose works, owned by Mr. Pulaski Carter, there lay a strip of meadow upon the bank of the Lackawanna, where was standing a small carding-machine. This building was quickly demolished, the wool and rolls being spun along the fields and woods for miles. Some were carried in an oblique direction to Cobb's Pond, on the very summit of the Moosic Mountain.

One of the most singular incidents, however, in the phenomenon of the hurricane, occurred to a young woman living half a mile from the village, on the route taken by the whirlwind. Like many timid ones of the town, tremulous at the approach of the lightning and thunder, she sought refuge in bed. While smothering in the feathers under the covering of the quilt, the bed on which she was lying was whirled from the house, just unroofed, and carried along by the force of the black current of air several rods, and landed safely in the meadow adjoining, before she was aware of her aerial and unjolting flight.

In 1849, Providence village was incorporated into a borough ; in 1866, consolidated into the city of Scranton, forming the first and second wards of this young metropolis of the Lackawanna valley.

DUNMORE.[1]

Like Scranton, Hyde Park, Green Ridge, Dickson, Olyphant, Pecktown, and Petersburg, Dunmore is one of numerous villages which sprang from the original township of Providence. Purchased of the natives in 1754 by the whites, long before the tomahawk was flung over the Moosic, the territory now embracing this village offered its solitude in vain to the pioneers seeking a home in the wilderness between the Delaware and the Susquehanna until the summer of 1783. At this time, William Allsworth, a shoemaker by trade, who had visited the Connecticut land at Wyoming for the purpose of selecting a place for his home the year previous, reached this point at evening, where he encamped and lit his fire in the forest where Dunmore was thus founded.

The old Connecticut or Cobb road, shaded by the giant pines extending from the summit of the mountain to Capoose, had no diverging pathway to Slocum Hollow, No. Six, or Blakeley, because neither of these places had yet acquired a settler or a name. From the "Lackawa" settlement, on the Paupack, some four and twenty miles from the cabin of Allsworth, there stood but two habitations in 1783, one at Little Meadows, the other at Cobb's, both kept as houses of entertainment. The need of more places of rest to cheer the emigrants toiling toward Wyoming with heavy burdens drawn by the sober team of oxen, induced Mr. Allsworth to fix his abode at this spot. While he was building his cabin from trees fallen for the purpose of gaining space and material, his covered wagon furnished a home for his family. At night, heaps of logs were kept burning until long after midnight, to intimidate wolves, bears, wild cats, and panthers inhabiting the chaparral toward Roaring Brook and Capoose. Deer and bear were so abundant for many years, within

[1] Named from the Earl of Dunmore.

sight of his clearing, that his family never trusted to his rifle in vain for a supply of venison or the substantial haunches of the bear. In the fall and winter months, wild beasts made incursions with such frequency, that domestic animals at night could be safely kept only in palisaded inclosures. These were a strong stockade made from the well-driven sapling, and generally built contiguous to the dwelling, into which all kinds of live stock were driven for protection after nightfall. Every farmer in the township of Providence, unwilling to see his home invaded and occupied by the common enemy at the dead of night, took this precaution less than eighty years ago. And even then they were not exempt from depredation at Mr. Allsworth's. At one time, just at the edge of evening, a bear groped his way into the pen where some of his pigs were slumbering, seized the sow in his brawny paws and bore the noisy porker hurriedly into the woods, where it was seen no more. The affrighted pigs were left unharmed in the pen. At another time, during the absence from home of Mr. Allsworth, a large panther came to his place before sundown in search of food. This animal is as partial to veal as the bear is to pork. A calf lay in the unguarded inclosure at the time. Upon this the panther sprang, when Mrs. Allsworth, alarmed by the bleat of the calf, seized a pair of heavy tongs from the fire-place, and, with a heroism distinguishing most of the women of that day, drove the yellow intruder away without its intended meal. The same night, however, the calf was killed by the panther, which in return was captured in a trap the same week, and slain.

The house of Mr. Allsworth, famed for the constant readiness of the host to smooth by his dry jokes and kind words the ruggedness of every man's daily road, became a common point of interest and attraction to the emigrant or the wayfarer. The original cabin of Mr. Allsworth stood upon the spot now occupied by the brick store of John D. Boyle.

The descendants of Mr. Allsworth have filled many places of trust and usefulness in the county, and adorned the various walks of social life. For twelve years this pioneer had no neighbors nearer than those living in Capoose or Providence. In the summer of 1795, Charles Dolph, John Carey, and John West began the labor of clearing and plowing lands in the neighborhood of *Bucktown* or the *Corners*, as this place was long called after the first foot-path opened from Blakeley to the Roaring Brook crossed the Wyoming road at Allsworth's.

Edward Lunnon, Isaac Dolph, James Brown, Philip Swartz and Levi De Puy, purchased land of the State between 1799–1805 and located in this portion of Providence Township.

The old tavern, long since vanished with its round, swinging sign and low bar-room, one corner of which, fortified with long pine-pickets, extending from the bar to the very ceiling, in times of yore, was owned successively by Wm. Allsworth, Philip Swartz, Isaac Dolph, Henry W. Drinker, and Samuel De Puy, before its destruction by fire, a number of years ago.

The external aspect of Dunmore, somber in appearance and tardy in its growth, with a clearing here and there occupied by men superior to fear or adversity, promised so much by its agricultural expectations in 1813, that Dr. Orlo Hamlin with his young wife, was induced to settle a mile north of Allsworth. He was the first physician and surgeon locating in Providence. This locality, fresh with hygiene from the forest, offered so little compensation to a profession without need or appreciation among the hardy woodmen, that the doctor the next year removed to Salem, Wayne County, Pennsylvania.

The population of Dunmore and Blakeley, doubling in numbers and increasing in wealth, warranted Stephen Tripp in erecting a saw and grist mill in 1820, on the Roaring Brook half a mile south of the village, the *debris* of whose walls, forgotten by the hand that reared

JOHN B. SMITH.

them, are seen at No. Six, favored with no thought of their former value to the community.

A store was opened at the Corners in 1820 under the auspices of the Drinker Turnpike; but the village, consisting of but four houses, had but a negative existence until the Pennsylvania Coal Company, in 1847-8, turned the sterile pasture-fields around it into a town liberal in the extent of its territory and diversified by every variety of life.

The immense machine-shops of this company, concentrating and fostering a vast amount of superior mechanical skill, are located at No. Six, and serve to give Dunmore additional note and character as a business village. In fact, Dunmore can congratulate itself not so much upon the internal wealth of its hills, as upon the vigor of the men who furrowed them out, and thus encouraged a town at this time deriving its daily inspirations wholly from this source. While Gen. John Ewen, President of the Pennsylvania Coal Company, especially looks after its affairs in New York with a zeal assuring his courage and fidelity, the general superintendence of the entire works in Pennsylvania has been exercised by John B. Smith, of Dunmore, through an administration of nearly twenty years, in a manner so discreet, popular, and yet withal so modest, as jointly to advance the interests of the company, impart strength of development to Pittston, Dunmore, and Hawley, and change the circumstances and fortunes of a large class of men employed along the line of the road, who looked and trusted to industry for reward.

Dunmore is now an incorporated borough, is connected with Scranton, Hyde Park, and Providence by a street-railroad, and enjoys an aggregate population of about five thousand souls.

HISTORY OF SCRANTON.

Nay-aug, or Roaring Brook, linked together by successive rapids and falls for many miles, emerges from the water-shedding crest separating the Delaware from the Susquehanna, and forms the noisiest tributary of the Lackawanna, which it enters at Scranton, one mile below the ancient village of Capoose. The woodland along the brook, unbroken on its gorgeous surface save by the achievements of the beaver, whose dams and villages deepened many a curve, had no fixed tenantry but beasts of prey until 1788.

NAY-AUG FALLS.

Across the Lackawanna, the skin-clad savages had vanished from their wigwams with a sigh, leaving their fertile meadows to be tilled by men efficient in industry, yet indifferent to fear, who used the jungle now marked by Scranton, to return the visits of the wolf and the bear coming often to them unannounced. Although the great war-path from the Indian villages on the Delaware to the tribes strolling over Wyoming, intelligence of which had been early gained of the wandering bowmen, entered Capoose at the eddy affording moorage for the warrior's canoe, no one looked upon the tamarack swamp, now hid in the interior of Scranton, as suitable for a dwelling-place, while the richer lands west of the Lackawanna, more easily cared for, invited occupancy and tillage.

Philip Abbott was the first settler in "Deep Hollow," as this place was designated from 1788 until 1798, when it took the name of *Slocum Hollow.* While the month of May charmed the glen with its foliage and fragrance, Mr. Abbott marked out his clearing. On a ledge of rocks, washed by the brook whose waters it overlooked, near where stands the old Slocum House, rose from the up-rolled logs the first cabin in the Hollow. It was simply a log hut or pen covered with boughs, formed but a single room, occupied in great part by a huge fire-place four or five feet in width and as many in depth, filled in the long evenings of winter with great sticks of wood before a back-log, which furnished both light and warmth to the hardy inmates. Philip was a native of Connecticut, had emigrated to Wyoming Valley with the Yankees before the Revolution, owned property under the Connecticut title, which he transferred to his brother James, both of whom were expelled by the Tories and Indians in 1778.

The settlers in Providence Township in 1788 were limited in numbers, yet their necessities sometimes pressing, found expression in the settlement of Deep Hollow. Corn and rye raised in the valley, had to be carried twenty miles to mill in Wyoming Valley, or half cracked by the pestle and mortar, and eaten almost whole. The wants of the inhabitants, multiplying gradually by the development of the settlement, and other causes wonderfully productive here in the wild woods, suggested to the practical mind of Mr. Abbott the erection of a grist-mill upon the Roaring Brook. Its waters were ample in volume and power; a dam easy of construction along its rocky grottoes. The Lackawanna, spanned by no bridge, could generally be forded during the summer months, unless swollen by rains; in winter an ice-bridge favored communication with the farmers living across the stream.

The construction of the mill was marked by strong simplicity. One millstone wrought from the granite of an adjoining ledge, slightly elevated by an iron spindle, revolved upon its nether stone as rudely and firmly adjusted upon a rock. A belt cut from skin, half wrapped on the drum of the water-wheel, passing over the spindle with a twist, formed the running gear of a mill fulfilling the expectations of its projector, and the hopes of those encouraging its erection. The mill building, upheld by saplings firmly placed in the earth, was roofed and sided by slabs hewn from trees and affixed by wooden pins and withes. Nails comprised no part of its construction, nor did the sound of the mallet and chisel take part in the triumph of its completion. No portion of the mill surpassed its bolt in novelty. A large *deer-skin*, well tanned and stretched upon poles, perforated sieve-like with holes, made partial separation of the flour from the coarser bran. The strong arm of the miller or the customer worked the bolt. An old gentleman, now deceased, informed the writer many years ago, that when he was a mere lad "he often went to Abbott's mill with his father, and that while the corn was being ground the old man and the miller got jolly on whisky punches in the house, while he was compelled to stay in the mill to shake the meal through the bolt." So primitive and unique was the construction of this *corn-cracker*, without tools or machinery, that it simply broke the kernels of corn into a samp-meal, which made a kind of food very popular in the earlier history of the valley.

The grist-mill, maintaining and even increasing its importance among the yeomanry scattered along the river, needed additional capital and labor to arrange and enlarge its capacity. These requirements came with James Abbott, in October of this year, and with Reuben Taylor in the spring of 1789, both of whom, with Philip Abbott, became equal partners in the mill. Mr. Taylor built a double loghouse on the bank of the brook, below the cabin of Abbott, which was the second dwelling erected in the Hollow. Owing to the want of glass, its high, small windows, like all the cabins of the frontierman, gave place to skins from the forests. Doors, beds, and blankets, and sometimes clothes, were made from the same rich untanned material. The forest trees in the forks of the two streams, yielding to the united assaults of ax and firebrand, opened a strip of land for the reception of wheat and corn, bringing forth its maiden crop in 1789. John Howe and his unmarried brother Seth, animated by the hope that independence would come from a life of honesty and labor, purchased the rights and good-will of the former owners, and moved into the thatched dwelling vacated by Mr. Taylor. On the uplands known throughout the valley as the "Uncle Joe Griffin farm," Mr. Taylor, after rescuing a few acres from the woodlands, disposed of his place for a trifle because of its seeming worthlessness.

The first saw-mill built in Providence Township was planned on Stafford Meadow Brook, half a mile below Scranton, in 1790, by Capt. John Stafford, from whom the stream derived its name.

While the farmers living around Capoose enjoyed the prosperity and rustic comforts they themselves had created, little or no progress toward enlarging the settlement at the Hollow had been made. No building of a public character, neither school nor a meeting-house had yet been fostered within the limits of Capoose, Providence, or the Hollow. The Lackawanna led on its way, unvexed by dam or bridge. In 1796, Joseph Fellows, Sen., a man of great resolution and intelligence, who had just gained a residence on the Hyde Park hill-side, aided by the farmers of Capoose, placed a bridge across the river, with a single span. The plank used upon it was the first production of Stafford's mill. It was located on the flats, where the slackened waters are still crossed by the throng.

That part of the certified Township of Providence now occupied by Hyde Park, originally reserved by the Susquehanna Company for religious and school purposes, was settled in 1794, by William Bishop, a Baptist clergyman of some eccentricity of character, whose log-quarters, fixed on the parsonage lot overlooking Capoose, in its rural simplicity stood where now stands Judge Merrifield's dwelling. Most of the land about the central portion of this thrifty village was cleared by the Dolphs. In 1795, Aaron Dolph rolled up his small log-house upon the present site of the Hyde Park hotel; his brother Jonathan then chopped and logged off the Washburn and Knapp farm, while the lands at Fellows Corner were brought to light and culture by Moses Dolph. The earliest house of entertainment or tavern in Hyde Park was opened and kept by Jonathan Dolph. In 1810, Philip Heermans, influenced by the community, which required a public point at which to hold town meetings and enjoy the largest liberty of franchise, turned his house into a *tavern*, where the spirit of frolic sometimes mingled with the more sober duties of the assemblage. Elections have been held at this place ever since. On the cold soil and bleak hill north of Dunmore, Charles Dolph, another brother, moved into the forest, where he sowed and reaped in due season.

The joint and double advantage of water-power and timber everywhere found along the Roaring Brook from its mouth up to its head-springs amidst the evergreens of the Pocono, could neither be overlooked nor resisted by Ebenezer and Benjamin Slocum, who purchased of the Howes, in July, 1798, the undivided land of Slocum Hollow. The father of the Slocums was Ebenezer Slocum, Sen. He had emigrated to Wyoming Valley previous to the massacre, was shot and scalped by the Indians, near

Wilkes Barre Fort, in December, 1778, with Isaac Tripp, Sen.

A domestic tragedy, casting a spirit of melancholy over the brook-side cabin, hastened and impelled the transfer of the property. Lydia, the eldest born of John Howes, depressed by some disappointed visions of girlhood, was found dead in her chamber, having hanged herself with a garter attached to her bedpost. The effect of this suicide —the first in the valley—removed every speculating consideration or cavil from a trade which placed the mill and the wild acres around it into the hands of the Slocums.

Benjamin was a single man; he afterward married Miss Phebe La Fronse. Ebenezer married a daughter of Dr. Joseph Davis, one of the most eccentric medical men ever known in the Lackawanna Valley. "*He was not,*" in the language of an octogenarian familiar with his oddities five-and-sixty years ago, "a great *metaphysical* doctor but a wonderful *sargant* doctor." Dr. Davis died in Slocum Hollow in 1830, aged 98 years.

There were now but two houses in the Hollow, and only that number of grist-mills from Nanticoke northward to the State line.

The Slocums, young, strong, and ambitious, infused new elements into the settlement. They named the place *Unionville,* but the name, having no descriptive interpretation or bearing to the glen, readily gave way to that of Slocum's Hollow, or Slocum Hollow. In 1799, after the mill, necessarily rugged in its interior and external features, had been improved, enlarged, and a distillery added thereto, Ebenezer Slocum and his partner, James Duwain, built a saw-mill a little above the grist-mill. A smith shop, built from faultless logs, rose from the margin of the creek, and the sound of the anvil, carried afar, blended joyfully with the song of the noisy water. Two or three additional houses, built for the workmen, the saw and the grist mill, one cooper shop, with the smith shop and the distillery, formed the total village of Slocum Hollow or

Scranton in 1800. Both dams were swept away by the spring freshet of this year, exhausting the courage of Mr. Duwain, who forthwith retired from partnership; Benjamin Slocum taking his place.

The interests of the community suffered but little, as the dams were promptly built by the aid of a *bee*, which called together every farmer in the township. The gristmill was patronized far and near. Farmers twenty miles away sometimes sought the mill with their grists, and when the work was pressing on the farm at home, they tarried and toiled while the wife, heroic and devoted, went to mill on horseback, with no equipage grander than the pillion.

The Pittston division of the valley owes no more kind remembrance to Dr. Wm. Hooker Smith for his vigorous efforts to extract iron from its hills, than the Scranton portion of it concedes to the elder Slocum brothers for the erection of the original iron-forge in the Hollow in 1800. Low down on the bank of the brook, beside the waterfall and yet above the flood, grew up the forge and trip-hammer, which, fed with ore gathered from gullies, brought forth the molten product in abundance.

The old landmark of Slocum Hollow, cherished with pride by the old settler, is the old "Slocum House" yet standing by the creek, with its stone basement and broad long stoop, as proudly as in days of yore. It is the oldest structure in Scranton, was built in the fall of 1805 by Ebenezer Slocum, well preserved even to its capacious hearth where the fagot blazed and reflected back the light of smiling faces half a century ago, where the jest and the song went around and the old hall rang to the very roof. The second *frame* house in the Hollow was built by Benjamin Slocum. Facing the brook, with its low porch extending along its entire front, it offered an admirable view of the forge and the sturdy artisans around it. With all these improvements along a narrow strip of clearing, Slocum Hollow was yet comparatively a wilderness. Deer, bear, and even panthers were hunted and killed here as late as 1816. Lands now occupied by the massive Round House and the Depots of the Delaware, Lackwanna, and Western Railroad, were cleared of the fallen tree and sown with wheat in 1816. Six years previous, a chopping had been made where Lackawanna Avenue runs, but the wolves issuing from their fastnesses in the tamarack jungle adjoining, prevented the Slocums from keeping sheep for their much-needed wool.

THE OLD SLOCUM HOUSE.

Elisha Hitchcock, a young mill-wright from New Hampshire, made his way into Slocum Hollow in 1809. He repaired the mill, married Ruth the daughter of Benjamin Slocum in 1811, an excellent lady who still survives him. Mr. Hitchcock was an honest man, who never wronged his fellow, and beloved by all for his exemplary qualities; he died a few years since.

A second still was put into operation in 1811. The tranquil succession of abundant harvests throughout Capoose—the absence of an approachable market for the grain, thrashed out by the flail—the frequent calls for whisky coming from Easton, Paupack, Bethany, Montrose, and the high banks of Berwick, abating none of its value and inspirations as a commercial agent, served to welcome the accession of the new still as a *public benefaction* worthy of the unhesitated and active patronage and favor accorded to it by every member of society.

Luzerne County, as now bounded, had but two post-offices in 1810—Wilkes Barre and Kingston. In 1811 four were established, viz.: at Pittston, Nescopeck, Abington, and Providence. The Providence office was located in Slocum Hollow, and Benj. Slocum appointed postmaster. The inhabitants of the valley working hard for coarse food and rustic homespun, sometimes had leisure to visit and reflect, but few books or papers to peruse. Scattered through Blakeley or over the mountain, they enjoyed no mail facilities other than those offered by this office, until the establishment of another one in Blakeley in 1824. The Slocum Hollow office was removed to Providence in this year, and John Vaughn appointed postmaster. The same year William Merrifield was commissioned postmaster of a new office established at Hyde Park. The mail was carried once a week on horseback from Easton to Bethany by Zephaniah Knapp, Esq., *via* Wilkes Barre and Providence; the entire mail matter for the Lackawanna settlements bore no comparison, in quantity, to the amount that very many business firms in the same vicinity are now daily the recipients of.

Frances Slocum, who was taken captive by the Indians in Wyoming Valley, in 1778, and whose subsequent history has been made familiar by Dr. Peck and Miner, was a sister of Ebenezer and Benjamin. When she was caught up in the arms of the savage that had just scalped a lad with the knife he was grinding at the door, a painted warrior rushed into the house of Jonathan Slocum "and took up Ebenezer Slocum, a little boy. The mother stepped up to the savage, and reaching for the child, said: 'He can do you no good; see, he is lame.' With a grim smile, giving up the boy, he took Frances, her daughter, aged about five years, gently in his arms, and seizing the younger Kinsley by the hand, hurried away to the mountains."[1] His release from the fickle savage, through the adroitness of his mother, was no more providential than his escape from as horrible a death in 1808. Losing his foothold while clearing the mill-race of drift-wood, he fell, and was carried by the rushing impulse of the current down the stream between the buckets of the water-wheel before he was rescued by his faithful negro. Mr. Slocum's weight exceeded two hundred, and yet, through this vise-like space, measuring scant *six inches*, he was forced with so little injury that he resumed his wonted labor within a week! Of such material, plastic yet withe-like, was made the men who carved and nursed the valley in its infancy.

In the manufacture of iron, no advantage was taken of the coal ramparts by the creek, because no knowledge of its use for this purpose had reached the public mind until 1836. Charcoal, made in the turf-clad pits by the woodside, everywhere at the furnaces asserted its prerogative as the heating agent. In fact, the timber about Scranton in the earlier part of the century was swept away, more especially to supply the charcoal demand of Slocum's forge, than for any remunerative gain its soil promised to the cultivators of the country.

Iron forges and furnaces having sprung up in various sections of country where Slocum Hollow iron, famous for its superior texture, had been favorably known and used; the dilapidated state of the works in use for six-and-twenty years; the cost of transporting ore over miles of roads sometimes rendered impassable by fallen trees or deepened ruts; all contributed to extinguish the forge-fire. The last iron was made by the Slocums in June, 1826; the last whisky distilled a few months later. Up to this time these primitive iron-works were, in the hands of

[1] Miner's History, p. 247

these unobtrusive men, yielding their conquests and diffusing a spirit of enterprise amidst accumulative difficulties, in a valley having no outlet by railroad, no navigable route to the sea other than shallow waters long skimmed by the Indian's canoe.

Ebenezer retired from business in 1828; in 1832, full of years, peaceful, trusting, he went to his grave, as a shock of corn fully ripe cometh in, in its season.

Joseph and Samuel Slocum, full of youthful enthusiasm, began to carry on farming and mill interests with the same spirit of earnestness distinguishing the elder Slocums.

The obliteration of the still and forge abridged the importance and checked the growth of the village. Three roads, or rather two, cut through the woods, too narrow for wagons to pass each other only in places prepared for turn-outs, diverged from the Hollow: one from Allsworth's, at Dunmore, led to Fellows' Corners; while the other crossed the swamp, along what is now Wyoming Avenue, on fallen logs, and found its way by Griffin's Corners to the acknowledged political center of the valley —Razorville village. Upper and Lower Providence, Abington, Blakeley, Greenfield, Scott, and Drinker's Beech, offering choice wild lands to all seeking a competency by a life of frugal industry, became the home of men whose hardihood, hospitality, and stanch virtues, carried cultivation and thrift into the borders of the forest, while Slocum Hollow, strangely intermingled with rock and morass, offered little to the husbandman, and nothing to the newcomer.

An effort was made in 1817 to improve the navigation of the Lackawanna, and a company incorporated at the time for this purpose; nothing more was done. In 1819, the late Henry W. Drinker—than whom no man surpassed in readiness to aid the needy pioneer or develop the resources of the country—explored the mountains and valleys from the Susquehanna at Pittston to the Delaware Water Gap, with a view of connecting the two points by a railroad to be operated over the Lehigh Mountain by hydraulic power achieved from the waters of Tobyhanna and the Lehigh.

While the Slocum Hollow settlement, being on the line of the proposed road, was expected to acquire some increased activity mutually advantageous, the interests of Drinker's Beech, watched carefully by Mr. Drinker, were more especially aimed at by the projectors of the road. A charter was granted in March, 1826; simultaneously a charter was obtained by Wm. Meredith, for a railroad to run up the Lackawanna to the State line from Providence village. Both were projected upon the plan of inclined planes.

The four pioneers obtaining railroad charters in the Lackawanna Valley were Wm. and Maurice Wurts, Henry W. Drinker, and Wm. Meredith. The first two gentlemen banded the mountain's brow with the flat rail; the last, owing to needless antipathies which aroused every impulse of selfishness, and embittered even the calm hour of triumph with its remembrance, were not able to infuse into charters easily obtained, advantage to themselves or to the places they sought to enrich and develop. These men were powerful in the day of first railroads; polished, opulent, and educated, and had there been united and harmonious action among them, the valley would hardly have been so reluctant in yielding the wherewithal to gladden the firesides of the land. Drinker, averse to a strife fatal to his cherished projects, shared none of the prejudices against the men who had rendered practicable an eastern outlet from the valley.

The North Branch Canal, fed by the idle waters of the Lackawanna, was begun in Pittston in 1828 by the State, and looked to as the great commercial avenue to the sea. The citizens of old Providence Township, restrained by the mountain's wall from all hope of public intercourse with Philadelphia or New York by a continuous railroad, withal too modest to expect a canal at the expense of the

State, asked the Legislature, having but a negative representation from the valley, to build "the *feeder* of this canal, or some other improvement up the valley as far as would be thought of service to our citizens and the Commonwealth."

This scheme naturally excited the public mind, because its prosecution under any circumstances would reach out benefits to every husbandman jealous of his own rights, yet taught by invidious men to distrust the power of "incorporated companies."[1]

The coal-clad slopes enjoyed repose. The cesarean drill had not yet fallen into the strong arms of the skillful miner. Up in the Carbondale glen, under the shelter of a ledge of rocks forming the western bank of the Lackawanna, a few hundred tons of surface coal had been mined by the Wurts brothers as an experimental measure. The operations of these weather-beaten, persecuted, yet hopeful men, were not recognized by the inhabitants of the lower townships as of any practical utility to any one but the miners themselves. Wood was abundant, and every hill-side offered fuel to the woodman who chose to gather it without cost. Coal had neither domestic value nor sale at home; no market abroad. A brighter aspect at length struggled its way into the valley, and the solitude of Slocum Hollow was gone.

"About 1836," says Mr. Joseph J. Albright, in a note to the writer, "at the suggestion of Geo. M. Hollenback I made the trip to Slocum Hollow for the purpose of examining the iron ore, coal, &c., with a view of purchasing from Alva Heermans the property (now Scranton) for $10 per acre. I took a box of the iron ore on top of a stage to Northampton County, where I was engaged in the manufacture of iron, and I contend that I shook the first tree, if I failed to gather its fruit. I believe the box of ore thus transported was the means of attract-

---

[1] See "Wilkes Barre Advocate," December 9, 1838

ing the attention of Messrs. Henry, Scranton, &c., to this tract. These facts are known and recognized by S. T. Scranton; had I been successful in persuading Dr. Philip Walter and others to join me in its purchase, I might have gathered ample reward."

Drinker's route for a railroad from the Delaware to the Susquehanna, surveyed in 1831 by Maj. Beach, awakened neither interest nor inquiry among the yeomanry having scarcely means to meet the yearly taxes or support families generally large and needy, and yet, strange as it may appear, the initial impulse toward a village at Slocum Hollow came from the friends of this project. William Henry,[1] one of the original commissioners named in the charter, was especially enthusiastic and active in his efforts to build up a town at this point for the purpose of advancing the interests of this unattractive project. His knowledge of the country was too thorough and general

[1] A tradition in the "Henry" family exists, where the Indian character appears in a more amiable light than that exhibited on the Western plains. "My grandfather," writes William Henry in a note to the author, "William Henry, late of Lancaster, Pa., in 1755 was an officer serving under General Washington, at General Braddock's defeat near Fort Pitt; he there saw a well-made, athletic Indian in jeopardy of his life, and by extraordinary effort and means, saved him; in the recognition, names were exchanged, and a friendship established; parting soon after they never met afterward, and nothing was known of the Indian until the commencement of the Revolution in 1774, when the rescued man called and made the acquaintance of my father, at Christian Spring, Northampton County, as the Chief *Killbuck*, whose life, he stated, was saved by Maj. Henry, relating all the incidents attending the disastrous battle-field, remarking that while ordinarily he did not expect to live many more years, but that 'Indian never forgets,' his own people and family would know how to pay a debt of gratitude.

"In the year 1794 my father and other gentlemen were commissioned by the U. S. Government to locate a quantity of lands donated to the 'Society for propagating the Gospel among the Heathen' in what then was Indian country and a wilderness; fortunately *there* resided the descendants of Chief Killbuck. The surveying party not knowing this, however, were the grateful recipients of bear's meat, venison, and other game, through the instrumentality of the Chief 'White Eye,' who subsequently made himself known as the leading successor of the Sachem Killbuck and his gratitude toward the son, whose father saved the life of his chief; about three months were occupied in the woods on the banks of the Muskingum in safety. A fuller detail and historical account, agreeing in every particular with the above, was given by the Indian family, now in Kansas, to Col. Alexander, late the editor of a paper at Pittston, then resident in Kansas;

to be without its stimulating influence, and yet this acquaintance of the mineralogical character of the western terminus of the route only enabled him to give decided expression to views neither adopted nor accepted by his friends.

Messrs. Drinker and Henry, undismayed by the cold, solemn avowal of the inhabitants occupying the valleys of the Delaware and the Susquehanna, that no such road was possible or necessary to their social condition, taking advantage of the speculative wave of 1836, called the friends of the road to Easton at this time to devise a practical plan of action. Repeated exertions in this direction had hitherto yielded a measure of ridicule not calculated to inspire great hopes of success. At this meeting, prolonged for days, Mr. Henry assured the members of the board that if the old furnace of Slocum's at the Hollow could be reanimated and sustained a few years, a village would spring up between the unguarded passes of the Moosic, calling for means of communication with the seaboard less inhospitable and tardy than the loitering stage-coach. This novel plan to achieve success for the road, although urged with ability and candor, met the approval of but a single man. This was Edward Armstrong, a gentleman of great benevolence and courtesy, living on the Hudson. In the acquisition of land in the Lackawanna Valley, or the erection of furnaces and forges upon it, he avowed himself ready to share with Mr. Henry any re-

---

by him a friendly message from them was received in remembrance of their and our fathers; conclusively to show that an 'Indian does not forget.'

"The appellation of 'Henry' is at this day the middle name of every member of the family, to wit:—

    Moses Henry Killbuck.
    Joseph "   "
    William "   "
    Josephine "   "
    Sarah   "   "
    John   "   "
    Rachel "   "

"These are all well-known persons in the West to the 'Moravian Missionaries.'"

sponsibility, profit, or risk. During the spring and summer of 1839, Mr. Henry examined every rod of ground along the river from Pittston to Cobb's Gap to ascertain the most judicious location for the works.

Under the wall of rock, cut in twain by the dash of the *Nay-aug*, a quarter of a mile above its mouth, favoring by its altitude, the erection and feeding of a stack, a place was well chosen. It was but a few rods above the *debris* of Slocum's forge, and like that earlier affair enjoyed within a stone's throw every essential material for its construction and working.

After the decease of Mr. Slocum, the forge grounds changing hands repeatedly for a mere nominal consideration, had fallen into possession of William Merrifield, Zeno Albro, and William Ricketson of Hyde Park, and had relapsed into common pasturage. Mr. J. J. Albright was offered 500 acres of the Scranton lands for $5,000 upon a long credit in 1836; for *such* land that figure was considered too high at that time.

In March, 1840, Messrs. Henry and Armstrong purchased 503 acres for $8,000, or about $16 per acre. The fairest farm in the valley, under-veined with coal, had no opportunity of refusing the same surprising equivalent. Mr. Henry gave a draft at thirty days on Mr. Armstrong, in whom the title was to vest; before its maturity, death came to Mr. Armstrong, almost unawares. He had imbued the enterprise, by his manly co-operation, with no vague friendship or faith, and his death, at this time, was regarded as especially disastrous to the interests of Slocum Hollow. His administrators, looking to nothing but a quick settlement of the estate, requested him to forfeit the contract without question or hesitancy. Thus baffled in a quarter little anticipated, Mr. Henry asked and obtained thirty days' grace upon the non-accepted draft, hoping in the interim to find another shrewd capitalist able to advance the purchase-money and willing to share in the affairs of the contemplated furnace. The late lamented Colonel Geo. W. Scranton and Selden T. Scranton, both of New Jersey, interested by the earnest and enthusiastic representations of Mr. Henry regarding the vast and varied resources of the Lackawanna Valley, of which no knowledge had reached them before, proposed to add Mr. Sanford Grant, of Belvidere, to a party, and visit Slocum Hollow.

The journey from Belvidere to the present site of Scranton took one day and a half hard driving, and was well calculated to test the self-reliance and vigor of the inexperienced mountaineer. The Drinker Turnpike, stretching its weary length over Pocono Mountain and morass, enlivened here and there by the arrowy trout-brook or the start of the fawn, brought the party on the 19th of August, 1840, to the half-opened thicket growing over the tract where now Mr. Archbald's residence is seen. Securing their horses under the shade of a tree, the party, amazed at the simple wildness of a country where green acres were looked for in vain, moved down the bank of Roaring Brook to a body of coal whose black edge showed the fury of the stream when sudden rains or thaws raised its waters along the narrow channel. None of the party except Mr. Henry had ever seen a coal-bed before. Assisted by a pick, used and concealed by him weeks before, pieces of coal and iron ore were exhumed for the inspection of the party about to turn the minerals, sparkling amid the shrubs and wild flowers, to some more practical account. The obvious advantages of location, uniting water-power with prospective wealth, were examined for half a day without seeing or being seen by a single person.

The village of Slocum Hollow, in 1840, yielded the palm to the surrounding ones. The Slocum house and its humble barn, three small wooden houses, and one stone dwelling, outliving the days of the forge, stood above its *debris;* a grist-mill, owned by Barton Mott, a seven-by-nine school-house squatting on the ledge, and a clattering saw-mill, made up the village twenty-nine years ago.

The exterior features of the Slocum property were any thing but attractive, yet, after some question and hesitancy, it was purchased at the price already stipulated. Lackawanna Valley achieved its thrift and fame from this comparatively trifling purchase of but yesterday, and Scranton dates its incipient inspirations toward acquiring for itself a place and a name from August, 1840.

The company, consisting of Colonel George W. and Selden T. Scranton, Sanford Grant, William Henry, and Philip H. Mattes, organizing under the firm of Scrantons, Grant & Co., began forthwith the construction of a furnace, under the superintendency of Mr. Henry, whose family immediately removed from Stroudsburg to Hyde Park.

None of the older portion of the community can forget the thriftless appearance of the four villages in Providence Township, exhibiting no reluctant spirit of rivalry. Hyde Park contained but a single store, where the post-office found ample quarters in a single pigeon hole; a small Christian meeting-house standing by the road-side, and six or eight scattered dwellings along the single roadway; neither physician, lawyer, nor miner, and but a single minister, without a church of his own, resided within its precincts. Providence, known far and wide by the *sobriquet* of *Razorville*, acknowledged as the seat of government for the county, had a dozen houses, two stores and a post-office, a grist-mill and a bridge, an ax factory, three doctors, no minister, and it did a snug business in the way of *horse-racing* on Sunday, and miscellaneous traffic with the round-about country during the week. Dunmore was the equal of Slocum Hollow in the number of its dilapidated tenements, sheltering as many families. Such were the towns that gave a negative welcome to the innovations of the unknown "Jerseyites," as they were termed, in half derision, by people hearing of their search and purchase around Capoose.

New men naturally introduced new names. When the white man first strayed into the valley, no other name than Capoose—an Indian signification of endearment—was heard until the connection of the Slocums with the rough hollow, in 1798, opening land and trade, fixed the appellation of *Slocum Hollow*. The memorable days of "hard cider" substituted the name of *Harrison* for that of Slocum Hollow. The Scrantons, not without ambition to popularize a name never dishonored, assented to the exchange of Harrison for *Scrantonia*. With the growth and triumphs of the iron-works, the brief vowels *ia* were erased, leaving plain Scranton in possession of the field. This name thus serves to perpetuate the memories of the founders of the town, but would not the aboriginal Capoose or the Indian names for their streams, *Nay-aug* or Lar-har-har-nar, have been more musical and appropriate?

The first day's work on the Harrison furnace was done September 11, 1840, by Mr. Simeon Ward. During the fall and winter months satisfactory progress attended it. A small wooden building, afterward enlarged for "Kresler's Hotel," was erected by W. W. Manness, who is yet in the employ of the company, and jointly occupied as an office, store, and dwelling. It was afterward torn down to make room for the blast-furnace engine-house. As the spring of 1841 opened, tenant-houses went up, and work went forward without cessation or abatement. Mr. Grant became a resident of Harrison, with his family, and for many years, when the tide was low, conducted the management of the store with such urbanity and studied regard for the interests of all, that he acquired consideration and popularity among the yeomanry of the county.

The interests of P. H. Mattes were represented by his son, Charles F. Mattes, who, from the time the furnace was put in successful blast, has been efficiently engaged at the head of one of the more important departments.

The liberal doctrines of Methodism, itinerated and diffused in the valley as early as 1786, were rarely practiced, and had but a feeble recognition in any way until 1793. "At this time," writes the venerable Rev. Dr. Peck, "William Colbert, a pioneer preacher, visited Capouse, and preached to a few people at Brother Howe's, and lodged at Joseph Waller's. Howe lived in Slocum Hollow, and Waller on the main road in or near what is now Hyde Park. In 1798 Daniel Taylor's, below Hyde Park, was a preaching place. For years subsequently the preaching was at Preserved Taylor's, who lived on the hill-side in Hyde Park, near the old Tripp place. When Mr. Taylor removed, the preaching was taken to Razorville, now Providence, and the preachers were entertained by Elisha Potter, Esq., whose wife was a very exemplary member of the church. Up to this period, preaching was held in private houses." School-houses, moderate in capacity, served for religious purposes until June, 1841, when a subscription was raised for the purpose of building a "meeting-house" at some suitable place within reach of missionaries and laymen. The great bulk of the subscription coming from Harrison Iron Works, governed the location of the church, which was built in 1842, and jointly and harmoniously used as a place of worship by Methodists and Presbyterians until the latter erected a place of their own. The Methodists have enjoyed the pastoral labors of A. H. Schoonmaker, Rev. Dr. Peck, B. W. Goram, G. C. Bancroft, J. V. Newell, J. A. Wood, N. W. Everett, and Byron D. Sturdevant.

The Presbyterians, now representing so much of the intelligence and wealth of the Scranton community, had no definite organization in Scranton until February, 1842. In 1827 missionaries were employed to preach at Slocum Hollow and Razorville twelve times a year, generally in school-houses and barns, and sometimes under the shelter of a friendly tree. Rev. Cyrus Gildersleeve, John Dorrance, and the bold, blunt Thomas P. Hunt, were thus employed alternately. The success attending the Methodists in building their church by subscription, animated the fewer Presbyterians to a similar effort in the same direction. The pressure of poverty among the farmers of the valley, combined with the weak condition of this denomination, having but *four* members at Harrison, influenced the committee appointed in 1844 to select a site for a church, to decide upon Lackawanna, three miles below Harrison, as the place best calculated to favor the majority of the Presbyterians. The church, built in 1846, was owned in common by the members at Lackawanna and Harrison. This latter place was a mere subordinate preaching point, and yet cared for so well by the young, gifted Rev. N. G. Parks, that in 1848 the Scranton portion of this organic body, acquiring influence and independence with the development of the village, sought a peaceful separation, and at once asserted its strength by the erection of an imposing church, costing $30,000, capable of seating 800 persons. Since Mr. Park, the Rev. J. D. Mitchell, John F. Baker, and the Rev. M. J. Hickok, have all creditably officiated within its walls. Mr. Hickok, whose purity of mind and blameless life endeared him to all, was hopelessly stricken with paralysis in the fall of 1867, thus leaving the church without an active pastor.

The spiritual wants of the Catholics in Scranton were first looked after by the Rev. P. Pendergrast in 1846. A small room in a private dwelling served for a gathering place until 1848, when a church, 25 by 35, was constructed. The constant accession of numbers rendered a larger place of worship necessary in 1853-4, under the attention of the Rev. Father Moses Whittey. The erection of a Catholic church in Providence and another in Dunmore, drew somewhat from a congregation yet so numerically strong in Scranton, that Father Whittey, well known for his calm deportment yet zealous devotion to the interests of his church, looking to the future want and welfare of his flock, began in 1864 to build a cathedral, at an estimated cost of $100,000. The edifice is built in the Grecian style of architecture, 68 by 158 feet, and will seat 2,300 persons. Few individuals in the valley could have turned so powerful an influence to the greater advantage of Scranton than has Father Whittey done in the erection of this edifice.

The first Baptist church here was built under hopeful auspices in 1859 ; in 1863, the Rev. Isaac Bevan, acting in concert with those fostering the project, increased his claim to public gratitude by the erection of a brick sanctuary, 50 by 80, at a cost of $40,000. The church numbers about 200 communicants.

St. Luke's Episcopal Church dates back only to 1852. Within the next eighteen months, a frame church and parsonage were finished and completed at a cost of about $4,000. St. Luke's is now so comparatively wealthy and popular in Scranton, that a new stone church is being erected for a Parish, at a cost of $150,000. This ecclesiastical body, eschewing politics and religious ultraism, has, under the ministerial administration of Rev. John Long, W. C. Robinson, and the Rev. A. A. Marple, the indefatigable, gentlemanly pastor, grown into public favor in an especial manner since its original existence here.

The German Presbyterian Church of Scranton was dedicated in 1859 ; the Evangelical Lutheran Zion Church, organized in 1860, purchased the First Welsh Baptist Church of Scranton in 1863.

The Liberal Christian Society have a respectable organization without enjoying a place of worship of their own.

The German Catholics, looked after by their worthy pastor, Rev. P. Nagel, built them a neat edifice in 1866, at a cost of $11,000.

The above-named churches, enumerating only those embraced within the old village proper of Scranton, are named in the order of their development.

The fact is indeed creditable to the Lackawanna Iron and Coal Company, that a great portion of the land occupied by these respective places of worship, was generously donated by them for this specific object.

In the Slocum furnace of 1800, nothing but charcoal was used for smelting purposes. Experiments, attended with failure and sometimes with derision, were made in Pennsylvania between 1837-9, toward the substitution of anthracite coal as a melting menstruum in the manufacture of iron, for the more expensive and perishable charcoal. The Iron Works upon the Lehigh inaugurated the change; the Danville artisans were the next to enlarge the province of stone coal. This long-delayed triumph of coal, wonderful in the grandeur of its results everywhere, governed the design of the new furnace at Harrison. It was contemplated from the first to use the *ball ore* found adjacent to one of the veins of coal running through the whole coal region; a brief trial proved it too expensive to mine. Upon the southeastern slope of the Moosic, about three miles from Harrison, a large body of iron ore was discovered in the spring of 1841, which with the intervening acres of land was purchased, and a railroad stretched from the mine to the furnace.

The erection of miners' houses, the increased cost of the iron-works awaiting blast, the unforeseen yet unavoidable outlay for lands and railroad unprovided for in the original estimate, exhausted the capital, and left from the very outset an embarrassing debt. Under such auspices, little calculated to encourage the enterprise, came Col. George W. Scranton into Scranton, as a resident, in the fall of 1841. A man of ardent faith, affable and persuasive address, full of honor and probity, whom no difficulties could discourage, no honors cause him to forget the good of the poor man, he was eminently fitted to aid Mr. Henry in the superintendence and experimental inauguration of the iron-works.

The first effort to start the furnace, owing to various

causes incident to a new, wet, defective stack, appalled the projectors with failure. Wood, charcoal, and even salt and brimstone, employed as auxiliaries to intensify the heat, brought no fulfillment of hopes or prospect of victory. A second effort led to the same result. The furnace was altered. The hot-air ovens were multiplied and enlarged, the machinery changed, and the practical knowledge and services of Mr. John F. Davis secured. On the 18th of January, 1842, the furnace was blown in, amid mutual applause and congratulation. About two and a quarter tons of pig-iron per day was made the first month.

The early trials and failures at the furnace, occupying three months of constant struggle, awakened an interest among the better class of people of the valley and elsewhere, honorable alike to their intelligence and humanity. Many, willing to check any and every advancement toward general prosperity, boldly pronounced "the *thing* a Jersey humbug!" as they prayed and predicted it would be. Even such skepticism, when the molten stream of iron issued from the furnace into bars, exciting astonishment and pride, vanished into silence; the people acquiesced in the good feeling of the proprietors, whose recompense thus far had been only hope deferred.

In the spring of 1843, additional fire-ovens, with other improvements, were added to augment its capacity, which thus far had yielded iron superior in quality, but deficient in quantity. Iron, when manufactured, found no market to any extent short of the distant sea-board, reached only by two roundabout routes, viz.: the Delaware and Hudson Canal, and the North Branch and Tide Water Canal, to Havre-de-Grace. In either case, the iron must be transported upon heavy wagons from Harrison, fifteen miles to Carbondale, then the terminus of the railroad leading to Honesdale, or to Port Barnum on the Susquehanna.

The first year's product was shipped by the latter route to New York and Boston, at a time when great commercial embarrassment pervaded the country, and threatened the annihilation of manufacturing interests in every section. Since the commencement of the forge, September 20, 1840, iron had fallen in value over forty per cent. Its demand and price continued to decline. More than this, Lackawanna Valley iron had neither name nor character in either of these places to carry itself into public estimation. Thus were men whose fortunes were pledged to foster and sustain a great development, greeted in advance by restrictions especially baleful and adverse to their success. Meantime, financial obstacles in Harrison increased. The *credit* system was popular in the valley. It attenuated its dubious length as an equalizing medium among the inhabitants unwilling to accord it to the company.

The darkest period in the history of the partnership was seen in 1842–3. In a remunerating sense, the iron speculation had proved a failure, and left the treasury worse than empty. Without character, money, or credit, its affairs began to look hopeless. Their notes given to individuals in lieu of money, were daily offered to farmers at forty per cent. discount in the uncurrent tender of Pennsylvania currency. Every petty claim of indebtedness was urged and pressed before the justices of the township with an earnestness really annoying.

It was at this time that the existence of the company was preserved and prolonged by a timely loan made them by Joseph H. and E. C. Scranton,[1] then of Augusta, Georgia.

The persons once expecting but a negative advantage themselves, expressed regret at their expected arrest and destruction; others looked calmly and coldly on the severe, unabated energy with which the Scrantons, forgetting every other consideration, fought for their bare integrity and financial preservation. Their failure at this especial time would have been of double signification and

---

[1] Killed by the cars, Dec. 29, 1866, at Norwalk, Ct.

injury, while the young, giant valley, far up among the hills, would have resumed the natural simplicity of its former character.

As the company faltered under the pressure of distrust, and danger menacing it from every side, Col. Scranton never exhibited the elastic and buoyant disposition ever characterizing the man, with such admirable advantage as now. He proposed to enhance the value of their iron 25 per cent., by converting it into nails and bars, by the aid of a *Rolling Mill* and *Nail Factory*, to be built on the brook below Nay-aug Falls. To accomplish this great project, Selden T. Scranton was sent to New York to negotiate for funds, if possible. This he successfully did. He thus obtained $20,000. The Rolling Mill and Nail Factory begun in 1843, was completed in 1844. The erection of these works with New York capital has indirectly led to an investment in coal lands in the Lackawanna basin, from the same quarter, of some one hundred and fifty millions.

The plan of the village of Harrison, laid out on a diminutive scale in 1841, by Captain Stott, a superior draughtsman of Carbondale, gave such brisk signs of life that the neighboring villages of Hyde Park, Providence, and Dunmore, feared that its continued growth might, at some future period, equal or possibly surpass their own!

It yet had no post-office. Hyde Park and Providence, a mile or two away, afforded the nearest mail facilities. Dr. Throop, then residing in the latter village, a warm, influential friend of the Scrantons and the improvements they were striving to inaugurate, attempted to get one established at this point. The Department at Washington, influenced by the known fact that a post-office had been suspended here a few years previous for the want of support, naturally gave the matter an unfavorable consideration.

Nor had the village a single minister, lawyer, or physician, within its boundaries. Dr. Gideon Underwood, now of Pittston, began professional life in Harrison in 1845; he abandoned the place after a few months, for the reason that it was "too small to support a doctor." The late Dr. Robinson was his only competitor in the township of Providence, where now no less than fifty physicians manage to keep soul and body together, and yet the entire practice failed to sustain a gentleman every way worthy of trust. Dr. Pier opened an office in the village in 1848; Dr. John B. Sherrerd in 1849. Drs. Throop and Sherrerd started the first drug-store in the town, which, after the death of Dr. Sherrerd, the next year, passed into the hands of L. S. & E. C. Fuller, two gentlemen who have, through a long series of years, obtained a comparative competency by their diligence and attention to business.

In the spring of 1844, Selden T. Scranton, who, like all the Scrantons already mentioned, originally came from East Guilford, now Madison, New Haven County, Conn., removed from Oxford Furnace, New Jersey, settled in Harrison, exchanging positions with his brother George. He was one of the men who shared in the acquisition of the Roaring Brook lands, four years previous to this, and who, by no idle stroke of fortune, succeeded in connecting his name with its remotest future. Gaining some knowledge of the mineral resources of the valley of the Lackawanna from his father-in-law, William Henry, he readily joined in the hazard of their successful development; and, by the happy exercise of a talent adapted admirably to win friendship or insure success, he contributed to sow the seeds, of which the fruits were to appear in less than a lifetime. Selden was uniform in his advocacy of all pertaining to the welfare of the valley, and yet so honorable and consistent were his efforts in this direction, that it can be said of him, as of few men, he never made an enemy or lost a friend. The celebrated Oxford Furnace is now managed and principally owned by him.

Under a new direction of mechanical industry, instituted at the Lackawanna Iron Works by its founders, the final struggle, which was life or death in a commercial sense to the inhabitants of the township of Providence, began to give way for actual remuneration. The T rail was first manufactured in the United States in 1845. Railroads, everywhere shod with the thin, flat rail, called for the T rail, the first of which was made in Harrison for the New York and Erie Railroad in 1847. This pioneer road through southern New York was then in operation no farther than Goshen. English iron, costing the Erie Company $80 per ton, had thus far been laid.

The presence of every variety of material cheaply attained, led the Scrantons to believe that as good, if not superior, T rail could be furnished by them, especially upon the Delaware and Susquehanna divisions, at a lower figure than the English iron-masters across the water had hitherto afforded.

Joseph H. Scranton, a man whose active mind for nearly a quarter of a century has been employed in guiding the iron enterprise which this company have developed, purchased the interests of Mr. Grant in 1846. Mr. Platt, who subsequently became a partner, filled the position vacated by Mr. Grant, and through the successive changes of firms, the expansion and enlargement of business, he has held the same satisfactory and creditable relation to the place he has filled so long.

The year of 1846 was auspicious in the history of Harrison. Col. Scranton returned, and aided by Joseph and Selden, negotiated a contract with the Erie Railroad Company for 12,000 tons of iron-rail, to weigh 58 pounds to the yard; to be made and delivered at the mouth of the Lackawaxen, in Pike County, during the years of 1847-8. This arrangement was mutually advantageous to both parties. It was of vital significance to that great road, now stretching its fibers from the lake to the sea. At the opening of the northern division of the Delaware, Lackawanna, and Western Railroad, Mr. Loder, then President of the Erie Company, stated in a public speech that nothing but the prompt fulfillment of this contract averted bankruptcy to the road, by enabling them within the specified time to open it to Binghamton. To the Scranton Company it evoked life-long results. The men whose common interests and joint sacrifices and struggles had bound them together in the unity of brotherhood, felt the invigorating and fervid influence of this great sale of iron, which gave to the valley a prospect and prominence it never had enjoyed before.

Mills and machinery of a corresponding character, with the wherewithal to erect them, were thus necessitated by compliance of the contract.

Several gentlemen, wealthy and warm friends of the Erie road, promptly came forward, and on the simple obligations of the Scrantons alone, with no security, but faith in their integrity, loaned them $100,000 to construct the requisite iron-works. Extraordinary activity was now displayed in Harrison, in every department of business, the active management of which passed into the hands of Joseph H. Scranton, who came here to reside in 1847.

Up until now the means of transportation to market of the now largely increased annual product of iron, remained as difficult as at the commencement, with the exception of the extension of the Delaware and Hudson Canal Company's railroad from Carbondale to Archbald, which reduced the hauling by teams to nine miles; the iron ore was carted three miles and a half from the mines; the limestone and extra pig-iron needed by the mill, purchased at Danville, drawn from the canal at Pittston, and the railroad iron, now the principal product of the works, was drawn to Archbald upon heavy wagons, requiring the use of over *four hundred* horses and mules. Even this large force, gathered from the farmers of Blakeley, Providence, and Lackawanna, sometimes at the expense

of agricultural interests, was able to move the first rail iron only with provoking tardiness.

Two large blast-furnaces were now in the course of construction, as well as a railroad to the ore mines on the mountain. This road was so graded that the empty cars could be drawn to the mines by mules, and when loaded with ore, return to the furnace by gravity power alone, over five miles and a half of this circuitous road.

On the south side of Roaring Brook, some three hundred houses had been built for the workmen; upon the the other, now the business part of Scranton, but a single dwelling, aside from the few owned and occupied by the company, stood. This had been erected by Dr. Throop for his brother. With the constant influx of new-comers, the doctor, who was recognized pre-eminently throughout the country as *the* doctor, removed from Providence to Harrison in 1847. On the old mill road leading from *Slocum Hollow* to *Razorville*, amidst the tranquil woodlands, he built his modest cottage. He lived here many years, with his family, with no house in sight of his own, surrounded by the low murmuring pines, where, after the professional drives of the day, he enjoyed the cheerful fireside and smoked his pipe in quiet, with no sound to disturb him, save the grave *bo-loonk-blonk* of the denizens of the adjacent swamp, tuning up their minstrelsy at each successive nightfall. The cottage, remodified and absorbed into business quarters, is yet seen in sound condition, near the Presbyterian church.

The Lackawanna Iron Company, organized under the general partnership law, consisted of George W. Scranton, Selden T. Scranton, Joseph H. Scranton, and J. C. Platt as the general partners, and several New York gentlemen as special ones. Edward C. Lynde and Edward P. Kingsbury, two gentlemen eminently qualified for any station, fill the respective positions of secretary and assistant treasurer.

To carry through the programme of manufacturing and

delivering to the New York and Erie Railroad Company, this quantity of iron, with the limited capital at command, required extraordinary exertion and energy. Extra work, additional machinery, and various expensive materials, augmented the necessity of more money and labor. Large iron contrivances which were essential to the works were drawn, by the jaded horse or stubborn mule, sixty or seventy miles over the rough, hilly roads for which upper Pennsylvania was formerly distinguished. Teams consisting of eight mules were used for this service with such vexatious experience, that willing and reliable drivers were rarely found or retained. When such were apparently secured, the company found it necessary to contract with the keepers of the small taverns along the road from Stroudsburg to the Hollow, to furnish meals for their drivers and feed for their teams, and forward bills each month to the office for payment. It was especially provided that *no liquor* should, under any condition or circumstance, be furnished the drivers. Yet bills properly attested for "sixteen glasses of *leming ayde* (lemonade), at sixpence a glass, and one pint of whisky," came from places where a lemon had never been heard of before or since.

The business of the company, so comprehensive in its character, so beneficial in its influence, made many a valley fireside exult with hopes and smiles. To witness a town spring from a pasture lot with such rapidity into a maze of founderies, furnaces, manufacturing works, and dwellings full of bright expectations, caused astonishment and pride among the inhabitants, unused to such rapid advancement. The rise in real estate along the Lackawanna Valley, as well as Wyoming, since the organization of this company, was at least one hundred per cent., while the relations of the Scrantons with the public were harmonious, and characterized throughout by *general* good feeling. It is true, there were then as there are yet, and ever will be, a class of croakers who gathered

in bar-room groups and gravely predicted that "the Scrantons *must* fail."

On the western side of the Lackawanna a line of four-horse stages ran up from Wilkes Barre to Carbondale, connecting at each place with a similar line *via* Milford and Morristown to New York, and *via* Easton to Philadelphia, and furnished the only mode of conveyance to or from the Lackawanna, and brought New York daily papers to Providence and Hyde Park in the forenoon of the *third* day after their publication.

The mills were completed; as they molded the hills into iron fiber awaiting no longer a market, the Lackawanna Iron Works stepped into the front ranks and established their character beyond cavil or peradventure. The first fifteen hundred tons of railroad iron was delivered at the mouth of the Lackawaxen. Here it was taken by canal to Port Jervis, and laid on the road between that place and Otisville. After that portion of the Erie road was opened to the public, the company, delayed by injunctions urged on by the cupidity of Philadelphians and the New York Central interests, in crossing the river into Pennsylvania at the Glass House rocks, finding their utter inability to open the road to Binghamton by the time specified without the delivery of the balance of the iron at different points along the route by the Scranton Company, arranged such terms of delivery, in pursuance of which the Scranton Company carted by teams some seven thousand tons of rail, which they delivered at Narrowsburgh, Cochecton, Equinunk, Stockport, Summit, and Lanesboro, an average distance of about fifty miles, thus enabling the company to lay the track almost simultaneously at all points along the Delaware division as fast as the grading was ready, and open the road for one hundred and thirty miles four days ahead of the appointed time. The difficulty of carting so large an amount of iron within so brief a period, can be inferred only by those familiar with the ruggedness of the mountain roads intervening.

A post-office, named *Scrantonia*, was established in Harrison in 1848, and John W. Moore appointed postmaster. The name of Harrison was dropped for that of Scrantonia. The same year the old names of *Capoose* and Slocum Hollow were disowned and forgotten by newcomers; the accidental and transient ones, Lackawanna Iron Works, Harrison, Scrantonia, were folded up and laid away forever for the briefer name of Scranton.

The rapid expansion and concentration of business at this point, as well as the absence of all necessary communications with the sea-board and the lakes, rendered an outlet east or west most apparent and desirable. The project of connecting the valley by railroad with the New York and Erie road, in a northerly direction, was frequently discussed by the general partners; in fact, it was the sanguine expectations of a line of public improvement being extended both north and south at no distant day, that went far toward deciding the original proprietors in locating here.

With a view of bringing the subject of railroad facilities, and connections with the valley generally, before the minds of capitalists in a manner both advantageous and effective, Col. George W. Scranton was detailed from the active engagement of the affairs of the Iron Company in the summer of 1848.

Valuable coal lands had been secured as a reliable basis of such an enterprise; large delegations of New York and New England gentlemen were persuaded from time to time to visit the valley and examine the vast mineral resources apparent along its border, and witness the dark croppings of coal, the fertile farms and luxurious intervale, the abundant water-power for mills or manufacturing purposes, the splendid sites and the fine timber; all of which, the moment a railroad outlet appeared, would be trebled in value. By many, the valley was considered too wild and remote, or too difficult of access, even for an exploring tour. Such never left the parental roof, and it was left for bolder hearts and stouter arms to plant and reap the harvest. An extra stage-coach, with its five miles an hour speed, now and then brought into the valley delegation after delegation from the East, which were hailed with friendly solicitude by the inhabitants. Often and always was the inquiry heard of that firm friend of the public interest, Sam Tripp, "When the *Yorkers* were coming?" All eyes, for a time, were directed toward the local movements of the Yorkers, and the hope of every honest citizen then as well as now was, that long life and prosperity would be the fortune of all who came.

Until 1847 no car had rolled nor had a single rail reached the remote Lackawanna, with the exception of those upon the Delaware and Hudson Canal Company's railroad from Carbondale to Honesdale. This road was a gravity one, worked by stationary steam-engines and horse-power, over the Moosic Mountain, and was built in 1826-8.

Drinker's route for a railroad from Pittston to Delaware Water Gap, surveyed in 1824, to develop which Scranton was originally planned, and ultimately reversed in relation and purpose, had yet no living functions given its indefinite existence. The line was run with a view of inclined planes operated by water, and perhaps a canal over the more level portion of the way.

Wurts Brothers, Meredith, and Drinker blazed the trees along the forest for their *gravity* roads through many a lonely nook shaded by woods; but the honor of conceiving and completing a *locomotive* road from Great Bend to the Delaware River, belongs to the late Col. George W. Scranton—the firm, fast friend of every industrial interest of the valley. Mountainous as were the general features of the intermediate country, formidable as appeared the idea of grading ranges offering stubborn resistance to such invasions of the engineer, he advanced and urged forward his scheme until he was able to see and share its substantial achievements and advantages. Under the immediate direction of Col. Scranton, a preliminary survey was made of the proposed route, which was found to be quite as feasible as his own personal observations had led him to expect, and, as the idle charter of Leggett's Gap Railroad would answer every practical purpose, after slight modifications, it was purchased.

The public mind, understanding only the rough topography of the country, without a single village of a thousand inhabitants, was instructed into the benefits to flow from the construction of this rail highway to the upper border of the State. The subscription books were opened at Kresler's hotel, in Scranton, in 1847, by the commissioners, and the whole capital stock promptly subscribed, and ten per cent. paid in. While these flattering movements argued well for the common welfare of the valley, and country adjacent, men of means were so shy of the enterprise, that it was the work of two long years of ceaseless labor amidst every possible discouragement, before any real capital could be calculated upon. The road was commenced in 1850, and pushed forward in the same spirit of earnest enthusiasm with which it was conceived. To overcome the objection that it would not pay as an investment, and reach and *make* a more northern market (for the first loads of coal taken hence, were *given away* in order to introduce the black stuff into general use), the Ithaca and Owego Railroad, one of the oldest roads in the country, was purchased by the Iron Company in 1849. This, like all railroads in the United States at this time, was laid with the *flat* or *strap* rail—a rail possessing neither strength nor safety, as one end of it sometimes becoming bent would dart up with lightning-like rapidity into the passing train, marking its progress with appalling slaughter.

A new company being now organized, called the Cayuga

and Susquehanna Railroad Company, for the purpose of building this road, Colonel Scranton was chosen President, who at once repaired to Ithaca and discharged the duties of the position with acknowledged prudence and success.

To carry out the original plan contemplated by the colonel, of connecting the iron-works with New York City by a locomotive road, a survey was made eastward in 1851-2, and the next year the present line, running parallel and sometimes embracing the Drinker route, adopted.

Thus far Scranton had but a single hotel. Mr. Kresler, popular as a landlord, could not in his abridged quarters meet the demands of the throng turning into the village. A large brick hotel, such as only courageous men could have planned in such a place, was erected in 1852, by the Iron Company, to which was applied the strange misnomer of Wyoming House. Mr. J. C. Burgess became the purchaser, and is the present owner. The next public house emerging from the forest, from which it derived its name—Forest House—was fitted up and kept by Joseph Godfrey, Esq. The St. Charles, Kock's, and the Lackawanna Valley House, appropriate in name, and a dozen others less familiar to the wayfarer, have anticipated the demand of the moving world until, to-day, Scranton can boast of the beauty, comfort, and healthfulness of its hotels, rarely equaled, and surpassed nowhere within the State.

The Iron Company reorganized in 1853, under a special charter, with a capital of $800,000, and Selden T. Scranton, now of Oxford Furnace, N. J., elected President, and Joseph H. Scranton, the present Manager and President, Superintendent.

After the Lackawanna and Western Railroad was consolidated with the Delaware and Cobb's Gap charter, under the name of the "Delaware, Lackawanna, and Western Railroad Company," work was commenced vigorously on the southern division of this road. On the 21st of January, 1856, the first locomotive and train of cars passed over the Delaware.

Rapid as has been the *sympathetic* growth of half a dozen villages from Pittston to Carbondale, theirs has been a snail's pace compared to the sturdier growth of Scranton. In July, 1840 *five* small brown tenements composed the town of *Slocum Hollow*, where now the young city of Scranton, perpetuating the name of its founders as long as the Lackawanna shall flow by the dwellings of civilized man, enumerates a population, constantly increasing, of five-and-forty thousand.

The stranger who visits Scranton may not find as much wildness and sublimity around it as when, from the Pocono Range, his eye first catches a glimpse of the truly bold outlines of the Delaware Water Gap, he will, nevertheless, as he walks along the walls of Roaring Brook, and gazes on the massive piles of furnace stacks, pouring out, day after day, ponds of rude or finished iron, from the ponderous bar to the delicate bolt, and sees the smooth, yet resistless motion of the largest stationary engine on the American Continent, feel proud and pleased with the sights of industry and thrift everywhere around him.

To get and appreciate a bird's-eye view of the town and valley, let the tourist ascend the high bluff near the Baptist Church in Hyde Park, overlooking the city, where the charming panorama that unrolls itself before him, will compensate in the highest degree for the trouble of the visit. He will then look down into a region interesting for its scenery, its strata of coal, its beds of iron ore, and its Indian history. The first impression is one favorable toward this portion of the valley, as there appears on every side evidence of animation and thrift.

Yonder the *noisy water* (Roaring Brook) takes a white leap from one of the loveliest and loneliest nooks carved from the mountain, before it splashes on the busy wheel of the manufacturer, and after being used three or four times in its passage through the city, mingles with the waters of the Lackawanna below. The huge, round, slate-roofed locomotive depot, filled with engines, at first strikes the eye, and reminds him of the Roman Coliseum; while the landscape, sprinkled with brown-colored depots, car-shops, and Vulcan-shops on every side; the chaste, imposing churches, the long white line of public and private architecture contrasting finely with the deep green of the surrounding trees, tastily left for shade; the trains of coal cars, serpentine and dark, emerging from the "Diamond Mines;" or skimming along the iron veins, down a grade of seventy feet to the mile, from the productive coal works at the "Notch," some two miles distant, on their passage to New York; the locomotives of the Lehigh and Susquehanna, the Lackawanna and Bloomsburg, of the Delaware, Lackawanna, and Western, of the Delaware and Hudson Railroads, rushing into Scranton like some fleet devils, carrying on their back the whole moving world whether they will or not; the villages of Hyde Park, Providence, Dunmore, and Green Ride, arrayed in thrifty garb, far up and down the valley; the Lee-har-hanna, with its modest throat and richer shade drawn like a belt of silver along the picture; the neat farm-houses, here and there nestling in some lovely meadow, or half hid among the blossoms of orchards, with the background of the unshorn mountain, swelling upward from Wyoming or the Lackawanna region, all make up a sight as beautiful as the Jewish ruler of old once witnessed from old Mount Nebo. Nor is this all. As he looks into the bosom of "Capouse Meadow," his eye wanders over coal lands which, fifteen years before the completion of a railroad outlet north from the valley, could have been purchased for fifteen dollars per acre, and which now are worth $800 and $1,000; and building-lots, which then no respectable man was willing to accept as a gratuity, now readily bring from one to five thousand dollars each.

The growth of Scranton has been marked by uniform decades.

In 1826, the Drinker Railroad wrought consternation among the pines of this secluded glen ; in 1836 the same measure, combined with the North Branch Canal and new county schemes, again awakened hopes partially fulfilled. In 1846, sales of iron made by the Scranton Company, enabled them to defy threatened bankruptcy ; in 1856, the first locomotive engine rolled from Scranton, just formed into a borough, to the Delaware River ; in 1866, incorporated into a city ; and in 1876, all the townships in northern and central Luzerne will probably take their places in the new county of Lackawanna, with the county seat at Scranton. In 1866, Scranton, Hyde Park, and Providence, were fashioned by the legislature of Pennsylvania into a city composed of twelve wards, with all the municipal rights and regulations necessary for its existence. E. S. M. Hill, Esq., was elected mayor.

The newspaper interests of Scranton, now so prominent a feature, had no place or foothold until fifteen years ago.

During he year 1845, a newspaper called the *County Mirror* was started in Providence (now the 1st and 2d Wards, Scranton), by the late Franklin B. Woodward. Harrison at this time had made so humble pretensions that but a single advertisement from the village found its way into this lively paper. In 1852, the *Lackawanna Herald*, a paper of more partisan bitterness than real ability, was issued in Scranton by Charles E. Lathrop. Three years later the *Spirit of the Valley* was published by Thomas J. Alleger and J. B. Adams for one year, when the two were consolidated under the name of the *Herald of the Union*, purchased and edited by the late Ezra B. Chase,—a gentleman of superior literary attainments. Declining health induced him soon after to sell out to Dr. A. Davis and J. B. Adams. In the spring of 1859, Dr. Davis purchased the interest of Mr. Adams, transferring it to Dr. Silas M. Wheeler, and the paper was managed by these medical gentlemen with a degree of originality and spiciness rarely seen in a country newspaper. Dr. Davis at that time moved into Scranton, building the first house erected on Franklin Avenue, and now occupied by Dr. G. W. Masser. This paper finally subsided into the *Scranton Register*, owned and edited by Mayor E. S. M. Hill, until the summer of 1868.

Theodore Smith established the *Scranton Republican* in 1856, conducting it in a highly creditable manner for two years, when F. A. McCartney became the proprietor. After being owned by Thos. J. Alleger, and conducted fairly and honorably, it passed into the hands of F. A. Crandall, then again into those of F. A. Crandall & Co., the present energetic and spirited owners. The *Scranton City Journal* came forth from the hands of Messrs. Benedicts in 1867, and from the acknowledged industry and qualifications of these gentlemen, the new paper can hardly fail to thrive.

The *Scranton Wochenblatt*, a German paper, was started, with a large circulation, January 1865, by E. A. Ludwig. It is now edited and published by F. Wagner, and presents a neat appearance. The *Democrat*—a bold, original, ultra-democratic paper—edited by J. B. Adams, has already secured the favorable consideration and good opinion of the people of the country.

The above named are and were all weekly publications.

One or two dailies and tri-weeklies have been born and buried within that period ; some of them, especially the *Morning Herald*, a daily published in 1866 by J. B. Adams, evidenced considerable merit. None of them however, exhibited the substantial prosperity shown by the *Scranton Daily Register*, edited by E. S. M. Hill, Esq., and managed in its *local* department by J. B. Adams with a bluntness and severity of thought, which, however creditable it might have been to his abilities as a writer, offended the erring rather than corrected the errors of the day. Messrs. Carl and Burtch, purchased the paper in 1868, converted it into an evening issue, and by its telegraphic features and the vigor of its young editors, without abating any of its democratic tendencies, it has already gained a place in the public heart.

In spite of the failures in every inland town and city in Pennsylvania to sustain a daily paper, with full telegraphic news, Messrs. Scranton and Crandall essayed forth the *Scranton Daily Republican* in November, 1867, as an experimental measure.

Its prosperity and success, at first jeopardized by a disastrous fire, is now fully assured in public opinion, and all concede to these gentlemen the credit of first offering to the people a daily country paper, with telegraphic news simultaneously enjoyed by the New York Associated Press. Its *local* department, managed by Mr. Chase, and its general editorials, somewhat ultra and positive in their character, bear evidence of vigorous thought.

Scranton abounds in industrial enterprises, which its remarkable growth have prompted and fostered.

FINCH & CO.'S SCRANTON CITY FOUNDERY AND MACHINE WORKS, situated on the Hyde Park side of the Lackawanna, was established, in 1856, by Mr. A. P. Finch. This establishment, representing high engineering attainment, is largely engaged in the manufacture of portable and stationary engines, mining machinery, circular sawmills, turbine water-wheels, iron fronts, &c., &c.

MACLAREN'S BRASS FOUNDERY, deriving its name from its founder and owner, John Maclaren, is located in Scranton, near the depot of the Lehigh and Susquehanna Railroad. Its establishment in 1866, to supply the demands of a wide section hitherto seeking New York or Philadelphia for the infinite variety of brass work needed in the interest of commerce, gave proof of sound judgment and a correct appreciation of the increasing wants of the Valley of the Lackawanna. This is one of the

LACKAWANNA VALLEY. 261

SCRANTON IN 1860.

most extensive brass founderies in the State, and while its success adds to the wealth and vigor of Scranton, the public are not indifferent to its general welfare.

The Capouse Works of Pulaski Carter, of Providence, known far and wide by the superior character of the *edge tools* issuing from them, as well as by the self-made man instituting on the low bank of the Lackawanna this *pioneer* mechanical enterprise; The Sash and Blind Manufactory of Messrs. Hand & Costen, of Providence; the Providence Stove Manufactory of Henry O. Silkman; the Scranton Stove and Manufacturing Company, of Scranton, and the various individual and associated operations and improvements within the city limits, establishes the reputation of Scranton as a manufacturing rather than a mining city.

The sketch of the history of Scranton can hardly be appropriately closed without a glance at the great iron works now in blast here, capable of smelting about seventy thousand tons of ore a year. The sizes of these blast furnaces may be inferred from the diameter of the *boshes*, which are respectively 18, 18, 19, and 20 feet, with a height of fifty feet. Into these furnaces air is forced by four lever-beam engines of vast power. The steam cylinders are fifty-four inches in diameter. The blowing cylinders are 110 inches in diameter, with ten feet stroke. The wind is forced by this apparatus into the furnaces, under an average pressure of eight pounds to the square inch. The huge fly-wheels which regulate the movements of this enormous apparatus weigh forty thousand pounds. In order to be prepared for any possible exigency, and have increased blowing power, the Iron Company have built appropriate apartments, and set up still another pair of engines upon the very ground where formerly stood, under one roof, the first office, store, and dwelling of Messrs. Scranton and Grant, in Harrison, subsequently known as "Kresler's Hotel."

This pair of engines have cylinders 59 inches in diameter, and blowing cylinders 90 inches. Each engine has two fly-wheels, 28 feet in diameter, weighing seventy-five thousand pounds. By this power they are able to force air into the furnaces under a pressure of eight or nine pounds to the square inch, a great advantage, as it is found by experiments that in order for a furnace to yield the greatest product, it must not only have a certain amount of air, but that the air, to be most advantageous, must be introduced under heavy pressure, and at many places simultaneously, when it is more equally diffused through the stack. The aggregate productive capacity of the Scranton furnaces is about sixty thousand tons per annum.

A walk of five minutes brings one to the rolling-mills, which also stand on the north side of the Roaring Brook. Midway between the furnace and the mills, down the bank of the brook to the right, is seen a railroad track leading into a mine directly under our feet, into which a few blackened coal cars, drawn by mules, disappear in midnight. This vein of coal, at this point, which is used in all the iron works now, is the very one first seen by the exploring party, in 1840, led by Mr. Henry, and which, in connection with the adjacent iron deposits, decided the Scrantons and Mr. Grant to purchase this property for sixteen dollars an acre. Entering the rolling-mill, one is surprised to see the magnitude and the precision of the whole arrangement. The principal product of the mills is T railroad bars, of which about 40,000 tons a year are finished. A great quantity of railroad spikes and chairs are made, besides some three thousand tons of merchantable iron.

About 200,000 tons of coal are mined annually by the Lackawanna Iron and Coal Company, and consumed at their works.

Some *general* idea can be formed of the imposing character of the iron-works by the fact that over two hundred thousand tons of anthracite coal per year are consumed by them alone, while they furnish employment to an effective army of two thousand men !

The amount of capital already expended by the Delaware, Lackawanna, and Western Railroad Company, in their railroad and coal property, including the Cayuga and Susquehanna Railroad, and the Warren Railroad, in New Jersey, is, at this time, over fifteen million dollars, and a large amount will yet be required to complete the double track and properly equip the road.

The influence of the opening of this great eastern and western outlet upon a valley so long shut out from the great world by mountain barriers, make as plain as noonday, facts of yesterday and to-day. It is visible in every hamlet, felt in every cottage by the wayside, and is written in vivifying lines everywhere along the Lackawanna; while the vast revolution it has effected in monetary affairs, finds expression in the grand aggregate of prosperity seen throughout every county in Pennsylvania and New Jersey through which the road passes. Much of this prosperity is due to Hon. John Brisbin, President of the road for the last ten years, and who has managed its affairs with singular sagacity and skill.

What Scranton lacks in *antiquity*, is compensated for in the design of the original village; in its fine streets, laid out with great regularity, and illuminated with gas —in its ample water works, supplying the purest water from the upper Nay-aug—in its street railroads, which traverse every portion of the city—in its free schools, surpassed by none in the State ; in its churches, representing so great a diversity of religious sentiment, in the magnificence or the modesty of their structures, that "none need fall among thorns or thieves;" in its doctors of medicine, sheltered by broad Latin diplomas, which all the dictionaries in the Vatican would not enable them to read, skilled in the wherewithal to heal the sick and invigorate the feeble; in its clever lawyers, blustering when opposed, and ever ready to mystify and perplex the simplest matter for a fee; in its doctors of divinity who, learned in biblical affairs, are ever ready

> "By apostolic blows and knocks
> To show *their* doctrine orthodox;"

in fact, by the general intelligence and thrift of its inhabitants everywhere observed within its borders. Wyoming Valley, worthy of the fame it has acquired the world over, boasts of its gray obelisk with an honest pride,—of its shire town, filled with elegance, wealth, and intelligence, deriving much of its celebrity from being the residence of some of the finest lawyers in the State, with its streets shaded by long lines of stately elms; and yet it lacks the marvelous and irresistible business impulse which makes up the enchantment of Scranton City. Located in the very midst of unbounded mineral wealth, it will naturally exact tribute from the surrounding country by the aid of the numerous railroads entering within its limits, until the villages that begirt it now will expand and commingle and involuntarily become merged into one of the greatest cities of the State.

THE DICKSON MANUFACTURING COMPANY.

The *first stationary steam-engine* used in the valley of the Lackawanna, between Carbondale and Wilkes Barre, where now no less than *five hundred* daily vindicate the name of Stephenson, was put up in the rolling-mill in Scranton in 1847.

The valley, at this time, had just become an object of desire and competition, which led to its more energetic development. One of the results of that development which has aspired to make Scranton the great commercial manufacturing emporium, is visible in the existence and operations of the Dickson Manufacturing Company, which was organized in 1856.

This company, with a capital of $500,000, absorbing the "Cliff Works" and "Planing Mill" adjoining it in

Scranton, and the large foundery and machine-shops of Messrs. Lanning and Marshall at Wilkes Barre, gives steady employment to nearly a thousand men.

Not only is its business immense in volume, but so diversified in its general character, that the huge, stationary engine that throbs its lay upon the Moosic, or the locomotive plowing the plain below—the mining machinery, and every mechanical contrivance that can be wrought from iron or wood by the skill of the artisan engaged in the works of this company, all promise a measure of future prominence and remuneration, creditable alike to mechanical genius, and its happy concentration and encouragement by Thomas Dickson, the President of this young, opulent association.

The following is a list of physicians who have, at one time or another, lived and practiced their profession within the area now embraced by the chartered limits of Scranton City :—

LACKAWANNA VALLEY.

Names.	Where Settled.	When Settled.	When Left.	Died.	Remarks.
Dr. Joseph Davis	Slocum Hollow	1800		1830	Dr. Davis originally settled near [Spring Brook.
" Orlo Hamlin	Providence	1813	1815		
" Silas B. Robinson	"	1823		1860	
" Daniel Seavers	"	1834	1837		
" Hiram Blois	"	1839	1840		
" Joseph Osgood	"	1839	1841		
" Benjamin H. Throop	"	1840			Now resides in Scranton.
" William H. Pier	Hyde Park	1845			Now resides in Scranton.
" Gideon Underwood	Harrison	1845	1845		Pittston.
" Nehemiah Hanford	Providence	1846	1846	1847	
" Horace Hollister	"	1846			
" William E. Rogers	Scranton	1849	1858		
" Henry Roberts	Providence	1850			
" Julian N. Wilson	Dunmore	1850	1853		
" John B. Sherrerd	Scranton	1851		1853	
" George W. Masser	"	1852			Surgeon in Army Potomac.
" Bennet A. Bouton	Providence	1852			Removed to Scranton, 1867. Pres.
" Johnathan Leverett	Scranton	1853	1854		[Med Society.
" John P. Kluge	"	1853	1853		
" George B. Seamons	Dunmore	1853	1865		Removed to Scranton, 1868.
" Augustus Davis	Scranton	1854			Hyde Park, Surgeon in Army.
" Lucius French	Hyde Park	1854	1859		
" George B. Boyd	Scranton	1854			
" William E. Allen	Hyde Park	1855			
" Ralph A. Squires	Scranton	1855			Asst. ex-Surgeon, 1865, Prov. Marsh, [office, Scranton.
" S. Burton Sturdevant	Providence	1856			Surgeon to the 84th Pa. Reg. during
" Asa H. Brundage	Scranton	1856	1858		Candor, N. Y. [the war.
" Albert M. Capwell	Dunmore	1856	1860		Resides at Factoryville, Pa.
" F. Bodeman	Scranton	1856			
" William Frothingham	"	1857	1861		New York.
" John W. Gibbs	Hyde Park	1857			
" Isaac Cohen	Scranton	1857	1858		Jewish Rabbi, Scranton.
" N. F. Marsh	"	1857	1860	1867	
" Charles Marr	"	1857		1865	Asst. ex-Surgeon, 1864-5, in Scran-
" Erastus W. Wells	"	1858	1859		[ton.
" William Green	"	1859	1862		
" E. B. Evens	Hyde Park	1859			
" W. H. Heath	"	1859			
" Thomas Stewart	Scranton	1860			
" J. M. Fox	"	1860	1865		
" Horace Ladd	"	1860			
" F. Wagner	"	1861	1867		Wilkes Barre.
" Wm. Gelhaar	"	1861	1867		
" P. H. Moody	"	1862	1867		Ex-Surg. dur'g the war, at Scranton.
" Willoughby W. Gibbs	Providence	1865			Coroner, Luzerne County.
" Peter Winters	Dunmore	1865			
" S. P. Reed	"	1865	1868		Scranton.
" John W. Robathan	Hyde Park	1865			
" N. Y. Leet	Scranton	1866			Surgeon during the war, 76th Reg.
" A. W. Burns	"	1866			[Pa. Vols.
" Harper B. Lackey	Providence	1867			
" J. B. Benton	Scranton	1867			
" C. H. Fisher	"	1887			
" L. F. Everhart	"	1867			
" N. B. Roberts	Hyde Park	1867			Surgeon 8th and 16th Pa. Cavalry.
" — McGinlie	Scranton	1867			
" William Barnes	"	1867			
" William Haggerty	"	1867			
" J. Williams	Providence	1868			

HOMEOPATHISTS.

Names.	Located.	Arrived.	Left.
Dr. A. P. Gardner	Scranton	1854	1859
" — Reynolds	"	1855	1855
" A. P. Hunt	"	1858	1862
" C. A. Stevens	"	1862	
" A. E. Burr	"	1865	1868
" J. S. Walter	"	1868	
Drs. Clark & Ricardo	"	1868	
Dr. Sidney A. Campbell	"	1868	

The superior or relative *status* of Providence and Scranton as business villages, five-and-twenty years ago, is plainly apparent in the enumerated list of medical and legal gentlemen, who, to advance their fortunes or achieve reputation, chose the former place for a residence, because of its real as well as its expected importance.

Lawyers who have for a longer or shorter period lived and practiced law within the city limits of Scranton :—

Names.	Original location.	When Admitted.	Remarks.
Lewis Jones, Jr.	Carbondale	August 5, 1834	Now of Scranton.
Charles H. Silkman	Providence	January 1, 1838	"
Peter Byrne	Carbondale	August 3, 1846	"
J. Marion Alexander	Providence	August 4, 1846	Kansas.
Elliot S. M. Hill	"	April 5, 1847	First May'r of Scranton.
David R. Randall	"	November 4, 1847	Late District Att'y Luzerne Co.
Daniel Rankins	"	August 7, 1850	Clerk of the Court.
Washington G. Ward	Hyde Park	November 10, 1851	
Samuel Sherrerd	Scranton	April 4, 1853	
Edward Merrifield	Hyde Park	August 6, 1855	
George Sanderson	Scranton	Sept. 14, 1857	Founder of Green Ridge.
*Ezra B. Chase	"	April 7, 1857	
Edward N. Willard	"	Nov. 17, 1857	Register in the Dist. Court of the U. S., for the Western District of Pa.
George D. Haugawout	"	January 18, 1858	
Wm. H. Pratt	"	January 4, 1859	
David C. Harrington	"	May 7, 1860	
Alfred Hand	"	May 8, 1860	Notary Public.
Frederick L. Hitchcock	"	May 16, 1860	
John Handley	"	August 21, 1860	
Aretus H. Winton	"	August 22, 1860	Notary Public.
Corydon H. Wells	Hyde Park	August 30, 1860	
Frederic Fuller	Scranton	Nov. 13, 1860	
W. Gibson Jones	"	April 1, 1861	
Charles Du Pont Breck	"	August 18, 1861	
Aaron A. Chase	"	August 20, 1862	
Zebulon M. Ward	"	August 17, 1863	
James Mahon	"	Jan. 6, 1865	Dist. Att'y Scranton.
M. J. Byrne	"	Dec. 5, 1866	
Francis D. Collins	"	Dec. 24, 1866	
Francis E. Loomis	"	Feb. 20, 1866	
Daniel Hannah	"	Feb. 21, 1867	
Jeremiah D. Regan	"	August 19, 1867	
Lewis M. Bunell	"	—— 1867	
J. M. C. Ranch	"		
Isaac J. Post	"		
Charles G. Van Fleet F. E. Gunstur, Wm. Stanton.	"	Sept. 21, 1868	

* Deceased.

BLAKELEY.

"This township was called Blakeley from respect to the memory of Captain Johnston Blakeley, who commanded the United States sloop of war *Wasp*, and who signalized himself in an engagement with the British sloop *Avon*."[1] It was formed in April, 1818, from "a part of Providence, including a corner of Greenfield, east of Lackawanna mountain."[2] It embraced Ragged Island (now Carbondale) and the lands of the Delaware and Hudson Canal Company, then brought into value by William and Maurice Wurts.

During the Revolutionary war, a bridle-path, afterward leading through Rixe's Gap into the county of Wayne, marked by trees, was made by the trapper and hunter, but no settlement was attempted within its yet unmeasured boundaries, until comparative tranquillity came to Wyoming and Lackawanna in 1786. In the summer of this year, Timothy Stevens, a war-worn veteran from Westchester, New York, who had served in the long struggle with courage and credit, moved into the Blakeley woods with his family. No Indian clearing was found, and but the vague trace of the deserted wigwam appeared on the bank of the stream, where he encamped and began a clearing for his home. Here, overshadowed by forest, where the pulse of the great world only throbbed in storms and winds, he uprolled his cabin from the rough timber felled, and lived many years with his family alone. In 1814, he erected a grist-mill upon the Lackawanna, subsequently known as "Mott's mill," the *debris* of which can yet be seen by the road-side, above the village of Price.

There came a strange character here in 1795, about whom for a time there was great mystery. He carried a gold snuff-box, from which he incessantly inspired his

---
[1] Chapman.   [2] Court Records.

nose, wore an olive velvet coat, was a man of considerable literary attainment; exhibiting a good deal of

"Grandeur's remains and gleams of other days,"

He had been a German merchant in Hamburg, received a classical education, and was withal a clever linguist. His name was Nicholas Leuchens. A man of culture, fond of display in early life, he expended a thousand pounds sterling at his wedding. He left his native shore to escape conscription, landed in Philadelphia, in August, 1795, and departed at once for Wyoming Valley, just emerged from internal discord. Reaching Wyoming, he strolled up the Lackawanna to the present location of Pecktown, where he established the first log-structure upon these exuberant lowlands. This was thirteen years previous to the formation of Blakeley into a township, and Leuchens was at this time the only inhabitant in this portion of Providence, with the exception of Stevens, living a mile or two down the valley. Finding no owner for the land, he took possession of about five hundred acres, of which he never acquired a title. Here rose his plain habitation, roofed with boughs and barks, containing but a single room, in which he piled successive layers of beds almost to the very roof, so as better to repel the approach of ghosts, ever inspiring him with special dread. In the winter of 1806, he taught a district school in the old jail-house, in Wilkes Barre, and one of his pupils[1] thus describes the school-house. On a little basin of water, called "Yankee Pond," lying back of the school-house, there was good skating after a cold snap, which the boys in their rustic freedom regarded as a healthier developer, both of muscle and mind, than the musty lore he aimed to inculcate. Leuchens had little control over his school; the larger boys starting off to skate without permission, assent would be given to others to follow, recruit after recruit

[1] Anson Goodrich

would be sent in vain after the delinquent pupils until none were left to do homage to the master. Vexed at his roguish and boisterous scholars, he would visit the skating pond himself. Being sixty years of age, and near-sighted at that, his appearance was greeted with a storm of snow-balls, which he was unable to restrain or trace to the mischievous authors.

The mental power and the forcep-like grasp of the German trader distinguishing him in other days, forsook him on his farm, with his fortune; he grew aimless, indolent, and disheartened, returned to Philadelphia, where he died, and was buried by the hand of charity.

Upon the road-side from Providence to Carbondale, between the village of Price and the Lackawanna, can be seen an orchard in the meadow where John Vaughn and his sons settled in 1797. One of the pioneers in this year was Elisha S. Potter. Learning of the rich wild lands sold for a song along the Lackawanna, he left his native place, White Hall, N. Y., and sought them. Potter was the first justice of the peace in the township, and so well were the vexatious and harassing duties of the magistrate performed by him, that litigating parties were generally satisfied with his judgment and decisions.

Moses Dolph, the grandfather of Edward Dolph, Esq., with the Ferrises, made a pitch here in 1798. Of the children of Dolph, none are now living.

There were yet no settlers farther up the valley than Leuchens, and sparse and poor indeed were the dwellings intervening toward Wyoming. Mt. Vernon, formerly the residence of Lewis S. Watres, Esq., was cleared and occupied in 1812.

The forbidding aspect of the country along the borders of the forest, the long severe winters, with their prodigious depth of snow, rising often with its long, white lines of drift, to the very tops of the cabins, and the absence of all roads to communicate with the settlement below, imposed upon the inhabitants the most exacting hardships. Markings upon trees along the woods directed the path of the pioneer. No bridge spanned the Lackawanna at this time other than the one at Capoose and Old Forge; all streams were forded, if passed at all. Once swollen by the lengthened rain or spring freshet, all intercourse with the neighborhood was delayed or suspended with as much certainty as when the wintery months rendered crossing formidable.

The earlier inhabitants enjoyed neither churches, school-houses, nor mills. The product of the soil, in the shape of corn and rye, was either mashed by the simple stone or wooden mortar and pestle, or cooked and eaten whole. Bear meat, venison, potatoes, and the scanty salt, comprised the luxuries of the day; potatoes sometimes became so scarce in the spring, that those planted for seed were re-dug in a few instances to sustain a family perishing with hunger.[1]

For many years, wolves were so bold and disastrous in their inroads upon all live stock left exposed at night, that cattle and sheep were driven into high, strong inclosures, around which fires were often lighted after nightfall for greater protection from these abundant animals, whose howl, prolonged with terrible distinctness and frequency at the very door of the cabin, made up one of the exciting features of border life.

Wilkes Barre, Stroudsburg, and Easton, furnished the only stores within a radius of fifty miles, and every spring, after a fine run of sap, was the ox-journey undertaken thither to exchange the maple sirup and sugar for tea, calico, and salt.

For many years, *sweet fern* was substituted for tea; browned rye and indigenous herbs appeared on the table for coffee. The pine knot, or "candle-wood," as the Yankees termed it, cheered the household at night, and blended its light with the friendly shadows of the moon.

---

[1] Moses Vaughn.

In 1824, a post-office was established in Blakeley, and N. Cottrill appointed postmaster.

Between Olyphant and Mr. Ferris's, on the back road running from Olyphant to Archbald, is seen a small clearing on the bank of a creek, with no house or trace of a cabin, occupied as late as 1820 by an Indian half-breed, with his squaw and children, skilled as an "Indian doctor." He never went from home, nor received compensation for his cures only in the shape of presents; and yet, in the low moss-covered cabin hid away in the edge of the forest, he received many visits from the credulous ones in the valley. He died soon afterward.

Blakeley has no scrap of local history. Originally embracing the primitive coal-works of the Delaware and Hudson Canal Company, its prosperity has steadily kept pace with the advancement of this company, until the villages of Archbald, Olyphant, and Rushdale, have gathered a population of hardy, industrious thousands, at whose touch the anthracite has been awakened from its dream and sent its allegiance from the wood-side down to the shore of the sea.

Peckville is prettily situated on the Lackawanna, does a snug lumber business, while its inhabitants, characterized by intelligence, good-nature, and liberal attachments, never yet have had a single breach in the social relations of the neighborhood.

Jessup, a thriving village in 1855, dwells in the memory of the inhabitants of the valley as a place which started into life with too sanguine expectations of coal mines, railroads, and iron developments, and was thus exposed to a shock fatal to its existence as a town.

One of the first churches in the valley was the Blakeley church. It was raised and inclosed in March, 1832, and remained unfinished for many years. Its completion was hastened by the ironical criticisms of a stranger who, upon passing it, remarked that he "had heard of the *house* of the Lord, but had never before seen his *barn*."

YANKEE WAY OF PULLING A TOOTH.

Long before doctors, armed with lancets and well-filled saddle-bags, went forth in the valley, empowered, like the beast in Revelations, "to kill a fourth part," at least, of those whom they might meet on the way, the more trivial duties of the physician necessarily fell upon the patient himself or the skill of some good-natured neighbor, or perhaps were assumed by some officious doctress, whose roots and "*yarbs*," gathered from meadow and mountain, had such wonderful "*vartu*" in their simple decoctions that no disease could deny or resist. Toothache, rarely treated with the inexorable dignity of turnkey or forceps, vexed many a nervous sufferer by its presence. Sometimes, however, its court was summarily adjourned by a process original, sudden, and cheap.

Among the settlers in Blakeley, at the time spoken of, was a long, lean, bony son of a farmer, troubled with that most provoking of all pains, or, as Burns called it—"thou h—ll o' a' diseases,"—the toothache.

The troublesome member was one of the wide-pronged *molars*, as firm in its socket as if held in a vise. The pain was so acute as it ran along the inflamed gums, that the usual series of manipulations with decoctions and "*int*-ments," alternated with useless swearing, failed to bring relief to the sufferer. As the ache grew keener with torture, a "*remejil*" agent was suggested and tried. One end of a firm hemp string was fastened upon the rebellious member, while the other, securely fixed to a bullet, purposely notched, was placed in the barrel of an old flint-lock musket, loaded with an extra charge of powder. When all was ready, the desperate operator caught hold of the gun and "let drive." Out flew the tooth from the bleeding jaw, and away bounded the musket several feet.

After this new way of extracting teeth had thus been demonstrated by one so simple and unskilled in the dental science, it became at once the chosen and only mode practiced here for many years.

THOMAS SMITH.

Among other resolute pioneers who sought the shores of the Susquehanna in 1783, appears the name of Thomas Smith, grandsire of the late T. Smith, Esq., of Abington.

On the east side of the river below Nanticoke, he laid the foundation for his future home. The great ice freshet of 1784, which bore down from the upper waters of the Susquehanna such vast masses of ice, overflowing the plains and destroying the property along the river, swept his farm of all its harvest product, leaving it with little else than its gullied soil. Hardly had his recuperative energies again made cheerful his fireside, when the "pumpkin freshet," as it was called, from the countless number of pumpkins it brought down the swollen river, again inundated its banks, sweeping away houses, barns, mills, fences, stacks of hay and grain, cattle, flocks of sheep, and droves of swine, in the general destruction, and spreading desolation where but yesterday autumn promised abundance.

Smith, not stoic enough to receive the visits of such floods with indifference, moved up in the "gore" (now Lackawanna Township) in 1786, "for," said the old gentleman, "I want to get above high-water mark."

His son, Deodat, intermarried with the Allsworth family in Dunmore, from whom sprung a large family of children.

THE SETTLEMENT OF ABINGTON.[1]

Of the highlands of Abington, lying between the Susquehanna River and the Lackawanna, now rendered productive by a comely and industrious people, little was known by the white man at the beginning of the

---

[1] Named from Abington, Connecticut.

century, else that its wild thresholds were crossed by the Indians' pathway from Capoose village to Oquago, N. Y.

In 1790 a party of trappers, consisting of three persons, penetrated the wilderness where now spreads out the rich sloping farm of the late Elder Miller, with a view of making a settlement, as trapping grew dull and furs became scarce. Here they felled the underbrush and a few of the forest trees, rolled them into a cabin roofed with boughs, while the great crevices, liberally seamed with wedges of wood and mud, imparted to the new structure a Hottentot appearance. Their provisions having become exhausted, and bear meat losing its relish, they shouldered their guns and traps before the close of summer and abandoned the enterprise, so that no permanent settlement was made until 1794. In the spring of this year Stephen Parker, Thomas Smith, Deacon Clark, and Ephraim Leach, father of E. Leach, Esq., of Providence, led by the intrepid John Miller, on foot, slung their packs and guns over their shoulders, and with ax in hand, first marked and widened this ancient pathway of the wild man through the mountain gap, known as Leggett's. This gap, in the low range of the Moosic, offered then, as now, the only natural eastern outlet to the township of Abington. Before the work was completed, it was abandoned because of the unvarying obstruction offered by trees to the passage of a cart or wagon, and the declivity rising from Leggett's Creek abruptly into the very mountain. The slighter depression in the range, half a mile south of Leggett's Gap, was then selected for a wagon road, even with the disadvantages of its treble height. In 1791 encroachments were made upon the warriors' path through the notch for the passage of a wagon, when the mountain road relapsed again into forest.

Near the location of the present grist-mill of Humphreys, the white man's clearing first emerged from the Abingtonian woods. This was made by Ebenezer Leach, who afterward sold out his right at this point, and moved down in the vicinity of Leggett's Gap, where he soon became a tenant of a small, low, log-cabin, remarkable only for its rude simplicity. A clearing was niched out upon the slope of a hill, where the corn soon sprouted from the fresh burned fallow, and the pumpkins, with their yellow sides and rounded faces, threw a Yankee and domestic look over a region naturally rugged and lonely.

Corn once raised and husked, was either cracked in stone or wooden mortars, for the brown mush, or carried in back-loads down to the corn-mill in Slocum Hollow, to be ground. Sometimes, when the snow was deep or drifted, the journey was made to the mill upon the slow and cumbrous snow-shoe.

The utter solitude of Leggett's Gap, interrupted only by the screech of the panther or the cry of the wolf, as they sprang along its sides with prodigious leaps, made even the trip to mill perilous in the cold season of the year.

"Many a time," said Leach, "have I passed through the notch, with my little grist on my shoulder, holding in my hand a large club, which I kept swinging fiercely, to keep away the wolves growling around me; and to my faithful club, often bitten and broken when I reached home, have I apparently been indebted for my life." At length he hit upon a plan promising exemption from their attacks.

Being told that they were afraid of the sound of iron, he obtained from the valley below, a saw-mill saw. To this he attached a strong withe, by which he drew the saw by one hand over a trail or road, as yet unconscious of the dignity of a sled or a wheel, making a tinkling alternately so sharp and soft as it bounded over a stone or plunged into a root as to inspire them at once with fear so great that his passage was only interrupted after this by their indignant growls.

During one of his mill trips to Capoose, a timid fawn

being pursued closely by two wolves, ran up to him, and placed its head between the legs of Leach to seek protection from its half-starved pursuers. This was done in a manner so abrupt and hurried, as to first convey to the *rider* a knowledge of the chase. The wolves came up with a bound, within a short distance of where the fearless arm interposed for the trembling animal, and, giving one ferocious view of their white, sharpened teeth, crouched away to their retreats.

So frightened had the fawn become, that not until the path opened distinctly upon the clearing of Leach, could it be induced to leave the side of its protector.

Deer and elk, at that period, thronged along the mountains in such numbers that droves often could be seen browsing upon saplings or lazily basking in the noonday sun.

The *Moose*, from which the mountain range bordering the Lackawanna derived its name of MOOSIC, were found here in vast numbers by the earliest explorers in the Lackawanna Valley. The clearing of Mr. Leach subsequently embraced the Indian salt spring, mentioned heretofore.

Parker and Smith located upon land north of this, while Clark, drawn by the delicious landscape of Abington's fairest mount, plunged into the woods, where now thrives a village honoring his memory, in the preservation of the name—Clark's Green.

On the summit of the hill commanding such a sweep of mountain, meadow, lowland, and ravine, as stretches to the eye turned to the south or the east, there then stood the straight pine and the shaggy hemlock, interspersed with the maple and the beech, where was erected the original dwelling-place of Deacon Clark. It was a substantial compact of unhewn logs, notched deep at either end, placed together regardless of beauty or timber. The floor came from ask-plank, full of slivers, unaided by the saw or plane—the keen ax alone being responsible for smoothness and finish. It was, withal, a comfortable affair built in the wood-side, some 1,300 feet above tidewater ; but energetic, contented, and industrious, the old gentleman passed under its humble roof many a pleasant hour in the long evenings of autumn, when the hearth glowed with the crackling fire, while his daily duties were to give thrift and culture to one of the finest farms in Abington.

John Lewis, James and Ezra Dean, Job Tripp, Robert Stone, Ezra Wall, and Geo. Gardner, also settled in the new region the same year. Job settled in the western portion of Abington while it possessed all its native ruggedness. Most of those who had plunged here in this old forest, were, like those who had commenced along the Lackawanna, so poor as to be unable to pay for their land, until from the soil, they could, by their honest industry and frugal management, raise the necessary means. Not so, however, with Job ; he had a little money, and was determined to make the most of it. He purchased a grindstone and brought it into Abington, which for six years was the only one here. This he fenced in with stout saplings, allowing no one to grind upon it unless they paid him a stipulated sum, and turned the stone themselves. This enterprise, although it was comprehensive in its design, and brought to his barricaded grindstone one or two dull axes a week of the toiling chopper, could not bring into play all the energies of his mind, so he fenced in much of the woods by falling trees, for a *deer-pen* or park, into which, after the deer had wandered for his morning browse, or had been driven by Job, the passage to the pen was closed, when the deer was to be slain, and dried venison and buckskin were to effect such a revolution in the commercial aspect of Abington, and he was to be the Midas who had brought it. The chase over the acres he had thus fenced proved more invigorating to his stomach than beneficial to his pocket, and the project of the old man died with him a few years later, marked only by the remaining *débris* of the fence yet seen around "Hickory Ridge."

Elder John Miller, a man alike eminent for his long services as a minister, and his virtues as a man, settled in Abington in 1802. He was born February 3, 1775, in Windham, Connecticut. Young, hopeful, and robust, he emigrated to the inland acres of Abington, where, for half a century, identified intimately with its local and general history, he gave cheer and character to society around him as much as the brook crossing the meadow imparts a deeper shade and more luxuriant herbage to its banks. The great influence he exerted over the people of the township up until the very day of his death, in February, 1857, in keeping alive the spirit of improvement, husbandry, and morality, can yet be observed along the farms of his neighbors, in the enterprise, intelligence, industry, customs, and habits of the yeomanry of Abington. Previous to the coming of Mr. Miller to "The Beech," as Abington was designated until the formation of the township in 1806, few had inclined toward its rigorous domain. He located upon the spot marked and vacated by the trappers twelve years before, purchased three hundred and twenty-six acres of land for *forty dollars*—$20 in silver, $10 in the customary tender of *maple-sugar*, and $10 in tin-ware.

The only store in the county of Luzerne was kept in Wilkes Barre by Hollenback & Fisher, offering a variety surpassed by the ordinary pack of the modern peddler of to-day. At this store, Elder Miller was furnished with the necessary tin, which he manufactured into such ware as the county called for.

Almost simultaneously with his arrival, he began to preach the gospel and "turn many to righteousness." During this long five-and-fifty years of spiritual labor, he married nine hundred and twelve couples, baptized (immersed) two thousand persons, and preached the enormous number of eighteen hundred funeral sermons before he was called to receive his reward on high. It was rare to witness a funeral in the valley when the elder was in his prime, and find absent from the mournful gathering his frank, friendly face, ever full of words of comfort and kind reminiscence of the dead.

For a period of twelve years he officiated in the valley as the only clergyman laboring here of *any* denomination.

Being a practical surveyor withal, there are few farms in the northern portion of Luzerne County he did not traverse while tracing and defining their boundaries. His wife —an estimable lady—was the fifth white woman living in Abington. Elder Miller, although he held his own plow and fed his own cattle, was the great representative of Abington, whose various qualifications to counsel and console, whose characteristic desire to do good, whose benevolence of heart, grave but kind deportment as a man of the world or the adviser of his flock, gave him an ascendency in the affections of the community attained by few.

While he has passed away, he left behind him in manuscripts events of his life, and incidents in the early history and growth of Abington, whose publication could not fail to interest all who knew him, and recall to the mind of the reader the gray head and kindly greetings of a man whose age, calm, deliberate air, whose venerable and unquestioned piety, and whose great sympathy in the hour of sorrow, made him one of the most remarkable persons ever living in Abington.

This township was the twelfth one formed in the county of Luzerne, and is sixty-three years old. At the Court of Quarter Sessions, held at Wilkes Barre, August, 1806, Abington was formed from a part of Tunkhannock, "Beginning at the southwest corner of Nicholson township, thence south nine and three-quarter miles east to Wayne County, thence by Wayne County line north nine and three-quarter miles," etc.

The original inhabitants were from Connecticut and

Rhode Island; and even now, after the lapse of over half a century with its mutations, the stern morality, the honest industry, and the social virtues literally impressed upon the hills of the parent State, are distributed and distinguished among their descendants. Although no evidence of coal or iron exhibits itself within the boundaries of Abington, it furnishes one of the *best* farming and grazing areas found in the county of Luzerne.

The only *colored* feature in the picture of Abington is a colony of negroes, which, in spite of the double disadvantage of prejudice and hereditary indolence, has drawn from the frosty hills thereabout the wherewithal to sustain animation in a very creditable manner.

ELIAS SCOTT, THE HUNTER.

Daniel Scott emigrated to the Lackawanna in 1792. His son Elias was widely known throughout the country forty years ago, as a successful Nimrod, but the encroachments of civilized life crowded the forest world from his reach with the same remorseless force that the Indians have been rolled up and frenzied to the very base of the Rocky Mountains.

Some years ago, while he was standing near the Wyoming House, in Scranton, in an apparently thoughtful and sorrowful mood, the writer asked him what was the matter.

"Matter! matter!" he exclaimed, as he looked up with a sigh, and pointed his wilted hand and hickory cane toward the depots. "See how the tarnal rascals have spiled the hunting-grounds where I've killed many a bear and deer."

In the autumn months he would take long hunting-jaunts, sometimes being absent a week from his home. Upon his left hand appeared unmistakable evidence of an encounter with a bear many years ago, while out upon such an excursion on Stafford Meadow Brook, running through the southern portion of Scranton. Encamped at night among the willows on the border of the run, with his leather knapsack for a pillow, his belt, keen knife, and long, heavy rifle for his companions, where the glare of his camp-fire startled the fawn as it browsed along the mountain side, or was chased by the wolf or more bloodthirsty panther down into the valley, he met old bruin at daybreak, as his bearship was gathering berries for his morning lunch. His organs of digestion, however, did not relish the tickling sensation of the bullet thrown from Scott's rifle, and he immediately approached the hunter with all the familiarity and warmth of an old friend, until he came frightfully close. Scott, declining his advances, retreated as rapidly as possible from the wounded and enraged brute, and by the frequent punches of his gun, now empty and broken, avoided the embraces of the bear. Walking backward from the animal, the heel of his boot caught in a treacherous root of a tree, and he fell to the ground. Before he could raise himself again, commenced the death-struggle. Bruin sprang on the hunter with such violence as to rupture an internal blood-vessel, and for a moment the copious flow of blood from his mouth threatened suffocation. Smarting with the wound of the bullet, the bear seized the left hand of Scott in his mouth, as it was uplifted to divert attention from his throat, while with his right arm he drew from his belt the well-tried trusty knife. This he plunged repeatedly into the bear, until, exhausted from the loss of blood, he fell dead on the mangled hunter.

Hunters then lived a life of plenty, for game of all kinds was so abundant at that period, that in the course one year's casual hunting, Scott killed one hundred and seventy-five deer, five bears, three wolves, and a panther, besides wild turkeys in great numbers. He has killed and dressed eleven deer in one day, three of them being slain at *one* shot.

Mr. Scott informed the writer that many years ago, finding a rattlesnake den on the upper waters of Spring Brook, he killed seven hundred and fifty of the reptiles in a single day; the next day he slew three hundred and seventy-five more; making a total of *thirteen hundred and twenty-five* of the bright occupants of the rocks thus fraternizing in this snake castle or rendezvous, and destroyed by the hand of a single man. He died in the summer of 1867.

EARLY HISTORY OF THE SETTLEMENT OF "DRINKER'S BEECH," NOW COVINGTON.

As the dweller in wigwams turned his footsteps toward the setting sun, in search of hunting-grounds better stocked than the Pocono, he left behind him no region more wild than the section of country lying between the Delaware and the Lackawanna, known as Drinker's Beech—a name made popular by the vast number of beech-trees growing upon lands owned by Drinker. No attention of the white man was directed to the tract until 1787. During this year, and that of 1791, Henry Drinker, Sr., of Philadelphia, father of the late Henry W. and Richard Drinker, purchased from the State some twenty-five thousand acres of unseated land in the Beech, now embraced by Wayne, Pike, and Luzerne counties. An effort was made in 1788 to turn this purchase to some practical account by opening a highway through the lands. It failed for want of means. Four years later, John Delong, a hardy woodsman of Stroudsburg, was employed, with other persons, to mark or cut a wagon-road to these beechen possessions, from at or near the twenty-one-mile tree on the north and south road, which was also called the Drinker road, from the fact that it was opened principally at the expense of Henry Drinker, Sr., who was an uncle of Henry Drinker, Jr., and was withal a large landholder in the more northern portion of the State.

The road cut by Delong extended in a westerly direction, passed that romantic sheet of water, Lake Henry, crossed the present track of the Delaware, Lackawanna, and Western Railroad, and thence taking a southerly course, terminated on a small branch of the Lehigh, called Bell Meadow Brook, near the old Indian encampment before mentioned, upon the edge of this run.

After the return of the choppers, the road grew full of underbrush, and forbade passage to all but the hunter and his game. In reopening it, in 1821, the name of "Henry Drinker, 1792," was found rudely carved upon a tree.

The late Ebenezer Bowman, Esq., of Wilkes Barre, was employed to pay taxes upon these lands as late as 1813, after which time Henry W. Drinker, as the agent, offered them for sale and settlement.

In the spring of this year, Henry Drinker, Sr., with his sons, Henry W. and Richard Drinker, visited Stoddartsville—a faint village brought into being by the late John Stoddard, who, being an alien, was impelled from the city of Philadelphia to a tract of land embracing the Great Falls on the Lehigh, where his lumbering operations eventuated into a village of considerable note in the days of the stage-coach over Wilkes Barre Mountain.

As the southern portion of the Drinker lands lay on the Lehigh and its upper tributaries, about twelve miles northeast of Stoddartsville, it was decided to open a communication to them from that place by a road nearly following the course of the river, if the same was found at all practicable.

Previous, however, to running any line of road, H. W. Drinker determined to ascend that stream in a small canoe or skiff, up to the very mouth of Wild Meadow Brook— now called "Mill Creek." This the old hunters and sturdy woodsmen declared impossible, as the stream in one place was completely closed by a compact body of drift-wood of very large size and great extent, on the top of which a considerable strata of vegetable and earthy matter had accumulated, and brushwood was growing luxuriantly; in other places there were swift and narrow rapids, beaver dams, and alder and laurel, twisted and interwoven over the very current in such a manner that it seemed as if no boat could ascend the Lehigh, unless carried upon shoulders the greater portion of the way, as the bark canoes of the Indians were sometimes taken. Notwithstanding these discouraging representations, by offering high wages, a resolute set of axmen were at length engaged to undertake this truly formidable task, and after the expenditure of no little energy and money, accompanied with some of the *hardest swearing* among the choppers, a boat channel to the desired point was opened in the course of two months.

The first encampment of the Messrs. Drinkers, with their choppers, was near the mouth of Wild Meadow Brook, where they erected a bark cabin, or shed, open in front and at the sides, and sloping back to the ground. Each man was furnished with a blanket, in which he rolled himself up at night, and while a large crackling fire blazed in front of the cabin without, the soft hemlock boughs within furnished invigorating repose after the fatiguing labors of the day. Now and then, they were annoyed by the serenade of a school of owls, attracted to the camp by the strange glare of the fire, or the piercing scream of the sleepless panther, watching the intruders; in damp, rainy weather, by the bite of gnats or "punks," as they were termed. Trout and venison were so abundant around them, that an hour's fish or hunt supplied the cabin for a week with food.

This encampment was made in 1815, when this new avenue along the Lehigh was sometimes used for boating and running logs. Provisions and boards were taken up the stream from Stoddartsville in a large bateau drawn by a tough old mare, hitched to the bow with a plow harness, and with a setting pole to assist her when there was a tight pull, and push *en derrière* when the speed slackened too much to suit the *Rear*-Admiral, as the hands called the driver and owner of the animal; sometimes swimming through deep beaver-dams, or scrambling along the narrow, rocky passes and rapids, to the astonishment of otters, minks, and muskrats, the soft-furred inhabitants of the banks of the stream.

> "And if a beaver lingered there,
> It must have made the rascal stare,
> To see the swimming of the mare."

In the summer of 1814, these lands were resurveyed by Jason Torrey, Esq., of Bethany, Wayne County, into lots averaging one hundred acres each. Lots were sold at five dollars per acre, on five years' credit, the first two years without interest; payment to be made in lumber, shingles, labor, stock, produce, or *any thing* the farmer offered or had to spare.

The first clearing was made in Drinker's settlement, in 1815, by the late H. W. Drinker, on a ridge of land, where he built a log-house, about a quarter of a mile south of the spot long adorned by his later residence.

During the year 1816 a road was surveyed and opened from the Wilkes Barre and Easton Turnpike, at a point about half a mile above Stoddartsville, to the north and south road, near the Wallenpaupack bridge, a distance of some thirty miles. This road is also known as the old Drinker road.

At the Court of Quarter Sessions, held at Wilkes Barre in 1818, Covington was formed out of a part of Wilkes Barre, embracing the whole of Drinker's possession. "In honor of Brigadier-General Covington, who gallantly fell at the battle of Williamsburg, in Upper Canada, the court call this township Covington."[1] H. W. Drinker being an intimate friend of General Covington, this name was given to the new township at his suggestion.

[1] Court Records, 1818.

Among the earlier settlers were John Wragg, Michael Mitchell, Lawrence Dershermer, Ebenezer Covey, John and William Ross, John and George Fox, John and Lewis Stull, Samuel Wilohick, Archippus Childs, John Lafrance, John Genthu, Henry Ospuck, John Fish, David Dale, Edward Wardell, John Thompson, Mathew Hodson, Peter Rupert, Wesley Hollister, John Besecker, Jacob Swartz, Nathaniel Carter, Samuel Buck, Richard Edwards, John Koons, and Barnabas Carey.

The Philadelphia and Great Bend Turnpike, originated by Drinker, whose name it still bears, was the first to gain admittance into the valley from the east as a public highway. This turnpike commenced at the Belmont and Easton road, some three miles above Stanhope, and ran thence a northerly course to the Susquehanna and Great Bend Turnpike, at a point near Ithamar Mott's tavern, in Susquehanna County.

The charter for this road, over sixty miles of vast inland frontier, was obtained in 1819, but the State, willing to foster an enterprise promising to enlarge its development and dignity, had so little faith in the civilizing advantages of this proposed road that it favored it with the limited subscription of only $12,000. The balance of the stock was taken by the Messrs. Drinkers, Clymer, Meredith, and other wealthy landholders. Drinker, who located the road, superintended its general construction, and was elected president of the company.

The four villages, Moscow, Dunning, Dalesville, and Turnersville, diversifying the agricultural centers among the hills and dales of the Beech, are all increasing in population and importance, and yet have ample room for expansion.

SETTLEMENT OF JEFFERSON.

Although Jefferson Township was only formed in 1836, from Providence, its settlement dates back to 1784, when Asa Cobb, taking advantage of the repose succeeding the

Revolution, located his cabin, and made a clearing at the foot of one of the larger and steeper elevations, deriving its name from him, Cobb's Mountain, as it sends down its steep slope to the old Connecticut road crossing the range at this high point. This cabin, offering its unwavering hospitality to friend or foe from Wyoming, was the primitive structure in Jefferson, and its former location is indicated by the mansion of his great-grandson, Asa Cobb. Between the solitary dwelling in Dunmore and the clearing at Little Meadows, in Wayne County, a distance of sixteen miles eastward, the cabin of Mr. Cobb was for many years the only one intervening. In 1795 Mr. Potter chopped a place for his home in the extreme eastern border of the township and county, upon a tributary of the Wallenpaupack issuing from Cobb's Pond.

Jefferson has achieved no local history of interest, yet its uplands were once familiar to the savage clans crossing from the Delaware to their Wyoming villages. Upon the very summit of the mountain, north of the old Cobb house, the camp and signal fires of the Indian often rose, as the hunter or warrior gathered around the resinous logs, while the flames of the fire glowing high and red among the tree-tops, were visible miles away to the eastward. At an early period, a large number of Indian implements, to smite an enemy or secure the game, were found commingled with the *débris* of these upraised encampments. The township is sparsely settled, and generally covered with timber, yet in spite of its altitude, it possesses a few farms of surprising fertility and beauty.

The Moosic or Cobb's Mountain, interposing its granite bowlders between Jefferson and the Lackawanna, has shut off all traces of coal formation, yet a coal mine was discovered *east* of this range, a quarter of a century ago, by a voluble, inventive genius, who was promised a farm by the owner of the land, should the explorer find coal in a certain locality. Making an excavation deep in the mountain side, he actually toiled weeks in *carrying* upon his shoulder baskets of anthracite for a distance of six miles before the blackened appearance of the drift gave satisfactory evidence of the existence of coal. The owner of this supposed coal property, always liberal in his gifts, cheered by his good luck in the discovery, promptly deeded a tract of land, from his many thousand acres, as a reward to the finder, who, like the kind-hearted possessor, lived long to join in the laugh at the joke.

The country east and southward of Cobb's, alternating with forest and meadow, possesses much of the gloom natural to the primitive wilderness in America when trodden by the warriors. Wild beasts, to a certain extent, inhabit the ravines and woods extending from this point to the head-waters of the Lehigh over the Shades of Death, on the Pocono, and haunt in places less accessible to the footsteps of the hunter, making now and then such demonstrations upon the farmers' sheep-pens as to satisfy the fastidious that the keen, frosty air of the mountain imparts a keener whet to the appetite than *rum*.

The winter of 1835 was one of great length and severity, from the vast quantity of snow which had fallen. It lay upon the ground for many weeks four and five feet in depth on the level, while drifts, crossed only upon snow-shoes, often rose to a prodigious height. Game perished on the mountains in large numbers, and wolves even sought the settlements for food. A gray, lean wolf, thus impelled by hunger, found its way into the barn-yard of the late John Cobb, Esq., in Jefferson, during the winter, while the members of the family, with the exception of Mrs. Cobb, were absent from home. The commotion among the sheep in the yard, some distance from the house, attracted her attention. With a heroism that rose instinctively with the occasion, Mrs. Cobb, though naturally a mild and slender lady, caught the pitchfork in her hand and hurried forth to repel or dispatch the intruder. This was comparatively an easy matter for the brave woman, as the brute, in its starved condition, had become enfeebled, and, although for a moment it turned its lurid eye and long, white, keen teeth upon the assailant, it soon fell a trophy to a woman whose sterling courage, thus displayed, exhibited in a broader and better light the requirements and qualifications of the earlier women of the country. For the scalp of the wolf, Luzerne County paid Mrs. Cobb the usual reward or bounty at that time of ten dollars.

There lived upon a time in Jefferson a man of fair mental endowments, upright and honorable, glib in speech, of unmeasured egotism, whose ambition led him to hope for a division of the great county of Luzerne and the selection of the green plateau of *his* plantation for the county seat. Visions of court-house, jail, and prominence, rose before him as he diffused his convictions among all parties throughout the county with a persistency worthy of success, urging the cutting in twain of its ancient boundaries for the especial good of the Beech and Jefferson, offering land gratuitously for the public buildings; and, as a final unanswerable counterpoise, the old gentleman, in his enthusiasm for his favorite scheme, exclaimed to the writer, "Rather than see the thing fail, I would consent to act as judge myself the first year or two for nothing."

CHASED BY A PANTHER.

To the east of Cobb's clearing, eight or ten miles upon the old Connecticut road, nestles down at the foot of a long hill a tract of low, swampy land, known in the ancient Westmoreland Records by the name of "Little Meadows." Two natural ponds, flooding hundreds of acres, lying a mile apart, divided by a strip of wild meadow-land grown over with coarse grass and willows, afforded the earliest pioneers to Wyoming a place to cheer their cattle with food, and led to the adoption of the name. The first settlement in the county of Wayne, aside from that upon the Delaware, was made upon the edge of this meadow. From this place to the Paupack settlement, a distance of less than a dozen miles, stretched the woods, unbroken save by a single farm-house, kept for a tavern, remarkable for its neatness within, and its slovenish appearance without. A portion of this distance is swamp-land, grown full of alder, laurel, beech, and the long, wrinkled hemlock, and is a continuation of the swamp or "Shades of Death," extending their desolating aspect for a great space along the Pocono.

Midway through this swamp flows the Five-mile Creek in the most sluggish manner, from which the land upon either side of it gradually ascends for a distance of three or four miles.

In the autumn of 1837, while the writer was passing from this tavern homeward on one bright, frosty midnight, accompanied by a friend, just as the clearing receded from the view, the horse and ourselves were startled by the loud cry of a panther, coming from the thicket along the road-side. The dry limbs cracked as the enormous creature sprang into the road behind us, and it is difficult to tell whether horse or the whitened drivers most appreciated the perilous condition. The moon shone bright down among the opening tree-tops, as over the road, frozen, steep, and stony, trembled the slender vehicle. Deeper and farther the forest closed up behind us, leaving little chance for us to reach Little Meadows in safety. Turning the eye backward, and the approaching form of the panther could be seen within a stone's throw, leaping along at a rate of speed corresponding with our own. The silence of the woods, stretching back in such utter loneliness, the sound of the nervous horse-feet, the jar of the wagon over the stones, the terribly distinct yells of the pursuing animal breaking in upon the surrounding gloom, and our own defenseless condition, made such an impression upon boyhood—that its mention here may seem a wide digression—it never was effaced or forgotten. We shot down hill after hill, around curve after curve, with fearful rapidity, without uttering a word or hardly drawing a breath, fearing every moment that the wagon would either prove treacherous to its trust, or that every leap of the panther would interrupt our ride. For three miles, down to the brook and over it, did the yellow beast follow up our trail, uttering as it came its shrill, appalling cries at intervals of every minute. Crossing the creek on a rude, log bridge here thrown across the stream, the horse, conscious of the danger, sniffed instinctively, hurried up the ascent with all possible speed, while the panther, slackening his pace perceptibly and ceasing his cries, led us to believe that the chase was abandoned. Not so, however. As we emerged from the woods into the edge of Little Meadows, where courage rose to a wonderful pitch, we gave one "hollo!" to ascertain the whereabouts of the animal, hesitating whether to leave or spring upon us. Hardly had the echo of our voices returned from the wood-side before the replying scream of the panther reached us, in accents so distinct and appalling as to remove all desire or effort to hold further intercourse with his panthership.

As for the panther, which had accompanied us six or eight miles during our moonlight flight, with no benevolent intentions, we took leave of his society with less regret than we had left the fair ones at the homestead on the Paupack.

DUNNING.

Madison Township, embracing an area of twenty-eight square miles, much of which is timbered with the knotted hemlock or the smoother beech or maple, was formed from Covington and Jefferson in 1845.

Pleasant Valley, lying ten miles east of Scranton, on the Delaware, Lackawanna, and Western Railroad, within this township, is a deep vale scooped out of the hills for the passage of Roaring Brook, in its descent to the Lackawanna, where the village of Dunning animates the spirit of industry, and carries on a profitable traffic with the people of Drinker's Beech. Like the Lackawanna region, this short and narrow valley bears evidence of once having been a lake, whose waters, enlivened by fish and water-fowl, were liberated with heavy murmur through the fractured mountain below. About one mile west of the village, "Barney's Ledge,"[1] a long, bold bending of vertical rock, rises up some five hundred feet at the door of Cobb's Gap, with rugged outlines, and, stretching its strong arms right and left, half encircles the village in its embrace. The old Drinker turnpike, once merry with the passing stage-coach, finding its way from Providence to Stroudsburg, and the light track of the Pennsylvania Coal Company, pass through it.

Hunter's Range, once famed for its trout-fishing and whisky, lies in the vicinity. Although the rough sides of Pleasant Valley, capable of great cultivation and production, if brought out by patient toil, are marked by an eruption of stumps wherever cleared, there is a fresh business air about the village, with its vast leather-trade and lumbering interests, that arrests the attention of the passer, and that gives assurance that when the scalping-ax disperses the forest farther from the brook, it will, in point of thrift and enterprise, excel many older towns upon the line of this great locomotive road.

Hon. Abram B. Dunning, who represented Luzerne County in the Pennsylvania Legislature in a manner so eminently satisfactory to his constituents during the years 1852-3-4, as to be *thrice* elected—a compliment seldom paid in this county—has grown up with the place, and given it a name and an impetus alike permanent and favorable in its character. Dunning enjoys the advantages of a depot, two stores, post-office, two hotels, and a

---

[1] Named from the late Barney Carey, who for many years kept a toll-gate on the Drinker turnpike, within view of this ledge.

large tannery of Eugine Snyders, able to convert quarter of a million's worth of raw hides each year into ready leather.

CARBONDALE.

Carbondale Township, underlaid with rich seams of coal, lies on the Lackawanna, twenty-four miles from its mouth, some 700 feet above the level at its confluence, and was formed from Blakeley and Greenfield, in April, 1831. On the eastern slope of the Moosic, near the present location of Waymart, Captain George Rix, whose name lives in the notch of the mountain, chose a dwelling-place, before Waymart had even a name. This led to the settlement of Ragged Islands (now Carbondale) by David Ailsworth in 1802. He was a farmer from Rhode Island. He fixed his habitation in the spring of this year upon the spot known since 1830 as the "Meredith Place," cut away and burned the forest for a single crop of corn he planted and secured by his little cabin: in the fall returned for his family. The backwoods became his permanent abode in 1803, and by the aid of his trap, gun, and new land productions, he lived a life of contented obscurity. His self-reliant wife wove and spun every yard of clothing material worn, other than that manufactured from furs and skins, secured with little trouble from the bold inhabitants of the woods. Franklin Ailsworth ascended the Lackawanna from Capoose, to share the fortune of his father, in 1806. A daughter of Mr. Ailsworth, 66 years old, familiarly called "Aunt Ruth Waderman," who accompanied her mother here in 1802, yet lives above Carbondale. The first white child born in Carbondale was born on the Meredith Place in 1806. The second family that ventured into the Carbondale wilderness was James Holden, who in 1805 chopped and logged a piece of land near Ailsworth. He abandoned it the second year, and moved into the Lake country.

Peter Waderman and James Lewis moved upon

Ragged Island in 1807. Lewis abandoned his clearing the second year, while Waderman reared up a bevy of sturdy youngsters. The attire of Mr. Waderman, when full, was imposing and unique. A bear-skin worn for a coat, the fore-legs serving for the sleeves, a fawn-skin vest, buck-skin pants, and a raccoon cap, with the tail hanging behind when worn, set off his tall figure to great advantage, and when he visited Capoose, to vote or carry his grist to Slocum's mill, children stood dismayed or fled to their mothers at his approach. Near where the toll-gate stands, below Carbondale, Roswell B. Johnson, from New York, who had married a Boston lady, took possession of land covered with the tall hemlock and the low thicket in 1809, and lived upon it for five years. The "big flats," now occupied by a portion of Carbondale, was never disturbed until 1809. During this year, George Parker and his son-in-law, Winley Skinner, both more familiar with the rifle than the ax, cut away the timber for a corn-patch early in the spring of 1809. A small, one story log-hut, warmed by the abundance of fuel lying at the door, supplied them with shelter the few months they inhabited it, when they abruptly withdrew from the place, in despair of ever seeing it emerge into civilization. The green logs soon rotted down, and the young saplings again triumphed in the place where the cabin stood.

In 1810 Christopher E. Wilbur, an ingenious wheelwright from Dutchess County, N. Y., became a resident of the farm now occupied by Horace Stiles. He emigrated here to manufacture wooden wheels, then used along the borders for spinning wool and flax, worked by the foot or hand. There was no other wheelwright along the Lackawanna other than him, and so clever was his hand in working wood for the use of the busy housewife, that every fireside in the valley was gladdened by the hum of his wheels. In 1812 he erected a miniature corn or gristmill upon the stream where he lived. It had no bolt, and but a single run of stone diversified its work; corn, crushed by its rudely wielded power, had to pass through a common seive before being fit for use. Mr. Wilbur was a plain, practical man, and his house afforded a place for a school and meetings as early as 1813; Elder John Miller and Mr. Cramer alternately itinerated their diverse doctrines at this point once a month.

Carbondale, by its origin and nature a mining village, as indicated by its name, owes the vigor of its development to the genius of William and Maurice Wurts. In 1814–15, these true pioneers in the valley, with compass and pick, a knapsack of provisions slung over their shoulders, penetrated and bivouacked along the eastern range of the Moosic, exploring every gorge and opening favoring the exit of coal, two bodies of which they found, and uncovered a few years later, by the aid of Mr. Nobles and Mr. Wilbur, one at Carbondale, under the bluff, on the western edge of the Lackawanna, the other on a strip of half-cleared land in Providence, since known as the Anderson farm. The wild land about Carbondale, originally owned by an Englishman named Russell, living at Sunbury, came into possession of William and Maurice Wurts at the time of these explorations.

In November, 1822, these men, in quest of honest reward for their labors, cheered onward by no friendly hand from the inhabitants of the upper or lower valley, laughed at for their perseverance in digging among rock and rattlesnakes for naught, erected a long, low log-house for the joint occupancy of themselves and their workmen. Up until this time but a single horse-path, showing its narrow and indefinite outline by marks upon trees, led to the site of Carbondale, and passed through Rixe's Gap to Belmont and Bethany.

Dundaff—named from Lord Dundaff, of Scotland—became a place of some note in the backwoods before Carbondale enjoyed even the honor of an appellation. Redmond Conyngham, an uncle of our excellent judge of the county of Luzerne, purchased the land where the village now stands in 1822, laid it out for a town, whose growth was to be stimulated by the rugged agricultural developments of the country, and by the considerable travel on the Milford and Owego turnpike, which passed through the place as a stage route. Three or four small houses stood here before this time.

The settlement expanded into a village of such prospect, that Mr. Stone Hamilton started a democratic weekly newspaper, called the *Dundaff Republican*, the first number of which was issued in February, 1828. It was the only paper, with the exception of one or two published in Wilkes Barre at this time, issued within the county of Luzerne.

James W. Goff, Esq., afterward sheriff of the county, raised the first frame-house in Carbondale, in October, 1828. For a series of years the development of the village, enriched by its subterranean possessions, surpassed in promise and rapidity every settlement within the county. Churches were built, a railroad, licensed by mountain planes, led its iron way to the waters of the Dyberry, and a spirit of thrift blended its impulse with the sober notions of the farmers of the surrounding townships, hitherto poor and embarrassed. Awakened thus by the activity of these brothers, whose spirit and effort unlocked the mountains of the Lackawanna, and gave luster to a name unhonored in their earlier achievements, the village, deriving nurture from the operations of the company, of which they were the organic head, compares favorably to-day with the towns of the lower valley.

The principal persons who found remunerative occupation in the new, prosperous coal settlement, prior to 1832, were James Dickson, Charles Smith, Thos. Youngs, Stephen Mills, Dr. Thomas Sweet, Salmon Lathrop, John M. Poor, Samuel Raynor, Stephen Rogers, D. Yarington, Esq., R. E. Marvin, Henry Johnson, Hiram Frisby,

James Archbald, H. Hackley, John McCalpine, and E. M. Townsend.

Carbondale is now an incorporated city, rugged somewhat in the general style of its architecture, and yet from the uplifted anthracite within and beyond its boundaries,

FIRST BAPTIST CHURCH IN CARBONDALE.

it gives employment, and even a comparative competency, to its thousands of inhabitants.

It abounds in churches, the first of which, the First Presbyterian church, was erected in 1829. However counter and diverse may be the religious convictions of the mass, ample scope for their harmonious enjoyment is here found in the different churches, representing every Christian denomination.

The oldest coal-mines of the Delaware and Hudson Canal Company are located at this point, which was for many years the western terminus of their railroad leading to the canal at Honesdale. The first car-load of coal passed over this road, October, 9, 1829.

Maurice and William Wurts, in 1816, attempted to transport a sample of coal across the mountain to the Paupack waters upon sleds, from a superficial body they had uncovered in Providence township, some five miles above Slocum Hollow, and failed. After this route was found to be impracticable, the irrepressible energy of these men turned to the Carbondale placer, where the first sled-load of stone-coal from the Lackawanna Valley left its bed, by the creek side, and was floated to Philadelphia upon rafts; and while its claimed attributes for heat, brought jeers from the passer to its patrons, it wore and won its way into favor after many struggles, as the stream, sometimes baffled in its upper waters, becomes serene and goes unwearied to the sea.

APPEARANCE OF THE VALLEY IN 1804.

A brief retrospective view of Lackawanna Valley, as it appeared to the eye in 1804, while shut out from the great world almost as much as the Icelander among his glacial peaks, will have a *local* interest, enhanced by the fact that the reader is indebted for the faithfulness of the picture to the memory of the late Elder John Miller.

In searching for material for publication, the writer visited the elder in May, 1856. He was found alone in the plowed field planting corn, dropping the seed from a huge, leather bag, made from a boot-leg, hung by his side; and although he then was *eighty-one* years of age, his extraordinary powers of vitality enabled him to fill the farmer's place as ably as one forty years his junior. Leaning his right arm upon his hoe, and successively raising handfuls of corn, to be dropped again in the bag through his fingers, he stood affixed for two long hours, describing the appearance of the country as he saw it sixty-four years before, interwoven with the remembrance of lively gossip and anecdote. It was done with that sober good sense and cheerful temper that always gave his conversation a charm suited to every taste, circle, and place.

The first house standing near the confluence of the Lackawanna with the Susquehanna, at this period (1804), was that of Ishmael Bennett, a blacksmith. He was a great Indian fighter and hater, having witnessed many of the cruelties practiced by them after the battle across the river. A huge elm-tree, seen a little east of the railroad depot at Pittston, indicates the original location of his dwelling. On the farm, now known as Barnum's, a little pretension in the potash and agricultural line was made by James Brown. Captain Isaac Wilson, who married a daughter of John Phillips, owned a narrow patch of land immediately above. Just as the road, skirting along the western border of the Lackawanna, below Old Forge, emerges from the strip of wood into the sandy plain, stood the residence of that old sunburnt veteran, Ebenezer Marcy. In 1778, he was engaged in the Indian battle, and his wife was among the fugitives who fled from Wyoming on the evening of the memorable 3d of July of this year. The tourist, as he passes down the valley, can not fail to observe, as he passes over the Lackawanna bridge, below the rapids, a deep, ragged, narrow passage cut through a rock, that here turns aside the waters of the stream as they come fretting and chafing over the rocky bed, like an ill-curbed colt. This channel, dug out as early as 1774 for mill purposes, now conveyed to the forge below motive power from the stream above. At this forge, standing a little below the bridge spoken of, Dr.

Wm. Hooker Smith and James Sutton lived and manufactured iron. Opposite this point lay the farm since known as Drake's, on which a cabin had been fashioned by Hermans, who claimed the land, while on the adjoining clearing there lived Deodat Smith, father of the late Thos. Smith, Esq., of Abington.

An old gentleman named Cornelius Atherton resided at Keys or Keiser's Creek.[1] He was a blacksmith by trade; and it is claimed that the first *clothier's shears* in the United States were made by him in Connecticut. His son Jabez was shot in the Indian battle at Wyoming, the bullet passing through the *femur*, or thigh-bone, without a fracture. One of those tragic episodes so frequent in the earlier history of Wyoming was enacted upon this creek, at the present location of Taylorsville. The day after the Wyoming massacre, the whites remaining unharmed fled from the plains of Wyoming by every path leading from it. To escape the knife or the merciless ax, homes were hurriedly left, and all fled toward the Delaware for safety. A party of six persons, two men, their wives and children, were thus urging their single yoke of oxen over this route, when they entered the glen with comparatively little apprehension, as the savages were supposed to be present at their bloody carnival below. Hardly had a draught been taken from the creek before the whoop and uplifted tomahawk announced the presence of the savages as they sprang from the ambuscade. Before the whites could raise their guns upon their foes, and defend their families or themselves, one man fell by the dash of the tomahawk, while the other darted away in the forest with such rapidity, as to draw away entirely from the rest of the party the notice of the pursuing Indians. It was now a moment big with peril. To flee at once was the only hope to escape captivity, or perhaps a lingering, barbarous death. Each mother gathered a

---

[1] This creek took its name from Timothy Keys, once living here, who was killed by the Indians in 1778.

child to her bosom, and instinctively hurried away in the deep, dark thicket of willows bordering this stream, as it flowed along that swampy lowland. From the knife, already gleaming and tried upon those they had loved so long, these bold women, with their nursing babes, successfully escaped. Although the stern wilderness frowned before them, and their assailants were prowling in their rear, they left their hiding-place at night; and, creeping from bush to bush along the Lackawanna, continued their journey over Cobb Mountain toward the settlements upon the Delaware. They subsisted upon roots and berries—the manna of the wilderness—and at night huddling together under some friendly tree, found wild-dreaming repose.

After passing every danger and enduring every hardship, heart-heavy, stripped, and starved, yet trusting in God, they arrived at the village of Stroudsburg in safety.

The Indians, as they returned from the chase, with the warm and dripping scalp in their hands, finding their victims beyond reach, cut out the lolling tongue of one of the oxen for a roast, leaving the other undisturbed, in which condition they were found the next day by some of the escaping settlers.

Along the path from this creek to Providence the woods retained their native aspect until the highland farm, now known as "Uncle Joe Griffin's," came in view. Upon this plateau, where the rich outlines of the Indian region rose up in every form of beauty, stood a log-cabin, with its roof running to the very ground—better to withstand the storms of winter. Reuben Taylor lived here at this time.

Mr. Lafronse had a possession right immediately above Taylor's, while Joseph Fellows, Sen., who came to the valley in 1796, had made a permanent residence on the slope of the hill, near the present family mansion of Turvy Fellows, Esq. Subsequently he received a commission as a justice of the peace, an office which he filled with ability and great satisfaction. His nearest neighbor up the valley was Goodrich.

Hyde Park, as a village, had no existence, and but a single cleared acre, half-hidden in the green park on all sides surrounding it, was inhabited. Upon the site of the residence of Hon. Wm. Merrifield, stood, in 1804, the unhewn-log habitation of Elder Wm. Bishop, who, as early as 1795, officiated as the first stationed minister in Providence.

With the exception of the "Indian clearing," and a little additional chopping around it, the central portion of Capoose Meadow, or Tripp's Flats, was covered with tall white pines. The road lay along the brow of the hill for nearly half a mile from the house of Bishop, when it reached the two-roomed log-tavern of Stephen Tripp, who at this time had a large distillery operating here.

Tripp was a man of singular evenness of temper. He never became boisterous or belligerent. The nearest approach to it occurred here at his *tavern*. A stranger stopping at his house, finding the landlord agreeable and full of social qualities, ventured to ask his name. He was told it was Tripp. "Trip, Trip, is it?" said the stranger, pleased with the reply; "that is a capital, capital name I know, for I have a dog by that name—and 'Trip' is a good dog!"

Entering a small, dark cabin, near where now lives Ira Tripp, Esq., there sat a short, gray-headed man, more cheerful and communicative than his associates of the day, whose earliest life was full of incident and hardships, and who emigrated from Rhode Island at the time of the formation of Luzerne County, in 1786. This was the father of Stephen.

About midway between this point and the Lackawanna River, a little to the northeast of the "Diamond mines," a small tract of rich land had been purchased by Lewis Jones from Wm. Tripp and John Gifford—a son-in law of Isaac Tripp—who lived here at this time. Jones's farm included that intervale where yet lies the *débris* of an old still-house. John Staples occupied the Widow Griffin farm—adjacent to that of Alderman Griffin—which soon after passed into the hands of Mathias Hollenback.

The Von Storch property, originally passing from the proprietors of the town of Capoose to Dean, and from him to Nathan Roberts, for a barrel of whisky, came into the hands of H. C. L. Von Storch in the spring of 1807, before coal lands had a name or a value in the valley. A strip of pines lay between the clearing of Von Storch and the cabin of Enock Holmes, standing on the site of the village of Providence. Where now stands the cottage of Daniel Silkman, lived Henry Waderman, who, as late as 1810, when the census was first taken in the valley by the Hon. Charles Miner a gentleman to whom all accorded the possession in a high degree of those frank, pleasing, and intellectual qualities, which seldom fail to secure the regard of every one—occupied the only dwelling he found *above* Providence. Mr. Miner recollected this more distinctly from the fact of staying over night with Waderman, whom he found cheerful, sociable, and fond of relating stories of Bonaparte.

Upon the flats, now known as the Rockwell farm, dwelt James Bagley, whose porchless abode gave welcome shelter to children, cats, and dogs. Bagley's fordway crossed the Lackawanna, near his dwelling.

At the mouth of Leggett's Creek, Selah Mead cultivated the narrow intervale, while Mr. Hutchins occupied a patch of land rising up from the brook, known now as the McDaniels' farm. The adjacent clearing, thick with stumps, marked the well-chosen location of Ephraim Stevens, who, bending and white with the years of almost a century, passed away a short time since, leaving his estate to his son Samuel, subsequently deceased.

Half a mile beyond, on the farm so long rendered productive by Colonel Moses Vaughn, one of the worthy descendants of Captain John Vaughn, lived John Tripp. The orchard spread over the meadow crossed by the Delaware and Hudson Railroad, on the western bank of the Lackawanna, planted by Captain Vaughn, denotes the place where he and his sons long drew nurture from the soil. Upon the Decker farm lived Wm. McDaniels, whose sluggish ideas of agriculture governed each successive inheritance until the property came into possession of Messrs. Pancost and Price, two Philadelphia gentlemen of education and fortune.

The village of *Price*, peopled by hardy and industrious Germans, stands upon a portion of the Decker farm. The first clearing made in Blakeley turned to practical account, was that of Timothy Stevens, who, about the close of the Revolution, began a chopping on the farm known as the Mott farm, where he "logged-off" land for a corn and potato patch, which yielded abundance to the wants of his family.

Nicholas Leuchens, the erratic genius before mentioned, lived at the present site of Peckville. Along the forests of the Lackawanna, above Leuchens, the ax had rung, only to mark the course of the trapper or trader coming from Pleasant Mount, and but a single hut or cabin stood between. Blakeley, Carbondale, Rushdale, Archbald, and Jessup, had no impulse even toward a settlement, nor was there a township formed in the valley north of Providence; a "chopping," with the fallen pines divested of their lesser limbs by fire, edged its way into the green woods, where in latter years the "Meredith Cottage," made rural and attractive by warm hospitality, stood and still stands, to gladden the wayside.

Having now reached the extreme point of the valley, on the west side of the Lackawanna, as far as settled in 1804, a glance of the eastern border, less sought after for a dwelling-place or heritage at this time, will be as briefly given. There are yet a few remaining who can bear testimony to the rugged, narrow path along the stream, overhung with interlocking trees, which led its way from Ragged Island to Capoose, with only here and there a break in the woodland for the occasional occupant. Upon the farm known as the Dolph farm, in Olyphant, lived Moses Dolph, father of Alexander and grandfather to the present owner, Edward Dolph; immediately below, Samuel Ferris, father of Samuel, William, and John, won by hard toil a resting-place for his young family. From the lands of Ferris it was nothing but woods, broken only within a single mile by the blackened fallow of John Secor, whose cabin, built from logs of great strength and size, served to dispel all fears inspired by wolves never slumbering about the clearing after nightfall. Between Secor's and Dunmore, two miles away, two rights had been improved respectively by Charles Dolph and Levi Depuy.

The Corners (Dunmore) had two houses only—the tavern of Widow Alsworth and the residence of David Brown. Between this point and Slocum Hollow, a log-house of John Carey's, with its huge, stone chimney and mud-chinked sides, had risen from the clearing, and the bevy of children issuing from the door to wonder at the occasional passer, or building dams of mud across the stream running at the door, made up the daily picture of domestic life at this solitary habitation between these two named places.

At Griffin's Corners, there lived an old man named Atwater, while on the Dings or Whaling property (now Green Ridge, where the Hon. George Sanderson has brought a town into being), stood by the brook-side the rude yet hospitable dwelling of Conrad Lutz, occupied by his son John. The old Connecticut road, familiar to the Wyoming pioneers, following the Indian trail, came into Capoose Meadow, and crossed the Lackawanna at Lutz's fordway. This fording-place, deriving its name from Mr. Lutz, was traversed from 1769 until 1826. Tall pines, alienated from Indian tenure, crowded upon the road leading to Slocum Hollow, where Ebenezer and Benjamin Slocum, with their less than a dozen employees, enumerated the entire white inhabitants of this tranquil and independent settlement.

James Abbott, whose iron energy had animated the glen of Roaring Brook, resided on the bank of Stafford Meadow Creek. Some two miles below Slocum Hollow, a tract of land improved as early as 1776, by Comer Philips, was tenanted jointly by David Dewee and David David. The latter met with a sudden death a year or two later. Engaged at the break of day in prying up a rock for a hearth-stone, he was mistaken by Dewee, in search of game, for a beast of prey, and shot dead upon the spot. His widow subsequently married Mr. Abbott.

John Scott, father of the great hunter Elias, lived upon the farm lying farthest down in the township of Providence. His nearest neighbor was Joseph Knapp, a brave old revolutionary soldier, spurning alike title or pretension. At the surrender of Burgoyne he received a wound long incapacitating him from active service. After the declaration of peace he resumed farming in Columbia County, New York, until 1790, when he emigrated to the valley and settled in the "gore."[1]

His son Zephaniah, attaining eighty years, yet lives among us. Much of his early life was spent in hunting and trapping various animals inhabiting the valley over half a century ago. Sometimes during the autumn months he was out alone for weeks, engaged in hunting, subsisting on the trophies of his gun, and finding on friendly leaves and boughs his only *bivouac*. He has kept a curious record of the number of bears and other wild animals he killed upon the Lackawanna; of the time and manner of their capture, with their respective weight, in a work of over one hundred folio pages; a work probably

---

[1] The *gore* was a narrow strip of land, lying between Pittston and Providence. It is now Lackawanna Township, set off as an electoral district, Feb. 25, 1795; into a township at the November sessions, 1838.

unmatched in novelty and interest by any manuscript of the kind found in the country. He has given it the inimitable title of "*The Leather Shirt.*"

This enumeration, embracing no particular creed nor politics, comprised the entire inhabitants of the valley four and sixty years ago. To many who may peruse these pages the foregoing particulars may seem out of place, but to those who visit the Lackawanna Valley, or make it their home, it will not be amiss to thus catch a retrospective glance of the days gone by, so as better to contemplate the changes years have wrought, and judge from the past how rapid and marvelous will be the prosperity of the future. Six years later the census was taken by the Hon. Charles Miner. Within the Lackawannian district existed but two townships, Pittston and Providence, the first having a population of 694, the last 589, or a total population of 1,283 for the entire valley in 1804. Abington had an inhabitancy of 511.

The same territory, divided and sub-divided into cities, townships, and boroughs, will furnish in 1870, according to the same ratio of increase, a population of *one hundred thousand.* Diffused along its living border, it falls to-day little short of eighty thousand, and a more enterprising, intelligent community, a more thrifty and successful people, remarkable alike for their love of liberty and their attachments to their country, can nowhere be found.

The thrift everywhere diffused along the intervale, no longer hid in its native fastnesses, has kept pace with the steady hum of its population. It is in fact impossible to contemplate the unvaried progress of the Lackawanna Valley for the last thirty years without astonishment and pride. It has been a progress at once so rapid, so liberal, so vast and comprehensive in its character, as to exhibit alike the importance of the valley, and the sagacity of those to whom its development has been intrusted. Buried deep in the forest of northeastern Pennsylvania, as it has been within a few years, walled in from the great world by natural mountain barriers, like the Northmen among their glimmering crags, with no outlet to the east or the west, but for the slow coach, swinging along at the rate of *four* miles an hour behind the jaded stage-horse, with no incitement but its slumbering wealth, it has risen like a man awakened from his slumbers, strong, refreshed, invigorated, until it has become one of the most commercial and prosperous valleys in the State.

FORMATION OF TOWNSHIPS UNDER PENNSYLVANIA JURISDICTION : PRIMITIVE MINISTERS.

> Pittston was formed in 1790.
> Providence was formed, August, 1792.
> Abington was formed, August, 1806.
> Greenfield was formed, January, 1816.
> Covington was formed, January, 1818.
> Blakeley was formed, April, 1818.
> Carbondale was formed, April, 1831.
> Jefferson was formed, April, 1836.
> Lackawanna was formed, November, 1838.
> Benton was formed 1838.
> Newton was formed 1844.
> Madison was formed 1845.
> Fell was formed 1845.
> Scott was formed 1846.

The same territory, divided into lots of 300 acres each, extending back two and a half miles, was covered by two towns, while under Connecticut jurisdiction, viz. : Pittston and Providence. Three hundred acres of land were appropriated or reserved in either of these original towns for the use of the *first* minister *in fee*, before other lots were offered to the settler. Before the ministerial occupancy of these reservations, the adjoining town of Wilkes Barre with that of Kingston, prospered under the spiritual pleadings of the Rev. Jacob Johnson, a Presbyterian minister, for whom a house was built by the colony in 1772, and whose salary this year was fixed at sixty pounds Connecticut currency.[1]

[1] Westmoreland Records.

After the annihilation of the Connecticut claim in 1782, by the court at Trenton, the commissioners allowed "The Rev. Mr. Johnson to have the full use of all the grounds he Tilled for two years, ending the first of May, 1785." [1] He refused the kindness of the favor in a spirit less chafing than biblical, as evinced by the following letter[2] of

"Jacob Johnson To the Com[te] of the Pennsylvania Landowners, &c. : Gentlemen,

I thank you for your distinguished Favor shewed to me the widows, &c., in a proposal of Indulgence, Permitting us to reside in our present Possessions and Improvements for the present & succeeding Year. Altho I cannot Consistly accept the offer, having Chosen a Com[te] for that purpose, who are not disposed to accept of or Comply with your proposals. However, I will for myself (as an Individual) make you a proposal agreable to that Royal President, Sam[l] 9th, 16th, & 19th Chapter, if that dont suit you and no Compromise can be made, or Tryal be had, according to the law of the States, I will say as Mepheboseth, Jonathan's son (who was lame on both his feet) said to King David, Sam[l] 19, 30, yea let him take all. So I say to you Gentlemen if there be no resource, Neither by our Petition to the Assembly of the State of Pennsyvania or otherwise, Let the Landholders take all. I have only this to add for my Consolation and you Gentlemen's serious Consideration, Viz : that however the Cause may be determined for or against me (in this present uncertain State of things,) there is an Inheritance in the Heavens, sure & Certain that fadeth not a way reserved for me, and all that love the Saviour Jesus Christ's appearing.

I am Gentlemen, with all due Respect, & good Will
your Most Ob[t] Humble Serv[t],
JACOB JOHNSON.

Wioming, Ap[l] 24th, 1783.
To the Gentlemen Com[te], &c.

[1] Pa. Arch., 1783–1786, p. 32.   [2] Ibid., pp. 34, 35.

N. B. it is my Serious Opinion if we proceed to a Compromise according to the Will of heaven that the lands (as to the Right of soil) be equally divided between the two Parties Claiming, and I am fully Satisfied this Opinion of mine may be proved even to a demonstration out of the Sacred Oracles. I would wish you Gentlemen would turn your thoughts and enquiries to those 3 Chapters above refered to and see if my Opinion is not well Grounded & if so, I doubt not but we Can Compromise in love and Peace—and save the Cost and Trouble of a Tryal at Law."

The doctrines of Methodism were occasionally expounded to the people of Pittston and Providence in 1790; in 1794 an Englishman named William Bishop, a fervid Baptist preacher, kindled his fire on the parsonage lot in Providence. This lot lay on the east side of Hyde Park, and extended over the marsh or pond which a few years since gave to the interior of Scranton such a piscatory appearance. The principal hotels and churches, as well as the greater portion of Scranton, stand upon these ancient church lands.

On the bluff, upheaved from the Lackawanna, whose waters so gracefully bend around its base, the log-house and church of Elder Bishop, combined in one, emerged from the forest. It was a rude, paintless affair. No bell, steeple, pulpit, nor pews, marked it as a house of worship; four plain sides, chinked with wood held by adhesive mud, formed a room where the backwoodsmen gathered in a spirit of real piety, sincerity, and an absence of display impossible to find to-day in the more costly and imposing sanctuaries around us.

The habits of the assemblage were in keeping with the character of the humble edifice. Women wore dresses made from flax and woolen, fitting them so closely and straight as a bean-pole. These were sometimes plain from the loom, but generally colored and striped with a domestic dye, giving to the woolen fabric every variety of finish and shade. Instead of the negative shoe worn nowadays, the old-fashioned ones then in use furnished to the wearer one of the essentials to long life and health —a generous warmth.

The shadowy and often senseless duties of the milliner were but slightly appreciated here at that time, for one instance is related to the writer of a woman whose bonnet, cut from pasteboard and trimmed as plainly as a pumpkin, was worn summer and winter for the long period of *twenty-two years*, with no other change nor "doing up" than the addition of a single new ribbon or string! Appalling and incredible as may appear the fact to the girl or the matron of the present time, the person yet lives in the valley who remembers this pious and economical mother well. The prudent wife and mother who understood the necessity of supplying the wants of the family from the scanty means within her reach, so united industry with economy as to exhibit in the most favorable light the qualities of the New England women.

Broadcloth coats were never seen unless brought from Connecticut. Their place was supplied by the rough, warm, honest homespun, or more frequently by a suit of bear, or the coveted deer skin. Hats and caps ingeniously constructed from the skin of wild animals found in every thicket, were universally worn in winter, while in summer the straw hat, braided from the well-thrashed rye, gave comfort and dignity to the wearer.

Men and boys went barefooted until they reached the place of meeting, carrying their shoes in their hands, putting them on during preaching, and after meeting would walk home, sometimes many miles, upon the bare feet, and the shoes were returned in the same manner in which they had been brought. Many of the settlers, pressed by the needs of the household, did not enjoy the luxury even of *carrying* shoes.

The women were always seated upon one side of the house, the men upon the other. The habit of the male and female portion of the community being seated promiscuously in a country school or meeting-house was indulged in here only within the last forty years.

PROPRIETORS' SCHOOL-FUND AND PRIMITIVE SCHOOLS.

The fund in the township of Providence, known as the "Proprietors' School-Fund," came from a provision full of forethought and wisdom. The original proprietors of the seventeen towns certified to Connecticut settlers in Westmoreland, in setting aside certain lots for religious and literary purposes, inaugurated a measure that speaks for itself. Nearly 2,000 acres were thus reserved by the Yankees in the town of Providence.

The commissioners appointed under the act passed in April, 1799, offering compensation to Pennsylvania claimants, issued certificates or patents for the land from the State to the committees for the said lots in trust for the use of the proprietors of said town or township, and the annual committee had from time to time sold or leased for a term of years a great part of such lots, reserving the remainder for the proprietors' use.

As the committees, however, were supposed by many to be invested with little or no legal powers, the sales and leases made by them were so little regarded, that some debts and rents, due the original Yankee proprietors, are yet remaining unpaid.

A portion of the land thus appropriated by the old Susquehanna Company for school purposes, was sold the 17th of September, 1795, to William Bishop, by Constant Searles, James Abbott, and Daniel Taylor, who acted for the township.

With a view of confirming such contracts and sales, which at the time were deemed advantageous for the school fund, the proprietors of the township obtained an act of incorporation from the Legislature during its session of 1835, similiar in its character to that obtained in 1831 by the townships of Wilkes Barre, Hanover, and Plymouth, clothing the trustees of the township with all the privileges and franchises of corporations. John Dings, Samuel De Puy, William Merrifield, Joshua Griffin, and Nathanial Cottrill were vested with the authority of trustees under this act, until after the annual election.

Although this act did not affect any sales previously made by individuals acting for the township, and consequently failed to reach and recover lands forever lost to it, yet it enabled the proprietors who were subsequently elected by the taxable inhabitants of the district, to sell the remainder of this land, lying in the vicinity of Hyde Park, for the sum of $3,300, which being secured by bond and mortgage upon the property, now furnishes by its yearly interest the "School Fund," a fund which contributes so justly toward the support and success of what is considered so essential to the promotion of national welfare—common schools.

The first house built in the valley with especial reference only to schools was erected in 1818, upon a plot of land now within the limits of Providence village. The building was nine by twelve, without paint, steeple, or bell, yet no college hall now offers more willing culture to the young than did this plain edifice beneath the murmuring pines, open its doors to the mischievous urchins of the valley just half a century ago.

In reviewing the history of the Yankee settlements in Westmoreland, much of the thrift and sprightliness of the New England character can be traced in the elementary education imparted to them from the cabin schoolhouse along the forest. Many of the pioneers were men of deep religious sentiment and principle, and after their families had been sheltered from the storms and the intrusion of the inmates of the wigwam, they made provisions for the school-house.

The school records of the various townships in the valley, present no striking peculiarity, but as far as any judgment can be formed from the contents and character of the former records, both of school and society, it leads unavoidably to the conclusion that there has been no relaxation of effort in the cause of education since the earlier settlers passed away. The standard which they created has not been overlooked, nor has the common interest of every citizen in the education of the community been forgotten. While the district and higher school arrangements in the Lackawanna Valley are justly looked upon as superior—and some are eminently so—they would suffer none to-day by a comparison with any school found within the precincts of the oldest settled counties in the State.

The schoolmaster was, at an early period, an object of terror to school-children, and of vast importance in a a small neighborhood where he "boarded around." The respected parson, frequent in his visits, and beloved by all for his good wishes and kind words, only received more courteous attention from the farmer and his wife, than did the country schoolmaster—especially a *new* one, whose reputation for "*licking*" his scholars had happily preceded him.

It is well for the timid, nervous child, that the barbarous and often surgical whip and ferule, and the triumphant blows of a master strong in muscle and weak in mind, have been exchanged for a more rational discipline.

While the writer recollects his own school-boy days, when he spent many an idle hour in the old school-house on the hill, surrounded on every side but one by saplings, whose branches were often applied to the coatless backs of the pupils by some itinerating vender of *a b c's*, after the boys had been seated upon a high, hard, hemlock bench, six or eight hours, half frozen in winter and quite boiled in summer, he can not but rejoice at the progressive character of *government* in our common schools, as well as in their grade.

PATHS AND ROADS—JOURNEY FROM CONNECTICUT TO PITTSTON IN 1793.

The general poverty of the earlier emigrants, united with the agitated condition of Wyoming while the Province of Pennsylvania acquiesced in British allegiance, restrained the inhabitants from planning and working roads needed for ordinary intercourse.

Mountain trails trodden by the red men centuries before, and by the whites seeking Indian homes for traffic in rum and skins, led over the Moosic toward Connecticut undisturbed until 1769, when a narrow road long called the "Cobbroad" was opened from the Province of New York to Wyoming. This was the great and only highway entering the valley eastward from 1769 to 1772. From the Lackawanna to the Great Council Fires of the Six Nations among the Lakes, there was no pathway other than the warriors' trail connecting Capoose with Con-e-wa-wah (Elmira), until 1788.

Among the traders roaming along this wood-wrapped avenue for traffic with its tribal masters, was the afterward celebrated John Jacob Astor.

The conflicting claims to the territory embraced by Wyoming and Lackawanna valleys, provoked a controversy between Pennsylvania and Connecticut, long and embittered. The claim of the Yankees being summarily disposed of by the Trenton Decree, Pennsylvania assumed jurisdiction over the valleys known as Westmoreland no longer. This obliteration of rival interest, however final and prejudged it might have been, gave the settlers who remained under the new order of things, leisure to repair roads sadly neglected during and after the war.

The first appointment by the justices in 1788 of the supervisors of roads in Pittston, was John Philips and Jonathan Newman; in Providence, Henry Dow Tripp.

At the September sessions, 1788, held in Wilkes Barre, a petition was received from "Job Tripp and others, praying that proper persons may be appointed to lay out a road in the town of Providence. It is ordered that Ebenezer Marcy, Isaac Tripp, Samuel Miller, Henry D. Tripp, Waterman Baldwin, and Jonathan Newman, be, and they are hereby appointed to lay out necessary roads in said town, and make return to this court at the next session." At the December session, 1788, they reported that they had laid out roads through Pittston, but had surveyed none in Providence, so their report was not accepted.

As the road was essential to the wants of the upper township, the court appointed six housekeepers to survey one fifty feet in width. This followed the old road leading up through the Capoose, constructed under Yankee jurisdiction. The next year, John Philips and David Brown were appointed supervisors of highways in Pittston, and Job Tripp and Wm. Alsworth in Providence.

It does not appear, however, that any *new* roads were laid out or worked up to this time, by any of these supervisors—old roads only being surveyed and repaired.

Job Tripp, Constant Searles, Jediah Hoyt, Daniel Taylor, and James Abbott, living in Providence, were appointed in 1791, to lay out roads here. The present road leading from Pittston to Providence was surveyed by them on the 4th and 5th of April, 1791. This began " on the northeast side of the Lackawanna River in the town of Providence, beginning at Lackawanny River, neare where Mr. Leggett now lives," and thence through Providence to the Pittston line. Gabriel Leggett then lived a short distance above the residence and mill of the late Judson Clark, in Providence.

The Lackawanna was yet bridgeless, and only crossed by fording. Different fording-places took their respective names from the respective owners of the land in the immediate vicinity. Thus at the Capoose Works of Mr. Carter, located a mile from the center of the ancient meadow by that name—was Bagley's ford; at Providence, near the mound of Capoose, Lutz's ford, etc.

Leggett's Gap road was laid out in 1795. The Lackawanna Turnpike Road Company was incorporated in 1817, and was the first *turnpike* along the valley.

The journey from Connecticut to the Lackawanna in 1793, through a half-opened wilderness of nearly two hundred miles, was no easy matter. A day's drive with the slow ox-team over a road barely answering its purpose, was but eight or ten miles. At nightfall, a camping ground was chosen by the road-side near some spring or rivulet, when fuel was gathered and the bright, welcome blaze of the fire in the woods lonely and deep, offered light and company while the supper was being prepared and partaken. If from the forest thronged with deer, none was secured for the evening's meal, bread and bacon issued from the chest, or corn-meal from the saddle-bags was readily converted into "Johnny cakes." Supper disposed of, and the oxen cared for by a liberal supply of *browse*, a few extra logs were piled on the fire as the party crowded under the cover of the wagon and found repose amidst the silence of night.

Along the Lackawack, whose sober waters no longer rocked the Indian's craft, this road offered few inducements to pursue it as it drifted toward Wyoming, passing through the "Lackawa" settlement, and crossing Cobb Mountain into Capoose. From the Paupack clearings to the Lackawanna there was in 1793 but three dwellings, at Little Meadows, Cobb's, and Alsworth's at Dunmore.

Several acres of land overgrown with wild grass and lying ten miles west of the Wallenpaupack in a rich intervale, were found inhabited by the red tribes when the whites explored it in 1769. A small creek stretches its languid line across the meadow into a neighboring pond, where the abundance of fish gave joy to the wigwams on the western edge of the meadow, from whence the warriors came forth with peace-pipe to smoke the friendly welcome. This point, because of its prolific growth of wild grass, was selected for a residence by

Seth Strong, in 1770. It was the first attempt to settle the territory, now known as Wayne County. Mr. Strong lived here at the time of the Wyoming massacre.

This farm is known as the Goodrich property, into whose possession it came in 1803. It was the birthplace of that eccentric genius, Phineas G. Goodrich, known in every nook and corner of Wayne, as "*long-nosed* Goodrich," who writes of Strong, "I had this from the early settlers on the Paupack, who in 1778 hid their effects in the woods and fled to Orange County, to escape the tomahawk and scalping-knife. There was a skirmish here on our old place (Little Meadow) between the whites and Indians. The whites were mostly slain. I remember the mound that was raised over their one common grave. Indians and whites were buried together. When a boy, I used to find the arrows and broken hatchets of the redmen around the mound and the hill."

In 1793 there lived a man here by the name of Stanton, whose one-roomed log-house, early styled an "Inn," furnished accommodation for the wayfaring man and beast. The structure itself, standing on the knoll rising westward from the meadow, was half occupied by a huge fireplace and chimney grouped from stone and mud. The guests, emboldened to ascend a ladder to the upper story where the bare rafters greeted the head of the aspirant, found only boughs and grass spread upon the pole flooring for their reception and repose.

Such was this rustic inn, whose counterpart was seen in many of the new settlements. Homely as was its fare, plain as were its pewter dishes and single hunting-knife, the venison or bear meat swinging from the trammels, hunger made always welcome.

Fox-meat was not so readily appreciated. A stranger passing the way, was drawn to the table by the smell of roasting meat. Taking a morsel of the smoking viand in his mouth, it stung him like cayenne. Thinking that the housewife had peppered one side of the roast too highly, he turned the dish around and took a slice from the other side with the same provoking result. He laid down his knife and fork, and asked the good-natured landlady, what kind of meat it was. "Why," replied she, very innocently, "this morning my husband killed a fox, so I thought I would roast the hind quarter." The stranger was furious. "D—n your fox!" he exclaimed as he dashed platter, grease, fox, and all to the floor, and hastily resumed his journey.

Bishop Asbury, after visiting Wyoming in 1793, returned to New York over this route by Strong's, and thus records it in his diary.

"*Monday* 8, 1793.—I took the wilderness, through the mountains up the Lackawanna, on the Twelve Mile Swamp; this place is famous for dirt and lofty hemlock. We lodged in the middle of the swamp, at S——'s, and made out better than we expected."[1]

Cobb's house on the slope of the Moosic Mountain, a distance of about eight miles from Little Meadows, was reached. The white cover of the wagon, jerking up or down as it mounted over a root, or plunged into a rut, passed over creeks never yet spanned by a bridge. The plain house of Cobb, floored, ceiled, and shingled with the split slabs, was too small to accommodate the emigrating party, who found in the hospitable wagon repose for the night. Asa Cobb made the first clearing here soon after the close of the Revolution. It was seven miles, or one day's journey from Cobb's, to where now stands the village of Dunmore. One green wave of tree-top was carried to the very summit of the mountain, disturbed by no clearing upon its western slope save that of William Alsworth, whose cabin half hid under hemlock and spruce, was also termed an inn. And, although the rude dwelling had little of the finish about it of modern times, the social comforts and the substantial meals and beds it furnished

---

[1] Dr. Peck's Early Methodism, p. 58.

to the casual emigrant, was evidence that Alsworth had lost none of the New England character. The good old man, who acted as landlord, hostler, and waiter, and doing every chore essential to household affairs, never was so delighted as when he saw gathered around him the happy face of the emigrant or his guests, and his greatest pleasure seemed to be, to smooth with his dry jokes and racy stories the ruggedness of each man's daily road.

Pittston, a tidy village on the Susquehanna of half a dozen houses, two only of which were *frame*, was thus reached after a journey of thirty-one days.[1]

THE RISE OF METHODISM IN THE VALLEY.

As the emigrants encamped upon Wyoming generally acquiesced in Presbyterian tenets, an organization friendly to their diffusion was easily effected under the ministrations of the Rev. Jacob Johnson, an officiating minister in the colony, as early as 1772, and who for many years was the only one, with a single exception, in all the wide territory lying between Sunbury and the Mohawk.

Not so, however, with the Methodists. As the noiseless border of the Lackawanna began to thicken with a population, whose physical wants for a time pressed those of a spiritual character aside, Sabbath morning, with its associations of youthful days in the old village church at home, came and went with better observance. Hunting, fishing, horse-racing, or wrestling for drinks for the crowd, were among the many ways chosen to wear Sunday away by a large proportion of the inhabitants many years ago, before religious influences crept into the new settlements of Capoose or Pittston. The birth of Luzerne County, in 1786, modified elements hitherto adverse to either the achievements of Methodism, or the favorable propagation of the doctrines of any organic religious interests.

One of those happy characters able to hew their way

---

[1] Mrs. Von Storch.

into a prominent usefulness emerged from a blacksmith shop in Kingston, and commenced to exhort and explain the liberal doctrines of Methodism to the world in 1787. This was Anning Owen. He had early emigrated from Connecticut to Wyoming with the pioneers; had fought beside the gallant Butler in the Indian battle on the plain until the day was lost, escaping only with his life. He accompanied the fugitives to the East after the massacre, where he remained for nine years before he again crossed the mountain and rolled up his log-cabin and shop on the bank of Toby's Creek, in Kingston. Never neglecting the duties of his shop until his appointments multiplied far and near, he officiated in the double capacity of blacksmith and exhorter for a few seasons before he became a circuit preacher of singular efficiency and power.

A Methodist class was formed at Ross Hill, Wyoming Valley, in 1787-8; three years later a similar society, fewer in numbers, was first organized in the Lackawanna Valley, at the forge of Dr. Wm. Hooker Smith and James Sutton, by the Rev. James Campbell, who had been sent hither by the Philadelphia Conference for this specific purpose. The group, composed of five members, were led by James Sutton as class-leader.

In the summer of 1792 Mr. Owen ascended the Lackawanna to Capoose and upper Providence, where he preached alternately at Preserved Taylor's and Captain John Vaughn's, in private houses. Captain Vaughn had imbibed the broad doctrines of Universalism, but their fallacious character was so demonstrated and proven by the plain blacksmith, that he forsook them forever, and became a zealous convert to Methodism. Meetings were also occasionally held in other log-houses or cabins along the stream, where the minister, generally poor and penniless, tarried all night, and enjoyed the abundant and real hospitality of the valley. Bishop Asbury, in his reconnoiter of the Lackawanna and Wyoming valleys in 1793, appointed Valentine Cook presiding elder.

In 1800, Methodist meetings were held once a month at the house of Preserved Taylor, in Providence, who lived upon the western border of Capoose Meadow. After Mr. Taylor's removal, the dwelling of Squire Potter, two miles farther up the valley, became a stated preaching point. In fact, the lonely school-house or the isolated cabin, afforded the only places for religious gatherings in the valley until the fall of 1828, when there was erected the first meeting-house in that very portion of it last settled —in Carbondale.

Meetings were sometimes held in cool groves or woods from bare necessity. Some shaded nook, watered by a spring or brook, was chosen for a camp-ground. Here, around a circle well cleared of underbrush and sheltered by hemlock or beech from the rays of the sun, rose the whitened tents like the wigwams of the cunning bowmen, in which were collected groups of old and young, whose pilgrimage to this wild, joyous Mecca was long remembered with pleasure and profit.

In 1803, two noisy itinerants went forth like John the Baptist, to prepare the way of the Lord. They preached at Kingston, Plymouth, Shawney, Wilkes Barre, Pittston, Providence, crossed the Moosic Mountain at Cobb's, journeying through Salem, Canaan, Mount Pleasant, Great Bend, and Tunkhannock, and preaching in all these places before returning to Wyoming. In 1807, a regular circuit was formed, and a portion of the same route was traveled over twelve times a year, or once in every four weeks. From 1810 until 1818, George Harman and Elder Owen officiated in this vineyard. One of the prominent members of the church here then was old "Father Ireland," as he was familiarly called, who emigrated to Providence Township in 1795, and settled upon what is now known as the Briggs's farm. He was a long time a class-leader. In his intercourse with the world, his kindness of heart, and his calm and virtuous life, until his sun passed behind the horizon after a long day, contributed no little toward softening the prejudices of the illiberal against the Methodist Society.

The two events marking their distinctive era in the development of Methodism in the valley were the visit of Bishop Asbury in 1793, and the accession to its strength of the young but bold and fervid presence of the Rev. George Peck, D. D., in 1818. He brought with him a fixed purpose to diffuse Christian truths in the new field before him, in the exercise of which he was made familiar throughout the country as the great champion of Methodism. "In less than a century," said he to Brother Taylor, as he was threading his way along the infant settlement, "this charming valley, from its beauty and fertility, will have a large population and need great conversion." Heaven, in its mercy, has given the venerable elder *fifty-three years in the pulpit*, with a yet firm step and bright eye, so that he has not only lived to witness the fulfillment of his prophecy, but has shared in the triumphs of faith with a fidelity and complacency enjoyed by few. Dr. Peck has achieved distinction as an author of great ability, as his numerous, popular volumes offered the public attest.

Although many of the uncharitable charge the spiritual advisers of this denomination, with mercenary views as they direct the wanderer on to the New Jerusalem, we find them as a body to possess as little selfishness, and quite as much true, honest, available capacity, and appreciation of the right, as can be found in the same number of men of any creed or profession in the country; and, although some within the writer's acquaintance command a fortune, few a competency, while very many are comparatively poor, thus affording a decisive commentary on the utter want of judgment of the illiberal. And, yet, beset, with every inducement, with no hope of personal advantage or emolument from their ministerial labors, and pressed by wants that pride conceals from the careless eye, how rarely do they wield their talents for money, position or power! And yet when a whole life has been spent to diffuse those sublime, simple truths which form the basis of all morals, how little security does the purity of character or the claim of age offer from the assaults of parishioners whose liturgy seems but a desire to exile their pastor, and whose devotions are the convenience or but the fashion of the hour!

SMELLING HELL.

Anning Owen was a son of Vulcan, a stout, swarthy, genuine specimen of earnestness, who spoke all he knew and sometimes more, in the most impulsive manner. He remarked often, that he preached as he hammered out hot iron, to make an impression. His sermons were always extempore; after he warmed up in his favorite subject, his eye grew animated, his voice full and clear, as he displayed eloquence of a high order.

The Methodists labored under many disadvantages. The self-sacrificing and sometimes boisterous itinerants who were toiling for their race merely for the sake of good, and no possible hope of pecuniary gain, with few thanks, little or no remuneration, often with scanty fare, were sometimes accused of ignorance, bigotry, and fanaticism, and yet under the effective appeals of Elder Owen, much of this common error was dispersed, while the church, augmenting in numbers, surpassed every other denomination in the extent of its prosperity. The loud "hallelujahs," "glories," and "amens," which pealed forth from the preachers in such sharp accents as to be heard at least half a mile from the stand at this period, was so different from the sober mode of worship of the more numerous Presbyterians, that many thought them crazy, and in one or two instances attempted to enforce silence by violent measures.

A good story is told of Elder Owen by an old uncle

of the writer, who heard him preach at a quarterly meeting, held at the court-house in Wilkes Barre, in the winter of 1806. Never closing his sermons without reminding sinners of the danger of *brimstone*, it had at length become so proverbial that the boys in a sportive mood (for there were sons of Belial in those days as well as now), had a living illustration of the virtues of his doctrine, at the elder's expense. In the south wing of the old court-house there was a large fire-place, in which smoked a huge beechen back-log. Behind this some of the boys had placed a yellow roll of the genuine article before the meeting commenced in the evening. The elder —or the Son of Thunder as he was called—opened his battery with more force than usual upon the citadel of Satan. He began to grow excited while elucidating the words of his text, "he that believeth not shall be damned." The flames of the fire began to penetrate the region where lay concealed the warming and wicked brimstone, the fumes of which spread through the room in the most provoking manner. The elder, with such a re-enforcement to his brain and his battery, felt inspired. Although ignorant of the joke the devil was playing upon him, he soon appreciated the odor of his resistless agent. Turning his eye upon the unconverted portion of the congregation, he exclaimed in a loud voice, "Sinners! unless you are converted you will be cast in the bottomless pit." Pausing a moment as he glanced indignantly upon the tittering ones who were enjoying the scene in an eminent degree, he raised himself to his utmost height, elevated his voice to a still loftier key, and at the same time bringing down his clinched fist with a powerful stroke upon the judge's desk, cried out, "Sinners, why don't you repent, *don't you smell hell?*"

It may be interesting to note that in 1833 the long-remembered patriarch, Lorenzo Dow, with his long white beard and imposing equipage, in passing down the valley to his Southern death-bed, preached to a vast assemblage in a barn in Providence. This barn was blown over by the great gale in 1834.

FORMATION OF ANTHRACITE COAL.

To the geologist or the philosopher, coal-formation affords great scope for theory and reflection. The generally accepted supposition of scientific men, is that the coal-fields, once densely covered with trees huge as the California giants, were submerged by volcanic action, forming a vast lake into which whirled chaotic material, separated in the molten body into alternate layers of coal, sandstone, and shale. Different seams or veins of coal are thought to have been formed at different periods in the world's history, but under similar circumstances, thus alternately elevated or depressed. The *progressive* character of fossils appearing in separate strata, proves their deposit at different periods ; and it is more than probable that centuries passed between their respective formations. Vegetable and organic remains found in one stratum, have no analogy in another. In the igneous or fire-rock no carboniferous element enters, while coal, viewed with a microscope, delineates the carbonized character of its origin. Many hundreds of extinct species of plants have been recognized in the secondary series of rocks. The fern is found in the greatest abundance, while the branching mosses—the calamites—the sigillaria—the cycades, and the palm appear in ceaseless profusion.

Geological examinations made in the Lackawanna coal basin seem to favor the idea that the rocks of this region, with their intervening coal strata, originally level in position, were crumpled or folded into their present form of alternate basins and ridges by the same tremendous convulsions or slow changes which crowded up the Alleghany ranges ; and that, since then, the action of diluvial and atmospheric agencies have worn away the upper or coal-bearing strata on most of the high and exposed points of the Moosic hills and mountains, leaving them only in the troughs or depressions which were sheltered by the mountain rock and left in the position now found by the miner. The contraction or cooling of the anthracite lakes, gave the dipping or broken appearance to many of the veins of coal. Coal destitute of bitumen, or *hard coal*, found only in a minute portion of the earth's surface, everywhere in the carboniferous series presents the same phenomena of fossils. The fern being identified in species and genus to all those found in coal bottoms, it is inferred that the earth in its primitive period was insular, and that the rank vegetable growing then was the result of the internal heat of the globe, which at that time was too uniform to affect the latitudes. In fact, the immense quantity of fossils brought to light along the Lackawanna, the remains of that by-gone time, attest how numerous the herd, and how hot and fertile the clime of that ancient epoch.

In the preparation of vegetable matter for coal, heat, pressure, and water, were probably the controlling agents employed millions of years ago in the great *cooking* laboratory of nature.

ORGANIC REMAINS IN COAL STRATA.

Vegetable fossil and organic remains have been found in various mines in the valley—more especially in the townships of Providence, Blakeley, and Carbondale—imbedded in the inclosing strata, preserving every original outline except the change effected by the vast pressure, from the rounded to the flattened form.

A large turtle family, fossil sea-shells, and fish resembling the gar-pike, or common pickerel, in size and shape, were found in Providence during the summer of 1856, by Captain Martin, while engaged in sinking a shaft, at the depth of some 200 feet. These were incased in the carboniferous strata in such relation to the older, deeper rock as to lead to the belief that the fish had once inhabited an open space of water communicating with a larger body or with the ocean itself, which by some upheaval of the earth became isolated, the waters of the lake were drained, while the fish perished and, intermingled with sand, shale, and stone, were translated into the petrified specimens, now unresistingly summoned by the miner's drill.

One large fish, more than a foot in diameter, and six feet in length, its fins, scales, and general structure yet distinctly recognized upon the stereotyping stone, was exhumed from its sepulcher, and blackened and brainless as it was found, takes us back to a period unknown and remote. This fish was broken while being blasted out by the miner, so that the skillful anatomist could soon determine, by the nature as well as by the number of the exposed vertebræ, its true species.

Rain-marks, foot-prints, stigmaria, and other characteristics of the coal-measure, have been furnished in interesting abundance, within a comparative small space, during the progress of the excavation at the shaft of the Van Stork Coal Company in Providence.

In 1831, while Captain Stott was driving a drift in the mines at Carbondale for the Delaware and Hudson Canal Company, the roof of the mine, becoming dislocated from the parent earth, fell in over a considerable surface, furnishing the richest aspect of vegetable and organic fossils. Deep in the fractured interstratifying stone and slate were imprinted innumerable delicate impressions of leaves, flowers, broken limbs, of the palm leaf and the fern, so remarkable in size as to indicate that the temperature of the earth's surface at the period of their growth was far too heated for human life; fallen trunks and branches of trees, so singularly dark and beautiful, that Daguerre could neither imitate nor improve; huge outlines and tracks of the *ichthyosauri*—the giant lizard, curious in anatomical structure and strength; snakes, ribbed and rounded, whose like is rarely known, and whose analogues are only found near the tropics; a class of amphibians intermediate between reptiles and fish—the *batrachian* tribe—the mammoth frog, foot-marks of which were displayed, exhibiting five toes before and four behind, marking their presence and passage in other times; all so distinctly and so terribly delineated upon this master-press of nature, as to convey to the mind some faint idea of the monsters once swarming the jungles, and whose courts on the low, wet, warm marshes were suddenly adjourned by the great phenomena of coal-formation.

MINERALS AND MINING.

The Lackawanna and Wyoming anthracite coal basin, walled by low ranges of the Alleghany, and drained by the placid Lackawanna and Susquehanna, is about fifty miles in length and averages four in width. Veins of the purest anthracite emerge from the foot of the mountains, its entire length and breadth. The lower strata, sunk at a mean depth of four or five hundred feet beneath the surface in mid-valley, show themselves higher up the mountain side than those located nearer the surface of the valley.

In its mineralogical character, the Lackawanna Valley is both varied and productive. Filled with the coal-measure from side to side, it not only presents a series of slate and shale interstratified with anthracite from a few inches to as many feet in thickness, but iron ore and limestone commingle and enrich the rugged acres of the intervale. Four of the great coal seams in the Lackawanna Basin, viz.: the 7, 8, 10, and 12 feet veins (least thickness), furnish a total thickness of 37 feet, or 44,000 tons per acre.

The productive character of this coal basin is exhibited by the following table prepared by Professor Rogers,[1]

---

[1] Report of the Geology and Mining in the Lackawanna Valley.

with especial reference to the coal-bearing in the township of Providence:—

TABLE.

Least Thickness.	Good Coal.	Yield of good Coal per Acre
5 feet.	3 feet.	4,000 tons.
7 "	4½ "	7,000 "
10 "	7½ "	12,000 "
6 "	3 "	5,000 "
12 "	9 "	15,000 "
8 "	6 "	10,000 "
6 "	4½ "	7,000 "
54 "	37½ "	60,000 "

These seven veins alone yield 60,000 tons per acre. Twelve distinct, separate beds underlying the entire valley, furnish about sixty feet of available coal,—a supply ample for as many generations, or until the day of ballooning shall bring forth a new discovery calculated to supersede the coal fire, as the old beechen back-log of times gone by has vanished into ashes.

While the center of the Northern and Lackawanna coal-field is regarded as being near Pittston—the bed of the ancient caldron once glowing with anthracite—mines were first successfully worked at Carbondale at least one thousand feet above the level of Pittston coal. About twenty-five miles in length may be considered as the extent of this field, running northeast and southwest with the great Appalachian chain.

COAL LANDS FIFTY YEARS AGO.

Between the villages of Hyde Park and Providence bristles from the road-side a clump of pines, swinging their green limbs over a low, faded cottage, once made attractive by the presence of a young and loving heiress. To the south of this cottage a few yards opens a glen, so worn by the rapid stream dashing through it after a heavy rain or sudden snow-thaw, as to make it look almost cavernous. Down this rock-rimmed ravine, where it expands into the ancient meadow of Capoose, there lived an old gentleman in 1800, named Stephen Tripp, who owned much of the land in the notch of the mountain, about one mile above this point, called Leggett's Gap.

Upon the brink of Leggett's Creek, passing through this gap, a small grist-mill was erected in 1805 by Joseph Fellows, Sen., the remains of which are yet visible by the road-side, but as the bank upon one side of the creek rose almost vertically into a full mountain, and upon the other ascended quite as abruptly hundreds of feet, covered with the stern hemlock, neither road, team, nor grist could approach the mill with safety, and the enterprise was reluctantly abandoned.

This mountain mill-site, with a quantity of the wild land in the vicinity of the "Notch," Mr. Fellows purchased of Tripp, sixty years ago, for five gallons of whisky; Fellows stipulating in the purchase to pay expense of survey and deed. The commercial worth of whisky being one dollar per gallon, this sale realized about *five cents per acre* for lands now owned and mined by the Delaware, Lackawanna, and Western Railroad Company, and worth at least five thousand dollars per acre. Some estimate of the value of coal lands at this period can be formed by the following incident. A then young man from Connecticut, who recently died in the adjoining county of Wayne, was passing along through Slocum Hollow (now Scranton), and observing a prominent cropping of coal by the road-side, asked the owner what it was, and what it was good for?

"Wal," replied the owner, who suspected it was no great credit either to his judgment or his pocket to possess such land, "they call it stone-coal, I believe, but I wish the *cussed black stuff* was off!"

THE DISCOVERY AND INTRODUCTION INTO USE OF ANTHRACITE COAL.

When lands passed from the natives to the whites, all knowledge of mineral deposits was rigidly withheld.

Tradition gives a definite place to mines of gold, silver, lead, iron, copper, and coal, in neighborhoods far up in the wilderness where the wild man dwelt in his silent realm, but so carefully did the Indians, who knew less of the crucible than the cupidity of the trader, baffle the whites in their concealment, that their existence or location has become the subject of strange tales. If the men skilled in the lore of the forest were familiar with precious metals or black stones, their worth was taught them by the whites.

Of the value, or even the existence of coal in America, all races were ignorant until about the middle of the seventeenth century. "At Christian Spring (near Nazareth) there was living about the year 1750 to '55 a gunsmith, who, upon application being made him by several Indians to repair their rifles, replied that he was unable to comply immediately; 'for,' says he, 'I am entirely bare of charcoal, but as I am now engaged in setting some wood to char it, therefore you must wait several weeks.' This, the Indians (having come a great distance) felt loath to do; they demanded a bag from the gunsmith, and having received it, went away, and in two hours returned with as much stone-coal as they could well carry. They refused to tell where they had procured it."[1]

That portion of Pennsylvania purchased of the Five Nations by the Connecticut Susquehanna Company at Albany, July 11, 1754, for "the sum of two thousand pounds of current money of the province of New York,"[2] embraced the Lackawanna and Wyoming coal district. Fourteen years later, November 5, 1768, the same territory was included in the Fort Stanwix purchase of the Indian Nations by the Proprietary Government of Pennsylvania. The strife between Pennsylvania and Connecticut over Wyoming resulted from these purchases.

As early as 1648, iron and copper mines were worked

---

[1] Wm. Henry. [2] See original Deed of Six Nations to Susquehanna Co.

in an imperfect manner by the Dutch and Swedes, at a small village on the Delaware called Durham, a few miles below Easton; but no mention of *coal* is made upon any map of Pennsylvania until 1770, when one published by Wm. Schull, of Philadelphia, bears the word "coal" in two places. Pottsville and Minersville are now located upon the points thus indicated.

On the original draft of the "Manor of Sunbury," embracing the entire western side of Wyoming Valley, surveyed in 1768 by Charles Stewart, in the Proprietary interests, appears the brief notation, "stone-coal," without further explanation.

A Yankee named Obediah Gore, who emigrated from Connecticut to Wyoming in February, 1769, began life in the new colony as a blacksmith. Friendly with the remaining natives from motives of policy, he learned of them the whereabouts of black stones, and, being withal a hearty and an experimenting artisan, he succeeded after repeated trials and failures in mastering the coal to his shop purposes the same year. He is believed to have been the first white man to give practical recognition and development to anthracite as a generator of heat. Mr. Gore, afterward an associate judge of Luzerne County, was one of the brave defenders of Forty Fort in 1778, when assailed by the British and their Indian-Tory allies. In the few blacksmith shops in Wyoming Valley and the West Branch Settlement, coal was gradually introduced after its manipulation by Mr. Gore.

When the struggle for American Independence began in 1775, the Proprietary Government of Pennsylvania found itself so pressed for fire-arms, that under the sanction of the Supreme Executive Council two Durham boats were sent up to Wyoming and loaded with coal at Mill Creek, a few miles below the mouth of the Lackawanna, and floated down the Susquehanna to Harris's Ferry (Harrisburg) thence drawn upon wagons to Carlisle and employed in furnaces and forges to supply the defenders of our country with arms. Thus stone-coal by its patriotic triumphs achieved its way into gradual use.

Beyond the limits of Wyoming, no discoveries of coal were made until 1791. During this year, "a hunter, by the name of Philip Ginther, who had built himself a rough cabin in the forest, on the Mauch Chunk Mountain, being out one day in quest of food for his family, whom he had left at home without any supply, meeting with but poor success, bent his course homeward as night was approaching, considering himself one of the most forsaken of human beings. As he trod slowly over the ground his foot stumbled against something, which by the stroke, was driven before him; observing it to be black, to distinguish which there was just enough light remaining, he took it up, and as he had often listened to the traditions of the country of the existence of coal in the vicinity, it occurred to him that this might be a portion of that *stone-coal* of which he had heard. He accordingly carefully took it with him to his cabin, and the next day carried it to Colonel Jacob Weiss, residing at what was then known as Fort Allen, now Weissport." [1]

Coal-pits were opened here in May, 1792, by the "Lehigh Coal and Mine Company," which gratuitously distributed the brittle compound into every blacksmith shop in this portion of the State willing to use it.

When the forest began to recede and the fresh charred land engaged the thoughts of the backwoodsman on the Lackawanna, stone-coal had neither value nor recognition among men, with but a single exception.

In 1815, there died an eminent physician and surgeon in Tunkhannock, who had formerly lived in the Lackawanna Valley, and who made the first purchase in the county of Luzerne of the right to mine coal here, of which record evidence is furnished. This was Dr. William Hooker Smith, who made a number of such pur-

---

[1] Henry's Lehigh Valley, p. 377.

chases for a mere song, between the years of 1792 and 1798.

A bushel of coal was sent to Christian Micksch, a gunsmith in Nazareth, in November, 1798, but after trying it for three or four days by repeated blowing and punching and altering the fire in every possible manner, he grew so impatient at his long, fruitless efforts, that he indignantly threw it into the street, saying to Mr. William Henry, of whom he had purchased a bushel, "I can do nothing with your *black stones*, and therefore I threw them out of my shop into the street; I can't make them burn. If you want any work done with them, you may do it yourself; everybody laughs at me for being such a fool as to try to make stones burn, and they say that *you* must be a fool for bringing them to Nazareth."

During General Sullivan's march through Wyoming in 1779, one of his officers wrote of the valley: "The land here is excellent, and comprehends vast mines of coal, pewter, lead, and copperas."[1] The last three named have never been found here. The first few ark-loads of coal, carried from Mauch Chunk to Philadelphia was purchased by the city authorities, placed under the boiler of an engine, where it "put the fire out, while the remainder of the coal was broken up and used for graveling streets."[2]

Knowing that there was value in coal, which, in spite of the universal prejudice against its encroachments upon the old wood-pile and fire, would be made manifest by moral firmness and persistent struggle, and that it would rescue their mountains from oblivion, the Lehigh operators, animated by no hope of *immediate* remuneration, mined a larger quantity of coal in 1806. The general distrust, however, of using *stony fuel* for domestic purposes was so prevalent even among intelligent persons, that comparatively none could be sold, little accepted as a gift,

---

[1] George Grant's Report, 1779.   [2] William Henry.

thus compelling these gentlemen to suspend operations, and calmly wait and watch for the public mind to become schooled in the treasures of the Lehigh. Men, however upright and honorable, who *talked* of its introduction into common use in Philadelphia, were deemed fanatics, and ridiculed accordingly; those attempting to *sell* the stuff for cash, compromised their integrity, and in some instances barely escaped arrest and maltreatment from the hands of the populace.

The late Hon. Charles Miner came to Wyoming in 1799, and for thirteen years afterward edited the *Luzerne Federalist*, a weekly newspaper published at Wilkes Barre, and conducted with such marked ability and success, that he soon became widely known as one of the strongest and most pleasing writers in the State. An accomplished scholar, an ingenious advocate, he combated the unsparing prejudices of the bigoted with an earnestness calculated to correct rather than offend.

No man labored with more unselfish fervor to unmuffle the coal-field or acquaint the masses with the grandeur of its character, than did the author of the *History of Wyoming*. Mankind, ever ready to embrace error, are slow to perceive great truths. The fallacy of employing *stones* gleaned from the mountain a hundred miles away for fuel, was so great, that the gray-headed octogenarian and the beardless youth—with all the intermediate conditions of life—laughed at the joke attempted to be played upon *them*. Old heads and young ones for once shared harmonious convictions as they arranged themselves as a unit on the orthodox side. Lectures delivered gratuitously explaining the power and character of the new combustible; certificates from Wyoming blacksmiths attesting its superiority; newspaper articles written with ability and patience, brought from the timid unbelievers not even a dull acknowledgment or approval. Or if a few assented to its *possible future* use in some capacity or another, they blended their assent with such a negative spirit as to be little less obnoxious than the blunt, open hostility accorded it everywhere in Philadelphia, the only place coal was sought to be introduced. Quakers, acquiring a competency by the slow accretions of patient toil, were the first to menace and oppose the innovation of coal. As this respectable body, generally calm in its judgment, represented the great bulk of Philadelphia enterprise and intelligence, its decision carried a weight fatal and conclusive in the matter. Meantime, stone-coal, better understood among feudal rocks, began to receive especial homage in the Valley of Wyoming.

Jesse Fell—afterward Judge Fell—a plain, modest reflective blacksmith, living in Wilkes Barre, gave it its first successful impulse toward general domestic use. In watching the light blue flame issuing from the furnace of his shop, made livelier by a draft of air from the hale lungs of a bellows, he conceived the idea of inaugurating a coal fire into an ordinary fire-place. His plan, just and reasonable as it appeared in his own mind for a while, faltered before the strong weapon of simple ridicule.

In the leisure hour of an evening, he built up a jamb of brick work in an old fire-place in his house, upon which he placed four or five bars of common square iron, with a sufficient number up in front to hold wood and coal. He filled this contrivance with hard wood, after igniting which, he piled on a quantity of coal, sought his bed and was soon lost in slumber. This was done late at night lest the people of the neighborhood might again laugh at him for the persistency of his folly. Early in the morning as he awoke, he was astonished and cheered to witness the coal fire announcing its own unconscious achievement. That fire, kindling a glow of anthracite throughout the world, carried the name of Judge Fell down in history. Such was the theme of universal rejoicing throughout the valley that the event was discussed at every fireside; the topic went with the people to church, and was diffused throughout the congregation at large;

by common assent, it entered for a while into all conversations at home and abroad; it silenced every adverse criticism as it gave the signal for long and mutual congratulations at the hospitable house of the judge, where friend and foe alike acquiesced in the truth that Wyoming was freighted with infinite fortune.

Judge Fell, long secretary of the Masonic lodge at Wilkes Barre, deeming the event worthy of note, wrote the following memoranda upon the fly-leaf of the Masonic Monitor, in the bold, beautiful off-hand style for which he was reputed:—

"February 11th, of Masonry 5808. Made the experiment of burning the common stone-coal of the valley, in a grate, in a common fire-place in my house, and find it will answer the purpose of fuel, making a clearer and better fire, at less expense, than burning wood in the common way. JESSE FELL.
"February 11th, 1808."

A few ark-loads of coal went down the Susquehanna with the spring freshets from Wyoming to Harrisburg, where it was treated with the same indifference or derision shown preceding cargoes to Philadelphia.

The intercourse between the inhabitants of Wilkes Barre and Philadelphia being considerable in the unhurried days of the stage-coach; and anthracite being found in abundance in 1812 on the upper waters of the Schuylkill, united auxiliary influences to bear upon the public mind in the city to such an extent, that the next year when Col. George M. Hollenback sent two four-horse wagon-loads of coal from Mill Creek to Philadelphia, it was sold with little effort to a few liberal patrons, among whom were the Wurtses, afterward conspicuous as pioneers in the Lackawanna coal-field.

Up the Lackawanna, coal was first burned in 1812, by H. C. L. Von Storch, of Providence. A bare body of it, washed by the high waters of spring, early exhibited its bald, blackened features by the side of the stream, near his dwelling. The same body or vein can yet be seen lying equidistant between the bridge crossed by Sanderson's railroad and Von Storch's slope. Ignorant of the laws of mining, Mr. Von Storch *dug* up the coal as ordinary earth is dug. In an awkward grate, contrived from iron made at Slocum Hollow, he used the coal as a substitute for wood. His success was so complete, that although the woods encircling his clearing offered its timber and coal for naught but the trouble of securing them, the superior genius of the latter, as an economical agent, was acknowledged even here.

This stratum of coal, half-hidden under its rocky pillow, at once changed the entire tenantry and business aspect of the valley. William and Maurice Wurts, the real *accoucheurs* of this coal basin, were impelled hither in 1812 in search of coal, and while exploring every gap and gorge, came across this prominent out-shoot. They desired earnestly to purchase, and had it fallen into their possession, as it possibly would have done had it not been for the success of Von Storch in burning coal found upon it, aside from the many changes it would have effected in all the relations of the valley, it is barely possible that Honesdale, Carbondale, Archbald, or Olyphant would have arisen from the wilderness, or grown into towns of their present importance.

Nor can it be supposed that Scranton, with its irresistible expansion, would have been even in existence to-day as *Scranton*, if, from the operations of the Wurtses on Von Storch's farm in Providence, "Wurtsdale," or some other town, had sprung into being, because the men whose name it bears—especially the late George W. and the present Joseph H. Scranton, who have contributed as much, if not more, to shape the varied industrial interests of this section of the valley than any other persons connected with its history—would have turned elsewhere their really effective energies.

Bituminous coal, used to a considerable extent in Philadelphia at this time, being withheld from Liverpool by the collision with England, intelligent men who had acquired coal property and privileges for almost nothing, aimed to supply its place with anthracite. Hon. Charles Miner and Jacob Cist, Esq., both prominent in the improvements of the day, sent down an ark-load of twenty-four tons of coal from Mauch Chunk to Philadelphia in the fall of 1814. By personal address and the necessities of manufacturing interests, they disposed of it all with but little loss to themselves. As the cost of transportation, fourteen dollars per ton, to an unwilling market, exceeded the receipts, these gentlemen soon withdrew from the proprietorship of the mines. While Mr. Miner promulgated and widened a knowledge of the qualifications of the new fuel, Mr. Cist, a merchant by profession, a natural genius and mechanic, was the first person to construct a pattern for burning coal in stoves. The stove was a high, square affair, uncouth in style, and yet a great step in advance of coal grates in use at the time.

While the coal, in ordinary grates, burned without smoke, spark, or flame, the flues of the chimneys built without adaptation to its use, proved so defective that the dust and sulphurous odor filling the low-roomed houses from the fires were almost insufferable. The venerable Dr. Peck informs the writer that when he came into the valley, in 1818, there were but two houses along the Lackawanna where stone-coal had made invasions upon the green wood pile and smutty fire-place. One was Preserved Taylor's, the other at Von Storch's. At no place in Wyoming was there at this time more than a single grate used in any dwelling. Joseph Slocum, Lord Butler, Philip Myers, Charles Miner, Jacob Cist, George M. Hollenback, and perhaps a half-a-dozen others, comprised the entire number of individuals having even a single grate in their houses fifty years ago in Wyoming Valley.[1]

[1] Dr. Peck.

The first coal taken from the valley of Wyoming in a canal-boat was started October 20, 1832.

WILLIAM AND MAURICE WURTS—EXPLORATION IN THE COAL-FIELD OF THE LACKAWANNA—CONCEPTION AND EARLY HISTORY OF THE DELAWARE AND HUDSON CANAL.

The war of 1812, dissolving many arrogant illusions across the water, was a powerful if not the chief auxiliary in the work of changing the passive and sedate character of the Lackawanna coal-fields.

This war, interrupting commercial intercourse with Liverpool and Virginia, cut off the supplies of fuel from those places so completely, that charcoal rose to a ruinous price. To the manufacturing interests of the country, the consequences were, of course, highly disastrous. Men familiar with the nature of anthracite coal attempted to relieve this embarrassment if possible, by the discovery and introduction among manufacturers of this new kind of fuel.

How their efforts were met and encouraged by the grand, great aggregate popular side in Philadelphia, the reader already understands.

Long before the coal heart of the Lackawanna was startled by the drill of the miner, there was occasionally seen in the valley a young, self-reliant, and determined man, who, trained by experience in steady habits and modest bearing, acquired the honor, in connection with his elder brother Maurice, of planning and maturing schemes under the shadows of the Moosic, which gave an impulse to the interests of commerce, whose influence was immediate and broadcast throughout the world. Energetic and active, enjoying sound judgment, a robust body that wavered only after long exposure in vindicating his theory by a practical development, he roamed for a series of years along the stream from its headsprings beyond the coal-measure down to its staid outgoing. This was William Wurts, a merchant of Philadelphia.

His first hope, founded upon the obscure knowledge attainable at that early day of the contour and geological structure of the country, was to trace the coal up the valley of the Lackawanna, in the direction of the general trend of the mountain ranges, to the Delaware River. Obliged to abandon this idea, and still retaining the Delaware in view as the grand highway for the transportation of his coal to market, his next conception was to reach the nearest tributary of that stream, the *Lackawaxen*, leading a quiet life upon the opposite side of the Moosic This barrier between the Lackawanna and Lackawaxen, guarded by woods and granite, like the calumet offered as a token of peace, increased rather than abated the fervor of his enthusiasm.

The explorations of Mr. Wurts, commencing about 1812, were extended by himself and subsequently by his agents over the central and northern portion of the valley while it was as rugged as when it offered no longer a home to the Monseys. None of the eastern passes in the Moosic, viz.: Rixe's, Wagner's, and Cobb's had ever been marked for a road, with the exception of the latter one. These he repeatedly examined, with a view of finding a passage from the coal-mines to the headsprings of the Lackawaxen, through whose waters it was supposed that coal could be carried toward an eastern market.

A trivial incident favored the researches and designs of Mr. Wurts. While searching up and down the Lackawanna he came across a hunter, named David Nobles, familiar with places where black stones could be readily pointed out. The State of Pennsylvania had not at this time withdrawn its prerogative of imprisonment for debt. David Nobles, struggling in vain with poverty he inherited, being threatened for a trifling debt by an extortionate neighbor in the county of Wayne, fled to the woods with his gun to avoid the officer and the jail. Mr. Wurts found him rambling over Ragged Island, heard his simple story, and, after giving him the wherewithal to secure his exemption from arrest, employed him to hunt coal and bring knapsacks of provisions over the mountain from the township of Canaan, where a few farmers lived. He became, during the summer months, the inseparable companion of the pioneer, sounding his way up the winding of the Lackawanna. His knowledge of the woods and location of coal territory made him competent as a guide and invaluable as an employee.

After the discovery of vast bodies of coal upon lands, the possession of which was essential in maturing the original purpose, Mr. Wurts and Nobles visited Northumberland to purchase them. As the shabby exterior of Mr. Nobles carried no dignity, nor awakened suspicions of wealth or any ulterior object, he was selected to make preliminary negotiations and the final purchase. Nobles intimated to the owner, who had no knowledge of the eyes glancing longingly over his waste of acres, that he and his numerous brothers desired to farm it on a large scale somewhere along the frontier, where a considerable tract of wild land could be bought for a trifle. The owner, eager to accept any definite offer for lands hitherto unsought by the settlers below, readily acquiesced in the terms of sale. Mr. Nobles, unable to make payment himself, called in "his friend" Wurts, in whose name the contract was signed for possessions, which gave him the key to a coal fortress first assailed in the valley.

By such artifices, honorable and ingenious as they were, Mr. Wurts secured control of several thousand acres of coal land in the county of Luzerne, in the year of 1814. The cost of the land at this time was but fifty cents to three dollars per acre. The giant timber spread over it was of no account, and much of it upon the site of Carbondale was felled and burned away to prepare it for the reception of the cabins of the workmen. These purchases made by an expenditure now considered nominal and vague, included the region where Carbondale and Archbald are located, with a portion of the intervening land, and a small section in Providence, on the Anderson farm, above Cobb's Gap; where, in 1814, he opened the seven and nine feet veins of coal to obtain specimens for exhibitions in Philadelphia, New York, and other sections of country.

Hon. Paul S. Preston, of Stockport, Pennsylvania, now hale and hearty, in his 73d year, a warm friend of the late Col. Scranton and the Erie road, who, in 1849, predicted "that the transit of coal north and west, within the next quarter of a century would exceed that of the present day to the south and the east,"[1] thus writes: "In 1804, my father run an exploration line from Stockport to Misshoppen, passing through what is now known as (I believe) Griswold's Gap. In crossing the Lackawanna Creek, he discovered stone-coal, with which he had become acquainted in Western Virginia and on the Monongahela as a surveyor previous to his location at Stockport.

"In the year 1814, I heard my father tell Maurice Wurts in Market Street, Philadelphia, 'Maurice, thee must hold on to that lot on the Lackawanna, that you took for debt of David Nobles, it will be very valuable some day as it has stone-coal on it and under it.' Whether Maurice was aware of that fact before, I know not. The lot, however, was *hung on to*. Its location was where Carbondale now stands." The next important event connected with the history of the earliest coal operations in the valley, was an attempt made by Wurts in the year 1815, to transport the coal he had mined at this isolated point, to the Wallenpaupack or some stream leading into it.

On the opposite side of the Moosic Range in the adjoining county of Wayne, threads along its base a narrow creek, whose dark languid waters are so hid by the rank alders and iron-like laurel, as to be concealed from the

---

[1] See Auburn "Daily Advertiser," Jan. 19, 1849.

view, until its marshy border is almost passed. This is "Jones's Creek," one of the upper and larger branches of the Wallenpaupack. Being eight or nine miles only from the coal-mines opened in Providence, this creek, from its convenient proximity, was selected as one of ample capacity, after the removal of ordinary obstructions, to carry light rafts and a small quantity of anthracite down to the Paupack. The whole summer of this year was spent by Mr. Noble in clearing this stream of the interlocking logs and drift-wood. After a raft had been lashed together, two sled-loads of the first coal ever carried from the Lackawanna, were loaded upon it.

A long, heavy rain had so swollen the volume of water, that when the raft swung out into the current with its glistening freight, it ran safely for the distance of nearly a mile, when, encountering a projecting rock, the frail float went to pieces, and the coal sank into the flood. Thus were the hopes of the young Philadelphian baffled at the very onset, and the busy world neither delighted nor grieved at the result.

The mind of Wurts, refusing rest, allowed no transient failure to alienate or defer the maturing of his specific scheme.

The old Connecticut road from the Delaware to Wyoming, in passing over Cobb's Mountain, came within a few miles of the two mines opened by Wurts. Over this, to the slackened waters of the Wallenpaupack, one of the tributaries of the Lackawaxen, and about twenty miles distant, coal was next drawn on sleds by the slow ox-team. Here rafts were constructed from dry pine-trees, on which coal was taken as far as Wilsonville Falls, where this stream, narrowing to about seventy feet in width at the top, leaps over three consecutive ledges of rocks of fifty feet each with singular force and beauty. The coal being carried around these falls upon wagons to the eddy in the Lackawaxen, was reloaded into arks and taken thence to the Delaware, and if these were not stove up in their downward passage reached Philadelphia, where nobody wanted the "black stuff," as all the blowing and stirring given to it did not make it burn.

But little coal, and this at a ruinous expense, was taken over this route, and it being abandoned as a complete failure, led to operations farther up the valley in the wilderness, in the vicinity of Rixe's Gap. Here we next find Maurice Wurts associated with his brother William, mining coal on the Lackawanna, at the spot now called Carbondale. This was in 1822, and eight years before the North Branch Canal was put under contract from Nanticoke to the mouth of the Lackawanna. The scene of their operations was a bluff which rises upon the western side of the town, then forming the immediate bank of the river, whose channel has since been diverted. Here these determined, far-seeing pioneers in the coal-fields kept their men at work until late in the fall, forming a sort of encampment in the woods, sleeping on hemlock boughs and leaves before a large camp-fire, and transporting their provisions for miles upon horseback. The mine was kept free from water by a rude pumping-apparatus moved by the current of the river, and when the accumulation of ice upon it obstructed its movements, a large grate made of nail-rods was put in blast, in which a fire of coal was continually kept burning and removing the difficulty. In this slow laborious manner they succeeded at great expense in taking out about eight hundred tons of coal, which they intended to have drawn upon sleds over the mountain through Rixe's Gap to the Lackawaxen during the winter, in order to be floated down the Delaware to Philadelphia in the spring. The winter of 1823 being unusually mild, snow remaining on the ground but few weeks in heavy drifts, only about one hundred tons were drawn over to the rafting-place, a distance of about twenty miles, via Cherry Ridge.

Instead of arks, found to be too expensive and easily broken in their downward passage, dry pine-trees were cut, rolled into the stream, and lashed together raft-like, upon which as much coal was deposited as would safely float, and thus taken down the Lackawaxen and Delaware to Philadelphia.

The price of anthracite coal in this city at this time was but ten or twelve dollars per ton. At these figures it was estimated that a remunerative profit awaited coal transported in this manner, or even in the unreliable ark, provided the navigation of the Lackawaxen was made safe by practical slack-water improvements.

In 1823, Maurice Wurts was authorized and empowered by the Legislature of Pennsylvania thus to improve the navigation of this short, wild stream. In the mean time, the supply of coal from the Schuylkill and Lehigh regions, small as it was, had so reduced the price as to preclude any hope of a profit such as would justify the expenditure, unless a new and better market could first be found or created.

The *demand* for coal at this time can be perceived from the fact, that during the entire year of 1820, only 365 tons of anthracite were sent to market—just *one* ton a day to supply every demand in the city of Philadelphia.

In 1823, only 6,000 tons of anthracite were carried to the sea-board in the whole United States, being considerably less than the amount now used in the Lackawanna Valley every day in the year.

New York and the Lackawanna Valley, linked together by the social chain of canal, railroad, and river, mutually dependent upon each other, knew no interest in common until schooled by the active and persistent agency of the Wurtses. The original plan of looking to Philadelphia for a source of revenue being frustrated by the reduced price of coal, Maurice Wurts, in whom the privilege of improving the navigation of the Lackawaxen was vested, and who had now become largely interested in the enterprise, conceived the project of reaching New York by a direct canal communication between the Delaware and

Hudson rivers. With the hope of accomplishing this object, the exploration of the route on which the Delaware and Hudson Canal has since been constructed, was undertaken by William Wurts alone; and, after such a superficial inspection as he could give it without an actual survey, he concluded that the favorable character of the ground, especially through southern New York, and the abundant supply of water-power at the very beginning of the route, would justify the prosecution of the enterprise.

The project of connecting the two localities by a water communication, favored and understood by few, received a primary and definite form, and although there seemed to have been no just appreciation of the difficulties to be surmounted, or the physical labor and expense incurred in maturing a scheme full of advantage and traffic to the valley, these two gentlemen determined to lend all their energies to its completion.

The needful legislation from the respective States of Pennsylvania and New York was obtained by their unaided efforts, and after an abortive attempt to interest residents upon the route, or those living in the valley, so as to obtain a general fund for the preliminary survey, they engaged Benjamin Wright, then the most experienced engineer in the country, to make the necessary surveys and estimate at their own expense.

The report of the engineer, made in 1824, confirmed the most sanguine calculations of the projectors as to the practicability of the work; but the estimate of its cost ($1,300,000) was discouraging, and to obtain subscriptions for such an amount of money, at that time, for such a work, seemed almost hopeless. Capitalists naturally viewed with distrust a proposition to construct a railroad over a mountain, whose cliffs seemed to exult over physical ingenuity and science; and when these energetic men began to talk of opening a canal navigation through an unknown region, at a period, too, when such undertakings were regarded, even under the most favorable circumstances, as unremunerative and of doubtful propriety, many persons, representing the current of popular thought, unconscious of the celebrity awaiting these gentlemen for their good judgment and cheerful perseverance, were active and clamorous in predicting ruin and dishonor.

Happily for the interests of the country at large and the valley especially, the inflexible men, inured to fatigue and encampment upon rocks, who had glowed with the hope of bearing the work across the country dividing the Hudson from the shallow Dyberry, inherited the requisite force and ability to urge it to a favorable issue. They recognized no opposition from any quarter. Conscious that a failure would compromise forever their positions as business men, and number their names among dishonest schemers, they concentrated every available resource to foster and advance the great enterprise.

Their plans, considered after repeated tramps over the mountain, was to cross the Moosic by inclined planes, connecting the railroad with the canal on its eastern side, at the greatest elevation at which water could be obtained from the natural ponds strung along the western terminus of the route.[1]

Almost on the very summit of the Moosic, nestles among the spruce and oak one of the loveliest sheets of water found anywhere in the country, known as "Cobb's Mountain Pond." Around it gathers the forest, nowhere broken by a clearing, and aside from the light step of the deer upon the margin, or the sail of the wild bird over its surface, no evidence of animated nature appears.

Upon one side of the pond, the waters are so shallow

---

[1] It may be interesting to the local reader to learn, that in the original survey of the proposed route, the western terminus of the canal was to be at Keene's, or Hoadley's Pond, in Wayne County, a distance of only four or five miles from the coal-fields. These ponds, estimated at a capacity of sixty acres, when united, were to be converted into reservoirs, and were supposed to be capable of furnishing the contemplated canal with the necessary supply of water at any extraordinary drought brought by summer.

that the tourist can wade hundreds of feet toward its center, over white sand, without even wetting the knee, while the northern side sends its bank down almost perpendicular for a great distance. In the center of this waveless sheet there exists a perceptible movement of the water or mimic maelstrom, able to swing around a log-canoe. The pond, fed by unseen springs, finds a considerable outlet, and forms the upper tributary of the Wallenpaupack. The idea was early entertained by William Wurts of bringing coal to this pond, some seven miles from Providence, using it as the highest reservoir for the canal. To carry out this plan, it was proposed that subscriptions should be opened for a capital stock of $1,500,000, and the Delaware and Hudson Canal and Banking Company be organized.

The undertaking was greatly in advance of the knowledge and comprehension of the day, and yet so lucid and convincing were the arguments of Maurice and William Wurts in relation to the coal subject, that when the books were opened in New York the subscriptions exceeded the amount authorized by the charter.

While wiser men were thus interpreting the wants of the world, by opening a way into the Lackawanna Mountains, the great popular mind had given little discussion to the theme. In fact, the first element of making coal-fires had to be taught in New York in the same spirit of Christian liberality and patience given to Philadelphia by Messrs. Miner, Wurts, and others, a few years before.

A few persons, spurning pupilage in so plain an affair as making a fire, failing to secure heat by putting the coal in the bottom of the stove and the *wood on top*, refused to have further dealing with the dusky invention.

Stoves and grates, adapted to the use of anthracite coal, being put up in New York, Philadelphia, and Albany, by the agency of these earnest gentlemen, not only demonstrated to the observer the great superiority of anthracite over charcoal and wood as a fuel, but, in spite of strong natural prejudices arrayed against the project, it found among reflecting minds a steady growth and advocacy.

The canal, commenced in 1826, was completed in 1828. Originally constructed for boats of thirty tons, it subsequently was enlarged for those of fifty tons, and within the past few years has again been so altered and improved as to admit boats of one hundred and thirty tons. The arrangements of this company have been judiciously made at different points, such as Carbondale, Honesdale, Olyphant, Providence, &c., for the accommodation of an extensive business. Their capital now exceeds fifteen millions of dollars.

To show how far the results of this pioneer enterprise from the valley have transcended the narrow views of the community of that recent period, both with regard to its capabilities and the use of coal, it may be stated, that the idea of transporting one hundred thousand tons of coal *per annum* over the railroad and canal (upon which idea the capacity of the former was at first based) was at first scouted by many as preposterous, as regarding both the disposal of, and the ability to deliver, such an unheard-of amount, whereas, during the last year (1868), there was transported over this highway, by the Delaware and Hudson Canal Company, nearly *two million* tons of coal.[1]

When this young enterprise was struggling its way into popular favor, equipoised between extermination and a possible triumph, it did not escape the jealousy of men engaged in transporting coal from the Lehigh. The product of the mines had to force itself into a market over the heads of envious and crafty competitors.

Unfortunately for the company, the small quantity of coal taken to New York from the coal-pits at Carbondale, in 1829, being surface coal that had lain for ages exposed to the action of the elements, furnished plausible grounds

---

[1] 1,840,681.06 tons.

apparently for the statements of rival companies, that the Lackawanna coal offered by the Wurtses was quite valueless, or if otherwise, it was boldly asserted that the works of this company were so imperfect in their construction, and so perishable in character, as not to be capable of passing a sufficient amount of tonnage to pay interest upon the original cost.

Indeed, to those who looked searchingly into the matter, with the imperfect knowledge possessed at that day, the Moosic Mountain range might well have proved a great stumbling-block in the way of this artificial outlet to the valley. Habit has now so familiarized us with the triumph of physical science over natural obstacles, that we have ceased to feel or express astonishment at results, which at that day were dismissed from the consideration of rational men as visionary, foolish, and forbidding. The mode of overcoming elevations by means of *inclined planes* was then almost untried, imperfectly known, and little appreciated. The works at Rixe's Gap were the first of this kind projected in this country on any considerable scale. Much credit is due to the engineers having charge of these works, and especially to Mr. James Archibald, for many ingenious and highly efficient contrivances connected with them.

There is one interesting feature connected with the early

FIRST LOCOMOTIVE RUN IN AMERICA.

history of this road. The *first locomotive engine* introduced and worked in America was run a short distance upon it in 1828, and Hone's Dale[1] offered its friendly glen for the purpose of conducting the experiment. This locomotive, called the "Stourbridge Lion," was built in England, of the best workmanship and material, and most approved pattern of that date. As compared with the powerful, compact, and simply constructed engines of the present day, it was complicated, unwieldy, top-heavy, and of inconsiderable power, as will be seen by the accompanying illustration, copied from an exact drawing of the original, in the hands of R. Manville, Esq., Superintendent of the Railroad Department.

The village of Honesdale, the eastern terminus of the railroad and the western of the canal, lies snugly in the bottom of a canal-like intervale, where, a single week before the conception of these works, rose one dark mass of laurel and hemlock, through which the Lackawaxen, once famous for trout-fishing, after meeting with the Dyberry, gropes silently along under Irving's Cliff.

The road passed out of Honesdale by a sharp southwesterly curve, with a moderate grade, and was carried over the Lackawaxen by a long hemlock trestling, considered too frail by many to support the great weight of the mysterious-looking engine all ready for the hazardous journey. As the crowd, gathered from far and near, expected that bridge, locomotive, and all, would plunge into the stream the moment passage was attempted, no one dared to run the locomotive across the chasm but Major Horatio Allen, who, amid exultation and praise, passed over the bridge and a portion of the road in safety. The engine, however, was soon abandoned, as the slender trestling, forming much of the body of the road, sufficiently strong for ordinary cars, was found too feeble for its weight and wear.

---

[1] Named from the late Philip Hone.

Major Horatio Allen, the engineer of the New York and Erie Railroad, gives the following account of the first trip made by a locomotive on this continent:—

"When was it? Who was it? And who awakened its energies and directed its movements? It was in the year 1828, on the banks of the Lackawaxen, at the commencement of the railroads connecting the canal of the Delaware and Hudson Canal Company with their coal mines—and he who addresses you was the only person on that locomotive. The circumstances which led to my being alone on the road were these: The road had been built in the summer; the structure was of hemlock timber, and rails of large dimensions notched on caps placed far apart. The timber had cracked and warped from exposure to the sun. After about three hundred feet of straight line, the road crossing the Laxawaxen Creek on trestle-work about thirty feet high, with a curve of three hundred and fifty-five to four hundred feet radius. The impression was very general that the iron monster would either break down the road, or it would leave the track at the curve and plunge into the creek.

"My reply to such apprehensions was that it was too late to consider the probability of such occurrences; there was no other course than to have a trial made of the strange animal which had been brought here at a great expense; but that it was not necessary that more than one should be involved in its fate; that I would take the first ride alone, and the time would come when I should look back to the incident with great interest.

"As I placed my hand on the throttle-valve handle, I was undecided whether I would move slowly or with a fair degree of speed; but believing that the road would prove safe, and preferring, if we did go down, to go handsomely, and without any evidence of timidity, I started with considerable velocity, passed the curve over the creek safely, and was soon out of hearing of the vast assemblage. At the end of two or three miles I reversed the valve and returned without accident, having thus made the first railroad trip by locomotive on the western hemisphere."

This primitive machine was finally switched off the track, a house built over it, and instead of being treasured as a relic of early engineering in the New World surpassed by no other, its rusted combination was partially destroyed and scattered, quarter of a century ago. Some portions of it are yet in use in Carbondale.

It might have been supposed by intelligent men, that after the authors of this canal and railroad had shown their operations to be practical and effective, when by vast expenditure of means, time, and labor, the most exhausting, their enterprise was completed, their physical efforts and mental anxieties would have been rewarded with respite and profit: subsequent events assured them that their labors had just begun. The cost of these improvements had far exceeded the original estimate, and a large debt had thus been necessarily contracted in their progress. The market for coal was so limited that a small amount supplied the demand, and if it did not forbode the disruption of the company, it alienated all hope of immediate gain or dividend. Before the resources of the company were developed, financial difficulties accumulated. More than this, the cry of monopoly was arrayed against it, at a time when the shares, first costing $100 each, had been six or seven years on the hands of the stockholders without yielding a single dividend, and had therefore, in effect, cost about $140 per share, could actually be bought in the market at the time for about $48 to $50 per share, or half what it had already cost.

The Wurts brothers, undaunted by these adverse auspices, abated none of their confidence in a cause whose fate involved their own integrity as well as the interest of every valley tenant, taught by the narrow-minded to distrust and oppose its success. Maurice Wurts (who had superintended the canal during its construction, and resigned his office when it was completed) undertook, in this exigency, the superintendence of an important department of the company's business, while his brother John, then a prominent member of Congress, of the Philadelphia bar, assumed the presidency. These gentlemen devoted their lives to promote and vindicate the material interests of the company, and the proud, high, firm position it has attained to-day, is much, if not mainly due to the constant care and industry with which its affairs, during a long series of years, sometimes hostile, were conducted by them. This was done in such a broad spirit of fidelity to the entire associated interests, that no charge of self-aggrandizement or greedy selfishness emanated from the most capricious.

Not only was the very existence of the company imperiled by financial dangers formidable in their character, but legislative bodies, moved by the leverage of personal jealousies and fancied rivalry, labored to crush it, and this too, at the instigation of men whose private fortunes and social positions in life, came wholly from the operations they were seeking to arrest and destroy. The benefits which have arisen out of this undertaking, the general and *generating* influences it has exerted in the Lackawanna Valley, are various in kind and character, and are diffused over a wide region of country, as well as concentrated in special localities. Prominent among these special localities, may be named New York City, and the Lackawanna Valley. Who can estimate the magnitude of the impulse which the introduction of cheap fuel has given to the growth of New York? To this great outlet, conceived and matured by Maurice and William Wurts, is this great city indebted for the cheapening and supply of this desirable and indispensable fuel. The history of the company struggling for many years through appalling difficulties, indicates that even here, neither the benefits nor instrumentality by which it was attained, were appreciated by the many recipients. But no estimate can be made of the power which a work like this exercises over the affairs of a nation, in encouraging private and stimulating public efforts for internal improvements. The material benefits thus conferred upon the valley, in the highest degree advantageous and practical to the expanding activities east of the Alleghanies, can be estimated readily by simply comparing the average value of coal land and property *now* and *before* the maturity of this enterprise. The entire length of the canal, including three miles of slack-water navigation, is 111 miles; the railroad from Honesdale to Providence, thirty-two miles.

This road, with but a single exception, the *oldest* in the country, represents more wealth, for one of its length, than any other one in America.

During the last year the company have entered into arrangements with the Baltimore Coal and Union Railroad Company, whereby they control the railroad from Providence to the Baltimore mines, near Wilkes Barre, together with the mines upon that justly celebrated property.

They have also completed an arrangement with the Northern Coal and Iron Company, for the coal in the property, recently purchased by the latter company of the Plymouth and Boston companies. This property is located on the west side of the Susquehanna, in Plymouth, and is considered to be one of the most valuable properties in Wyoming Valley.

The canal company also control the railroad and bridge of the Plymouth and Wilkes Barre Railroad and Bridge Company, which connects the property upon the west side of the river with the system of railroads upon the east side.

These alliances, with other recent acquisitions, give the canal company a position from which it can ship coal in *all* directions, and place it in the front rank of the great coal corporations of the country.[1]

---

[1] Statement of Coal mined and forwarded by the Delaware and Hudson Canal

The Delaware and Hudson Canal Company, preserving the same wise policy inaugurated by William and Maurice Wurts, of giving great discretionary power to their officers at the primary or mining end of the line, have prospered beyond expectation or measure under the judicious management of Thomas Dickson, vice-president of the road, and his able assistant managers, E. W. Weston, R. Manville, and C. F. Young.

George T. Olyphant, of New York, is now the president of this company; its vast interest in the Wyoming Company for the year ending December 10, 1868, with sources whence received:—

SENT NORTH.
Delaware and Hudson Canal Company's Mines.

Carbondale	330,770 12
Grassy Island	97,724 14
Olyphant	294,041 19
Providence	316,301 04
	1,038,838 09

Contractor's Mines.

John Jermyn	171,298 10
Eaton & Co	141,418 10
B. & L. C. Co	95,182 13
Elk Hill Coal Co	62,753 04
Filer & Co	12,347 17
Mineral Spring Coal Co	541 04
	483,541 18

Baltimore Coal and Union Railroad Company's Mines.

Mill Creek	111,722 04
Baltimore	53,770 09
	165,492 13
Total	1,687,873 00

SENT SOUTH.
Baltimore Coal and Union Railroad Company's Mines.

Mill Creek and Baltimore Mines	152,808 06
Total production for 1868	*1,840,681 06
Total production for 1867	1,468,314 10
Increased production for 1868	372,366 16

* or 2,061,565 tons of 2,000 pounds.

and Lackawanna valleys, however, come under the jurisdiction of Thomas Dickson, of Scranton. The village of *Olyphant* derived its name from one, while the young mining town of *Dickson* received its appellation from the other. With a clear head and a disposition to turn hard work to some account, Thos. Dickson came from Scotland, quarter of a century ago, to try his fortune in the mountain ranges of Pennsylvania. Although not "to the manor born," he has, by the aid of a practical turn of mind and steady habits, made his way from the humble place of a *mule-driver*, in the Carbondale mines, to the honorable position he now occupies, with a rapidity and steadiness almost romantic—thus presenting to the young men of the country an illustration of the triumphs of a life of probity and ambitious industry worthy of emulation.

FALLING OF THE CARBONDALE MINES.

Those who have never entered the midnight chambers of a coal-mine, far away in the earth, where no sound is heard but the miner's drill or the report of a blast in some remote gallery, and no light ever enters but the lamps on the workmen's caps, which are seen moving about like will-o'-the-wisps as the men are mining or loading the coal into little cars, can not understand how perilous the miner's occupation, or how much the place he works in reminds one of the great pit itself, only this, in the language of the miner, is free from "the *hate* of summer." Some of the mines are mere low, jet-black coal-holes, gloomy as the tombs of Thebes, while others have halls and chambers of cyclopean proportions, along which are constant openings into cross-chambers or galleries, some sloping downward, some upward, in which roll along cars, drawn by mules, accompanied by a boy as driver. Accidents not unfrequently happen in the mines, by the explosion of powder, as the lamps are continually around it ; by the falling of slate or coal, before props are placed to support the treacherous roof; and sometimes by the falling in of the mines themselves. After all the coal is taken from one stratum or vein, miners frequently remove the pillars or props from the chambers, so that the mines can fill in—this, in miner's language, is called "robbing the mines."

During the winter of 1843 and '44, a portion of the Delaware and Hudson Canal Company's mines, at Carbondale, "fell in" upon the workmen. Some days previous to the final crash, the mine, in the phrase of miners, began to "work," that is, the occasional cracking of the roof over where the men worked, denoted the danger of a fall. It came, and such was its force that all the lights in the mines were extinguished in an instant, while the workmen and horses, which were entering or retiring from the black mouth of the cavern, were blown from it as leaves are swept by the gale. The men who were at work in their narrow chambers farther in the mine, heard the loud death-summons, and felt the crash of the earthquaked elements, as they were buried alive and crushed in the strong, black teeth of the coal-slate.

One of the assistant superintendents of the mines, Mr. Alexander Bryden, was on the outside at the time the low, deep thundering of the rocks within came upon his ear. He hastened in to ascertain the cause of the disaster or the extent of the fall. Penetrating one of the dark galleries a short distance, he was met by three miners, who informed him that the mines had broken, killing and wounding many, and that they had just left behind them about twenty men, who were probably slain by the crushing slate. Although urged by the retreating men to turn back and save his own life, as there was no hope of rescuing their companions from death, the determined Scotchman pushed along the gloomy passage, amid the loosened and hissing rock, which, like the sword of the ancient tyrant, hung over his head. He reached the edge of the fall. Earth and coal lay in vast masses around him, and here and there a body becoming detached from the parent roof, came down with sullen echo into the Egyptian darkness of the mines. Bryden, inured to danger from his youth, was not deterred. The dim light from his lamp revealed no passage, save a small opening made by the huge slabs, falling in such a manner by the side of the floor of the gallery as to form an angle. Through this aperture he crept upon his hands and knees; as he proceeded he found it so narrow that he was barely able to force himself along by lying prostrate upon his abdomen.

About one mile from the mouth of the mines he reached the "heading," or the end of the chamber, where he found the twenty imprisoned miners uninjured, and inclosed in one fallen, black, solid body of coal! One mile of wall between them and the outer world! The brave Scotchman, whose lips whitened not until now, wept like a child, as he found among the number his own son! The boy had the genius of the father. When one of the three retreating fugitives who had escaped from the mine proposed, as they left, to take away the horse confined here with the workmen, young Bryden, who feared the torture of starvation in that foodless cell, replied, "Leave him here; we shall need him!"

Bryden was upon the point of leading out his men when he learned that another lay helplessly wounded, still farther beyond this point, in the most dangerous part of the fall. On he continued his perilous mission until he entered the lonely chamber. A feeble cry from the miner, who was aroused from his bed of slate by the glimmer of the approaching light, revealed a picture of the miner's life too familiar with the men who face danger in these cleft battle-grounds. Almost covered by the fallen strata, he lay half delirious with agony, blackened with coal-dirt, and limbs gashed and fractured with rock. Lifting the wounded man upon his shoulder, Bryden retraced his steps. For rods he bore him along, with the broken, flaccid arms of the miner dangling at his side.

When the rock was too low to permit this, he first crawled along the cavern himself, drawing his companion carefully after him. Through perils which none can appreciate who have not strode along the gloomy galleries of a coal-mine, he bore him full one mile before he reached the living world.

The fall extended over an area of about forty acres, and although neither effort nor expense were withheld by the company or individuals, to rescue the living, or to recover the bodies of the dead, the remains of a few have never yet been found. One man was discovered some time afterward in a standing position, his pick and his dinner-pail bearing him company, while the greater portion of the flesh upon his bones appeared to have been eaten off by rats.

Others, without water, food, or light, shut in from the world forever by the appalling wall of rock, coal, and slate around them, while breathing the scanty air, and suffering in body and mind, agony the most intense, clinched tighter their picks, and wildly labored one long night that knew no day, until exhausted they sank, and died in the darkness of their rocky sepulchers, with no sweet voice to soothe—no kind angel to cool the burning temples, or catch the whispers from the spirit-land.

Eight dead bodies were exhumed, and six were left in—one, the only son of a dependent widow. Mr. Hosie, one of the assistant superintendents of the mines, was in them at the time of the disaster, and escaped with his life. Creeping through the remaining crevices in the break upon his hands and knees, feeling his way along the blackness of midnight, where all traces of the general direction of the mine had disappeared, he often found himself in an aperture so narrow, that to retreat or advance seemed impossible. Once he was buried middle-deep by the rubbish as he was digging through. Another convulsion lifted up the mass and relieved him. After being in the mines two days and nights, he emerged into sunlight, the flesh being worn from his finger-bones in his efforts to escape from the tomb-like captivity.

EARLIEST MAIL ROUTE IN THE VALLEY.

When the first and only post-office was established in the Lackawanna Valley in 1811, the mail was carried once a week on horseback from Wilkes Barre, *via* Capoose or Slocum Hollow, to Wilsonville, the original shire town of Wayne County, at the head of the Wallenpaupack Falls, returning *via* Bethany, Belmont, Montrose, and Tunkhannock. In 1762, or fifty years previous to this, the Rev. David Zisberger, sheltered only by trees and friendly wigwams, made his way along the Indian pathway, from Fort Stanwix, New York, to Wyoming and Philadelphia, for a slight consideration, as can be seen by the following receipt:—

"Received ten pounds for my journey with Sr. Wm. Johnson's Letter to Teedyuscung at Wyomink, & bringing his answer to Philadelphia. DAVID ZISBERGER.

"APRIL 5th, 1762."[1]

Mail matter for the settlements upon the northeast branch of the Susquehanna and its larger tributaries came from Philadelphia, *via* Sunbury or Easton, to Wilkes Barre, whence it was diffused tardily through the broken openings of northern Pennsylvania.

The inhabitants being few, and poor withal, scattered over a wide range of territory, the post-office for the township was sometimes located at a point where there stood but a single cabin, yet this did not render the operations of the office any the less harmonious or effective.

There yet lives in the valley an old gentleman who prided in the duties of mail-boy from 1811-24, and who, during these dozen of years encountered dangers in fording streams swift and swollen, traversing roads lined with stumps and stone, and yet, characterized by a natu-

---

[1] Documentary History of New York, p. 310.

ral cheerfulness and love of fun himself, he sometimes forgot the loneliness of his journey as he encountered humanity in its most amusing aspects, at the stopping-places on his route.

"At one point," writes our informant, "the office was kept in a low, log bar-room, where, after the contents of the mail-pouch were emptied on the unswept floor, all the inmates gave slow and repeated motion to each respective paper and letter."

Sometimes the mail-boy, finding no one at home but the children, who were generally engaged drumming on the dinner-pot, or the housewife, unctuous with lard and dough, lol-li-bye-babying a boisterous child to sleep, was compelled to act as carrier and postmaster himself.

At another point upon the route, the commission of postmaster fell upon the thick shoulders of a Dutchman, remarkable for nothing but his full, round stomach. This was his pride, and he would pat it incessantly while he dilated upon the virtues of his "krout" and his "frow."

It would have been amazingly stupid for the Department to have questioned *his* order or integrity, for as the lean mail-bag came tumbling into his door from the saddle, the old comical Dutchman and his devoted wife carried it to a rear bedroom in his house, poured the contents upon the floor, where at one time it actually took them both from three o'clock one afternoon until nine the next morning to *change* the mail! Believing with Lord Bacon, that "knowledge is power," he detained about election time, all political documents directed to his opponents. These he carefully deposited in a safe place in his garret until after election day, when they were handed over with great liberality to those to whom they belonged, provided he was paid the postage.

"At another remote place where the office was kept, the mail-bag being sometimes returned to the post-boy almost empty, led him to investigate the cause of this sudden collapse in a neighborhood inhabited by few. The prolific number of ten children, graduating from one to twenty in years, all called the postmaster "dad," and as none could read, letters and papers came to a dead stop on arriving thus far. As these were poured out on the floor among pans and kettles, each child would seize a package, exclaiming, this is for me, and this for you, and that for some one else, until the greater bulk of mail-matter intended for other offices was parceled out and appropriated, and never heard of again."

THE PENNSYLVANIA COAL COMPANY.

The definite and successful character of the coal schemes devised by the Wurts brothers, tested amidst every possible element of discouragement and hostility, inclined capitalists to glance toward the hills from whence coal slowly drifted to the sea-board. Drinker and Meredith, aiming at reciprocal objects, and alive to venture and enterprise, each obtained a charter for a railroad in the valley, which, owing to the absence of capital, proved of no practical value at the time to any one.

Twenty-one years after coal was carried from Carbondale by railroad toward a New York market, the Pennsylvania Coal Company began the transportation of their coal from the Lackawanna. This company, the second one operating in the valley, was incorporated by the Pennsylvania Legislature in 1838, with a capital of $200,000. The proposed road was to connect Pittston with the Delaware and Hudson Canal at some point along the Wallenpaupack Creek in the county of Wayne.

The commissioners appointed in this act organized the company in the spring of 1839, and commenced operating in Pittston on a small scale. After mining a limited quantity of coal from their lands—of which they were allowed to hold one thousand acres—it was taken down the North Branch Canal, finding a market at Harrisburg and other towns along the Susquehanna.

Simultaneously with the grant of this charter, another was given to a body of gentlemen in Honesdale, known as the Washington Coal Company, with a capital of $300,000, empowered to hold two thousand acres of land in the coal basin. This last charter, lying idle for nine years, was sold to William Wurts, Charles Wurts, and others of Philadelphia, in 1847.

In 1845, the first stormy impulse or excitement in coal lands went through the central and lower part of the valley. Large purchases of coal property were made for a few wealthy men of Philadelphia, who had reconnoitered the general features of the country with a view of constructing a railroad from the Lackawanna to intersect the Delaware and Hudson Canal near the mouth of the Paupack.

The preliminary surveys upon the proposed route had barely commenced, before there sprang up in Providence and Blakeley, opposition of the most relentless and formidable character. Men who had hitherto embarrassed the company mining coal in Carbondale during its infancy, found scope here for their remaining malignity. The most plausible ingenuity was employed to defeat the entrance of a road whose operations could not fail to inspire and enlarge every industrial activity along its border. Meeting after meeting was held at disaffected points, having for their object the destruction of the very measures, which, when matured, were calculated to result as they did to the advantage of those who opposed them. It was urged with no little force, that if these Philadelphians "seeking the blood of the country," were allowed to make a railroad through Cobb's Gap, the only natural key or eastern outlet to the valley, the rich deposits of coal and iron remaining in the hands of the settlers would be locked in and rendered useless forever. Such fallacious notions, urged by alms-asking demagogues with steady clamor upon a people jealous of their prerogatives, inflamed the public mind for a period of three years against this company, but after such considerations as selfish agitators will sometimes covet and accept tranquilized opposition, those amicable relations which have since existed with the country commenced.

In 1846, the Legislature of Pennsylvania passed "an act incorporating the Luzerne and Wayne Railroad Company, with a capital stock of $500,000, with authority to construct a road from the Lackawaxen to the Lackawanna."

Before this company manifested organic life, its charter, confirmed without reward, and that of the Washington Coal Company being purchased, were merged into the Pennsylvania Coal Company, by an act of the Legislature passed in 1849.

This road, whose working capacity is equal to one and a half million tons per annum, was commenced in 1848; completed in May, 1850. It is forty-seven miles in length, passing with a single track from the coal-mines on the Susquehanna at Pittston to those lying near Cobb's Gap, terminating at the Delaware and Hudson Canal at the spirited village of Hawley. It is worked at moderate expense, and in the most simple manner for a profitable coal-road—the cars being drawn up the mountain by a series of stationary steam-engines and planes, and then allowed to run by their own weight, at a rate of ten or twelve miles an hour, down a grade sufficiently descending to give the proper momentum to the train. The movement of the cars is so easy, that there is but little wear along the iron pathway, while the too rapid speed is checked by the slight application of brakes. No railroad leading into the valley makes less noise; none does so really a remunerative business, earning over ten per cent. on its capital at the present low prices of coal; thus illustrating the great superiority of a "gravity road" over all others for the cheap transportation of anthracite over the ridges surrounding the coal-fields of Pennsylvania.

The true system, exemplified twenty years ago by its present superintendent, John B. Smith, Esq., of uniting the interests of the laboring-man with those of the company, as far as possible, has been one of the most efficient measures whereby "strikes" have been obviated, and the general prosperity of the road steadily advanced.

Through the instrumentality of Mr. Smith this has been done in a manner so uniform yet unobtrusive, as to make it a model coal-road. It carries no passengers.

This company, having a capital of about $4,000,000, gives employment to over three thousand men.

FROM PITTSTON TO HAWLEY.

A ride upon a coal-train over the gravity road of the Pennsylvania Coal Company, from Pittston to Hawley, is not without interest or incident. Starting from the banks of the Susquehanna, it gradually ascends the border of the Moosic Mountain for a dozen miles, when, as if refreshed by its slow passage up the rocky way, it hurries the long train down to the Dyberry at Hawley with but a single stoppage.

Let the tourist willing to blend venture with pleasure, step upon the front of the car as it ascends Plane No. 2, at Pittston, and brings to view the landscape of Wyoming Valley, with all its variety of plain, river, and mountain, made classic by song and historic by her fields of blood. The Susquehanna, issuing from the highland lakes of Otsego, flows along, equaled only in beauty by the Rhine, through a region famed for its Indian history—the massacre upon its fertile plain, and the sanguinary conflict between the Yankees and Pennymites a century ago. The cars, freighted with coal, move their spider-feet toward Hawley. Slow at first, they wind around curve and hill, gathering speed and strength as they oscillate over ravine, woodland, and water. Emerging from deep cuts or dense woods, the long train approaches Spring Brook. Crossing this trout stream upon a trestling thrown across the ravine of a quarter of a mile, the cars slacken their speed as they enter the narrow rock-cut at the foot of the next plane. While looking upon the chiseled precipice to find some egress to this apparent cavern, the buzz of the pulley comes from the plane, and through the granite passage, deep and jaw-like, you are drawn to a height where the glance of the surrounding woods is interrupted by the sudden manner in which you are drawn into the very top of engine-house No. 4.

The Lybian desert, in the desolation of its sands, offers more to admire than the scenery along the level from No. 4 to No. 5. Groups of rock, solitary in dignity and gray with antiquity, are seen upon every side; trees grow dwarfed from their accidental foothold; and only here and there a tuft of wild grass holds its unfriendly place. The babbling of a brook at the foot of No. 5, alone falls pleasantly upon the ear. As the cars roll up the plane, the central portion of the valley is brought before the eye on a scale of refreshing magnificence. The features of the scenery become broader and more picturesque. The Moosic range, marking either side of the valley, so robed with forest to its very summit as to present two vast waves of silent tree-top, encircle the ancient home and stronghold of Capoose. As you look down into this amphitheater, crowded with commercial and village life, catching a glimpse of the river giving a richer shade to a meadow where the war-song echoed less than a century ago, evidences of thrift everywhere greet and gladden the eye.

At No. 6, upon the northern bank of the Roaring Brook, are located the most eastern mines of this company, being those which are situated the nearest to New York City. These consist of a series of coal deposits, varied in purity, thickness, and value, but all profitably worked. The largest vein of coal mined here is full eight feet thick, and is the highest coal mined on the hill northwest of plane No. 6.

Upon the opposite range of the Moosic Mountain in

the vicinity of Leggett's Gap, this same stratum of coal is worked by other companies. Each acre of coal thus mined from this single vein yields about 10,000 tons of good merchantable coal.

The Delaware, Lackawanna, and Western Railroad, crosses that of the Pennsylvania at No. 6, giving some interest to the most flinty rocks and soil in the world. No. 6 is a colony by itself. It is one of those humanized points destitute of every natural feature to render it attractive.

On either side of the ravine opening for the passage of Roaring Brook, the sloping hill, bound by rock, is covered with shanties sending forth a brogue not to be mistaken; a few respectable houses stand in the background; the offices, store-house, workshops, and the large stone car and machine shops of the company are located on the northern bank of the brook. Some sixty years ago a sawmill erected in this piny declivity by Stephen Tripp, who afterward added a small grist-mill by its side, was the only mark upon the spot until the explorations and survey of this company. This jungle, darkened by laurels blending their evergreen with the taller undergrowth, was more formidable from the fact that during the earlier settlement of Dunmore it was the constant retreat of wolves.

Over this savage nook, industry and capital have achieved their triumphs and brought into use a spot nature cast in a careless mood. At the head of No. 6 stand the great coal screens for preparing the finer quality of coal, operated by steam-power.

Up the slope of the Moosic, plane after plane, you ascend along the obliterated Indian path and Connecticut road, enjoying so wide a prospect of almost the entire valley from Pittston to Carbondale, that for a moment you forget that in the crowded streets elsewhere are seen so many bodies wanting souls. Dunmore, Scranton, Hyde Park, Providence, Olyphant, Peckville, Green Ridge, and Dickson appear in the foreground, while the Moosic, here and there serrated for a brook, swings out its great arms in democratic welcome to the genius of the artificer, first shearing the forest, then prospering and perfecting the industrial interest everywhere animating the valley. The long lines of pasturage spotted with the herd, the elongated, red-necked chimneys distinguishing the coal works multiplied almost without number in their varied plots, give to these domains a picturesqueness and width seen nowhere to such an advantage in a clear day as on the summit of Cobb Mountain, two thousand feet above the tide.

Diving through the tunnel, the train emerges upon the "barrens," where, in spite of every disadvantage of cold, high soil, are seen a few farms of singular productiveness. The intervening country from the tunnel to Hawley, partakes of the hilly aspect of northern Pennsylvania, diversified by cross-roads, clearings, farm-houses, and streams. Here and there a loose-tongued rivulet blends its airs with the revolving car-wheel humming along some shady glen, and farther along, the narrow cut, like the sea of old, opens for a friendly passage. Down an easy grade, amidst tall, old beechen forests half hewn away for clearings and homes of the frugal farmers, the cars roll at a speed of twelve miles an hour over a distance of some thirty miles from the tunnel, when, turning sharply around the base of a steep hill on the left, the cars land into the village of Hawley, a vigorous settlement, existing and sustaining itself principally by the industrial manipulations of this company.

A little distance below the village, the Wallenpaupack, after leaping 150 feet over the terraced precipice, unites with the Lackawaxen, a swift, navigable stream in a freshet, down whose waters coal was originally taken from the Lackawanna Valley to the Delaware in arks.

It is fourteen miles to Lackawaxen upon the Delaware, where, in 1779, a bloody engagement took place between

John Brant, the famous chief of the Six Nations, and some four hundred Orange county militia.

The Tories and Indians had burned the town of Minisink, ten miles west of Goshen, scalping and torturing those who could not escape from the tomahawk by flight. Being themselves pursued by some raw militia, hastily gathered from the neighborhood for the purpose, they retreated to the mouth of the Lackawaxen. Here Brant with his followers formed an ambuscade. The whites, burning to avenge the invaders of their firesides, incautiously rushed on after the fleeing savages, ignorant or forgetting the wily character of their foe. As the troops were rising over a hill covered with trees, and had become completely surrounded in the fatal ring, hundreds of savages poured in upon them such a merciless fire, accompanied with the fearful war-whoop, that they were at once thrown into terrible confusion. Every savage was stationed behind the trunk of some tree or rock which shielded him from the bullets of the militia. For half an hour the unequal conflict raged with increasing fury, the blaze of the guns flashing through the gloom of the day, as feebler and faster fell the little band. At length, when half of their number were either slain or so shattered by the bullets as to be mere marks for the sharp-shooters, the remainder threw away their guns and fled; but so closely were they in turn pursued by the exultant enemy that only thirty out of the entire body escaped to tell the sad story of defeat. Many of these reached their homes with fractured bones and fatal wounds. The remains of those who had fallen at this time were gathered in 1822, and deposited in a suitable place and manner by the citizens of Goshen.

The New York and Erie Railroad have sent up a branch road from a point near this battle-ground to Hawley, thus giving to the Pennsylvania Coal Company an unfrozen avenue to the sea-board, besides dispensing in a great degree with water facilities offered and enjoyed until the completion of this branch in 1863.

From 1850 to 1866, 9,308,336 tons of coal was brought from the mines to Hawley, being an average of 581,775 tons per year.[1]

While a great part of the coal carried to Hawley acknowledges the jurisdiction of this branch road, a limited portion is unloaded into boats upon the Delaware and Hudson Canal.

Once emptied, the cars return to the valley upon a track called the *light* track, where the light or empty cars are self-gravitated down a heavier grade to the coal-mines. Seated in the "Pioneer," a rude passenger concern, losing some of the repelling character of the coal car, in its plain, pine seats and arched roof, you rise up the plane from the Lackawaxen Creek a considerable distance before entering a series of ridges of scrub-oak land, barren both of interest and value until made otherwise by the fortunes of this company. Leaving Palmyra township, this natural barrenness disappears in a great measure as you enter the richer uplands of Salem, where an occasional farm is observed of great fertility, in spite of the accompanying houses, barns, and fences defying every attribute of Heaven's first law. About one mile from the road, amidst the quiet hills of Wayne County, nestles the village of Hollisterville. It lies on a branch of the Wallenpaupack, seven miles from Cobb Pond, on the

---

[1] Report of Coal transported over the Pennsylvania Coal Company's Railroad for week and for year ending December 31, 1868, and for corresponding period last year:—

By Rail, week ending December 31	12,786 03	
" Previously	912,063 10	
		924,849 13
By Canal, week ending December 26	Closed.	
" Previously	29,004 19	
		29,004 19
Total by Canal and Rail, 1868		953,854 12
" To same date, 1867		861,729 15
Increase		92,124 17

JNO. B. SMITH, Superintendent.

mountain, and ten miles above the ancient "Lackawa" settlement. AMASA HOLLISTER, with his sons, Alpheus, Alanson, and Wesley, emigrated from Hartford, Connecticut, to this place in 1814, when the hunter and the trapper only were familiar with the forest. Many of the social comforts of the village, and much of the rigid morality of New England character can be traced to these pioneers. Up No. 21 you rise, and then roll toward the valley. The deepest and greatest gap eastward from the Lackawanna is Cobb's, through which flows the Roaring Brook. This shallow brook, from some cause, appears to have lost much of its ancient size, as it breaks through the picturesque gorge with shrunken volume to find its way into the Lackawanna at Scranton.

This gap in the mountain, deriving its name from Asa Cobb, who settled in the vicinity in 1784, lies three miles east of Scranton. It really offers to geologist or the casual inquirer much to interest. This mountain rent, unable longer to defy the triumphs of science, seems to have been furrowed out by the same agency which drew across the Alleghany the transverse lines diversifying the entire range. Like the mountain at the Delaware Water Gap, it bears evidence of having once been the margin of one of the lakes submerging the country at a period anterior to written or traditional history. Emerging from beech and maple woodlands, you catch a glimpse of a long, colossal ledge, bending in graceful semicircle, rising vertically from the Roaring Brook some three hundred feet or more. Its face, majestic in its wildness, as it first greets the eye, reminds one of the palisades along the Hudson. As it is approached upon the cars, the flank of the mountain defies further progress in that direction, when the road, with a corresponding bend to the left, winds the train from apparent danger, moving down the granite bank of the brook deeper and deeper into the gorge, enhanced in interest by woods and waterfall. The hemlock assumes the mastery of the forest along the brook, whose waters whiten as they pour over precipice after precipice into pools below, which but few years since were so alive with trout, that fishing half-an-hour with a single pole and line supplied the wants of a family for a day with this delicious fish. In the narrowest part of the gap, the cars run on a mere shelf, cut from the rock a hundred feet from the bed of the stream, while the mountain, wrapped in evergreens, rises abruptly from the track many hundred feet.

Greenville, a fossilized station on the Delaware, Lackawanna, and Western Railroad, and once the terminus of the Lackawanna Railroad, lies on a slope opposite this point.

The great *pyloric* orifice of Cobb's Gap, once offering uncertain passage to the Indian's craft, illustrates the achievement of art over great natural obstacles. Roaring Brook, Drinker's turnpike, now used as a township road, the Pennsylvania and the Delaware, Lackawanna, and Western Railroad, find ample place under the shadow of its walls.

A ride of an hour, far up from the bottom of the valley through a forest trimmed of its choicest timber by the lumbermen and shingle-makers, brings the traveler again to Pittston, renovated in spirits and vigor, and instructed in the manner of diffusing anthracite coal throughout the country.

DELAWARE, LACKAWANNA, AND WESTERN RAILROAD.

Historical Summary of the Susquehanna and Delaware Canal and Railroad Company (Drinker's Railroad)—The Leggett's Gap Railroad—The Delaware and Cobb's Gap Railroad Company—All merged into the Delaware, Lackawanna, and Western Railroad.

Imperfect as was the knowledge of the value of coal forty years ago, large bodies of it being discovered here and there in the valley, mostly upon or near the surface, led the late Henry W. Drinker to comprehend and agitate a plan of connecting the Susquehanna River at Pittston with the Delaware at the Water Gap, by means of a railroad running up the Lackawanna to the mouth of Roaring Brook, thence up that stream to the placid waters of Lake Henry, crossing the headsprings of the Lehigh upon the marshy table-land forming the dividing ridge between the Susquehanna and Delaware, and down the Pocono and the rapid Alanomink to the Water Gap, with a view of reaching a market.

This was in 1819. The contemplated route, marked by the hatchet over mountain and ravine profound in the depth of their solitude, had no instrumental survey until eleven years afterward, but an examination of the country, with which no woodman was more familiar than Drinker, satisfied him that the intersecting line of communication was not only feasible, but that its practical interpretation would utilize the intervening section, and give action and impulse to many an idle ax. In April, 1826, he easily obtained an act of incorporation of the "Susquehanna and Delaware Canal and Railroad Company." The charter implied either a railroad operated up the planes by water, or a canal a portion of the way. The "head-waters of the river Lehigh and its tributary stream," were prohibited from being used for feeding the canal, as it might "injure the navigation of said river, from Mauch Chunk to Easton." By reference to the original report and survey of this road, it appears that horses were contemplated as the motive power between the planes, that toll-houses were to be established along the line, and collectors appointed, and that the drivers or conductors of "such wagon, carriage, or conveyance, boat or raft, were to give the collectors notice of their approach to said toll-houses by blowing a trumpet or horn."

Henry W. Drinker, William Henry, David Scott, Jacob D. and Daniel Stroud, James N. Porter, A. E. Brown, S. Stokes, and John Coolbaugh, were the commissioners.

Among the few persons in Pennsylvania willing to welcome and recognize the practicability of a railroad route in spite of the wide-spread distrust menacing it in 1830, stood prominently a gentleman, by the aid of whom, the Indian Capoose region of *Slocum Hollow* changed the ruggedness of its aspect—William Henry. In fact, Messrs. Henry and Drinker were two of the most indefatigable and energetic members of the board.

In 1830, a subscription of a few hundred dollars was obtained from the commissioners; in May, 1831, Mr. Henry, in accordance with the wishes of the board, engaged Major Ephraim Beach, C. E., to run a preliminary line of survey over the intervening country.

By reference to the old report of Major Beach, it will be seen that the present line of the southern division of the Delaware, Lackawanna, and Western Railroad is, in the main, much the same as that run by him at this time. Seventy miles in length the road was to be made, at a total estimated cost of $624,720. Three hundred and thirty-six wagons (cars), capable of carrying over the road 240,000 tons of coal per year, were to be employed.

Coal at this time was worth $9 per ton in New York, while coal lands in the valley could be bought at prices varying from $10 to $20 per acre.

It was not supposed by the commissioners that the *coal* trade alone could make this road one so profitable, but it was originally their object to connect the two at these points, so as to participate in the trade upon the Susquehanna. For the *return* business it was thought that "iron in bars, pig, and castings, would be sent from the borders of the Delaware in Pennsylvania and New Jersey, and that limestone in great quantities would be transported from the same district and burned in the coal region, where fuel would be abundant and cheap."[1]

Simultaneously with this survey was the route of the

---

[1] Commissioners' Report of the Route, 1832.

Lackawannock and Susquehanna, or Meredith Railroad, leading from the mouth of Leggett's Creek in Providence up to that graceful loop in the Susquehanna, called Great Bend, forty-seven and a half miles away, undertaken and surveyed by the late James Seymour, four years after the granting of its charter.

Near the small village of Providence these two roads, neither of which contemplated the use of locomotives in their reliance upon gravity and seven inclined planes, were to form a junction, and expected to breathe life and unity into the iron pathway that was to grope its way out of a valley having scarcely a name away from its immediate border. Neither road proposed to carry passengers.

The report of the commissioners, presenting the subject in its most attractive light, failed to excite the attention it deserved. Men reputed as reliable looked upon the scheme as unworthy of serious notice. Those who had achieved an indifferent livelihood by the shot-gun or the plow, saw no propriety in favoring a plan whose fulfillment promised no protection to game or greater product to the field.

The few who felt that its success would interweave its advantages into every condition of life, were not dismayed.

In the spring of 1832, a sufficient amount of stock having been subscribed, the company was organized: Drinker elected president, John Jordon, Jr., secretary, and Henry, treasurer. At a subsequent meeting of the stockholders, the president and treasurer were constituted a financial committee to raise means to make the road, by selling stock, issuing bonds, or by hypothecating the road, &c. The engineer's map, the commissioners' report, and newspaper articles were widely diffused, to announce the material benefits to result by the completion and acquisition of this new thoroughfare.

The Lackawanna Valley, set in its green wild ridges,

known in New York City only by the Delaware and Hudson Canal Company, then in the fourth year of its existence, confounded often with the *Lackawaxen* region lying upon the other side of the Moosic Mountain, neither Drinker's nor Meredith's charter was received with favor or attention.

The advantages of railroads were neither understood nor encouraged by the inhabitants of the valley in 1832, because the slow ox-team or jaded saddle-horse thus far had kept pace with its development. To render the scheme, however, more comprehensive and general in its character, and make more certain the building of the Drinker railroad, a continuous route was explored for a gravity railroad, "from a point in Cobb's Gap, where an intersection or connection can be conveniently formed with the Susquehanna and Delaware Railroad, in Luzerne County," up through Leggett's Gap, and running in a northwesterly direction to the State of New York.

This was the Leggett's Gap Railroad, an inclined plane road which, when completed, was expected to receive the trade along the fertile plains of the Susquehanna, Chenango, and the Chemung, now enjoyed so profitably by the New York and Erie Railroad.

H. W. Drinker, Elisha S. Potter, Thomas Smith, Dr. Andrew Bedford, and Nathaniel Cottrill—the last two of whom are now living—were among the original commissioners.

Public meetings were now called by the friends of the Drinker road, at the Old Exchange in Wall Street, New York, to obtain subscriptions to the stock of the company, and, while many persons acknowledged the enterprise to be a matter of more than common interest to the country generally, as it promised when completed, to furnish a supply of coal from the hills of Luzerne County, a county where thousands of millions of tons of the best anthracite coal could be mined from a region of more than thirty-three miles in length, and averaging more than two miles in width, underlaid with coal probably averaging fifty feet in thickness, and besides this, unlike most other mining portions of the world, it abounded in agricultural fertility.

While these facts where generally conceded, they produced no other effect, than bringing from capitalists the favorable *opinion* that final triumph probably awaited their hopes. In Morristown, Newton, Belvidere, Newark, and other places in New Jersey ; at Easton, Stroudsburg, Dunmore, Providence, and Kingston, in Pennsylvania, meetings were called to draw the attention of the public mind and acquire the requisite means to open this highway through the wilderness, where the wolf, crouched in the swamp, bestowed with his gray eye as friendly a glance upon the project as many capitalists were inclined to give it. Every sanguine hope, every flattering promise made in a spirit of apparent earnestness languished and died like the leaves of autumn.

At length, engagements were made with New York capitalists to carry the matter forward to a favorable termination, provided that Drinker and his friends would obtain a charter for a continuous line of gravity railroad up the Susquehanna, from Pittston to the New York State line. In 1833, a perpetual charter for such a road was obtained by their agency, and the first installment of five dollars was paid, according to the act of Assembly. In itself it was considered, that in connection with other roads, at or near the Delaware Water Gap to New York City, it would be with its terminus at Jersey City eastwardly, and the State line near Athens, in Pennsylvania, westward, the shortest and the best line the natural avenues indicated from New York west. It was shown by the official report of a survey made in 1827, by John Bennett, of Kingston, Pennsylvania, that the distance from the mouth of the Lackawanna of eighty-six miles had but two hundred and fourteen feet fall, or about two and a half feet per mile, the acclivity for the whole distance being in general nearly equal, and beyond this to the city of Elmira at about the same grade.

The vast project of the New York and Erie Railroad was agitating southern New York at this time. Of the seven commissioners, John B. Jervis, Horatio Allen, Jared Wilson, and William Dewy urged the adoption of the present route, while F. Whittlesey, Orville W. Childs, and Job Pierson reported adversely to it.

The New York gentlemen interested in Drinker's route, having full faith in the realization of an idea promising control of a line reaching the same point on the New York and Erie Railroad (as laid down by Judge Wright, civil engineer, but on which nothing more had yet been done), at a distance of eighty-one miles *short* of this line, while running through both the anthracite and bituminous coal districts upon easier grades, were greatly encouraged to hope for success; several sections in the "Susquehanna Railroad" law were, by supplements, so amended by legislative enactments as to fulfill upon that point every expectation.

In October, 1835, the services of Doctor George Green, of Belvidere, who was a friend of this improvement, and who originated the "Belvidere Delaware Railroad," were procured. William Henry's note, indorsed by Henry W. Drinker, accepted and indorsed by the cashier of the Elizabeth Bank as "good," was taken by the doctor to the Wyoming Bank at Wilkes Barre as a deposit and payment, in compliance with the law called the "Susquehanna Railroad" act of Assembly of 1833.

In consequence of the commercial embarrassments alienating credit and confidence throughout the entire country in 1835-6, the New York party, impoverished and appalled by the shock, could give no further thought to the road. Other parties being prostrated by insolvency or death, the positive spirit, inaugurating the company, carried with it thus far a success decidedly negative and skeptical.

Ten years had thus escaped, and not a single tie nor rail

had shod the road ; here and there a few limbs clipped from the forest-tree to aid the surveyor, and a few rods graded for the flat iron bar, bore evidence of the hope of the directors.

In the summer of 1836, there was traveling in the United States an English nobleman named Sir Charles Augustus Murray, who, learning of the important character of this proposed road from one of his friends, became interested in its success. A correspondence ensued, which led to a meeting of the friends of the project, at Easton, June 18, 1836 ; Mr. Drinker and Mr. Henry on the part of the railroad company, and Mr. Armstrong of New York, Mr. C. A. Murray, and Wm. F. Clemson of New Jersey, wrote out articles of association ; the railroad committee fully authorized Mr. Murray to raise, as he proposed to do, 100,000 pounds sterling in England, conditional that the company should raise the means to make a beginning of the work. Mr. Henry accompanied him to New York, and furnished him with the power of attorney, under seal expressly made for the purpose, and on the eighth of August, 1836, Mr. Murray sailed for Europe. Mr. Henry at once met and made arrangements with the Morris Canal Board of Directors to raise $150,000 on stock subscriptions to commence the road, but before these arrangements had matured, discouraging news came from England through Mr. Murray, who informed the company that the prostrated monetary affairs of Europe rendered any assistance by him out of the question.

To this meeting, which lasted three days, in the village of Easton, can be traced the starting of the iron-works in Slocum Hollow, whose varied and wide-spread prosperity have animated the entire domain of the Lackawanna.[1]

The first iron-works in Scranton after those of Slocums', were erected in 1840. In the summer of 1842, after the artificers gathered around the Scranton furnaces had

---

[1] See History of Scranton.

learned to smelt iron with the lustrous anthracite, the directors of the railroad held only annual meetings. Drinker and Henry had each expended nearly their entire resources to fructify a project whose magnitude found no place or conception in the public mind; this being done in vain, postponed further sacrifices and efforts to stretch the iron fiber from river to river, until greater wants from the sea-board came up to the coal heaps, and established mutual confidence instead of general distrust.

The simple acquisition of Slocum Hollow, in 1840, by a New Jersey company, had but little interest outside of parties concerned in the purchase. Who were taxed for the rough pasture-land cleared on Roaring Brook, none cared to inquire. Its purchase, however, originally suggested by Mr. Henry with especial reference to the furtherance of Drinker's road, favored that result sooner than was anticipated. With the concentration and expansion of capital here at this time, a business was generated which called for a better communication with the sea-board than the ox-team or the sluggish waters of a canal frozen up at least six months of every year.

Col. Scranton, in the simplicity of whose character the whole country acquiesced and felt proud, representing the interests of the iron-makers in Scranton, yet willing to give power to a measure full of public good, conceived the project, in 1847, of opening communication from the iron-works northward to the lakes by a *locomotive* instead of a *gravity* road run by plane, stationary engine, and level, as Drinker's, Meredith's, and the Leggett charters all contemplated. The charter of the last-named road, kept alive by the influence of Dr. Andrew Bedford, Thomas Smith, Nathaniel Cottrill, and other spirited gentlemen, was purchased by the "Scranton Company" in 1849, by the suggestion of Colonel Scranton. A survey was made the same year; the road was commenced in 1850.

For the purpose of giving favor and strength to a project unable to make its way to a practical solution without capital from abroad, a road was chartered in April, 1849, to run from the Delaware Water Gap to some point on the Lackawanna near Cobb's Gap, called "The Delaware and Cobb's Gap Railroad Company." The commissioners, Moses W. Coolbaugh, S. W. Schoomaker, Thos. Grattan, H. M. Lebar, A. Overfield, I. Place, Benj. V. Rush, Alpheus Hollister, Samuel Taylor, F. Starburd, Jas. H. Stroud, R. Bingham, and W. Nyce, held their first meeting at Stroudsburg, December 26, 1850, choosing Col. Geo. W. Scranton president.

The northern division of "The Lackawanna and Western Railroad Company," carried by genius and engineering skill for sixty miles over the rough uplands distinguishing the country it traverses from Scranton to Great Bend, was opened for business in October, 1851, thus enabling the inhabitants of the valley to reach New York by a single day's ride instead of two, as before.

Travel and traffic, hitherto finding its way from the basins of Wyoming and the Lackawanna to Middletown or Narrowsburg by stage, and thence along the unfinished Erie, now diverged westward, *via* Great Bend, sixty miles away, before apparently beginning a journey eastward to New York. This unphilosophical and wasteful manner of groping among the hills in the wrong direction before *starting* for New York, directed the intelligence of the mass toward the purpose of Col. Scranton, of planing a continuous roadway direct to New York, *via* the celebrated Delaware Water Gap.

The original charter of Drinker's railroad was purchased of him in 1853, by the railroad company, for $1,000. Immediately after this, a joint application was made by the "Delaware and Cobb's Gap Railroad Company," and the "Lackawanna and Western Railroad Company," for an act of the Legislature for their consolidation, which was granted March 11, 1853, and the union consummated under the present name of "The Delaware, Lackawanna, and Western Railroad Company."

Of this consolidated road, the late George W. Scranton was unanimously elected President: how well he filled

DELAWARE WATER GAP FROM THE KITATINNY HOUSE.

this position until compelled to exchange it for the invalid's shelf, let the movement of the iron pathway across a valley which would be comparatively idle to-day without it—let the mutually satisfactory adjustment of every conflicting interest arising in the progress of this great road—let the spirit of his administration, characterized by qualities both sterling and comprehensive—more than this, let the simple fact that he, inspiring capitalists with the same confidence he himself had acquired and cherished, was able to draw forth the wherewithal to complete a road deriving its origin and vigor from him, bear ample and praiseworthy testimony.

The vast business of this road, which in the year of 1868 carried 1,728,785.07 tons of anthracite, requires one hundred locomotives, about five thousand coal-cars, and gives employment to over 5,000 men. Its total disbursements at Scranton alone, through H. A. Phelps, the courteous paymaster of the road, amounted, during the last year, to over $4,000,000, while a considerable sum diffused itself through the treasury department in New York.

The same efficiency and ability with which Hon. John Brisbin acquired popularity as the president of the great primitive locomotive railroad in the Lackawanna Valley, from 1856 to 1867, has been continued and even augmented by Samuel Sloan, Esq., its present vigilant president, and formerly the presiding officer of the Hudson River Railroad, whose admirable management of the interests of the Delaware, Lackawanna, and Western Railroad, has placed it upon a basis reliable and remunerative, and given it a character, even beyond the States it traverses, enjoyed by few, if any, railroads in the country.

The lease of the Morris and Essex road by the Delaware, Lackawanna, and Western, for an almost indefinite term of years, establishes more intimate relations between the Lackawanna Valley and the sea-board than ever enjoyed before, and marks an era in the history of coal transportation, second only in importance to the conception of the original gravity railroad stretched like a rainbow over the Moosic in 1826–8 by Wurts brothers.

Hitherto, the former road, vigorous with local traffic, strove only to compete with a diverse railway for doubtful dividends, without a wish to advance or retard the welfare of the valley. By a stroke of policy seldom surpassed in the grandeur of its results, all this was changed in January, 1869, by the practical foresight of President Sloan and his associates. The consolidation of these two roads gives a future interest to the Delaware, Lackawanna, and Western road far beyond the appreciation of the hour. It abbreviates distance, offers a continuous and controllable rail from the mines to New York, increases the value and tonnage of the road almost fourfold, while the travel over it for all time to come will make one steady, living stream of various lineage and faith, steady, remunerating, and thus commemorate the wisdom of the men who inaugurated the movement. The superintendency of the Morris and Essex division of the line has fallen into the experienced hands of Hon. John Brisbin.

THE LACKAWANNA AND BLOOMSBURG RAILROAD.

After the locomotive railroad from the Lackawanna Valley had become a fixed fact by the genial efforts of those to whom its failure or its success had been intrusted, other roads began to spring into a charter being. Among such was the Lackawanna and Bloomsburg Railroad. An act incorporating this company was passed in April, 1852, but not until some valuable and essential amendments were obtained for the charter the next year, by the able efforts of one of the members of the Pennsylvania Legislature— Hon. A. B. Dunning—did it possess any available vitality. This road, running from Scranton to Northumberland, is eighty miles in length, passing through the historic valley of Wyoming, where the poet Campbell drew, in his Gertrude, such pictures of the beautiful and wild. It also passes along the Susquehanna, over a portion of the old battle-ground, where, in 1778, a small band of settlers marched forth from Forty Fort, in the afternoon, to fight the spoilers of their firesides, and where, after the battle, the long strings of scalps dripping from the Indian belts, and the hatchets reddened with the slain, told how sore had been the rout, and how terrible the massacre that followed. The dweller in wigwams has bid a long farewell to a region so full of song and legend, and where can be found the one to-day who, as he looks over the old plantation of the Indian Nations, once holding their great council fires here, upon the edge of the delightful river, surrounded by forest and inclosing mountain, can wonder that they fought as fights the wild man with war-club and tomahawk, to regain the ancient plains of their fathers?

Wyoming Valley, taken as a whole, compensates in the highest degree for the trouble of visiting it. The grand beauty of the old Susquehanna and the sparkling current of its blue waters nowhere along its entire distance appears to better advantage than does it here. Along the Po or the Rhine, there loom up the gray walls of some castle dismantled and stained with the blood of feudal conflict; here on the broad acres of Wyoming turned into culture, humanity wears a smile nowhere more sweet or lovely.

The tourist who wishes to visit this truly interesting valley, can step into the cars of the Lehigh and Susquehanna, or the Lackawanna and Bloomsburg Railroad Company, at Scranton, and in twenty minutes look "On Susquehanna's side, fair Wyoming!" Across the river, half a mile from Campbell's Ledge, near the head of the valley, is seen the battle-ground. About three miles below Pittston, left of the village of Wyoming, rises from the plain a naked monument—an obelisk of gray masonry sixty-two and a half feet high, which commemorates the disastrous afternoon of the third of July, 1778. Near this point reposes the *bloody rock* around which, on the evening of that ill-fated day, was formed the fatal ring of savages, where the Indian queen of the Senecas, with death-mall and battle-ax, dashed out the brains of the unresisting captives. The *débris* of Forty Fort, the first fort built on the north side of the Susquehanna by the Connecticut emigrants, in 1769, is found a short distance down the river from this rock.

The Lackawanna and Bloomsburg Railroad, while it is a valuable auxiliary to the Delaware, Lackawanna, and Western Railroad, in whose interests it is operated, enjoyed all the advantages of travel between central Pennsylvania and the Lackawanna Valley until the Lehigh and Susquehanna and the Lehigh Valley railroads, bounding over the mountain with the celerity and speed of a deer, alienated a portion of the trade and travel.

Having the advantage of collieries with an aggregate yearly capacity of a million tons of coal, threading its way along the green belt of the Susquehanna over rich beds of iron ore, worked in Danville by ingenious artificers who have adopted science as their patron, it will ever stand prominent among the railroads of the country.

While the Delaware, Lackawanna, and Western Railroad, with its greater length of thirty-three miles, carried 187,583 passengers during the year 1867, the Lackawanna and Bloomsburg transported 269,564—an excess of 81,981 persons.

No railroad in the country of its length, lined with scenery always exhilarating, would better repay the visit of a few days in summer or autumn, than will this. It is, in fact, all picturesque, while portions of it are really magnificent. Thundering along the border of the river and the canal, at a rate of thirty miles an hour, a glimpse is now caught and then lost, of old gray mountain crags and glens, covered with forest just as it grew—of sleepy islands, dreaming in the half-pausing stream—of long, narrow meadows, stretched along with sights of verdure and sounds of life, and now and then a light cascade, tuned by the late rains, comes leaping down rock after rock, like a ribbon floating in the air! How the waters whiten as they come through the tree-tops with silver shout from precipice to precipice in the bosom of some rock, cool and fair-lipped! The scenery is especially grand at Nanticoke—the once wild camp-place of the Nanticokes—where Wyoming Valley terminates, and where the noble river, wrapped up in the majesty of mountains, glides along as languidly as when the red man in his narrow craft shot over the ripple.

Mr. James Archibald, life-long in his earnest devotion to the interests of the Lackawanna Valley, is president of the road.

SKETCH OF THE EARLY HISTORY OF THE LEHIGH AND SUSQUEHANNA RAILROAD.

This road, running from Providence to Easton, a distance of 120 miles, threads a section of country surpassed by no other in the State for the grandeur of its scenery or the interest of its history.

When the Indian civilizers first began to fraternize with the sachems of the Lehigh at Fort Allen or Gnadenhutten (now Weissport) in 1746, all knowledge of anthracite coal was so limited, that the word "coal" was noted upon but a single map within the Province of Pennsylvania. The casual discovery of coal, half a century later, near this settlement, gave fetal life to the Lehigh Coal and Navigation Company, and a prominence to the history of this region not otherwise enjoyed.

At the confluence of the Ma-ha-noy (the loud, laughing stream of the Indian) with the Lehigh, this fort was located, eighteen miles above Bethlehem, forty miles by the warriors' trail from Teedyuscung's plantation at Wyoming. It was the first attempt of the whites to carry civilization into the provincial acquisitions of Penn above the Blue Mountain. Why a region so rough in its general exterior should have been chosen for a sheltering place, can be accounted for upon no other theory than that the gray rock here bordering the Lehigh, took the place in memory of the Elbe in their fatherland emerging from the crags of the Alps.

This place, often visited by sachem and chief, whom the missionaries first conciliated, then endeavored to Christianize, "numbered 500 souls in 1752."[1] Braddock's defeat, two years later, opened the forest for the uplifted tomahawk. Some of the Six Nations, exchanging wampum and whiffs of the calumet with their Moravian brothers, danced the war-dance before Vaudreuil, Governor of New France (New York State). "We will try the hatchet of our fathers on the English," said the chiefs at Niagara, "and see if it cuts well."[2]

The obliteration of the village, with the death or expulsion of its inmates, January 1, 1756, attested the trial of both fire-brand and hatchet.

After a lump of coal found near Mauch Chunk, in 1791, by Ginther, had been analyzed and pronounced as such by the *savans* of Philadelphia, the following persons, Messrs. Hillegas, Cist, Weiss, Henry, and others, associated themselves together, without charter or corporation, as the "Lehigh Coal Mine Company," for the purpose of transporting coal to Philadelphia, in 1792. They purchased land, cut a narrow road for the passage of a wagon from the mine to the river, and sent a few bushels of anthracite coal to Philadelphia in canoes or "dug-outs." None could be sold; little given away. Col. Weiss, the original owner of the land, spent an entire summer in diffusing huge saddle-bags of coal through the smith-shops of Allentown, Bethlehem, Easton, and other places. From motives of personal friendship, a few persons were induced to give it a trial, with very indifferent success.

Under the sanction of legislative enactment, some $20,000 was expended to prepare the Lehigh for naviga

---

[1] Miner's Wyoming, p. 41.   [2] Vaudreuil to the Minister, July 13, 1757

tion. No more coal, however, was carried down the stream until 1805, when William Turnbull, by the aid of an ark, floated some 200 or 300 bushels to Philadelphia. As the coal extinguished rather than improved the fire, the great body of citizens refused to buy or make further attempt to burn it, or be imposed upon by the black stuff.

Messrs. Rowland and Butland were the next to lease the mines, and fail.

The success of Jesse Fell, of Wilkes Barre, in 1808, of burning coal in a common grate, led two of the representative men of the day, Charles Miner and Jacob Cist, to lease the Ginther mine in 1814, with a view of shipping coal to Philadelphia.

On the 9th of August of this year, the first ark-load of coal started from Mauch Chunk. "The stream," writes Miner, "wild, full of rocks, and the imperfect channel crooked, in less than eighty rods from the place of starting the ark struck on a ledge, and broke a hole in her bow. The lads stripped themselves nearly naked, to stop the rush of water with their clothes. At dusk they were at Easton, fifty miles."

The impetuous character of the river, untamed by art, and the absence of any demand for coal, induced these pioneers to retire from the Mauch Chunk coal-mines. "This effort of ours," says Charles Miner, "might be regarded as the acorn, from which has sprung the mighty oak of the Lehigh Coal and Navigation Company."

In 1817, three energetic gentlemen, Josiah White, George F. A. Hauto, and Erskine Hazard, profiting by each preceding failure, originated the plan of floating coal down the inky, turbulent current from Mauch Chunk to the Delaware by the aid of slackened water.

From Mauch Chunk to Stoddartsville, not a single cabin rose in the wilderness; the abandoned warrior's trail alone intervened.

In 1818, the Legislature of Pennsylvania empowered

these gentlemen as the "Lehigh Navigation Company," "to improve the navigation of the river Lehigh" by constructing wing-dams and channel walls along the more rapid and shallow portion of the stream, so as to narrow and contract the current for practical purposes. In October, 1818, "The Lehigh Coal Company" built a road from the Lehigh to the old Ginther mine on Summit Hill.

Arks of coal were carried down in the spring freshet; in the summer months when water was low, bear-dams were constructed from tree-tops and stones, "in the neighborhood of Mauch Chunk, in which were placed sluice-gates of peculiar construction, *invented for the purpose* by Josiah White, by means of which the water could be retained in the pool above until required for use. When the dam became full, and the water had run over it long enough for the river below the dam to acquire the depth of the ordinary overflow of the river, the sluice-gates were let down, and the boats which were lying in the pools above, passed down with the artificial flood."[1] Some 100 tons of coal thus found its way down the Lehigh in 1818.

The partial success of a plan alike novel and unreliable, led to a more systematic slack-water navigation from Mauch Chunk to Easton, forty-five miles.

The people of Philadelphia, educated reluctantly in the use and art of anthracite, finding this avenue from the coal-mines inadequate to the demands of commerce, lent a hand to calm the swift waters of the Lehigh for coal traffic. The Legislature of the State, influenced by men able to bring greater political influence to bear than this sterile region could then offer, granted to Messrs. White, Hauto, and Hazard, the privilege of improving the navigation of the Lehigh as far as White Haven; reserving, however, the right of *compelling* the company to make a continuous slack-water navigation to Stoddarts-

---

[1] Henry's "Lehigh Valley."

ville, a sprightly lumbering village, fifteen miles farther up the stream.

The Lehigh Coal and Lehigh Navigation Company were consolidated in the spring of 1820. During this year 365 tons of coal, lowered down the Lehigh in arks by some fifty dams, found its way to a tardy market. A few years later, 400 acres of land was stripped of its stately pines annually for the construction of the necessary arks: these were manipulated into building material in Philadelphia, while the iron was returned to Mauch Chunk for repeated use. This destruction of wood, now seriously felt, and the waste of time in building boats for a single trip, subsequently led to a more practical method of navigation.

The slack-water (canal) navigation was opened to Mauch Chunk simultaneously with the Delaware and Hudson Railroad, eastward from the Lackawanna Valley, in 1829, to White Haven, in 1835.

As the Lehigh Coal and Navigation Company, already embarrassed by the expensive dams they had built, could see no benefit to accrue by the extension of their works to Stoddartsville, it asked to be released from this particular part of the agreement, through the same body that had so ungraciously imposed it. Objections and remonstrances poured into the Legislature from Stoddartsville and from almost every township in the county of Luzerne. Andrew Beaumont, representing the expression and interests of Wyoming Valley, with a strength and ingenuity for which he was ever remarkable, interposed means to frustrate the wishes of the company. The matter was finally compromised; the Navigation Company agreeing to erect a single dam on the stream above Port Jenkins, and carry channel walls and wing-dams from pool to pool for the passage of rafts and logs from Stoddartsville, and build a gravity railroad over the mountain from White Haven to Wilkes Barre. The Legislature now withdrew or repealed so much of the former act as required the completion of the slack-water navigation to Stoddartsville.

The valley of Wyoming ramifying with competing railways, gained its first one by this scramble with a company with which its relations have subsequently become pleasant and profitable. This railroad was begun in 1837.

A stream, rapid and treacherous as the Lehigh, passing for miles through a mere fissure of vertical rock, bore restraint with deceitful demeanor. Danger concentrated in every dam. A sudden snow-thaw forced an infuriated volume down the Lehigh, January 8, 1839, at the expense of the company and their employees; on the same day of the month in 1841, another thaw released the snow from the mountain and swelled the torrent with loss of life and property; the freshet, however, of 1862, resistless and unparalleled in the extent of its ravages upon life and property, appalled and smothered with a single wave every lock-house and its inmates, every dam, boat, or bridge, attempting to interrupt its passage. About 300 persons living along the river perished in that cold, dark, memorable night.

The Lehigh Coal and Navigation Company, with but little left but the bare stream exulting over its liberation, actuated by humane and practical impulses as well as the wishes of the Lehigh Valley inhabitants, who everywhere opposed the reconstruction of the dams because of their danger, made the Lehigh a safer companion by constructing along its berme bank, or the *débris* of the canal, a locomotive railroad. While the immense forest around White Haven, slashed into by the lumberman without regard to economy or foresight, annually assured the road considerable traffic, the gravity railway from Wilkes Barre, terminating here, could not fairly compete with other routes diverging to the sea-board from northern Pennsylvania.[1] Years of reconnoissance of the interpos-

---

[1] LEHIGH AND SUSQUEHANNA RAILROAD.—Report of coal shipped south, for week ending Dec. 31, 1868:—

ing mountain enabled the engineers to descend with a locomotive into the plains of Wyoming triumphantly, as the Jewish ruler of old came down from the sacred mount.

If there is grandeur in the bold outlines of precipice and forest in the coal-fields of Pennsylvania, then the scenery along the entire road is truly exhilarating, while the view in ascending or descending the slope between Penobscot and Wilkes Barre is singularly beautiful and unique. The broad expanse of Wyoming Valley, with

Shipped from	Week.	Total.
Harvey Brothers....................................		184 11
Lances' Colliery....................................		3,264 15
New England Coal Co...............................		1,129 02
Morgan Mines......................................		92 18
Parish & Thomas...................................		19,100 12
New Jersey Coal Co................................	356 09	18,193 04
Gaylord Mines.....................................		245 01
Lehigh Luzerne Coal Co............................	220 01	5,010 03
Lehigh & Susquehanna Coal Co.....................		15 10
Germania Coal Co..................................		20,866 08
Franklin Coal Co...................................		243 18
Wilkes Barre C. & I. Co............................	4,772 01	335,544 17
Union Coal Co.....................................		2,040 07
Mineral Spring Coal Co............................	454 15	11,022 07
H. B. Hillman & Son...............................	103 19	2,768 14
Bowkley, Price & Co...............................	288 16	3,808 05
Wyoming Coal & T. Co.............................	286 14	4,375 16
Henry Colliery.....................................	356 02	9,490 08
J. H. Swoyer		5,405 08
Everhart Coal Co..................................	482 06	3,406 17
Morris & Essex Mut. Coal Co......................		78 19
Shawnee Coal Co..................................	219 14	20,297 05
Delaware & Hudson Canal Co......................		11,447 06
Pine Ridge Coal Co................................	325 05	12,898 04
Consumers' Coal Co................................		5,272 18
Albrighton, Roberts & Co..........................		10,606 03
Other shippers....................................	197 18	12,469 03
Total Wyoming Region............................	8,064 00	519,279 19
Total Mauch Chunk...............................	4,118 04	49,086 15
Total Hazleton....................................	49 10	332,817 06
Total Upper Lehigh...............................	2,389 12	141,499 06
Grand Total.......................................	14,621 06	1,042,683 06
Corresponding week last year.....................	5,280 06	485,501 00
Increase...	9,341 00	557,182 06

her dozen villages sleeping quietly in her bosom:—the Susquehanna making a low bow and bend around Campbell's Ledge at the head of the valley, dividing the rich bottom for twenty miles before it gathers in a measure of its beauty and retires from the eye at Nanticoke, and the green farms, dotted here and there with quaint homesteads telling their story of strife and skirmish in olden time, all make up a landscape rarely offered to the eye of the traveler.

Steel rails, stretched over a great portion of the road, impart a degree of security that must popularize it as a great thoroughfare. In fact, the same far-seeing sagacity that this pioneer company carried into the Lehigh Valley a quarter of a century ago, to secure and develop anthracite, has led them to make a railroad in such an excellent and thorough manner as to be a marvel among American railroads, reflecting equal credit upon the engineers and managers who matured this great enterprise.

John Leisenring, Esq., of Mauch Chunk, ably filled the united position of superintendent and engineer of this road until the summer of 1868. John P. Ilsley, a gentleman who enjoyed high consideration as the superintendent of the Lackawanna and Bloomsburg for many years, succeeds Mr. Leisenring in the superintendency of this road.

HON. GEORGE W. SCRANTON.

Col. George W. Scranton was too universally known and beloved throughout the country to be overlooked in a work aiming to do justice to men who have gained glory by carrying reformation and development to the valley of which it treats. The following biographical sketch of Colonel Scranton, prepared especially for this volume, is from the able pen of Rev. Dr. GEORGE PECK:—

Col. Scranton descended from *John Scranton*, who was one of the colony who settled in New Haven in 1638. The Scranton family was distinguished in the French and

Revolutionary wars, some of them as privates and others as commissioned officers. Col. Scranton was born in Madison, Ct., May 11, 1811. At an early period in life, he exhibited extraordinary qualities both of intellect and heart. His opportunities for an education were embraced within the privileges of the common school and two years' training in "Lee's Academy."

In 1828, he came to Belvidere, N. J., and the first employment he obtained was that of a teamster, for which he received eight dollars per month. His great industry and general good conduct excited the attention of business men, and he was soon employed as a clerk in the store of Judge Kinney, where his great business tact and winning management not long after gained him the position of a partner in the concern.

On the 21st of January, 1835, Mr. Scranton was married to Miss *Jane Hiles*, of Belvidere. After his marriage, he engaged in farming, in which business he continued until 1839. At this time Mr. Scranton, in partnership with his brother Selden, purchased the lease and stock of Oxford Furnace, N. J., and, contrary to the predictions and fears of their friends, they succeeded in the business, and maintained their credit through the season of embarrassment to business which followed the terrible crash of 1837.

In 1839, Mr. William Henry, being impressed with the advantages of the manufacture of iron in the Lackawanna Valley, purchased a large tract, including what was called *Slocum Hollow*, or what is now the site of the city of Scranton. It contained "the old red house," two other small dwellings, and a stone mill. With the exception of a few acres of cultivated land, the tract was covered with timber, a dense undergrowth, and a perfect tangle of laurel.

The attention of the Scranton brothers was attracted to this place, and, Mr. Henry not being able to comply with the conditions of his purchase, they, in connection with

other parties, in May, 1840, entered into a contract for the property.

The practicability of smelting ore by the agency of anthracite coal, as yet was hardly established by successful experiment. Two furnaces only now produced iron through heat generated by anthracite, and that under embarrassments and in limited quantities. The young company in which the Scranton brothers were the leading spirits, was now to take a prominent part in a series of experiments which were destined to contribute in no small degree to one of the practical arts which has communicated a new and an undying impulse to modern civilization.

The first experiment was made in 1841, and proved a failure; the second was likewise unsuccessful, but in January, 1842, a successful blast was made; others followed with increasing encouragement. The practical difficulties in manufacturing iron by anthracite were now considered as overcome, but the price that the triumph had cost, few understood, and none would ever understand, so well as George W. Scranton. He was the genius which presided over the struggles of many months, and even years, of hope deferred and of distrusting doubt which finally ended in complete success.

The scientific difficulties were no sooner overcome than financial problems were to be encountered. They could make iron, but how could they make it pay? The future *city* of Scranton was a straggling assemblage of huts, at a distance from every great market, and without convenient outlet. These difficulties, with those arising from want of funds, would have broken the spirits of ordinary men, but our young adventurers, nothing daunted, resorted first to one experiment and then to another, until they were able to exclaim, with Archimedes, *Eureka—I have found it.* A bootless effort to manufacture bar-iron and convert it into nails finally gave way to the project of a rolling-mill for the manufacture of railroad iron.

The great address of Col. Scranton succeeded with the leading men interested in the New York and Erie Railroad in making the contract to furnish rails needed by the road, at a lower rate than they could be procured elsewhere, upon the condition that the directors of the road would advance funds to enable the Scrantons and company to proceed with the business of making rails. This arrangement untied the Gordian knot of the Scrantons' financial troubles.

Success in the iron business was not an occasion for Col. Scranton to abate his energy in business. The manufacture of iron was but one of his great business projects —it was but a part of a great system, which, when fully carried out, was to reform the entire business interests of this portion of the country, and to change the whole face of society. His plan was to enlist capital abroad, to concentrate it in the Lackawanna Valley, and then to create outlets by railway east with North and South; and he lived to see his project succeed.

Col. Scranton was not in the ordinary sense a politician, although he was a thorough student of political economy. He had been an old-line Whig, but for years had paid no attention to party politics. There was one principle which he maintained against all opposers, and that was, *protection to home industry*. Upon this issue he was sent to Congress, in 1858, by a majority of 3,700, from a district ordinarily polling 2,000 Democratic majority. He directed himself incessantly to his favorite theme through the term, and was elected a second time.

We are obliged to pass over a multitude of interesting incidents in the life of Col. Scranton for want of space, and must now proceed to a brief estimate of his character. In marking the character of a great man, it will be found that it is only a few qualities which distinguish them from other men and give them prominence. Such is the fact with the great and good man of whom we are now speaking. We begin with the *great moral integrity of the man*. He was sincere—he was honest—his views were transparent. When in Congress he could get the ear of the most ultra free-traders. "Southern fire-eaters" would listen to his arguments on protection and free labor. They would often say to him, "Scranton, we can hear *you* talk, for we believe you are honest." You might differ from his opinions, but you could not avoid believing in the man. His zeal was that of conviction. His heart was upon the surface—it was "known and read of all men."

His *energy* was inexhaustible. He never yielded to discouragements, or acknowledged a total defeat. He sometimes failed, but always tried again; and, if necessary, again and again, and triumphed at last. He often spent the night in concocting a scheme, and early dawn found him upon the path of its execution. Due time usually brought success, but delay never staggered him. He was fastened to his purpose, like Prometheus to the rock, and there he hung, until mountains of difficulty melted away, and the sun of success illuminated his path. A man of less hope would have been despondent where he was confident, and one of a weaker will would have fainted when he was firm as a rock.

Another trait of character holds the highest position. Col. Scranton had the rare faculty of *impressing his own ideas upon the minds of other men*. This power depends upon an assemblage of qualities. An honest expression is essential to it. This expression means confidence. A sympathetic nature. His earliest sympathy in return, and sympathy exercises a marvelous control over the judgment. Draw a man into sympathy with your feelings and wishes, and you can lead him wherever you please. Blandness of manner is another attribute of this great power. A pleasant countenance, a happy face, has more power than logic. Good conversational powers is of the first importance in this enumeration. There must be definiteness of view, lucidness of description, brevity in the statement of facts, naturalness and beauty in the illustrations, command of language, perfect ease in manner, and an expression of confidence both in your cause and in your success. You must never for a moment doubt the good sense and receptibility of the party you would win over. All these attributes of character Col. Scranton possessed in an eminent degree.

The crowning glory of Col. Scranton's character was that he was a true Christian. All who knew him acknowledged this. His conversation and his manners were those of a true Christian gentleman. He lived beloved, and died regretted by all. His great mental labors undermined his naturally sound constitution, and in the midst of his usefulness, and at the zenith of his fame, he was called to his reward.

THE LEHIGH VALLEY RAILROAD.

A wild ridge of rock and forest twenty miles in width, cuts off the Lehigh from the Lackawanna, and forms the line of demarkation between the great northern anthracite coal-basin and the first southern or Schuylkill coal district of Pennsylvania. For many years it served the purposes of the hunter and the lumberman, and frowned on daily intercourse between the people of the two sections of country.

The first road to greet the Lehigh with an iron rail was the Lehigh Valley Railroad. While it crosses but a mere edge of the Lackawanna Valley whose commerce it aims to reach and partake, it has, by its immense traffic and the admirable management of its interests, formed for itself a character well known in the two valleys it connects and traverses.

This great road, incorporated in 1846, under the name of the Delaware, Lehigh, Schuylkill, and Susquehanna Railroad, languished for years simply because the idea was generally accepted, that the rocky chasm, washed

Henry Roberts M.D.

sometimes rudely by the Lehigh, could be by no possible legislation or engineering turned to any practical railroad account. A bare organization of officers of the contemplated road existed from 1846 until 1851, up until which time $444.37½ had been expended conjointly in surveying the route and building a fraction of a mile of the road merely for the protection of its charter. No distinctive step toward smoothing the Lehigh ledges for a locomotive was undertaken until those elements of a positive and substantial character, which were introduced more especially by Hon. James M. Porter, of Easton, and Hon. Asa Packer, of Mauch Chunk, began to be developed and felt.

In 1833, Asa Packer, a young, ambitious boy, born in Connecticut in 1805, moved into Mauch Chunk from the sap-woods of Susquehanna County, Pennsylvania, with a single jack-plane, hammer, handsaw, and a suit of rustic homespun, as his whole inheritance. He had neither friend nor acquaintance in the village, but being a man of clear discernment, excelling in the art of industry and frugality, distinguished for sobriety and sober sense, he devoted himself zealously to various industrious pursuits, until he became well known as one of the most efficient business men in the State, and rose rapidly in the confidence of the inhabitants of the Lehigh Valley, whom he served on the bench and in two successive Congresses. Such was the man whose earnest qualifications inspired this then unpopular project with organic life and triumph, and whose liberality, exercised in the broadest spirit, gave to the public an institution of learning which will transmit the name of Packer down to all time.

"On the 31st of October, 1851," writes Mr. Henry, in his interesting history of the Lehigh Valley, "Asa Packer became the purchaser of a large amount of the stock which had been subscribed, and commenced efforts to get additional stock subscribed and the road constructed. On the 13th of September, 1852, Robert H. Sayre was appointed chief engineer for the construction of the road; and on the 27th of November, 1852, Judge Packer submitted a proposition for constructing the railroad from opposite Mauch Chunk, where it would intersect the Beaver Meadow Railroad, to the river Delaware at Easton, where it would intersect the New Jersey Central Railroad and the Belvidere Delaware Railroad for a consideration, to be paid in the stock and bonds of the company, which was accepted by the stockholders, at a meeting in which all the stockholders, representing 5,150 shares of stock, were present.

"On the 7th of January, 1853, the name of the company was changed by act of Assembly to that of the Lehigh Valley Railroad Company, and on the 10th of that month, James M. Porter was re-elected president, John N. Hutchinson, secretary and treasurer, and John N. Hutchinson, Wm. Hackett, Wm. H. Gatzmer, Henry King, John T. Johnston, and John O. Sterns, managers.

"Although the formal contract with Judge Packer for the construction of the road was not signed until the 12th of February, 1853, yet he began the work immediately after the acceptance of this offer, on the 27th of November, 1852, by commencing the deep rock cut at Easton. The work was prosecuted with vigor by Judge Packer himself, at some of the hardest cuts, and by sub-contractors at other places, until its completion, September, 1855.

"Judge Packer, in the construction of this road, encountered great difficulties and embarrassments, from the rise in the price of provisions and necessaries for the hands—the sickliness of some of the seasons, the failure of sub-contractors and the necessary re-letting the work at advanced prices, and the difficulty of raising money upon and disposing of the bonds of the company, from the stringency of the money market; but, with an energy and perseverance seldom met with, he worked through it all."

A trifle less than 15,000,000 tons of anthracite coal was

the entire shipment within the United States during the year 1867. An aggregate of 4,088,537 tons of this amount was taken from the Wyoming coal-basin, a portion of which, 2,080,156 tons, swelled the tonnage of this young giant railroad.[1] 2,603,102 tons of anthracite found its way over the Lehigh Valley road during the year 1868, being an increase of 522,956 tons.

[1] Some idea from whence this road derives its coal tonnage can be had by reference to the following report for a single week.

LEHIGH VALLEY RAILROAD.—Report of coal transported over the above road for the week ending December 26, 1868.

FROM WYOMING REGION.	WEEK. Tons. Cwt.	TOTAL. Tons. Cwt.
Franklin Coal Co.	1,461 02	4,502 17
Audenreid Imp. & C. Co.		
Lehigh & Susquehanna Coal Co.		
Germania Coal Co.		
Wilkes Barre C. & I. Co.	203 18	595 15
Warrior Run Mining Co.	307 12	964 10
Parrish & Thomas.		76 15
New Jersey Coal Co.	202 01	1,088 10
Union Coal Co.		
Wyoming Coal & Transportation Co.	703 14	3,442 16
Newport Coal Company.		
Morris & Essex Mutual Coal Co.		
Everhart Coal Co.		
Plymouth Coal Co.		
H. B. Hillman & Son.	418 14	1,408 17
Bowkley, Price & Co.		
Mineral Spring Coal Co.	487 14	1,247 10
Enterprise Colliery.	1,181 07	4,377 14
Burroughs.	472 02	729 06
J. H. Swoyer.		
Linderman & Co.		
Washington Mutual Coal Co.		
West Pittston.		73 14
Barclay Coal Co.		
Shawnee.	698 09	934 15
Consumers' Coal Co.	275 17	1,133 15
Harvey & Brother.		
Wyoming Valley.	443 08	1,368 17
Henry Colliery.		
New England.	329 16	1,266 10
Delaware & Hudson Coal Co.		
Maltby Colliery.	74 18	74 18
Gaylord Colliery.		

This road, originally intended to connect only Easton with Mauch Chunk, now runs up the Susquehanna River to Waverly, New York, passing through some of the most picturesque scenery in the State. Emerging from the Lehigh ravine, it traverses the entire length of Wyoming Valley, on the south bank of the river, running within a stone's-throw of the celebrated Monocasy or "Monockonock Island," crosses the Lackawanna at its mouth, and leads its quiet way under a ledge familiar with the sad, heroic scenes of Wyoming so touchingly portrayed in Campbell's Gertrude, then follows Gen. Sullivan's route and the old Indian pathway from the Great Plains to the plantation of the dusky queen, whose memory, cherished only to be despised, has been rendered infamous forever. No part of this thoroughfare is destitute of historical reminiscence or interest to the traveler.

It would be difficult, and probably impossible, to find a railroad in Pennsylvania whose ramifications and feeders are more numerous and important, along its entire length, than this. Forming one of the strong links in the great chain of communication between central and lower

Chauncey Colliery	282 02	1,372 18
Fall Creek	45 05	321 11
Ravine Colliery P. & E.		
Butler, H. S. M.		
Maryland Anthracite	50 12	266 07
Morgan Colliery		
Tompkins	92 04	92 04
Rough & Ready		
A. McJ. Dewitt		
Rock Tunnell		
Butler Colliery		207 09
Other Shippers		9 06
Total Wyoming Region	7,729 15	25,560 14
Total Beaver Meadow Region	6,733 08	26,563 19
Total Hazleton Region	14,422 16	70,509 06
Total Upper Lehigh	159 12	922 06
Total Mahanoy Region	1,095 10	8,814 14
Grand Total	30,139 01	132,370 19
Increase	1,614 05	

Pennsylvania and southern New York, it derives additional consideration and strength from the many active railroad tributaries swelling the volume of its traffic. Almost every valley whose drainage fertilizes the Lehigh, rolls its tonnage and travel into this road with a bounteous hand.

The Wyoming division of the Lehigh Valley Railroad opens a new channel to internal commerce, and, in the earnest hands of its superintendent, Robert A. Packer, Esq., maintains the same character enjoyed by the older portion of the road, and, like that, cultivates those relations which connect the anthracite coal-basins of our State with the broad interests of the world on terms of mutual usefulness and advantage.

APPENDIX.

I.

INDIAN RELIC CONTROVERSY BETWEEN STEUBEN JENKINS AND H. HOLLISTER, RESULTING FROM THE FOLLOWING EDITORIAL IN THE "SCRANTON REGISTER," JUNE 22, 1865.

THE red man has left us forever, but we did not suppose that so many memorials of a departed race could be collected in the entire country, as has been gathered in Luzerne and Wyoming counties by Dr. Hollister, of Providence. His rare cabinet of Indian relics embraces some *ten thousand* implements used by them in peace and war. Of the stone kind it is undoubtedly the largest in the world, and of great value to the antiquarian. The doctor has refused the modest little sum of $2,000 for it, from a Massachusetts college. The articles are stone, flint, and burned clay, tomahawks which have slain many a foe, skinning stones, rare pipes of exquisite workmanship, huge and small pestles, javelins or spears, arrow-points of the most delicate finish, beads, death malls, quoits, hoes, gouges, sling-stones, Indian pots, broken pottery rudely ornamented, rings, birds, amulets, hammers, battle-axes, war-clubs, mortars, stones for weaving nets, bone needles, and a hundred stone contrivances which made life in the wigwam so agreeable to the poor Indian: all make up a collection really unique, interesting, and inviting to all, and more especially to the antiquarian. We have looked the collection through repeatedly, and would recommend to our readers to call and examine them. His collection is open and free to all, and the doctor takes great pleasure in showing them to such as have a taste in that direction.

We would note here that there appears to be a sort of rivalry between the doctor and Steuben Jenkins, Esq., of Wyoming, who is said to possess a large collection, but the doctor says it is hid away in old boxes and barns in such a manner that no person can imagine what a glance would reveal. Now, if these gentlemen will unite their collections and place them alternately at Wilkes Barre and Scranton, they will enable thousands to see their interesting collections, and by that means determine what the parties themselves can not do, which is the richest, the rarest, and the best. This is the only mode of determining the question, and the determination of the question is one in which our whole community is interested. We hope they will consent to the proposition

---

The following letter explains itself. It will be seen that friend Jenkins is not to be stumped out of the belief that his collection is *the* collection.—ED. *Register.*

WYOMING, *June* 30, 1865.

EDITOR " SCRANTON REGISTER "—DEAR SIR:—I noticed in your issue of the 22d inst. an article upon the subject of "Indian Curiosities." I take a great interest in every thing pertaining to the "Indians," and the relics of their early manners, customs, and arts, and particularly their stone implements of husbandry, the chase, war, &c. I have been gathering articles of this kind for more than thirty years past, from all parts of the United States, and, as you suggest, have succeeded in getting together considerable of a collection. I was somewhat surprised, however, to learn that Dr. Hollister, of Providence, had " a cabinet embracing some *ten thousand* implements, which is undoubtedly *the largest in the world.*" Did you ever calculate how many "ten thousand" are? Did you ever properly conceive what the largest thing in the world was? Sit down and think of it awhile before you state such things, and do not let your imagination run away with your better judgment. I am afraid you have been talking with the doctor lately about his collection. His enthusiasm frequently gets the better of him, and may have some influence over you.

Now, I don't want it understood that there is any rivalry existing between the doctor and myself upon the subject of the largest collection. When I commenced making my collection, I had never heard of such a man as Dr. Hollister. My object in collecting was to get at the history and character of the Indian race, as they were delineated in their implements of husbandry, the chase, war, and ornament, and, through them, taking up the discoveries of such things all over the earth's surface, endeavor to trace out the antiquity and origin of the race. Enough has been discovered to satisfy those who have given the subject careful consideration, that the whole earth was once peopled with a homogeneous race, who used stone implements for all the purposes of life, which are similar, and in many cases identical, with those used by our Indians, and which the doctor pretends to have found in such abundance that he now has *ten thousand* specimens.

I don't know but that the doctor has the "ten thousand" spoken of. I don't know but that he has more than I have. It may be he has. It may be he has the largest collection in the world. It may be. I don't wish to detract from either the doctor's number or size. I have an offer to make, however. I will place my collection alongside of the doctor's in any hall in Scranton, provided one large enough can be had there, and will then leave it to the public, who visit them, or to any three or more persons the doctor and I can agree upon, to say which has the largest collection—the best collection—the collection which best delineates the Indian character in every respect, as mechanics, as husbandmen, as huntsmen, as fishermen, as warriors, as artists, &c. The one in whose favor the decision is made shall then take both collections. Of course I should expect the doctor to leave out of his exhibition every thing not properly belonging to a collection of that sort—every thing not legitimate. I would not want any imposition of any sort practiced upon the public in the matter.

I shall want it fairly understood, before entering into competition with the doctor, that the judges selected shall be free from prejudice against my collection, because it has been kept in boxes, sheds, and barns, for the reason that it was too large to be kept in a pill shop. The fact is, I never kept my collection for show; never made a show of it; nor do I intend to do so very soon, unless there is a point to be gained by it, or a purpose to be subserved.

Can you get the doctor to agree to the proposition I make? If you can I will meet him at your office some time soon, and settle the preliminaries. Yours, very respectfully,

STEUBEN JENKINS.

In reply to Mr. Jenkins's letter of last week, we make room for the following from Dr. Hollister. We do this most cheerfully, as we are in hopes that the discussion as to which has the largest and best collection of Indian relics, will eventuate in affording our citizens an opportunity of becoming judges in the matter. A sight of the collections is something to be desired.

THE INDIAN RELIC CONTROVERSY.

Editor " Scranton Register"—Dear Sir :—As you have called public attention toward my collection of Indian relics, and as Steuben Jenkins, Esq., of Wyoming, in your last paper, questions the correctness of your statement, a word from me seems necessary. Friend Steuben is a very good *theoretical* Indian, and deserves the gratitude of all antiquarians, more for his zeal in *gathering* so many remembrances of the bravest race the world ever saw, than he does in *hiding* them under a bushel and barns. We occasionally visit Steuben to see his Indian cabinet, which is large and invaluable. He goes to a drawer, unlocks and exhumes a rare tomahawk or two, watching your throat closely lest you might swallow a pestle or hatchet, and then he takes you to some secluded corner, and from an old box guarded by cobwebs, gives you a half-glimpse of some memento of the departed race, and then to the shed, where he draws out of barrels many relics, as the angler draws the sturdy bull-head from the sluggish stream.

His collection is said to be magnificent, by those who have peeped into all his boxes and drawers, but mine is arranged in a "pill shop," where anybody can see it cheerfully and gratuitously, and it is too fine and valuable to be hid away for "thirty years" in obscure nooks. They are imperishable in their character, and mostly made from stone—as iron and copper implements of the later Indian period have little or no value.

Steuben objects to my relics being kept in a "pill shop," as he calls their unpretending abode, and yet he proposes to make a big show in Scranton. Well, suppose we have one. At considerable expense and labor, mine are now arranged in Providence. Let his be so arranged in Scranton. Or let the directors of the Wyoming fair, this fall prepare a safe, suitable place for each collection to be exhibited by Steuben and myself, then a committee chosen by us can determine which cabinet, by its size and variety, gives the best illustration of the character and customs of the wild race, once sheltered by our grand old forests. The one whose collection as a grand whole shall be deemed best, shall receive a certificate or diploma, and the one second best, must pay $50 to the Home of the Friendless or some other charitable institution in Luzerne County.

If I should possibly lose — (of which there is no danger, as my collection is undoubtedly the largest in the world of its kind), I should have the pleasure of knowing that the public had *seen* his relics, which were "too large for a pill shop," but just the size for miserish boxes and remote shed-corners.

Aside from this, it would not only bring dollars to the fair, but it would also diversify the character of that concern, which is usually made up mostly by Steuben and Bill Miner. The first one generally contributes a few bunches of fine grapes, and the last one furnishes a ride on horseback.

H. HOLLISTER.

PROVIDENCE, *July* 20, 1865.

WYOMING, *July* 22, 1865.

EDITOR OF THE "SCRANTON REGISTER"—DEAR SIR:—It is the fate of genius to be misunderstood and undervalued. Lofty pretensions and brusque impudence command greater consideration, and insure more certain rewards than the mightiest genius, unattended with patronage or place. It seems to be the fate of some men, to be misapprehended and belittled, because they stand aloof from, and, in their business pursuits and particularly in their recreations, rise above the ordinary level of mankind. Their motives are not the motives of other men, and as other men can not appreciate them, they generally decry them. I have been led to these reflections, from the fact that since Dr. Hollister and I have been brought before the public in your very able paper, as possessors of very fine collections of the relics of the Indian races that once roamed monarch of this mighty Western world, not a few persons have been found who laugh at the idea that the collections are of real importance and value. Not a little of this have I heard and seen in my presence, and I always feel a pity for the man who indulges in it—from the fact that their views are on the dollar and cent basis. If they were dollars that they could count, and there were "ten thousand" of them, they would hold their breath and stare in mute astonishment, but being "only ten thousand" relics of a once great and noble people, who scorned submission to or affiliation with a higher type of their species—they can only laugh at their possessors.

The doctor and I, it appears, are fast drifting into a complication of affairs, that will need wise and cool heads to unravel. I proposed to the doctor an exhibition of our respective collections, side by side, in some hall in Scranton, provided one could be obtained there large enough for the purpose—and the one having the best and largest collection, by a decision of the umpires, to take both. This the doctor declines, but makes this suggestion. He has at considerable expense and labor arranged his collection in Providence. He wants me at considerable expense and labor to arrange mine in Scranton, and then submit the decision to the people, who visit them. Well, suppose we do. I think I see mine arranged in a hall in Scranton, and then thrown open to the public examination. After a full and fair examination of my collection the immense throng start in procession to Providence. I see the long procession wending its way thither, down by the sand-banks, past the cemetery, on by the mud-hole, and turning the corner, commence winding their weary way up the high hill on which Providence is seated. The file-leader of the grand procession meets a denizen of the town, and inquires, "Where is the Indian—"

"What! have we an Indian among us?"

"I mean where is the Indian—"

"Exactly, but have we an Indian among us?"

"Hold a moment, I mean where is Dr. Hollister's Indian collection."

"Oh, yes, I understand you now, you turn up by the store, pass on down by the church, till you get to the foundery—then on the left you will find the doctor, with the latest story always out, his collection on exhibition, and the doctor always ready to expatiate on its merits, and declare it to be 'the largest in the world.'"

Here is where the doctor would have me. Lawyers always understand this if doctors don't. They always think that the last chance at a jury is worth twice as much as the first. I know that it is generally said that first impressions last the longest. While lawyers may believe that first impressions last the longest, they also believe that last impressions are the strongest. The doctor can't catch me in this way.

The other suggestion made by the doctor is to place our respective collections on exhibition at the agricultural fair this fall. To this I have no objection under proper arrangements, but the idea that he or I at the end of the exhibition shall give $50 to the Home of the Friendless, or to any other institution, is the highest absurdity of which the doctor has lately been guilty. How long has the doctor been engaged in laboring for other people, and then paying some one else for what he has done? I quit such things some time since. I find my labors better appreciated, and the results more satisfactory to myself when I get paid for my labor, than when I work for nothing, or give the fruits of my labor to some one who has no claims upon me for them. No! I don't go into arrangements by which I, at least, shall labor a week or two for nothing with the privilege of throwing in $50 at the end of time. Doctor, you knew you couldn't catch me with such a preposterous proposition. I am too old for that, and you ought to have known better than to have proposed it. I will see if some reasonable arrangement can't be made to exhibit at the county fair this fall, but I care nothing about this myself. I now have a silver cup, awarded to me by the Pennsylvania State fair, for my collections of Indian relics, as far back as 1860. I don't see how my honors would be added to by a diploma from the county fair, but to meet the doctor I am willing to exhibit at the county fair this fall under proper arrangements.

I didn't think the doctor was so observant as to note the watchful care I bestowed on my collection when he visited it. But he watched as well as I. The fact is, Indian relics disappear, when the doctor is around, in a wonderful manner. They go as quietly and as rapidly as "Trout glide along the mountain streams." The doctor knows this, and the trouble is, I know it; hence my watchfulness when he is about.

Very respectfully yours,

STEUBEN JENKINS.

THE INDIAN RELIC CONTROVERSY.

Editor of the "Scranton Register"—The Indian's side of history has never yet been written, only in traditions perishing with the race that knew them. It never will be written, only in the rude stone memorials they have left behind them. We shall read of homes reddened by the tomahawk, and of hearths blackened by the fagot, but not of the wrongs urging the wild man to defend the plain where his wigwam stood. For one, I do not believe that the same treacherous, thieving savage, rendered desperate by misfortune and impoverished by the whites, emerging from the dark passes of the West, are like those whose bones lie buried among us. Had we ever pursued toward the red men that humane, upright, consistent policy of Penn, instead of crowding them inch by inch southward and westward from homes they fought hard to protect, all the conflict with a race the American nation can not afford to lose, would have been avoided. For no race like this the world ever saw before or will ever know again. So much of calm courage—so much of true nobility—so much of unselfish friendship, could not be found in any other race or people on earth, and yet these memorials of another day and another race are the only visible evidences we have among us of the former occupants of our valleys.

Men whose souls are built of wood, and whose pockets are unctuous with traffic, can form no idea of Indian lore and history, as taught by these relics, and it is not for such persons that Steuben Jenkins immures his in sheds, or that mine are shown to the world. Such undervalue them, because a man of dollars and cents can not understand their worth or philosophy, when in fact each tomahawk and spear-point—each pipe and battle-ax—each and every implement of the earlier Indian stone period has a meaning and a language interpreting its history with as much faithfulness as the hieroglyphics along the Nile tell us of ancient times and glory. If I had space, article upon article could be written upon the part implements like these have played in history since Cain swung the war-club upon his brother Abel; but the purpose of this article is to reply to Steuben's last, and while I am at it I might as well trim up two or three limbs on the tree.

Some New York plagiarist has just issued a new book, which

is sold on the cars, describing portions of our valley, and he copies page after page from my "Contributions to the History of the Lackawanna Valley," without a word of acknowledgment or comment. Now is not this a cheap way of giving interest to a volume made from spoils? The Historical Society of Wilkes Barre, whose cabinet of Indian relics is even inferior to that of Steuben's, had no existence until my little volume appeared, and my suggestions urging it had been seen, and yet how little credit do I get there.

The "Nay-aug" companies of Scranton steal my names as if they were bastard words, and now brave Steuben comes along and presumes to put in battle-array his boxes and barns, stuffed with the Lord only knows what, against my fine Indian collection! Old rusty Wilkes Barre, how depraved and pretentious thou art in thy decrepitude!

Steuben and I, however, are going to have no quarrel, because he is as generous with his pen as he is covetous of his Indian traps, and my object in writing has been to smoke them out of their holes. As he virtually acknowledges my collection to be finer than his (tin cup and all that he got at the fair "*far* back as 1860"), there will be no necessity for their exhibition at the fair this fall, to settle this point, because their removal would involve much expense, beside necessitating the attendance of several watchmen, as Steuben's memory is exceedingly defective and his hands very awkward around Indian relics.

In conclusion, I would say to my friends, who have either read or laughed over these articles, that my collection (the largest in the world of its kind) is found in the airy village of Razorville, under the shadows of no protecting barn or box, but in a large office wholly devoted to their free exhibition (and to Dr. Hollister's Family Medicines), arranged finely in glass cases, always open, except when Steuben is known to be in town, when they are immediately locked, as I have observed that he is a liberal provider for those hungry and mysterious coat-pockets of his.

PROVIDENCE, *August* 3, 1865.   H. HOLLISTER.

INDIAN RELICS.

EDITOR "SCRANTON REGISTER"—DEAR SIR:—Dr. Hollister has finally reached the goal of his ambition. He has backed down entirely from his lofty pretensions of having "ten thousand specimens" of Indian relics—"the largest collection in the world"—and fails in every way to respond to the offers I made him to decide the question of the respective merits of his collection and mine. I here renew the offers I have made, and agree to give the doctor all the benefit of any doubt that may exist in the minds of the persons that may be chosen to decide. A friend of the doctor's, who has seen both collections, says that the doctor was foolish for thinking of competing with me. It would seem that if that was really the doctor's purpose, he had got fairly caught at it. But his last article shows pretty conclusively what the doctor has been at all the while, and shows, too, that the doctor has not been very foolish in the operation. His object was to puff up his collection of Indian relics, which I must admit is a very respectable one for the time the doctor has been engaged in making it, and advertising his Family Medicines and his History of the Lackawanna Valley, all of which he has managed to do very cleverly and without cost. I feel that I have been taken in a little by the doctor, but you, friend Hill, have been taken in and done for so much nicer than I, that I can not but laugh at your position. You, a long resident of Razorville, knowing the character of its inhabitants, to permit yourself to be used by one of them to advertise his nostrums for nothing, I am astonished at you. If I laugh at your verdancy, I can not help it, and I hope you will not be offended.

I attended the State fair at Easton, last fall, and while there I called upon Dr. Swift, of that place, who has a very large and well-selected collection of Indian relics, in every respect superior to Dr. Hollister's; and before leaving, the doctor gave me a stone hammer, found in the vicinity of the Ontonagon River, in the Lake Superior copper region. This hammer was made of a hard cobble-stone, that would weigh about three to four pounds, with a groove cut around it, to which the handle was attached with a withe. It was pretty well battered up with hard usage. Copper wedges and chisels are found in connection with the hammer, in the ancient workings of the copper mines in that region. One of these chisels was presented to me last week by Mr. Chambers, of Philadelphia; so that I now have both a hammer and a chisel, both exceedingly rare and difficult to be obtained. Dr. Hollister, I presume, has neither

The Lake Superior copper region seems to have been resorted to and worked by a race of men long before it became known to the white man. Whether these miners—the mound builders of the West, I have no doubt—and the Indians of the country were the same race or not, is matter for conjecture. That they were the mound builders who worked in the copper mines, I have no hesitancy in believing, from the fact that hardly a mound has yet been explored, in which something made of copper has not been found. Priest, in his "American Antiquities," says: "A vast many instances of articles made of copper, and some of silver, have been met with in opening these mounds. Circular pieces of copper, intended either as medals or breastplates, several inches in diameter, have been found, very much injured by time." Rev. Robert G. Wilson, D. D., of Chillicothe, Ohio, furnished the Antiquarian Society with information of a mound which once stood near the center of the town. "Its height was fifteen feet, circumference 180 feet, composed of sand. In excavating this mound, on a level with the surrounding earth, they found a human skeleton, overspread with a mat manufactured from weeds or bark, but greatly decayed. On the breast of this person lay *what had been a piece of copper*, in the form of a *cross*, which had become *verdigris*."

The Historical Society of Wilkes Barre have a copper arrow-point, which was found on the site of the fortification which once stood on Toby's Creek, in the borough of Kingston, described by Chapman in his history of Wyoming.

Foster and Whitney, in their report of the explorations of the Lake Superior copper region, say: "It is well known that copper rings, designed for bracelets, are frequently met with in the western mounds. We have several of these relics in our possession."

Samuel O. Knapp, agent of the Minnesota Company, in the spring of 1848, explored an ancient mine on the Ontonagon River. He gives this account of it: He found a depression twenty-six feet deep, filled with clay and a mass of moldering vegetable matter. When he had penetrated to the depth of eighteen feet with his excavations, he came to a mass of native copper ten feet long, three feet wide, and nearly two feet thick, and weighing over six tons. On digging around it, the mass was found to rest on billets of oak, supported by sleepers of the same material. The wood is dark-colored, and has lost all of its consistency. A knife blade may be thrust into it as easily as into a peat-bog. The earth was so packed about the copper as to give it a firm support. The ancient miners had evidently raised it about five feet, and then abandoned the work as too laborious. Every projecting point was taken off, and the exposed surface rendered perfectly smooth.

Trees are found growing on the heaps of rubbish thrown out of these ancient mines. Mr. Knapp counted three hundred and ninety-five annular rings on a hemlock which he felled on one of these heaps. He speaks of finding these stone hammers, the largest of which was $12 \times 5\frac{1}{2} \times 4$ inches, and weighed $39\frac{1}{2}$ pounds. In addition to these, a copper gad, with the head much battered, and a copper chisel, with a socket for the reception of a handle, were found, containing the fragment of a wooden handle, which crumbled soon after being exposed.

In clearing out one of these pits, at the depth of ten feet, a fragment of a wooden bowl was found, which, from the splintery pieces of rock and gravel imbedded in its rim, seemed to give evidence that it had been used in bailing water.

At the Phœnix mine, a copper knife was discovered in the explorations of an old working.

At Keweenaw Point and at Isle Royale, similar discoveries have been made.

All must admit that the facts set forth above in regard to the excavations, and the stone and copper implements found therein, assign to them a very high antiquity; but whether made by a race distinct from the Indians is a question about which there is some doubt, but I incline strongly to the opinion that we can not, nor need not, look beyond the Indians for a solution of the problem. I think it is their work.

How fortunate to be the possessor of specimens of their stone and copper implements, used by them in their copper-mining operations so far back in the history of this country.

Yours, very respectfully,
STEUBEN JENKINS.

INDIAN RELIC CONTROVERSY.

EDITOR OF "SCRANTON REGISTER:"—Indian Steuben is on the war-path again with his *copper* weapons; but as I intend to take off his scalp before long, if he remains in war costume, you need fear no danger.

Some weeks ago, Steuben took up your suggestion of exhibiting our respective collections of Indian relics side by side in Scranton, and he suggested that the one having the largest should take the other; but as I was too magnanimous to thus deprive him of the results of thirty years' labor, I declined the offer, but proposed that we exhibit them at the Wyoming fair, and that the one whose collection should be the best calculated to throw light upon the customs, habits, and life of the aboriginal race, should receive a diploma, and that the one second best must pay $50 to the Home of the Friendless, or some other charitable institution. This offer he not only declined, but attempted to throw ridicule and suspicion upon my motives of philanthropy in offering to bestow charity upon any one in this manner.

So your readers can see *who* is backing down. Instead of performing any such retrograde movement, I am determined if possible to draw his frozen contribution boxes out in daylight where his copper traps can be seen without a tallow candle, and then "the goal of my ambition" will have been reached. And now I not only renew my offer of their exhibition at Wyoming the coming fair, provided that assurance be given me two weeks before the fair that a safe, suitable place will be provided for them, but I would here choose Steuben Jenkins one of the umpires to decide the matter, because I believe that he would give an honest decision, however "mysteriously Indian relics disappear when he is around." It is true he has every advantage of me, because he has made many a pilgrimage to Razorville to see my vast collection and learn how to arrange his, besides this he tells you that he has visited the collection of Dr. Swift, in Easton, but failed in his loquacious mood to say why he visited it. Knowing that he could not successfully compete with mine, he goes to Dr. Swift to get the *loan* of his for the purpose of exhibiting them as his own! Now, Steuben, this is not a graceful way to launch your canoe after a lost battle; besides, how dangerous for Dr. Swift, if his collection is of any value!

Goldsmith imparts vanity to the one writing of himself, but I did not suppose that I was so vain as to write my relics into notice for the sake of getting my book and "nostrums advertised for nothing " until Steuben discovered it. The volume spoken of has been out of print since 1857, and can be purchased nowhere now; and as to my family medicines, I can not possibly supply the great demand for them now, and why should I seek gratuitous advertisement, when you know, Mr. Hill, that I am in the habit of paying liberally for what I get in that line.

I concede that Steuben makes out a strong case for himself on paper (and what sharp or lazy Luzerne lawyer could not?) and that he has a few *copper* hatchets—probably of French manufacture—which I have not, but I regard the wooden, iron, and copper implements found along our cataracts and caverns as of little or no value to the antiquarian, although I have a few copper arrow-points myself, which were found in an Indian's grave near Tunkhannock, and presented to me with many other relics, some years ago, by J. M. Robinson, Esq., of Meshoppen.

Important archæological explorations pursued with admirable vigor and extraordinary success in the West—in South America, and along the lakes of Zurich and Neufchatel in Switzerland, adduce evidence that the construction of the *copper* relics sometimes found in western mounds, belonged not to any of our known Indian races. In fact, the Indian knew nothing of the use and value of copper till taught by the whites.

Their creation pertains to the bronze period, which some of the Swiss archæologists have concluded to represent an antiquity of from two thousand nine hundred to four thousand two hundred years; the age of stone from four thousand seven hundred to seven thousand, and the whole period of from seven thousand four hundred to eleven thousand years.

I have some rare *stone pipes*, some elegant *stone chisels* for removing the char from canoes, and a singularly beautiful *stone bird* or idol, found along the Indian path crossing the farm of Dr. Throop, in Blakeley, and presented to me by Mr. Shaw. I have never seen or heard of any thing of the kind ever being found in the country before. I also have a curious *death-mall*, constructed from a huge ovoid pebble, weighing twelve pounds, similar to that used by the Indians to kill their captives. After the battle of Wyoming, in 1778, an instrument like this and a war-club in the hands of Queen Esther, malled and slew the captives around Bloody Rock.

APPENDIX.

While the copper utensils spoken of by Steuben give nothing but a faint conjectural idea of the occupancy of the county at the time of their deposit, and belong to a period subsequent to that of which I write, the antiquity of the stone weapons of war is alike instructive and wonderful.

The bow and the arrow are spoken of in Genesis and many other places in Holy Writ. Arrows were first made of reed; then of strong, light wood, with a stone arrow-point fastened to the end. Among the Hebrews, especially among the tribes of Ephraim and Benjamin, archers were numerous.

Among the ruins of the Temple of Luxor, on the Nile, two or three thousand years old, one apartment exhibits a great battle, in which the Egyptians, armed with bows and arrows, gained a great victory over their Asiatic enemies equipped with javelin and war-club.

In one battle between the Persians and the Tartars, 800 B. C., it is related by Persian historians that their great chief Rustam, with his own war-club, slew 1,160 of his foes!

Fragments of Nineveh, now in the British Museum, introduce us to their monarchs thirty centuries ago, clad in costume of war and armed only with the arrow and the bow.

The javelin or spear was a missile weapon, and took the place of our swords and guns. It is often mentioned in the Bible in connection with light-armed troops. It could be thrown at the enemy at a great distance, and in the great conflicts between the Persians and Macedonians, the white javelins flew and fell like snow-flakes upon the contending legions. When Xerxes crossed the Hellespont with his gleaming millions, he was dared and checked by the Spartans, armed with such missiles and animated by no common courage. The Medes were celebrated for the use of the bow, with which they fought on horseback with terrific effect. Their arrows were poisoned with a bituminous liquor which burned with such intensity that water increased the heat. This is the first record we have of the poisoned arrow used so much by the red warrior. I have several poisoned arrows in my collection.

"The sword," sang Mahomet twenty-four centuries ago, "is the key of heaven and hell, courage then my children, fight like men, close up your ranks—discharge your arrows and the day is your own!"

In the hands of Tell, the arrow saved his son and gave freedom to the land of the Alps.

The Hungarians threw a small stone ax or tomahawk with such dexterity at a hundred paces that a victim always fell. As late as 1461 arrows tipped with Steuben's copper were used by the English nation as a weapon of defense.

A tribe of Indians in Paraguay, South America, with these rude weapons have maintained their independence against all the power and treachery of the Spaniards for three hundred years.

The exploring party for the Pacific Railroad, in 1856, found along the Colorado many of these stone tomahawks yet in use among these savages.

Up the old Nile and along the track of the brave and lamented Speke, the black warrior still goes forth thirsting for blood, with club and lance and ever-beating drum. Is it strange then that these *stone* relics running along the history of so many strange centuries, should be gathered and cherished? And if it "is fortunate to be the possessor of" a few *copper* trinkets relating to a people and an epoch alike indefinite and uncertain, how much greater the pleasure to know that you can glance each day over *stone* relics whose antiquity carries us back to the earliest periods of traditional or written history!

H. HOLLISTER.

PROVIDENCE, *August* 17, 1865.

INDIAN RELICS.

EDITOR OF "SCRANTON REGISTER"—DEAR SIR:—I have read the whole of Dr. Hollister's last letter relating to the "Indian relic controversy." It is true I read it in a state of great trepidation and alarm, for the arrows, spears, tomahawks, axes, death-malls, scalping-knives, &c., that the doctor hurled at me from his vast magazine, whizzed and buzzed so about my head, as to keep me in a perpetual dodge, and yet I read it—all of it. You will wonder, and so do I, as I look back at the dangers through which I passed in doing so. Happily, however, I escaped unharmed, and a careful examination convinces me that my scalp is still on.

The doctor renews his proposal, "that we exhibit our collections at the Wyoming fair this fall, and that the one whose collection should be the best calculated to throw light upon the customs, habits, and life of the aboriginal race should receive a diploma, and that the one second best must pay $50 to the Home of the Friendless Children in Wilkes Barre, or some other charitable institution, provided that assurance be given him two weeks before the fair, that a safe, suitable place will be provided for them."

This offer I no longer refuse, but accept of the same, and assure the doctor that a safe and suitable place will be provided for his collection, and I will get this assurance in writing from the officers of the society and forward to him in a few days.

The Indian relic controversy, so far as the doctor and I are concerned, is now ended. The point I aimed at, and which the doctor seemed to desire,—a public exhibition of our respective collections, side by side, and a decision as to which has the best and largest collection,—is now provided for.

It remains, however, for me to say a word in reference to the doctor's very extraordinary learned disquisition upon the subject of Indian relics. I must confess my great surprise at the antiquity of the age of stone. I was aware that it commenced with man, nearly but not quite six thousand years ago, but until I read the doctor's article I was not aware that it extended back some five thousand years before man appeared upon the earth—altogether some "eleven thousand years." Man was, as I have stated—taking the *best* authority we have upon the subject—created a little less than six thousand years ago. I wish the doctor or some one else would inform "the whole world and the rest of mankind," who made stone implements eleven thousand years ago, who they made them for, and what use they made of them? Not more surprised was I to learn from the doctor's article, for the first time in all my reading, that "Mahomet sang *twenty-four centuries* ago." As I understand it, Mahomet flourished but a little over twelve centuries ago. I wish the doctor would inform me in what song of Mahomet he finds the language he attributes to him. I have Mahomet's writing, and have not as yet seen the song containing the language the doctor attributes to him. But it was *twenty-four centuries* ago. The doctor may forget in so long time where to find it. But where does the doctor get his new chronology? The stone period, extending back "eleven thousand years!" Ma homet singing "*twenty-four centuries ago!*" I can't understand it. The fault is mine, I doubt not. I feel sometimes—and I don't know why I should not feel so now, as I stand before the mighty mass of learning the doctor has accumulated before me—somewhat as the great and learned Laplace did at the close of his long and brilliant career, "that what I know is little, while what I do not know is immense." I hope to live and learn yet for a time, and with the doctor as a teacher, I have no doubt I may get to know something.

The doctor says "he has a *curious death-mall*, constructed from a huge ovoid pebble." When I read that, I thought myself that the doctor had a *curious-mall* that would be the *death* of somebody yet. I came near laughing myself to death the first time I saw it, and I came a little nearer to it when I read the doctor's last article. The fact is, I was confined to my house with illness for four days afterward, and I can give no other cause for it than that *curious mall*—a mere water-washed stone, having no more marks or signs of Indian workmanship upon it than the doctor's phiz has.

If the doctor will read history a little more carefully, he will find that it was the Parthians and not the Medes who were celebrated for the use of the bow and arrow on horseback. Does the doctor know what David killed Goliath with? Has he any weapon of that sort in his collection?

In my last, I made the suggestion that while it was matter of doubt among archæologists whether the people who built the mounds were the same that inhabited the country when first discovered by the whites—I was satisfied that they were one and the same people. But few facts can be gathered on which to found a hypothesis, either way, but those facts, however few, when discovered should have their full weight. Schoolcraft, the learned Indian antiquarian, who made, in August, 1843, an elaborate examination of the mounds found at Grave Creek, Virginia, says that "several polished tubes of stone were found in one of the lesser mounds. They were about one foot long, one and a fourth inches in diameter at one end, and one and a half at the other. They are made of a fine, compact, lead-blue steatite, mottled, and constructed by boring in the manner of a gun-barrel. This boring is continued to within three-eighths of an inch of the large end, through which but a small aperture is left. If this small aperture be looked through, objects at a distance are more clearly seen. Its construction is far from rude, and it was probably designed as a telescope."

Joseph Tomlinson, who settled at Grave Creek in 1770, first discovered the mounds there. His son, A. B. Tomlinson, in 1837 commenced excavating the larger mound, and in it, among other things, he found a lot of beads, made of a kind of porcelain, similar in appearance to the material out of which dentists manufacture artificial teeth. I have in my collection a polished tube of stone, exactly like the one described by Schoolcraft, which was found some three years ago at Northumberland, in this State, in excavating for the railroad; and I also have a very large and beautiful string of beads, of the kind found by Tomlinson, which were dug out of some Indian grave at Wilkes Barre a year ago. In addition to these are the facts of pottery and copper implements being common to the mound and to our Indians, the inference and proof are, therefore, very strong that the mound-builders and the Indians were one and the same people, and that they were I have no doubt. The proof is all in that direction.

Another word to the doctor and I am done. He should be certain of his facts before he states them as such, or draws conclusions from them. This is the great duty of every inquirer after truth.   Yours truly,

STEUBEN JENKINS.

THE INDIAN RELIC CONTROVERSY.

As Steuben Jenkins wishes to bury the hatchet for the purpose of saving his own scalp, and as I value copper trinkets too lightly to desire the possession of the top of his head, which for the last few weeks has been quivering with scalping dreams, we will smoke the calumet awhile, so that this article will be the last one upon Indian relics the public will have for some time; not but what very much could be written about the former occupants of our valley and their memorials: but how comparatively few care for the relics of the red men! although as long as spring can awaken flowers from the meadow, these memorials will have their interest and value to the antiquarian.

I will briefly answer Steuben's objections in the order of their appearance.

1st. The ridiculous importance he gave to his *copper* hatchets, &c., some weeks ago—which were all of European manufacture—vanished the moment I exhibited their utter want of claim to antiquity, as shown by Squier, Charlevoix, Bartram, and Brabeuf, leaving Steuben nothing to do but to sing "the song of Mahomet twenty-four centuries ago." Mahomet was born 569 A. C., and his flight took place 622 A. C., as every student of history knows, but the typographical error made my article read *twenty-four* instead of twelve centuries ago. Steuben writes too much, and reads too little in his Koran to acquire or impart knowledge, or appreciate the historical facts I have so liberally brought to his view.

2d. I am sorry that I once exhibited that "curious death-mall" to him, because I fear that it has knocked him senseless forever, and yet that stone implement of death attracted him once to Providence, and then how his eyes wished and his mouth watered as he gazed on its vast proportions safely reposing under glass, while the key was safe in my own pocket! And when he found that no persuasion could allure this unique and valuable stone into his collection (of boxes hid in sheds), he discovered that it was nothing more than "a mere water-washed stone!" Steuben, the fact is, that the *upper end* of the county is too much for your fussy *copper* kettles, even after a very clever Pittston doctor helped you scour them up.

3d. It is true that the Parthians or Scythians—now the Tartar race—were among the most skillful archers in the world on horseback, and shot their arrows with unerring precision even on a gallop; but if Steuben will look into the same history he refers me to, he will find that the first historical fact known of the Parthians is that they were the subjects of the Medes, from whom they learned their skill in archery. This was before the Tartars became powerful under the great Tamerlane.

4th. Would it not be creditable for Steuben to read something of chronology and archæology, as well as to interpret correctly what I write? I stated that "the *Swiss* archæologists have concluded that the age of bronze may represent an antiquity of from 2,900 to 4,200 years, the age of stone from 4,700 to 7,000 years, and the whole series a period of from 7,000 to 11,000 years."

All must acknowledge the imperfection of archæological record, and presume that a mere definite chronology will eventually be established. Kenedy, in his Scriptural Chronology, says that 300 different opinions, founded upon the Bible, may be collected as to the length of time that has elapsed between the creation and the birth of Christ. Fabricius, in his Bibliotheca Antiquaria, has given a list of 140 of these calculations. I would refer Steuben to these works, also to the chronological works of Dr. Hale, Prof. Playfair, and Desvignolles. And although the literature of the Swiss is merged into that of France and Germany, friend Steuben would find great information in perusing the works of Lavater, Sismondi, Haller, Euler, Le Sage, Necker, and other Swiss authors.

The "stone polished tube" in Steuben's possession, he thinks was used by the Indians as a telescope. If it were possible to conceive of any thing more comical than an Indian, inhabiting the forest so dense that he could not see his own nose, looking through Steuben's "polished tube" as a telescope into the thicket, it might be found in the idea of Steuben's, that the "long polished tube" was ever used by the aborigines for such a purpose!

> "Lo! the poor Indian whose untutored mind
> Sees God in the forest," through Steuben's long tube!

Schoolcraft no doubt drew an honest inference in the matter from the light accessible then, but there is no possible evidence in Indian histories or antiquarian explorations of any such use being made of these "polished tubes." I have a broken portion of one in my possession, which from my knowledge of Indian character and habit, I am satisfied was used, like all these tubes, by their medicine-men to render their incantations more potent and effective. Spectacles nor telescopes never vexed an Indian's eye. So much for Steuben, who has switched himself off the track, where I am sorry to leave him—out on the switch.

In Wyoming Valley, where the Indian fought with tomahawk and war-club to save his hunting-grounds, fortifications exist whose history has been lost even to tradition.

Along the Lackawanna, Indian tribes left no such trace.

Although from careful explorations there appears to have been no less than seven Indian villages along the Lackawanna—all standing upon its eastern bank—but a single mound denotes their place of burial. Evidences of villages are found in implements of stone and clay scattered along the river, generally where some tributary comes in. One peculiar feature appears in the fact, that where the broken pottery is most abundant, no stone utensil other than a corn pounder or pestle is found within twenty or thirty yards—showing that the braves practiced archery away from the shadows of their wigwams. Near the late Dr. Robinson's, a little stream puts into the Lackawanna, on the bank of which, rising into a gentle knoll, many relics are seen, and yet no culinary utensils are found. Near this point is seen a small elevation which I have named *Capoose Mound*, as it stands at the head of the old Indian meadow of Capoose. At the time of the first settlement of Providence by the whites, in 1770, there were about a dozen graves here. In 1799, however, a party of persons, one of whom still survives, opened these graves. A small copper kettle of European manufacture, large quantities of wampum and arrow-heads were exhumed, carried away and lost.

Of the Indian's mortar, or mill, for pounding *na-sump*, or samp, but few are found in the country unbroken. Whoever has had the patience to toil up the mountain side to Bald Mount in Newton, will find in a huge rock projecting over the precipice a number of holes or Indian mortar-places, made in the stone by the patient wild man, which no doubt were used by them for domestic purposes. Some have the capacity of a gallon. Of course portable ones were generally used by them, sometimes made of wood, but oftener of stone.

This height was no doubt chosen for a camp-place, so as to enable the Indians a chance to look down into the forest through those "polished tubes."

How long the Indian smoked his pipe along the Hudson or Mohawk before the discovery, we know not, but the white man was first cursed with the knowledge of tobacco in 1492. No article of luxury was constructed with more care—cherished with holier memories—loved with more constant fervor than the Indian's pipe. Their calumet, or pipe of peace, was among the most prized and sacred articles of all the stone implements of the wigwam. I have in my collection a large number of pipes of rare and exquisite workmanship.

I also have some elegant moose-skin robes, such as were worn by Rocky Mountain chiefs, porcupine necklaces, and hunting-belts for stringing scalps and trophies, medicine bags, and war caps in full plume—but these perishable things, while they attract the superficial eye, have no more real value than copper implements. So much for Indian stone relics, which some day will gather around them more interest than they can possibly command now. And yet "what are they good for?" asks some jingler of dollars. If every line of written history was obliterated forever, the presence and progress of races—their character and conquests—the diffusion of tribes—their relative approach to or departure from civilization—most of their habits, and many of their religious notions could be plainly elucidated by the aid of these relics, which to the unpracticed eye seem like rude, unmeaning stone. Upon the fairest face that ever smiled or wept, beauty will perish, and lips proudly glowing with hopes of many summers, dissolve into untroubled earth, forgetting and forgot, while these sad memorials of another day and another race, whose voice gives back no echo from the wild, neglected by many, despised by more, and treasured but by few, when many a voice is still, and many a heart is cold, these simple relics will remain perfect in their integrity, and beautiful in their silence!

H. HOLLISTER.

Sept. 7, 1865.

The following report of the Committee on Indian Relics, exhibited at the late fair of the Lucerne County Agricultural Society, will prove of interest to our readers.—[EDITOR *Lucerne Union.*]

The Committee appointed by the Lucerne County Agricultural Society to report upon the Exhibition of Indian Relics, made by Dr. Hollister and Steuben Jenkins, Esq., at the recent Annual Fair on the Society's grounds, near the Wyoming battle-field, take unusual pleasure in saying that the exhibition was in every respect far superior to any thing anticipated or looked for. The respective collections of these gentlemen are a monument to their untiring industry and love of science. They will challenge the admiration of all men in all places where hereafter they may be exhibited.

To the man of science and learning they are a *volume* of American history, to be read and studied nowhere else. A single glance over these splendid collections gives almost every implement used by the red man, whether in the fight, or the chase, the wigwam or the corn-field, for there are the bow and the arrows, the knife and the tomahawk of the warrior, the rude mortar and pestle for the squaw, and the delicate arrow-head for the early practice of the Indian boy. Here the book, and the only book of centuries of aboriginal savage life, in war and in peace, unfolds to the eye the living history of a people fast disappearing from their ancient grounds toward the setting sun. We congratulate the Agricultural Society in having been permitted to furnish to its numerous visitors at their fair, so unique a display, awakening in the bosoms of many of them such thrilling recollections of the bloody tragedy once enacted on this same field. We have heard on all sides since the opening of the exhibition but one continued expression of praise and thanks to Messrs. Hollister and Jenkins. We are certain that every man, woman, and child, who have been gratified by a sight of these relics, will not only join the Committee in thanks to those gentlemen, but will co-operate with them in the work in which they are engaged. In judging upon the comparative size and merits of the respective collections, the Committee, after a careful examination, concluded that the difference between them was but slight, and as the one in whose favor that difference seemed to predominate, desired that the Committee, if practicable and satisfactory to the Society, should render no decision upon that point, but should treat both collections as equally meritorious and entitled to the consideration of the Society, they have concluded to adopt this view of the subject. The Committee would therefore recommend that the special thanks of the Lucerne Agricultural Society be extended to both Dr. Hollister and Mr. Jenkins, and that in addition thereto there be awarded to each of those gentlemen, by the Society, a silver pitcher or goblet, of value not less than fifty dollars, with suitable inscriptions thereon to commemorate the facts.

E. W. STURDEVANT,
C. DORRANCE,
C. PARSONS,
ADW. T. MCCLINTOCK,
JOHN N. CONYNGHAM,
Committee.

II.

THE LACKAWANNA VALLEY FIFTY YEARS AGO AND NOW.

Scranton, settled less than a century ago, named after the original Scrantons, and incorporated into a city in 1866, is the largest one of its age in its commercial and industrial development and in the growth of all the elements of civilization of any city east of the Mississippi River.

When the writer first passed through it in 1837 it had but two dwellings, inhabited by Barton Mott, the miller, and the elder Slocums. It had no church, no store or tavern, saloon or post-office, and even the stage-coach, on its tri-weekly trips from Wilkes Barre to Carbondale, ran no nearer to it than Hyde Park, half a mile away. A single narrow wagon-road, crouched upon either side with low, dense shrubbery, led the way through it. Between Dunmore and Scranton stood but two solitary houses.

In the old Wurts and Drinker maps of the valley of 1826, now in my possession, made by those gentlemen with a view of running their proposed railroads from the Susquehanna to the Delaware, this section was simply marked "Slocums," commending itself to the eye only by the half-employed, excellent water-privileges of the wild-throbbing and trout-filled Nay-aug.

In 1840 the population of Scranton was about 100 persons, but the census report as late as 1850 gave the population of Providence township, without giving Scranton either name or notice because there was no Scranton to name. Three years later it was estimated at 3000 souls. In 1860 it was 9223. The percentage of its growth from that time until now, owing to the iron and coal industry, has been marvellous. In 1870 its population was 35,092; in 1880, 45,850; in 1881, 48,672; in 1884, 67,062; in 1885, 70,000 and over.

The entire city has a territorial area of $19\frac{1}{2}$ miles. It is five miles square and twenty miles in circumference, with five hundred streets, named and numbered, which are over one hundred miles in length.

Scranton is situated in what is known as the Northern Anthracite Coal Field, embracing an area of 198 square miles, or 126,620 acres of coal which is from thirty to fifty feet thick, yielding about 6000 tons to the acre, making a total of 7,603,200,000 tons. Up to the present time but three hundred million tons of this has been mined and marketed. The rest lies embedded in the bosom of mother earth.

"With such a basis for prosperity," says the Rev. David Spencer, to whom, as well as to Colonel Price, we are indebted for many of the facts herein stated, "it is impossible to predict any limit to the grand future of Scranton and the Lackawanna Valley."

Its streets are wide and straight, and, considering the youthfulness of the city, have many things about them superior to streets in older seaport cities. Give Scranton time for more development, and we can have the finest streets of any city in the world. Our municipality now expend $10,000 a year on our highways, less than $500 for each of the twenty-one wards.

Our postal facilities, which were introduced in 1884, through the instrumentality of Hon. JOSEPH A. SCRANTON, our present popular member of Congress, and postmaster, EDWARD C. FULLER, work to the satisfaction and advantage of all, and are very conducive to the 75,000 or 80,000 inhabitants of the city.

THE CHURCHES OF SCRANTON.

The churches of Scranton are numerous and generally well patronized.

Adams Avenue M. E. Church.—Adams Avenue. Rev. L. C. Muller, pastor.

Anshe Chesed (Jewish Church).—Linden Street. Rev. S. Freudenthal, rabbi.

Chestnut Street Baptist Church.—Chestnut Street. Rev. Owen James, pastor.

Christian Church.—N. Main Avenue. Rev. C. W. Cooper, pastor.

Church of the Good Shepherd (Episcopal).—Monsey Avenue. Rev. Joseph P. Cameron, S.T.B., rector.

First German Baptist Church.—Pittston Avenue. Rev. J. H. Meyers, pastor.

First M. E. Church of Providence.—N. Main Avenue. Rev. A. J. Van Cleft, pastor.

APPENDIX. 447

First Presbyterian Church.—Washington Avenue. Rev. S. C. Logan, pastor.

First Presbyterian Church of Providence.—Church Avenue. Rev. George E. Guild, pastor.

First Welsh Baptist Church.—S. Main Avenue. Rev. J. W. Williams, pastor.

German M. E. Church.—Adams Avenue. Rev. Jacob Kolb, pastor.

Grace Reformed Episcopal Church.—328 Wyoming Avenue. Rev. G. Albert, rector.

Green Ridge M. E. Church.—Corner Monsey Avenue. Rev. J. V. Newell, pastor.

Green Ridge Street Presbyterian Church.—Rev. M. F. Stahl, pastor.

Holy Trinity Lutheran Church.—Services held in Y. M. C. A. Hall, Lackawanna Avenue. Rev. M. L. Zweizig, pastor.

Hyde Park M. E. Church.— N. Main Avenue. Rev. G. M. Colville, pastor.

Jackson Street Baptist Church.—Rev. N. E. Naylor, pastor.

Methodist Episcopal Church.—Hampton Street. Rev. G. C. Lewis, pastor.

Park Place Chapel (M. E.).—Court Street. Rev. H. H. Dresser, pastor.

Penn Avenue Baptist Church.—Penn Avenue. Rev. David Spencer, D.D., pastor.

Plymouth Congregational Church.—Jackson Street, near S. Main Avenue. Rev. Jonathan Edwards, pastor.

Primitive M. E. Church.—E. Market Street. Rev. H. G. Russell, pastor.

Providence Welsh Baptist Church.—N. Main Avenue.

Second Presbyterian Church.—Jefferson Avenue. Rev. T. R. Beeber, pastor.

St. David's Church (Episcopal).—Tenth Street. Rev. Joseph P. Cameron, S.T.B., rector.

St. Luke's Church (Episcopal).—Wyoming Avenue. Rev. J. Philip B. Pendleton, S.T.B., rector; T. F. Hunt, senior warden; A. D. Holland, junior warden. Vestrymen: John Jermyn, G. L. Dickson, S. M. Nash, B. H. Throop, and J. H. Bessel.

St. Mary's Church (Catholic).—William Street. Rev. M. Whitty, pastor; Rev. Thomas Kernan, assistant.

St. Mary's Church (German Catholic).—River Street. Rev. John Schelle, pastor.

St. Patrick's Church (Catholic).—Price Street. Rev. J. B. Whelan, pastor.

St. Peter's Evangelical Lutheran Church.—Ash, corner Prescott Avenue. Rev. Eugene Weisskopff, pastor.

St. Vincent's Church (Catholic).—Wyoming Avenue, corner Linden Street. Rt. Rev. William O'Hara, Bishop of Scranton Diocese and pastor; Rev. R. A. McAndrews, rector; Rev. T. F. Coffey, 1st assistant; Rev. P. F. Broderick, 2d assistant; Rev. Dr. McManus, 3d assistant.

Washburn Street Presbyterian Church.—Washburn Street, corner S. Hyde Park Avenue. Rev. W. I. Steans, pastor.

Welsh Calvinistic Methodist Church.—S. Main Avenue. Rev. R. Faulk Jones, pastor.

Welsh Congregational Church.—W. Market, above Brick Avenue. Rev. R. S. Jones, pastor.

Welsh Congregational Church.—S. Main Avenue. Rev. Lot Lake, pastor.

Zion Lutheran Church (German).—Mifflin Avenue. Rev. P. F. Zitzelmann, pastor.

The total sittings of the churches in Scranton approximate to thirty-five or forty thousand persons, while the membership is considerably less.

OUR SCHOOL SYSTEM.

The public and private school institutions are thorough and complete. In the city there are thirty public school buildings, with a seating capacity of seven thousand nine hundred and twenty, all erected at a cost of $332,000, including the value of the lots upon which they stand. Two hundred and five teachers are employed at a total salary of $8009 per year, or about $40 per month. In 1879 there were five thousand four hundred and forty-eight scholars upon the rolls, while in 1884 there were seven thousand five hundred and eighty-three, with an average attendance of six thousand seven hundred and seven. In the case of school attendance the increase exhibits the very rapid growth of the city in population during the five years. In no department is the permanent prosperity of a locality more distinctly located.

HEALTH OF THE VALLEY.

The general health of Scranton is excellent. Located seven hundred and fifty feet above the level of the sea, surrounded by mountains two thousand feet high, it enjoys the advantages of an invigorating atmosphere, pure water, and ample drainage, and yet eighty physicians manage to sustain an indifferent degree of thrift and prosperity. Epidemics and endemics, such diseases as distract our seaboard cities, are unknown, while typhoid fever is rarely seen in the valley. Pulmonary troubles are not indigenous. Unless inherited and brought in the system from some other section of country, it is rare to see a case of consumption among us. Sheltered by the Moosic Mountains upon either side from the cold winds of March and December, the Lackawanna Valley, with its genial air and its coal-mines, affords to those predisposed to phthisis the best prospect for hope, recuperation, and longevity of any known place.

OUR CHARITIES.
THE LACKAWANNA HOSPITAL.

An institution originating solely through the agency of Dr. B. H. Throop, one of the oldest in Scranton, was incorporated in 1871, and it has done and is still doing a vast amount of good to the poor, unfortunate occupants of the city. This year (1885) it received an appropriation of $15,000 from the State. Charles W. Roesler is president, E. C. Fuller treasurer, and N. D. Green secretary.

THE MOSES TAYLOR HOSPITAL.

The Moses Taylor Hospital was the result of the thoughtfulness and benevolence and means of that noble man whose name it bears. It was started in 1884. When completed, the maimed and suffering will have occasion to rejoice over the measures of relief afforded them through its instrumentality. Mrs. Payne, his liberal daughter, supplemented this generous gift by donating $100,000 in addition.

DEAF AND DUMB INSTITUTION.

Scranton looks thoughtfully after the needs of the unfortunate children found within its precincts. Our young and talented senator, Hon. L. A. Watres, and his able assistants urged a bill through the Legislature in the spring of 1885, appropriating $45,800 for the establishment in this city of an oral school for deaf-mutes. Governor Pattison, however, ignorant of every generous thought or impulse, vetoed the bill because he had the right to do so without the reason. The money thus appropriated was to have been used in the erection of suitable buildings for the maintenance of the school for two years. The oral system was to be taught in preference to the sign system used in all continental Europe except France.

Progress has discovered a much better method, and, instead of the pantomimic action of the fingers, what is called the oral system has been introduced, by which words may be read and ideas communicated by the mere movement of the lips.

The oral school for deaf-mutes was established in this city nearly two years ago, and since that time has been supported by private subscriptions on the part of the directors and others. But thirteen pupils are enrolled, as many mutes from this vicinity attend the institution for deaf-mutes in Philadelphia. According to the census there are in this section between eighty and one hundred deaf-mutes of school age. Applications for admission to the school have lately come from many places in the neighborhood, and one was received from Lynchburg, Va. The school-house is situated on the alley between Jefferson and Adams Avenues, near Vine Street. The building used is the first church building that was erected on the Scranton side of the river. It served as a place of worship for many congregations, and finally became the property of the German Methodists, who moved it on the rear end of their lot. The new building was to be erected on Washington Avenue, on the lot presented the directors by the Pennsylvania Coal Company. The lot consists of between four and five acres, and is pleasantly located.

The directors of the school are as follows: Hon. Alfred Hand, President; Henry Belin, Jr., Secretary and Treasurer; William T. Smith, Rev. Moses Whitty, John B. Smith, William Connell, Fred. W. Gunster, R. J. Matthews, B. G. Morgan, Hon. L. A.

Watres, Rev. T. R. Beeber, Colonel E. H. Ripple, Charles H. Welles, Benjamin Hughes, J. C. Platt, H. M. Boies, E. B. Sturges.

HOME OF THE FRIENDLESS.

Probably there is no institution in Scranton or within the State which is devoted to a theme so lofty and dear, a charity so broad and wholesome, as that of the Home of the Friendless, at which all look with a feeling of satisfaction and pride. It was chartered in 1873. Managed by liberal, self-sacrificing ladies, of whom Mrs. Thomas Moore seems the leading spirit, the rugged pathway of the lives of helpless children and women is rendered less rough and lonely by the zealous, silent work of these ladies.

The following are the officers: Mrs. James Blair, President; Mrs. George L. Dickson, Vice-President; Mrs. Thomas Moore, Chief Manager; Mrs. W. D. Kennedy, Recording Secretary; Mrs. C. P. Matthews, Corresponding Secretary; Mrs. D. Langstaff, Treasurer; Managers: Mrs. A. E. Hunt, Mrs. J. R. Fordham, Mrs. C. B. Scott, Mrs. C. D. Simpson, Mrs. W. W. Winton, Mrs. E. S. Moffitt, Mrs. B. F. Fillmore, Mrs. W. H. Perkins, Mrs. S. N. Stetler, Mrs. Jas. P. Dickson, Mrs. L. B. Powell, Mrs. T. H. Dale, Mrs. O. P. Clark, Mrs. Joseph Ober, Mrs. S. A. Brightman, Mrs. E. G. Judd, Mrs. R. W. Luce, Mrs. J. L. Stelle, Mrs. J. Genter, Mrs. H. A. Loveland, Mrs. Wm. Von Storch, Mrs. H. A. Masser, Mrs. A. Chamberlain, Mrs. Hendricks; Auditors: Mrs. R. W. Luce, Mrs. Wm. Connell.

Standing Committees.—Advisory Committee: Mr. H. A. Knapp, Mr. H. S. Pierce, Mr. James P. Dickson; Members of Executive Committee: Mrs. W. W. Winton, Mrs. E. S. Moffitt; Committee on Finance: Mrs. C. B. Scott (Chairman), Mrs. H. A. Loveland, Mrs. Joseph Ober, Mrs. J. Genter, Mrs. O. P. Clark, Mrs. J. L. Stelle, Mrs. E. G. Judd, Mrs. J. R. Fordham, Mrs. W. H. Perkins, Mrs. C. D. Simpson, Mrs. B. F. Fillmore; Committee on Fuel: Mrs. R. W. Luce (Chairman), Mrs. S. N. Stetler, Mrs. A. Hendricks; Committee on Repairs and Improvements: Mrs. James P. Dickson (Chairman), Mrs. A. E. Hunt, Mrs. L. B. Powell, Mrs. W. H. Perkins, Mrs. H. A. Masser.

Assistant Manager, Mrs. S. A. Brightman; Matron of Home, Mrs. Sarah E. Hopkins.

BOARD OF TRADE.

Incorporated in 1871, this body has done very much to develop the latent resources of the valley in general and of Scranton in particular. With its indefatigable president, Colonel Price, it has given an impetus to various manufacturing industries. It has given importance to the huge piles of culm which disfigure our valley as a heating agent and as a fertilizer, and it has been the means of attracting a large amount of capital to this locality. It has made its resources and attractions known both at home and abroad.

The following gentlemen are the officers: Colonel G. A. Price, President; L. N. Kramer, Vice-President; A. W. Dickson, Treasurer; R. W. Luce, Secretary.

Such men as H. S. Pierce, Judge Handley, Hand, Archbald, Hon. Lewis Pughe, Hon. Wm. R. Halstead, Hon. J. E. Barrett, Hon. L. A. Watres, Dr. Throop, John B. Smith, A. H. Vandling, Wm. Cornell, John Jermyn, Thos. Moore, Ed. Merrifield, E. N. Willard, W. H. Richmond, Ira Tripp, H. M. Bois, R. J. Matthews, J. C. Platt, Colonel Ripple, Thos. Sanderson, B. Hughs, and nearly one hundred and fifty others, including the most prominent and enterprising men in the city, are enrolled as members.

OUR WATER.

One of the future problems of our coal region is the question of pure water for culinary and other purposes. Forty years ago the Lackawanna, stocked with trout, gave an ample supply of clear water to every human want; now it is the small, fishless stream, unfit for any but sewerage purposes. Its corrosive character will destroy the best boiler in a few months; its filthy properties almost turn the beast away from it with thirst.

Carbondale, Jermyn, Archbald, Jessup, Peckville, and Olyphant all have water-works, but none of them can compare with the Providence or Scranton Water Companies in the purity or the abundance of water.

The capacity of the Providence Water Company is three million gallons daily. The great reservoir or gravel-pond in South Abington, fed by the streams of those green uplands five hundred feet above Providence, gives ample pressure for conflagrations and all other purposes. It is exempt from typhoid impurities, without sediment, and non-corrosive. The main reservoir has a capacity of one hundred million gallons, with a district reservoir of three million of gallons. Other reservoirs, already in view, can be constructed of almost unlimited capacity.

On the Roaring Brook, some four miles from Scranton, a great substantial reservoir of this city is built, with a capacity of three hundred million of gallons daily. This brook, issuing from the springs of the Pocono, two thousand feet above tide-water, gives Scranton the purest water in the world. The reservoir yields five million gallons daily, and holds two hundred million gallons, which can be increased to any amount required in future by the wants of the city. The waters of both companies come from beyond the coal measures, are free from all mineral impurities, and are superior for drinking or manufacturing purposes.

THE LAKES OF THE COUNTY.

Among the larger lakes in the county there are but three worthy of mention,—Paupack Lake, on Moosic Mountain, sometimes called Cobb's Pond or Moosic; Crystal Lake, between Carbondale and Dundaff; and Lily Lake, in North Abington. Paupack is the original Indian name. On the Wurts map of the valley of 1826 it is marked Paupack Pond. It is fed by springs, and gives rise to Paupack Creek, which develops into the Wallen-paupack (slow and swift water of the Indian), and, after running some thirty miles through three counties, empties into the Lackawanna at Hawley.

Crystal and Lily Lakes are both favorite summer resorts, each having a hotel, and a small steamboat to give attraction to their waters. White lilies in great profusion and varieties are found on Lily Lake, which was formerly known as Wall's Pond.

PRECIPICES.

Of the cliffs and ledges of Lackawanna County and vicinity there are but few, viz., Barney's Ledge, Ball Mount, and Campbell's Ledge.

Barney's Ledge, between Dunmore and Dunning, named from Barney Cary, who kept the toll-gate on Drinker's pike, at

Hunter's Range, forty years ago, resembles Irving Cliff, in Honesdale, in height and appearance. This ledge has nothing to attract the eye of the visitor but an Indian spring bubbling up from the surface and full of legendry.

Ball Mount, five miles westward from Scranton, in Newton township, rises many hundred feet from the surrounding country, and affords to the eye a wide scope of territory. Shorn of its forest by heavy winds, the precipice for a long distance is comparatively bald. One large rock, perforated with holes of various capacities, was used by the Indians for grinding or pounding corn into samp for domestic use. This point will in time become a favorite resort for parties.

Campbell's Ledge, at the junction of the Lackawanna with the Susquehanna River, was named by a man who never saw its beauties or trod its borders. It is full of traditions, as will be seen by the illustration upon page 26, of white men, pursued by Indians, jumping off to escape, and of wild deer in droves hovering around its base. It has been made renowned by Campbell's "Gertrude of Wyoming." Like the other ledges, it was probably made by the action of water in the later period of the world's history. It is well worthy of a visit.

BUILDING DEVELOPMENT.

The Moosic Mountains bordering the Lackawanna were upheaved previous to the carboniferous era, and belong to the igneous and early sandstone deposits. As a natural consequence, building material, composed of conglomerate, blue and white sandstone, is abundant and cheap. Nothing is equal to the rough beauty of the white sandstone found on the side of the mountain a mile west of Providence in great abundance and quarried at little cost.

The building boom in Scranton has assumed gigantic proportions this year. In 1884, 1400 new buildings were erected, while this year this number will be largely increased. The new jail, the Moses Taylor Hospital, the Young Men's Christian Association building, the store building of John Jermyn, and hundreds of others are now in the course of erection.

It is impossible to predict the future of Scranton. With its two mammoth and best-managed Bessemer steel-works in

America, its busy silk-works, its street railway; with its nineteen newspapers, its $4,000,000 in bank subject to check, its scale, terra-cotta, and fire-brick for stoves; its electric light, its internal revenue receipts of over $133,000, its factories, foundries, and furnaces; its iron-, brass-, and glass-works, its button factory, its mills, and its countless industries that enliven capital and labor, it is bound to become one of the first cities of the Union.

Scranton, by the momentum of her population, by the inevitable operations of natural causes, is pushing up and down the valley with its building operations, and will, in the course of the next half-century, cover all the unoccupied territory.

FIRE DEPARTMENT.

About one hundred and twenty-five thousand dollars' worth of property was destroyed by fire in Scranton during the year 1884. This comparatively small sum would have been greater had it not been for the service of our efficient and voluntary fire department. The telephone and steam-gong announce the presence of fires. Horses are kept in readiness at the engine-houses to move at the first signal of alarm.

The entire force comprises three hundred and ninety men, divided into companies, as follows:

NAMES OF COMPANIES AND MEMBERS OF EACH.

Nay-aug Hose Company	40	Columbia Hose Company	35
Franklin Fire Company	16	Gen. Phinney Engine Company	36
Liberty Hose Company	23	Eagle Engine Company	26
Crystal Hose Company	25	Excelsior Hose Company	40
Neptune Engine Company	30	Invincible Hose Company	30
Relief Engine Company	27		
Phœnix Hose Company	32	Total	390
Niagara Hose Company	30		

MAYORS AND THE JUDICIARY.

From 1826 to 1834 there was but a single justice of the peace in the valley between Pittston and Carbondale, and this one was Elisha S. Potter, whose small office stood in the village of Providence, now the First Ward in Scranton City. Before this simple court, before whom no lawyer had ever appeared, less than a dozen cases were tried each year. There were no national jealousies nor prejudices then; and the few white men scattered along the stream were all brothers, and the duties upon the farm demanded more attention from the good-natured settlers than useless litigation.

Then came Esquire Fellows, Heermans, Slocum, Bristol, Potter, Leach, Ward, Derby, Jay, Spencer, Koon, Von Storch, Miller, Collings, and many others prior to the development of Scranton into a place demanding a Mayor's Court.

The first mayor of the city of Scranton was E. S. M. Hill, editor of the *Scranton Register*, who was elected in 1866 for three years; the second was William N. Monies, elected in 1869 for three years; the third was M. W. Loftus, elected in 1872 for three years; the fourth was R. H. McKune, elected in 1875 for three years; the fifth was T. V. Powderly, elected in 1878 for two years, re-elected in 1880 for two years, and again re-elected in 1882 for two years; the sixth was F. A. Beamish, elected in 1884 for two years.

W. G. WARD, a shrewd and able lawyer, was elected the first judge to preside over the Mayor's Court in October, 1870, and he entered upon the discharge of the duties of his office the 1st of December, 1870. He resigned, to take effect the last day of November, 1875.

His court lacked in dignity, but the good, honest sense and ways of the judge served the people well, and made him popular as a judge, and gave his court great character for fairness and impartiality.

A single incident will illustrate the character of his court. In a commonwealth suit, where a woman was on trial for selling liquor without license, after one or two witnesses had been sworn upon each side, it was apparent to the judge that the woman was guilty. To save time he directed that the jury return such a verdict from the box. In passing a paper along for the jurymen to sign, one man shook his head and refused to sign such a verdict, but wished to retire and consult. The judge saw the hesitating juryman, and, raising and crossing his legs upon the table before him, exclaimed, "Wishes to retire and consult! Why, any juryman who fails to bring in a verdict of guilty under such evidence is guilty of perjury!"

He was followed by HON. W. H. STANTON, who filled the

position very creditably until he resigned his commission some three years afterwards. He is now practising law and editing the *Scranton Democrat*.

In 1874, Hon. John Handley was elected judge. He took his seat upon the bench in 1875, and served faithfully until his term expired in 1885. During the most critical and exciting period in the history of Scranton, Judge Handley presided with singular judicial grace and ability, and his rulings, covering thousands of cases, simple and intricate, were those dictated by sound sense, a clear perception of law and justice, and were considered fair to both sides. He retired from the bench with all the honors earned by the lamented Judge Mallory, Jessup, Conyngham, and Woodward, of old Luzerne, carrying with him the respect of the bar and the people without regard to politics. The time will come when he will be accorded by all men the place in the history of Scranton to which he is entitled as the foremost jurist that the county has ever produced.

Bentley was appointed judge of Lackawanna County the 21st of August, 1878, and organized his courts on the 2d of September, 1878, which he presided over until the 14th of October, 1878, when the Supreme Court decided he was acting without authority, and ordered a peremptory mandamus to Judges Harding, Handley, and Stanton to organize and open the courts in Lackawanna County, which they did on the 24th of October, 1878.

Hon. Alfred Hand was elected judge of Lackawanna County in 1879. He went upon the bench in 1880. He wears his judicial robes with honor, and for the last five years he has been acting in this capacity has fulfilled the expectations of his many friends. It is rare to find a man to question his opinion as a thorough and lucid jurist.

Hon. Robert W. Archbald was elected judge in 1884, and was inducted upon the bench in 1885. He is a young man of promise, one of broad mind and liberal views, but he has had no time as yet to demonstrate his fitness for the position he fills; yet he is the son of a remarkable man, whose life was spent to benefit his fellow-man, and whose conduct and character were such during a long life that the world where he was known felt a loss at his death.

The legal fraternity are represented in Scranton to the number of seventy-six.

OUR PHYSICIANS.

Thirty-nine years ago, in 1846, there were but two doctors between Pittston and Carbondale, DR. SILAS B. ROBINSON, who died in 1860, and the writer. Dr. Throop had removed from Providence to Carbondale, where Dr. Thomas Sweet and Dr. Raferty resided, while in Pittston Dr. Anson H. Curtis practised.

Dr. Gideon Underwood, now of Pittston, was the first medical man to locate in Scranton, in the summer of 1846, but as the town was too small and the practice too poor to support a physician, he removed to Northmoreland, Wyoming County, Pa. Dr. W. H. Pier settled in Hyde Park the same year. Since that time until now doctors have rushed into Scranton, and at the present time there are eighty of them here.

In 1855 a medical society, embracing the physicians of the upper end of then Luzerne County, was formed in Scranton, with such able men as B. A. Bouton, A. Davis, Silas M. Wheeler, Washington G. Nugent, and George W. Masser—all sleeping in the silent hills—as members. It dissolved in 1868. A few years since a new society, with the veteran Dr. Throop as president, sprang into being, and it bids fair to become an organization of mutual advantage both to the public and the profession.

THE DELAWARE AND HUDSON CANAL COMPANY.

This corporation belongs neither to New York nor Pennsylvania. It was the joint product of both States,—a reciprocity of mutual interests. Who can estimate the impulse given to the city of New York by the introduction of anthracite upon the island of Manhattan by this company, and who would have fathomed the solitude of the Lackawanna if the moneyed men of this city had withheld the material aid whereby its coal development was inspired and hastened? Without the fuel-beds of Pennsylvania to respond to the demands of New York City, there would have been no right of way for canal or railroad solicited from the Keystone State by individuals able to conceive an enterprise that, with all their intellectual status, they

DR. SILAS B. ROBINSON.

were unable to mature without the assistance of the more advanced and magnanimous capitalists of that city.

Much of the brain-power was Pennsylvanian; most of the money entering into the corporation, first and last, came from the Empire State. Thus conceived by men of one State and vitalized by those from another, much of its present management and inspiration comes from Pennsylvania.

MAURICE and WILLIAM WURTS, occupying the frontispiece of early coal literature in the Lackawanna Valley, who educated the mountains to extend a warm hand to inland and seaboard cities everywhere, were Pennsylvanians. THOMAS DICKSON, late president of the company, who carved legible and lasting characters of success upon the growth and history of the corporation, although cradled among the Scottish hills, was claimed as a Pennsylvanian in everything but birth; while President OLYPHANT and COE F. YOUNG, of Honesdale, General Manager; A. H. VANDLING, of Scranton, Superintendent of the Coal Department; JOSEPH J. ALBRIGHT, of Scranton, Sole Agent Southern and Western Department; R. MANVILLE, Carbondale, Superintendent of the Railroad Department; EDWARD W. WESTON, Providence, General Agent of Real Estate Department; HENRY F. ATHERTON, General Paymaster of the Pennsylvania Division; ASHER M. ATKINSON, Honesdale, Superintendent of the Canal Department; JARED M. CHITTENDEN, of Scranton, General Outside Superintendent of Coal Breakers; E. R. PECKENS, of Plymouth, Assistant Outside Superintendent; CHRIS. and ED. SCHARAR and ANDREW NICHOLS, Mining Engineers, are all Pennsylvanians by birth, with two exceptions, and it would be folly to question the wholesome qualifications of these gentlemen, or the executive ability with which their respective departments at the coal-producing terminus of the company are managed year after year.

In a broader sense than mere local pride, it matters little which commonwealth preponderates in coal or capital as long as both States share advantageously by the union.

This organization finds no parallel in America. It stands alone. No other association of men so clearly illustrates what harmonious capital and labor can accomplish as does this. The first one in America that introduced and then abandoned a locomotive, the second one ever constructed upon the continent, it has in its development excited jealousy and admiration, range praise and open hostility, while it ever and always paid dollar for dollar, inaugurated the system of monthly cash payments, and maintained its high character for fairness and good faith in dealing with its employés and the public that was established by the managers of the company at its inception.

In 1826, when the corporation was sadly embarrassed, the State of New York, impelled by the wise policy which had given character to the administration of Governor De Witt Clinton, loaned its credit to the company for $500,000. When this became due, principal and interest were paid promptly, and this instance is recorded as the only one where indebtedness to the State was thus ever paid.

According to Mine Inspector Blewitt's annual report for 1884, this company operate sixteen collieries, employ 4291 men, and mined and carried to market last year 1,624,444 tons of anthracite. Its main office is in Scranton.

COAL WASTE AND COAL-BREAKERS.

No old resident of the coal region can forget the time when no other kind of coal was seen or sold but lump coal. The miner or laborer, immured in his lengthened chamber, with pick and drill, broke up the larger lumps in the mine simply to facilitate easier loading into mine cars. In this form anthracite was carried to market, and broken only as it was used, without waste. Until within comparatively a short period no prepared coal found its way into recognition and use. Each piece was fractured by hand with the same patient labor that wood, drawn from the forest in logs, required repeated strokes from the axeman to fit it for the fireplace.

One of the greatest conspirators of modern times against economy is that invention of the devil known as a *coal-breaker*, an institution that inaugurated a system of waste and loss of anthracite beyond repair and almost beyond measure. When posterity contemplates the flattened hills and culm-filled valleys a century hence, this enemy will be taunted as the great robber of the continent.

It was a disastrous day for all anthracite regions when competing coal men assented to waste a third part of the coal by breaking and screening it, for the sake of saving the remaining two thirds in a prepared form. The eruptions of culm piles, heightened into pyramids, all formed of the purest coal, around every breaker from Carbondale to Nanticoke, exhibit the certainty and rapidity with which our streams are being choked and our mountains turned wrong side out by a process alike exhausting and wasteful. True, it offers its advantages to the indolent consumer, but how fatal to the interior and exterior of our unresisting hills and valleys!

The actual loss in coal while the iron teeth and tireless jaws of the breakers subdue lumps into ordinary stove coal has been estimated by Daddow at 20 to 25 per cent. Some estimate the waste at 30 per cent., and some lower. Colonel Price, who has given the subject great attention, fixes the percentage at 20 per cent.

The total output of the four great companies mining coal in the Lackawanna Valley being 146,218,150 tons, would exhibit a total loss of 29,243,630 tons of culm deposit. This estimate is too small according to more competent judges. JARED M. CHITTENDEN, a gentleman who was born in Mount Pleasant in 1823, and whose unquestioned good judgment and official position in the Delaware and Hudson Canal Company cause him to be regarded as the best judge in the Northern Coal-Field, has investigated this matter for a lifetime. After the most careful research, he found the volume of loss in coal while preparing it by the usual grinding or breaking process to be precisely $29\frac{5}{10}$ per cent., or about one-third of its real weight.

This appalling amount is a total loss to coal territory, to all companies engaged in its production, and to the world at large. Before half of the coal owned by companies in the valley is mined, the culm piles, which already smother villages and cities along the Lackawanna, will close up the valley with ground coal, and obliterate the fair vale from the sight of coming generations.

Within the Schuylkill, Lehigh, Lykens, Wyoming, and Lackawanna coal area lies sufficient culm to pay the national debt if it could be utilized with judgment and economy.

Within a radius of three miles of the Scranton court-house

are two hundred and fifty boilers where steam is generated exclusively from culm for power purposes. The manufacturers save at least $25,000 each month in this manner. Still, in spite of this, 6000 tons of the purest coal are wasted every day in the year, and thousands of tons accumulated in culm dumps.

The false economy of breaking up coal by machinery began under the auspices of the Delaware, Lackawanna and Western Company, in Scranton, in 1852.

The first annual report of this company, made in January, 1854, says "that during the present year the steam-power coal-breaker at Diamond mines has been completed, the influence of which will be stated hereafter." Some years later a coal-breaker rose from the mines of the Delaware and Hudson Company. In 1855 the Von Storch lands in Providence were leased by Pittston men. In 1857 a company was organized, who sank the Von Storch shaft and erected a steam coal-breaker, with a view of sending coal over the Delaware, Lackawanna and Western Railway.

These Von Storch lands were desired by Maurice and William Wurts when first exploring the valley for coal. Could these gentlemen, in 1812–15, have purchased this rich tract as they aimed to do, opened mines, sought Cobb's instead of Rix's Gap for an outlet, tenanted the unploughed acres by encouraging and developing a manufacturing town, there would have been no Carbondale or Honesdale, and the forests then standing upon their sites might yet have rung with the merry notes of wild turkeys and singing birds.

In 1857 this shaft fell into the hands of the Delaware and Hudson Company, and the breaker removed to the river, half a mile away, where it ran until 1874. In this year, after masticating some 2,000,000 tons of coal and leaving its Alpine mark between Providence and Scranton, it was removed to make room for a new one of greater capacity and greedier proportions.

WILLIAM P. MINER, editor of the weekly Wilkes Barre *Record*, was the first man in the country to direct attention to this and other destructive features of the coal trade, in 1855, in an able and earnest editorial.

No man in the country has given more thought and attention to the study of coal waste than COL. J. A. PRICE, of Scranton.

He proposes by dry steam and a proportionate quantity of air to employ culm as a heating agent.

He says, "The construction of the apparatus is very simple. It consists of a closed ash-pit, into which one end of funnel or cone-shaped pipe is inserted, the larger end being upon the outside. At the mouth of the cone is placed a steam jet, which when turned on directs its volume to the neck of the cone, and the tendency of the steam to spray as it leaves the jet orifice carries with it a large quantity of atmosphere. The air, passing through the fire, is drawn by the chimney-suction, being assisted by the steam-blast pressure, and thus supports combustion, while at the same time the steam passes with it, is decomposed in passing through the fire-bed, and resolved into its original elements of hydrogen and oxygen, both powerful adjuncts of combustion. The hydrogen gas, the most powerful of the heat generating elements which is formed, is exploded at the surface, and the oxygen unites in the ordinary manner with the carbon, altogether producing a fierce cutting temperature in the fire-box."

A large number of gentlemen engaged in the manufacturing business have given favorable testimonials to the colonel's plan of utilizing culm as a heating agent; but even if it can be used to a considerable extent as a fertilizer or a generator of steam, the naked fact is still apparent that the present generation, while preparing coal, is robbing succeeding ones of nearly one-third of the value of the products of our mountains and valleys without disturbing us in the least.

HENRY ROBERTS, M.D.

Dr. Roberts was born in Wyoming County, Pa., in 1820, read medicine, and began practice in Lacyville. He soon after removed to Providence. In 1857 he ran and was defeated for the Legislature.

In 1859 he visited California, and while *en route* a thousand miles beyond the Missouri he lost the use of his right arm by the accidental discharge of a gun. After his recovery he visited for six months various places in California before he returned to Providence in 1861. During the invasion of the State in 1863 he enrolled a company of men in twenty-four hours, accompanying them to Harrisburg as volunteer surgeon. In April of the same year he was appointed one of the Examining Surgeons, a position he held for twenty years. In 1868 was elected a member of the Select Council of Scranton, and for nine consecutive years was re-elected. In April, 1868, was appointed postmaster of Providence, and was only removed in 1884, after the city of Scranton had practised the game of Jonah on the whale in Providence.

Dr. Roberts is regarded as a man of excellent judgment, and he stands high as a physician and as a man.

HON. LEWIS PUGHE.

The city of Carbondale has contributed many of its best business-men to the growth and development of Scranton within the last three decades,—the late Colonel Monies and Joseph Gillispie, two energetic men, William H. Richmond, of the Hillside Farm, Notary Public John M. Poor, Horatio S. Pierce, the successful banker,—but none of them have been brought more prominently before the public than Mr. Pughe.

Truth, a most able newspaper, published in Scranton by HON. JOHN E. BARRETT, paid the following tribute to this prominent stove manufacturer:

"The Hon. Lewis Pughe, who was recently the recipient of numerous congratulations on the celebration of his sixty-fifth birthday, is a happy illustration of the self-made man who owes his success to honest industry and careful business management. He was born in North Wales in 1820, and came to this country in 1844, when he settled in Carbondale, the pioneer city of the Lackawanna Valley, of which he had the honor of being elected first city treasurer, and subsequently alderman and associate judge of the Mayor's Court. A valuable tribute to his popularity with all classes was his election as a Republican to the Pennsylvania Legislature in the year 1859, at a time when the district comprised the entire county of Luzerne, with a Democratic majority of over 2500. In 1867 he became a resident of Scranton, and a partner in the well-known and eminently successful firm of Monies & Pughe. In the year 1872 he was elected a member of the Pennsylvania Constitutional Convention, and in that body was generally esteemed by his associates for his fine social qualities, as well as for his comprehensive

Yours truly
Lewis Pughe

views on all public questions, and the thorough knowledge of the needs of the people, which he brought to the consideration of all the important provisions which now form the organic law of the State. It was in that convention that the way was paved for the creation of a new county, and to the earnest labors and convincing arguments of Lewis Pughe in resisting propositions which, if adopted, would prove fatal to the project and prevent the necessary legislation, the people of this valley are indebted for the existence to-day of the flourishing county of Lackawanna, with its capital in this city. All the power of Wilkes Barre was directed against such a measure at the outset. But when the late Chief-Justice Woodward, who was a member of the convention, listened to Mr. Pughe's convincing argument, bristling with statistics showing the wonderful resources that made old Luzerne an empire in itself, he was so well pleased, and so deeply impressed with the grand tribute paid to the county's greatness, that he immediately declared to Mr. Pughe that he would not interpose any obstacle that might prevent the division of the county. Mr. Pughe was one of the Presidential electors on the Hayes and Wheeler ticket in 1876. He was one of the originators of the Scranton Board of Trade, and to his efforts the Scranton Poor District is indebted for the wholesome reforms which have made the Hillside Farm the model institution of its kind in the State. His recent election to the Board of Health gives promise of needed reforms in that body. Whatever he undertakes to do he believes in doing thoroughly, and as he is still active, mentally and physically, it is right to predict for him many years of usefulness. Mr. Pughe takes a deep interest in educational as well as charitable matters. He was a school director in Carbondale for ten years; was a member of the board of the old Fourth District, this city, and recently served a term on the Scranton School Board, where he was a valued and progressive member. He is president and one of the largest stockholders of the Pittston Stove Company, one of the most successful manufacturing establishments of its kind in the country, with a capital of $100,000. Mr. Pughe's nature is cosmopolitan, and he knows neither sect, creed, nor nationality in doing good."

THE STRIKES.

Throughout the entire Northern Coal-Field mining was suspended from the middle of May, 1869, to the middle of September. If the good effects of the war in stimulating the extraordinary yet artificial demands for coal that it did, and beguiling unneeded labor to the coal-fields that now creates its own embarrassment, were once acknowledged by all, then it must be confessed that whatever apparent advantage was gained by its existence at the time has been thrice counterbalanced by subsequent strikes, stops, and suspensions that have followed each other, and that must inevitably follow while the means for producing coal are so far in excess of its demands and consumption.

About the first of December, 1870, all the coal-producing companies of this region ordered a reduction of wages. This resulted in a strike known as the long strike, whose baneful influence still shadows bankrupt merchants with hopeless indebtedness as a reward for trusting in credit. All mines but private ones for local trade were idle and silent. The immediate cause of the strike was the reduction of wages of miners and laborers; the remote cause, the great excess of mine labor. The plain truth is, that for the amount of coal now demanded there are, by far, too many miners and too many mines for its production.

When the fresh agricultural grounds of the West or the warmer acres of the South invite the personal and permanent attention of at least one-third of our miners and laborers, the remainder can find remunerative employment, and prosperity will then, and not till then, return to enrich and enliven the banks of the Lackawanna.

The system of suspension inaugurated in 1869 by the miners, whose association embraced the entire anthracite region, for the avowed purpose of curtailing the production, was alike disastrous to coal companies, to the miner, and to the consumer.

The only safe remedy for over-production is the natural law of trade, and to mine no more coal than can be readily sold and consumed, for coal is a necessity rather than a luxury.

Concessions were made upon each side and work resumed in the mines upon terms considered more favorable to the miners than before.

The great excess of mine labor and other causes made itself felt beyond precedent in 1877. It resulted in the greatest suspension on record among us.

At noon, July 23, the employés of the rolling-mills, steel-works, and machine-shops of the Lackawanna Iron and Coal Company discontinued work and made a demand for an increase of 25 per cent. on their wages. In the afternoon the firemen employed by the Delaware, Lackawanna and Western Railroad and the engineers in the yard made a demand on Superintendent Halstead, which not being complied with, the engines were run into the round-house and the men ceased work.

On the arrival of the morning train on the Delaware, Lackawanna and Western road, July 24, a committee of the firemen detached the passenger cars from the mail and express cars, and then informed Mr. Halstead that the mail and express cars could go through. Mr. Halstead informed them that the entire train must go or none at all.

During the day the trains on all the roads leading into the city were discontinued. On the 25th a committee from the mine employés made a demand for an increase of 25 per cent. of wages. The excitement in the valley and adjacent coal-fields began to be intense. ROBERT H. McKUNE was mayor of the city of Scranton, and upon him all parties looked for relief and safety.

Samuel Sloan, President of the Delaware, Lackawanna and Western Railway; Thomas Dickson, President of the Delaware and Hudson Canal Company; W. W. Scranton, General Manager of the Lackawanna Iron and Coal Company; W. R. Storrs, General Coal Agent for the Delaware, Lackawanna and Western Railway; and F. S. Lathrop, Receiver of the Central Road of New Jersey, all importuned the mayor by telegraph or letter for the protection of property they respectively represented, while he was engaged in consulting Governor Hartranft, Colonel Osborne, and others in authority, for assistance and for a solution of the increasing trouble.

Idleness in the valley was supreme. It was a long, dull Sabbath day. No coal trains, no men at work, little business, and no confidence; merchants, men, and operators were impoverished, trade stood still, and all parties suffered. July 26, Governor Hartranft having made a request for United States troops, the President issued a proclamation ordering General Hancock to furnish them. During the day a meeting of the mine employés was held at the Round Woods, in the lower western limits of the city. The shops of the Delaware, Lackawanna and Western Railroad Company were all idle. Strong men doing nothing, many of them strangers, loitered along the streets with no definite object in view. On the morning of the 29th a head-house, No. 5, on the Pennsylvania Coal Company, was burned by an incendiary. A bridge on the line was also burned, thus rendering this road from Pittston to Hawley inoperative, and debarred the shipment of 30,000 tons of coal per week. The idle mines were being flooded, and the outlook was gloomy and ominous.

On the next morning, July 30, the mayor sent for the executive committee of the firemen and informed them that he had determined that if Mr. Halstead had men to run a train to New York, one should leave the city that afternoon; that he so far had refused military aid that had been proffered, and he hoped that he would not have to call upon troops to protect the trains. A meeting of the firemen was held at two o'clock, at which this proposition was made known and discussed, and by a decided vote it was resolved to resume work after a seven days' suspension. The miners and shop hands still stood out.

JOHN BRISBIN, who died February, 1880, was the only prominent man in the valley who had the entire confidence of the miners, men, and the corporations. He had the singular faculty of making everybody his friend. He believed that the miners had rights equally to be respected with those of the company he represented.

The committee of mine employés appointed at the Round Woods meeting chose Mr. Brisbin, whom they met at Mayor McKune's office, as arbitrator, where, after discussing their differences for two hours, an agreement satisfactory to both parties was concluded.

A full statement of their grievances was made by the committee; the discussion was carried on in the most cordial manner, and at the breaking up of the conference the committee cordially thanked Mr. Brisbin for the fair and manly course he had acted towards them.

When the conference broke up the best of feeling prevailed

upon both sides. When the result was announced upon the streets every one was happy, and the mayor was heartily congratulated upon the results of the good work.

Early on the morning of August 1 the streets leading to the silk-works were filled by miners and others going to the meeting called at this point. Six thousand persons were present, incendiary speeches were made, and it was resolved to stop by force the various works of the machine-shops, furnaces, and foundries at once.

At this time Mayor McKune appeared upon the streets. As he reached the corner of Lackawanna and Washington Avenues he was met by a messenger from Mr. McKinney, the foreman of the railroad car-shop, asking for his presence at the office. He and his friends then went in that direction. The whole space from the office to the main railroad tracks was filled by at least five thousand persons, who were going through the shops, driving away the few who were willing to work. As the mayor, on his return, was opposite the main entrance of the shop the angry crowd was emerging. Around him quite a multitude had gathered. The leader of the gang cried out, "Who is it?" "The mayor," some one replied. The leader then shouted out, "Kill him! He has no business here!" Immediately several pistol-shots were fired, and the mayor was struck in the back with a club, which caused the blood to spurt from his mouth, and was also hit by a number of stones. He was promptly surrounded by workingmen, who strove earnestly for his safety. They were nearly overpowered, when the REV. FATHER DUNN, of St. Vincent's Cathedral, arrived upon the scene, who, taking the arm of the mayor, proceeded towards Washington Avenue. They had gone but a few steps when a man jumped in front of McKune, struck him a severe blow with a slung-shot, breaking his upper jaw and fracturing the roof of his mouth. By this time the excited crowd overpowered those in the rear and rushed upon the unarmed mayor. A portion of it caught up Father Dunn, and carried him away from the scene of conflict.

In the mean time the mayor passed under the railroad culvert. On arriving at the corner of Lackawanna Avenue he was met by some of the posse that had been organized at the commencement of the strike, and for whom he had sent when first attacked. They were coming to his assistance. He beckoned to them to come on. He intended to make a stand at his office, two blocks down the street. As he turned to go down the avenue he was struck a blow on the head by a hammer, which for some minutes rendered him unconscious. He was carried by his police into the Merchants' Bank, where he regained consciousness soon after.

In the mean time the pursuing populace was following the avenue, and began an attack on the armed posse that had issued from the company's store. A few shots were fired over the heads of the crowd for the purpose of intimidating it, but it failed to do so. When the posse had reached the corner of Washington Avenue it halted and formed. Pistol-shots were fired by the crowd, wounding Sheriff Bortree and Carl McKinney. Orders were now given to fire. The company wheeled, and out of forty muskets flashed the fatal bullets. Some aimed over the crowd, others fired into it, killing four and wounding a number of others.

This unexpected shot dispersed the people in every direction, but volley after volley was fired until the streets were clear.

The scene of conflict presented a warlike spectacle. On the corner of the street lay a man with the top of his head blown off, and his brains and blood reddened the sidewalk, while three others in the middle of the street were struggling in the last agonies of death, and the wounded were being carried home or into drug-stores by their friends.

About two o'clock crowds again began to assemble on Lackawanna Avenue. The report had gone out that the mayor had been killed, and that no other person was qualified to direct and control the posse. He, however, in company with Colonel Ripple, at the head of the police and a detachment of the half-organized squad, marched down the avenue, and cleared the streets of people.

Early the next morning, General Brinton, with three thousand troops, arrived from Pittsburg, and were stationed here for several weeks. The presence of this force insured order and safety to persons and property that was salutary upon all sides.

Mayor McKune, maltreated by persons who sought his life simply because he was mayor and nothing else, discharged his

ATTACK UPON THE MAYOR OF SCRANTON, PENNSYLVANIA.

duties faithfully and fearlessly during this critical and exciting episode in the history of Scranton, as the testimonials of thousands of the citizens gave him written assurance afterwards.

For several weeks after this lamentable occurrence in Scranton, idle men gathered in groups and discussed the situation, deploring the affray of August 1, while in the lower end of Luzerne County, at Wilkes Barre, Plymouth, and Nanticoke, the vexed question of capital and labor was dangerously discussed for a time. The presence of the militia, followed by regular troops, stationed in Providence for a month, brought wiser counsels to bear in this region, and from that time until now have produced those harmonious relations between the workingmen and their employers that now happily exist.

THE THIRTEENTH REGIMENT.

The long strike, while it accomplished no real good to anybody, and defined no policy for future agencies, brought into being the Thirteenth Regiment Infantry, Third Brigade, National Guards. The genius of our people is not military, and nothing but the necessity of military power, made apparent by the events in the summer of 1877, developed this regiment.

On the 14th day of August of this year the Scranton City Guards were organized by the union of Company A, Captain Bryson; Company B, Captain S. C. Merrian; Company C, Captain H. A. Courson; Company D, Captain E. H. Ripple, under the command of Major H. M. Boies and Adjutant F. L. Hitchcock.

In October, 1878, the regiment was organized upon the foundation offered by the battalion of the Scranton City Guards.

The original officers of the regiment were:

Field and Staff.—Major H. M. Boies, Commandant; First Lieutenant F. L. Hitchcock, Adjutant; Captain H. A. Kinngsburry, Commissary.

Non-Commissioned Staff.—H. N. Dunnell, Sergeant-Major; S. G. Kerr, Quartermaster-Sergeant; G. H. Madox, Commissary-Sergeant; W. W. Ives, Hospital Steward; M. D. Smith and Edward Brady, Principal Musicians; and John J. Coleman, Battalion Clerk.

Line Officers.

Company A.—Captain, A. Bryson, Jr.; First Lieutenants, D.

Bartholomew, H. A. Knapp; Second Lieutenant, William Kellow.

Company C.—Captain, A. H. Courson; First Lieutenant, J. E. Brown; Second Lieutenant, L. A. Watres.

Company D.—Captain, E. H. Ripple; First Lieutenant, J. A. Linen; Second Lieutenant, Samuel Hines.

Subsequently other companies were added to the battalion, which was then organized into a regiment, composed of young men of Scranton, Stroudsburg, Honesdale, and Factoryville, whose character for sobriety, integrity, and every manly element compares favorably with any other regiment within the State. The regiment went into camp for instructions and drill at Long Branch, N. J., in August, 1879, and in Lebanon, in July, 1885, for seven days, where its appearance and demeanor were highly commended by all. At two inaugurations it has appeared in Washington, eliciting admiration by its soldierly bearing and its gentlemanly deportment. The following are the officers:

Field and Staff.—Colonel, F. L. Hitchcock; Lieutenant-Colonel, E. H. Ripple; Major, H. A. Coursen; Adjutant, C. C. Mattes; Quartermaster, John P. Albro; Surgeon, H. V. Logan, M.D.; Assistant Surgeons, A. J. Connell, M.D., C. L. Frey, M.D.

Non-Commissioned Staff.—Sergeant-Major, E. J. Dimmick; Quartermaster-Sergeant, A. P. Bradford; Commissary-Sergeant, L. M. Horton; Hospital Steward, Edward Evans.

Line Officers.

Company A.—Captain, L. A. Watres; First Lieutenant, George F. Barnard; Second Lieutenant, M. J. Andrews.

Company B.—Captain, William Kellow; First Lieutenant, H. R. Madison; Second Lieutenant, W. S. Millar.

Company C.—Captain, James Moir; First Lieutenant, William B. Henwood; Second Lieutenant, Charles W. Gunster.

Company D.—Captain, George B. Thompson; First Lieutenant, William A. May; Second Lieutenant, ——

Company E (Honesdale).—Captain, Henry Wilson; First Lieutenant, W. H. Stanton.

Company F.—Captain, Roger L. Burnett.

Company G (Factoryville).—Captain, Charles W. Depuy; First Lieutenant, E. O. Smith; Second Lieutenant, Abel D. Gardner.

Company H (Providence).—Captain, J. B. Fish; First Lieutenant, W. B. Rockwell; Second Lieutenant, Charles T. Weston.

Company I.—Captain Burke, of Parnell Guards.

A large armory has been erected in Scranton for its accommodation.

Company H, Captain J. B. Fish, of Providence, has also built a substantial stone armory in the Second Ward, for the use of the company and for public purposes.

AN INDUSTRIAL POINT.

Scranton is one of the best industrial centres in America. It is a great railroad centre. Over sixty trains a day come and go over the roads passing through it, carrying at least one thousand passengers,—the DELAWARE, LACKAWANNA AND WESTERN, the Erie Railway, the Philadelphia and Reading Company, and the Delaware and Hudson. The Lehigh Valley and the Pennsylvania Railroad are already making towards the valley, and are within a few miles of the centre of the locality. The Pennsylvania Coal Company and the Bloomsburg Branch of the Delaware, Lackawanna and Western road may be mentioned.

While the Delaware, Lackawanna and Western is one of the best constructed roads in the United States, it is also the shortest route between New York and Buffalo, being 44 miles shorter than the Lehigh Valley, 31 miles shorter than the New York Central, and 14 miles shorter than the Erie. Nearly half a million of persons a year arrive and depart from its railroad depot.

This magnificently-equipped road of four hundred and nine miles of double track, reaching from the lakes to the sea, managed with singular ability and success by its president, HON. SAMUEL SLOAN, and his able and judicious superintendent, W. F. HALSTEAD, gave the first impulse to Scranton as a village in 1856, and now fosters and gives greater encouragement and vitality to the business interests than any other factor operating here. Its army of fifteen thousand men, along the main line and branches, and all others, all attest to the excellence of its general management.

Three of these companies pay out over twelve million of dollars per year, besides vast sums of money being paid by its other business interests. About forty thousand tons of anthracite are mined and shipped each week from this vicinity, aggregating some 12,000,000 tons as the output for this year, thus illustrating the importance of Scranton as a great business centre.

This company has twenty-one collieries, employing 6086 men, and mined in 1884, 2,025,530 tons of coal.

Over one hundred million pounds of freight come to this city over three railroads every month, while about thirty million pounds of freight are dispatched from here.

Our railroad facilities place us within five hours' ride of New York or Philadelphia, within eight hours of Buffalo and Oswego and Saratoga, and within ten hours of the capital of the country, indicating how accessible we are to the great business and fashionable world, and to the best markets in America; so that our own markets can be stocked with the early luxuries of the South, while the late productions of the colder North, with every variety of fish from the sea and the rivers of the South as well as from the lakes and streams of the North, with all the outcome of Eastern manufacturers and the growth of our Western prairies.

Aside from the millions invested in Scranton by the various railroads and coal interests, over twenty millions are employed in manufacturing interests.

THE INDUSTRIES OF SCRANTON.

THE DICKSON MANUFACTURING COMPANY.

Early in 1855 the anthracite coal business of the Lackawanna Valley had assumed such proportions that it was deemed necessary that a shop for repairing mining machinery and doing what little new work was needed should be started in the then southern portion of the Lackawanna coal region; and consequently, in February, 1856, Thomas, John A., and George L. Dickson, Maurice and Charles P. Wurts, Joseph, Benjamin, and C. T. Pierson, came to Scranton from Carbondale, and began the erection of foundry and machine-shops, under the name of "Dickson & Co.," and in May of the same year ran the first heat of iron in their foundry, the amount melted being about two tons. They started with about thirty men, the greater number of which were employed in the foundry. They also had a machine-shop and small blacksmith-shop. The first few years of the business were not very encouraging, and the complement of men remained about the same, with an average monthly pay-roll of about $1200. A small boiler-shop was soon added to the works, but this increased the number of men only by about three, most of the work in that department being repairs for coal-works. Notwithstanding the depression of 1857, the works managed to keep in operation, and were enlarged from time to time.

In 1862 the company was incorporated under the name of The Dickson Manufacturing Company, with an actual capital of $150,000, and an authorized capital of $300,000. The first officers of the company were: President, Thomas Dickson; Secretary and Treasurer, George L. Dickson; Master Mechanic, John A. Dickson. The number of men employed the first year, i.e., 1862, was about 150; the average daily melting of iron, three tons; monthly pay-roll, about $7500; and the sales for the first year were $200,000.

As the output of anthracite coal increased, the business of the company increased with it, and in 1862 they purchased of Messrs. Cooke and Co. the locomotive-shops known as "The Cliff Works," which then had a capacity not exceeding five locomotives per year. In 1864 the planing-mill adjoining the Cliff Works was bought, and the manufacture of cars begun. At this time (1865) they employed about 400 men, the daily heats of iron were about four tons, the monthly disbursement to men about $16,000, and the sales over $600,000. In 1866 the foundry and machine-shops of Messrs. Lanning & Marshall, at Wilkes Barre, were purchased, and a branch established there. At these shops were manufactured car-wheels and axles, and such repairs were executed as were needed about the coal-works, the number of men employed there at that time being about sixty.

The business of the company had so increased that in this year the capital was enlarged to $600,000, which, however, was not all issued till 1870.

In 1867, Mr. Thomas Dickson retired from the presidency, and George L. Dickson was elected president in his stead. Mr. John C. Phelps, of Wilkes Barre, was made vice-president, and William H. Perkins, secretary and treasurer.

With the rapid growth in the valley the company kept pace, the locomotive-shops were enlarged, and in 1869 a large brick foundry was built at the Penn Avenue shops; this helped the business of the Cliff Works as well as the general work, and as additions had from time to time been made to the locomotive-shops, their capacity was, in 1870, four engines per month. The company then employed about 500 men at their three places, the daily heats of iron aggregated about seven tons, the pay-rolls were about $20,000, and the sales amounted to about $975,000. In 1874 the Cliff Works were destroyed by fire, entailing a large loss to the company. The work of rebuilding was at once begun, and very much improved buildings replaced those burned down, new tools of the most modern design were put in, and the capacity of the shops increased to sixty locomotives per year. In 1876 the capital stock of the company was further increased to $800,000, at which amount it now stands. In 1878 a large brick building, three stories high, was erected on the corner of Penn Avenue and Vine Street, to be used as a store for the sale of shop and mine supplies, general offices and storage-house, and the upper floors for the storage of patterns. The depression of business from 1873 to 1878 was, of course, greatly felt, but all departments were kept at work with a not very large decrease of force. In 1880 about 600 men were employed, with a monthly pay-roll of about $30,000, and the sales amounted to about $740,000 per year.

In 1882, Mr. G. L. Dickson resigned from the chair of president, and Mr. H. M. Boies, who is known as one of the best business men in the country, and as a gentleman of unblemished character and reputation, was elected. In that year the work of rebuilding the Penn Avenue shops was commenced; a new machine-shop was built, which is conceded by experts to be the best-arranged shop, for the class of work done, in the country. It covers 223 feet by 100 feet of ground, of which space the machine-shop proper occupies 196 feet by 97 feet, together with two galleries 25 feet wide running lengthwise of the building on both sides, giving altogether an available floor-space of nearly 29,000 square feet. The remaining part of the ground on the Vine Street end of the building is occupied by a four-story building. In the first story of this building are found, besides the foreman's office in the tower, a large room for the storage of tools and finished work, and also a very well appointed wash-room. On the second (or main) floor are the superintendent's office, a large reading-room for the men, and the paymaster's office. On the third floor is the office of the mechanical engineer, which has large storage facilities for drawings, the room being fire-proof, and adjoining his office is a large, well-appointed draughting-office. A new brick pattern-shop was also built, four stories in height, including the basement, 145 feet by 63 feet, the basement being used for storage of lumber, etc., and here also is the power for driving the shop. The first or main floor is used entirely for pattern-work, and the upper floors for storage of lumber and patterns. The Penn Avenue shops were equipped with new tools of the best and most modern design. There was placed in the boiler-shop the Tweddell hydraulic system for flanging and riveting.

In 1883 the company's sales amounted to over $1,400,000, while the average heat of pig-iron was twenty-five tons per day. At present about 1200 men are employed, with an average monthly pay-roll of $50,000. The capacity of the different shops at the present time is about as follows:

Penn Avenue Shops.—600 tons of iron melted per month; 100 stationary engines of all kinds, with cylinders over 22-inch diameter; mining machinery of all kinds; blast-furnace and steel-works machinery; blast-engines and air-compressors; rolling-mill machinery of all kinds; machine-shop machinery of all kinds; contractors' machinery of all kinds; water-works machinery of all kinds; 20 large boilers per month, including locomotive boilers; 500 steel plate car-wheels per month.

Cliff Works.—100 locomotives per year.

Wilkes Barre Shops.—150 stationary engines of all kinds, with cylinders under 22-inch diameter; mining machinery of all kinds; wire-rope making of all kinds; Cornish pumps of all sizes; 50 cast-iron plate car-wheels per day; 200 cylinder-boilers per day.

For generating steam the company use culm, and thus save many thousand dollars.

Their locomotives are spread over the globe. Along the rugged Andes, in South America, they mutter up the sides like the antelope; on the broad prairies of the West they skim along, and toil over the rocky barrier to the Golden City; and from the great Valley of the St. Lawrence to the city of Mexico the legend, "Dickson Manufacturing Co., Scranton, Pa.," appears upon engines unsurpassed in beauty, speed, or excellence by any other locomotives either in Europe or America. The officers are H. M. Boies, President; W. H. Perkins, Secretary and Treasurer; and Sidney Broadbent, Superintendent.

SCRANTON BRASS- AND FILE-WORKS.

These works were founded in 1853 by John McLaren. In 1871, James M. Everhart became interested, when the firm began largely to manufacture brass-works for water, gas, and steam, also a patent superior file.

Mr. McLaren died in 1873, when Mr. Everhart became sole proprietor. By the introduction of improved machinery, skilled labor, and by strict attention to his affairs, he has given a high character to the brass industry of this portion of the State. The works give employment to a large number of men.

SCRANTON CITY FOUNDRY.

On the Hyde Park side of the Lackawanna, above the railroad bridge, is located the large foundry of Finch & Co. Upon the death of A. P. Finch, in 1881, Mr. I. A. Finch became sole manager. The firm manufactures stationary and portable engines, circular saw-mills, mining machinery, iron fronts for buildings, and all kinds of steam-heating apparatus. Their machinery is driven by a forty horse-power engine of their own construction. Mr. Finch is a reliable man, and one of the best business men in Scranton.

PLANING-MILLS.

Among the enterprises of Scranton belonging to a single individual the planing-mills of Joseph Ansley excel all others in the variety and excellence of machinery for fashioning lumber into doors, sash, flooring, blinds, siding, and mouldings. His buildings and his lumber-yards occupy one acre and a half on the Hyde Park side above the railroad. The works were begun in 1848, and purchased by him in 1866. A seventy-five horse-power engine drives the necessary machinery for dressing and manipulating lumber into every possible shape.

In 1884 his mills and yard were destroyed by fire, but his indomitable energy immediately replaced them with great improvement. He sustains the highest character for probity and fair dealing, and is considered an excellent citizen.

PROVIDENCE PLANING-MILL.

This old and well-known sash- and blind-factory is now managed by Miller, Coleman & Co. It is located in Providence, the First Ward of the city of Scranton. It was established by Hand & Von Storch in 1848. In the following April, Chauncy Hand sold his interest to William and Gregory Von Storch, and they continued the business until 1851, when it passed into the hands of E. J. Hand & Son. The next year L. White joined the firm, whose name was changed to Hand, White & Co. In 1862 the firm was Hand, Ward & Co.; in 1863, Hand & Bristol, by Judge Bristol, now of Wilkes Barre, coming in; in 1865, Hand & Costen; in 1868, Hand, Costen & Co.; in 1872, Costen & Spencer; in 1876, H. B. Rockwell; in 1879, Wm. B. Rockwell; and in 1884 by its present proprietors.

The works are run by steam-power, with the most improved machinery for converting wood into every desired shape for use, and through the intervening change of firms has enjoyed and still enjoys a large trade in the Lackawanna Valley. Jason H. Johnson and his partners, Messrs. Miller and Coleman, enjoy the reputation of honorable business men.

SCRANTON STOVE-WORKS.

In 1840 there was but a single foundry in the valley where stoves were cast. Where the present Capouse Works of the late Mr. Carter, in Providence, stands, Mr. Tilston made two patterns of stoves. Grates were in general use, and were cast in great abundance.

Stephen and John Tunstall afterwards opened a stove-foundry

in the village of Providence, which, after a time, passed into the hands of H. O. Silkman. It was finally burned.

Among the very largest interests of this city, the Scranton Stove-Works stand conspicuously in the foreground. It is not in the sense of manufacturing exclusively that these works have served to very materially develop the local resources of our city, but in the general and positive upholding of the many advantages Scranton possesses for all classes of manufacturing and wholesale features of trade.

The unremitting exertions to develop the unfathomable resources lying at our very doors have not only served to demonstrate scientific facts regarding it, but have been the source which has carried the name of Scranton beyond the boundary lines of this continent.

From nine to thirteen tons of stove-castings are turned out per day. This product takes the shape of this famous cook and heating stoves, dockash series, which are known beyond the Mississippi River, as well as through the Eastern markets. The works cover an area of two acres, and give employment to 150 hands.

No compliment which we can bestow would be greater than to say that, among the leaders of this trade in the country, the works in question have no rivals, which is borne out by the great extent of their trade, and certainly no statement is more merited, or will be more readily endorsed by their numerous patrons. It remains for us to say that the firm has every facility for doing the largest trade in stove-castings between Philadelphia and Pittsburg. The roster is composed of J. A. Price, President; J. A. Lansing, Secretary; A. C. Fuller, Treasurer.

GREEN RIDGE.

In 1868, GREEN RIDGE had no name or being. Upon the ancient lands of John Dings, Joshua Griffin, Henry Whaling, and Michael Lutz, embracing a green slope on the east side of the Lackawanna, opposite the Indian meadow of Capoose, a mile from the court-house, this village or appendage of Scranton has emerged within the last two decades. HON. GEORGE SANDERSON, the founder of it, a man of strong, good sense and great public spirit, enriched himself by purchasing a portion of these acres several years ago, and encouraging a village, which, tidy and hospitable as the home of a wealthy class, depends upon Scranton proper for its subsistence, trade, and mail. It is the northern terminus of the Lehigh and Susquehanna Division of the Philadelphia and Reading Railroad. It has its churches, schools, stores, and street railway, and enjoys the advantages of the Delaware and Hudson Company's railroad passing through it. The new jail is being erected within its border.

SCRANTON GLASS COMPANY, LIMITED.

This young and vigorous company is located at this point. The works comprise ten lots and are run by a thirty horse-power engine and forty power boiler. The furnace-house is 80 x 100 feet, with nine ovens, which show a daily capacity for handling 8000 pounds of metal. This is shown every night in the form of 125 gross of bottles, in turn representing druggists' glassware, beer and soda bottles, wine glasses, and flasks. Eighty-five men and boys are employed throughout the furnace-rooms, packing-houses, batch-house, box-shops, crucible-shop, and sand- and crusher-house. The annual product will reach a value amounting to $100,000. They have a standing order from one large establishment in Chicago for all the ink bottles they can make. A special force is kept on this order. Mr. Samuel Hinds is president; Charles Henwood, treasurer; and M. A. Goodman, superintendent.

GREEN RIDGE IRON-WORKS, A. L. SPENCER, PROPRIETOR.

With a capital of $60,000, these works are run by three engines, one of which is fed with culm, while the others use coal costing $1.80 at the bed. An annual output of about four thousand tons of wrought iron, which appears on the market in the form of rails, bar-iron, toe-cork steels, strap-rails, band-iron, horseshoe iron, truck- and car-axles, with something of a specialty in twenty-five pound iron T rails. A force of thirty men are employed. Scrap-iron is purchased by Spencer to any extent, and contracts are solicited by the Green Ridge Iron-Works for working over scrap-iron.

Here are again displayed the direct and positive facilities held out by Scranton's peculiar location and other undisguised natural advantages for the successful conduct of iron manufacturing.

While Lackawanna and adjacent counties supply the market for the products of these works, other sections of this and adjoining States would be equally quick to respond to a greater and more diversified product. It can be added that flat, round, and square iron is shown by these works.

The scrap-iron manufactured by Mr. Spencer is superior in texture and durability.

UP THE VALLEY.

CARBONDALE.

This place was named before the Wurts's had erected a cabin upon its site. The name was compounded by these gentlemen in Philadelphia, in 1822, from *carbon* found in the *dale*. D. Yarrington, an old gentleman living in Carbondale, was boarding upon the mountain, in Rix's Gap, at that time when a lumber two-horse wagon loaded with tools, powder, and camp paraphernalia, driven by a weary teamster, stopped at the Mountain Inn to rest after his long journey. The teamster, upon whom devolved the task of finding the unnamed, unknown place, being asked where he was going with his strange load, replied, "To Carbondale." No one knew where this was, but his loaded stuff was prominently marked in large letters, "*Carbondale*, 143 *miles from Philadelphia on the Lackawanna River, Luzerne County, Penna.*"

Mr. Yarrington, knowing that some fellows with vague notions of stone coal had been digging in the woods down by the Lackawanna, some three miles from the Mountain Inn, directed the bewildered teamster to the camp-ground under the hemlock-trees, and then christened Carbondale.

William Wurts the elder paid me a visit in 1857, and gave me the above facts. He then had a bad cough and was exceedingly feeble. He died in 1858.

The city was the first to be incorporated within the limits of Luzerne County, the act of Assembly creating it bearing date March 15, 1851. On the 15th of December, 1850, a large fire destroyed the greater portion of the village, which contained about five thousand inhabitants.

APPENDIX.   489

The present population of the city is estimated at 9000. It had a court-house, but the division of the county extinguished its court in 1878. It has two banks, with an aggregate capital of $160,000, twenty public schools, two newspapers, seven churches, a superior water-works, and two military companies. HORATIO S. PIERCE, although a resident of Scranton, is president of the First National Bank, and is regarded as one of the most popular and prosperous men in the Lackawanna Valley.

THE SOLDIERS' MONUMENT.

In May, 1885, Carbondale erected a suitable monument upon the square for her patriotic dead. It was the first city in Lackawanna County to place a stone to commemorate the men who died to save the nation when in peril. The W. H. Davis Post, Commander J. M. Alexander, and the citizens, generally, liberally contributed to the expense of its erection. The monument was dedicated on Memorial Day, May 30, with the most impressive ceremony by various Posts and by the people of the upper end of the county. Its erection was alike creditable to the patriotism and the liberality of the citizens of Carbondale.

VAN BERGEN & CO.'S WORKS.

These works are located here. They are the oldest in the county of Lackawanna, being established in 1833, under the influence of the Delaware and Hudson Canal Company.

In 1850, J. Benjamin & Co. conducted the business. In 1873 the present firm entered, and made many alterations and improvements both in men and machinery. Five acres of land are occupied by the machine-shops, pattern- and smith-shops, storage-houses, store, and other necessary buildings. Throughout the entire works the machinery is of modern design and most improved kind, all driven by an engine of sixty horse-power. A large force of qualified mechanics and machinists are constantly engaged in building engines and all kinds of mining machinery. Castings of iron and brass and car-wheels and other fixtures are turned out in large quantities, while repairing machinery in general is made a specialty. The firm is also engaged in the sale of general hardware goods, water-, gas-, and steam-pipe of every description.

Mr. J. B. VAN BERGEN was born in the State of New York, but for many years has been a resident of Carbondale, filling several offices of trust, and was elected mayor for four consecutive terms, from 1869 to 1873.

JERMYN.

Five miles below Carbondale stands the quiet village of Jermyn. A small brook, called Rush Brook, rushes through a defile in the mountain, and from thence the name of Rushdale was applied to the place; afterwards called Baconville, then Gibsonburg, and finally Jermyn, from John Jermyn, who operated here in coal a few years ago. Like all the villages along the Lackawanna, its life depends upon coal-mining, which is carried on by the Delaware and Hudson Company, whose railroad runs through it. Excellent water from a mountain stream comes into the village, which is supplied with churches, schools, stores, hotels, and drug-stores, enjoying a population of about three thousand.

THE JERMYN COFFIN- AND CASKET-WORKS.

These works are located here, and, in spite of strikes, suspensions, and hard times, furnishes peaceful homes for the occupants of a vast territory. John Jermyn is president of the company, which employs thirty-five skilled workmen the year round.

MOOSIC POWDER-WORKS.

Half a mile below Jermyn is located the Moosic Powder-Works. There are three powder-mills within the county in an area of fifteen miles,—one on Spring Brook, at Moosic, one on the mountain south of Olyphant, and this one.

The capital of this company, which was organized in 1865, was $100,000, and it had a capacity of two hundred kegs a day. In 1869 the firm of Laflin, Boies & Yurik, owners of the old Raynor Works at Moosic, was consolidated with the Moosic Powder Company, and the capital was increased to $300,000. The present capacity of the works is 1000 kegs per day. It is in a thrifty condition. H. M. Boies is president of the company, and J. C. Platt treasurer. Both gentlemen are well known and highly esteemed. Their main office is in Scranton.

ARCHBALD.

In the winter of 1844 civilization dawned slowly upon Archbald, which was named from JAMES ARCHBALD. The narrow interval, shaded by forest of pine and enlivened by the clear waters of Lackawanna and White Oak Run, was known as a *deerway*, where buck and doe, driven from the mountains by pursuing hounds, attempting to ford the river to escape, fell an easy prey to the rifles of Blakely hunters forty years ago.

A smith-shop to sharpen drills and miners' picks was built on the eastern bank of the stream in 1844 by D. G. Sligh, which

ARCHBALD IN 1844.

was torn down in 1885. Under the auspices of the coal company two or three plain dwellings emerged from the fresh stumps and fallen logs near the outlet of the run, where Messrs. Archbald and Clarkeston had discovered coal. A bridge was thrown across the Lackawanna by R. S. Benjamin before a foot of land had been cleared upon its borders. It was the wildest place in the coal-field chosen for a habitation, and considerations of necessity rather than those of beauty of landscape governed the selection of Archbald for a village site. A bridle- or foot path led along the stream from Mount Vernon (now Winton) to

Baconville, but neither pike, road, house, or bridge ventured near the waterfalls of White Oak Run.

The growth of Archbald from that time until now has been steady, and it now enjoys a population of over two thousand. The Delaware and Hudson Company mine and send off a large quantity of coal from here, while Jones, Simpson & Co. are also engaged in mining coal and in a general mercantile business. Their mines consist of a slope, drift, and a shaft, connected with their breaker by a railroad two miles in length. Ten engines are employed in operating these mines and in running the breaker, working the pump, and in moving the cars. Three hundred and fifty men and laborers are employed by the firm, and 150,000 tons of coal annually shipped. Mr. George Simpson, of the firm, died last year. Mr. JAMES J. WILLIAMS is the general manager of the business, and by his fair dealing and the upright manner he conducts all transactions has made himself universally popular.

KNITTING-FACTORY.

This factory, the only one of its kind in the valley, was started in 1881 by Messrs. Linderman & White. They manufacture woollen and cotton hosiery, jackets, hoods, making a specialty of seamless socks. The works give employment to a large number of females, and is a great acquisition to the village.

The purest spring-water is brought from a mountain run to the town, and it enjoys all the advantages of a high-school, the Delaware and Hudson Railroad, and some commodious churches.

WINTON.

A mile down the stream from Archbald, in a sunny glade, lies the young mining village of Winton, with its post-office, store, and a colliery supplied with coal by the Pierce Coal Company's opening on the mountain half a mile east of Archbald and about two miles away. In the immediate vicinity coal has not proved to be of the first quality, and yet the village, named from W. W. WINTON, one of the most liberal gentlemen of Providence, is tenanted by a hardy and contented population. Two locomotive roads pass through it. The Dolph Coal-Works are located here, as is the quarry of stone from which the county jail is built.

PECKVILLE.

Named from Samuel Peck, deceased. This village is one of the prettiest found in the valley, and less dependent upon mining than any other. Its post-office, two churches, two drug-stores, schools, and stores supply the wants of its residents in every direction, while a grist- and saw-mill, and a planing-mill, all run by water-power, occupy the attention of many of the artisans of the place.

Peck, Wise & Co. carry on the business, and, owning the saw-mill, they are enabled to secure the remaining pine forest between this point and LAKE PAUPACK, on the summit of the Moosic, saw, kiln-dry, plane, and manufacture the lumber into doors, sash, blinds, flooring, siding, and mouldings as the carpenters and builders may desire. The members of this firm are all recognized by the people of the valley as business men of very high order and as excellent citizens. This mill was burned in 1884; rebuilt in 1885.

OLYPHANT.

A mile below Peckville stands Olyphant. In 1840-44 a mill-pond, a saw-mill, and three houses, two of which are yet standing, inhabited by Messrs. Barber, Travis, and Ferris, constituted Olyphant. The lands fell into the hands of William Hull, a rich farmer, living across the river, who refused to sell or lease them to the Delaware and Hudson Company.

In August, 1858, Lewis Pughe, of Scranton, Edward Jones, of Olyphant, and Abel Barker, of Wyoming, made a lease with William Hull for some 500 acres of coal-lands in Blakely, and the same year the same parties made a contract with Mott, Vosburg, and Newton for other coal-lands in the township of Blakely, now Olyphant. The first-named party at once made a contract with the Delaware and Hudson Canal Company to furnish it with 150,000 tons of coal per annum, at 12½ cents per ton royalty, until the coal from these two tracts was exhausted.

Some thirty years before this, Wm. Wurts had purchased coal-land from Jonathan Silsbee, below Hull's farm, on Eddy Creek, but it was not until the acquisition of these lands in 1858 that the company began to develop the place, which was then named

Olyphant, from President Olyphant, of the Delaware and Hudson Company.

The growth of the borough has been rapid since then, and it has at the present time every element of prosperity to make desirable homes for the industrious dwellers of the village. The Delaware and Hudson Company bring out a large quantity of anthracite, while the private works of Johnson & Co. exhume very many tons for local and foreign markets.

Churches, a high-school, four doctors, two drug and other stores, good hotels, and a post-office accommodate the citizens, while three railroad tracks pass through it. Water is brought over two miles from the Moosic range, and amply supplies the demand.

PRICE.

Down the Lackawanna, half a mile below Olyphant, this settlement appears upon the old farms of Luke and Michael Deckers of twenty-five years ago. It is the newest village in the valley. Eli K. Price, Prof. Pancost, and Dr. B. H. Throop owned the fields where the town is situated. From Mr. Price it took its name. Its first inhabitants were Germans.

In 1880, John Jermyn sunk a shaft and erected some expensive coal-works here, which gave to trade and building lots great impetus and activity in every branch of business. Mr. Jermyn ships a large quantity of coal from this point to New York each year. A single church, a fine school building, a drug-store, post-office, three hotels, and four stores enliven the village, which is the thriftiest one in the valley. A railroad depot and a school-house stands midway between Price and Dickson City.

DICKSON CITY.

This place, where Peter A. Snyder was the sole occupant in 1844, and yet resides here, deigned to be called VAUGHN, then HOLLISTER, but these gentlemen objected to have their names thus perpetuated. It was called Dickson, from the late Thomas Dickson.

Messrs. Pughe, Baker, and Jones leased the coal-lands at Dickson, and subsequently sold their lease to WM. H. RICHMOND and Charles P. Wurts. This change of property gave birth to Dickson as a village and to the Elk Hill Iron and Coal Company,

WILLIAM MERRIFIELD.

of which Richmond was president, until the breaker was burned in 1882. Mr. Richmond has recently erected a breaker in the Second Ward of the city of Scranton, where he is mining coal to great advantage.

The post-office department added city to the village, to distinguish it from other towns in the State by the name.

The Delaware, Lackawanna and Western Railroad have sunk a shaft here that will keep busy and give sustenance to a large number of men.

The old Indian apple-tree, described in this volume, page 61, was blown down on the night of September 23, 1885. It was the oldest tree in this section of the State.

THE INCEPTION OF LACKAWANNA COUNTY.

Lackawanna County was erected out of Luzerne under an Act of Assembly approved April 17, 1878. At an election held in August, 1878, out of 11,601 votes, 9615 were cast in favor of the new county.

As early as 1837 the citizens of Lackawanna Valley living above the bridge at Pittson began to agitate the question of a division, which was only settled after forty years of dissension. The sentiment of the upper townships was in favor of carving Lackawanna County out of Luzerne. In fact, there was no measure, no matter how meritorious, so fixed and popular in the public mind as was this. No communication with Wilkes Barre was had only by the tri-weekly stage or the slow wagon, horseback or on foot, and litigants who sought redress by law were compelled to stay there a week, at considerable expense, before their cases were reached or postponed until another term.

In 1843, Hon. WILLIAM MERRIFIELD, of Hyde Park, was elected to the Legislature. He served three consecutive terms, greatly to the advantage and satisfaction of his constituents. He was the real father of the new county. He was the first one to give it shape and animation, in spite of strong opposition from old Luzerne, which had great influence at Harrisburg because of the ability and shrewdness of their ever-present politicians. At the session of 1844 he succeeded in passing through the House of Representatives the first bill for the erection of the County of Lackawanna.

Providence Village deserves more credit than any other part of the territory for its steady efforts in establishing a new county.

In 1840, Charles H. Silkman and Dr. B. H. Throop removed from Honesdale to Providence, which at this time was considered the political Mecca of the valley. Nathaniel Cotrill's tavern, now the Bristol House, as it was termed, was the place where Bidlack, Beaumont, Butler, Fuller, Samuel P. Collings, Kidder, Wright, Merrifield, and other genial politicians of lesser light, were wont to meet annually before election for their country's good. In 1844-45 the valley was alive with excitement. The friends of the new county purchased a press and type in Carbondale, and started the *Providence Mirror and Lackawannian*, with Frank B. Woodward as its editor, although young Randall, Rankin, and Hill,—all deceased now, and all law students of Silkman then,—and others contributed largely to its editorial and local columns. Silkman had three distinct objects in view: *First*, the defeat of the Delaware and Hudson Canal Company from coming down the valley to Archbald with their gravity railroad from Carbondale; *Second*, to aid the Erie Road, then being surveyed, whose agent he was, to come up the Lackawaxen and Paupack, through Hawley and Cobb's Gap, Leggett's Gap, and follow the line now used by the Delaware, Lackawanna and Western Railroad to Great Bend, instead of going to Narrowsburg; and *Third*, the division of the county of Luzerne. He had little or no legal business, and his whole time was devoted to the accomplishment of these three objects. During the winter of 1845-46 meeting after meeting was held at least once a week at either Green's hotel, in Hyde Park, Cotrill's tavern, in Providence, at Waite Cannon's, now F. Keifer's place, in Price, or at the hotel of Levi Lillibridge, in Blakely. There was no Archbald then. Not a tree had been felled upon its site until the winter of 1845.

At these meetings Silkman, who was a fluent, persuasive, incisive speaker, full of vigor and venom, was the moving spirit. He called the meetings to order, appointed committees, made speeches, wrote resolutions, and reported them for the *Mirror and Lackawannian*, now on file in my office. The people of the valley were fevered with an agitation unparalleled before or since.

APPENDIX.

In 1852, Hon. A. B. Dunning, then residing in Providence as a merchant, was sent to the Legislature for three concurrent sessions without advancing the interest of the new county in the least, owing to the determined and bitter opposition of Buckalew, then a power at Harrisburg, and other selfish persons in old Luzerne, naturally inimical to a measure not calculated to advance their interests. Had the proposed new county been erected at this time, Providence instead of Scranton would have been the county-seat.

After its defeat, Silkman, beguiled into a purchased silence, retired from the contest. The *Mirror*, with its editor, removed to Virginia, where he soon after died of consumption.

It was not until 1873, when the Constitutional Convention was held, that Lewis Pughe and A. B. Dunning brought it favorably before the public. Especially was it due to the able and convincing speech of Mr. Pughe that the objectionable feature which required a submission to the vote of the whole county was defeated.

James Archbald, F. L. Faries, P. Blewitt, and A. Bryson, Jr., were appointed commissioners to survey the boundary line between the old and new counties.

FIRST OFFICERS OF THE COUNTY.

President Judge, Benjamin S. Bentley;* Prothonotary, F. L. Hitchcock; Sheriff, A. B. Stevens; Treasurer, Col. William N. Monies; Clerk of Courts, Joshua R. Thomas; Recorder, A. M. Renshaw; Register, John L. Lee; District Attorney, F. W. Gunster; County Surveyor, P. M. Walsh; County Commis-

---

* The appointment of Judge Bentley was made on the ground that Lackawanna County, the moment it was erected, became, under the provisions of the Constitution, a separate judicial district. A mandamus was issued by the Supreme Court, wherein it was decided that the Constitution did not execute itself, but that legislation was necessary before a new district could be created, hence the appointment was illegal and void. By the provisions of the New-County Act, the new county was to remain in the same judicial district with the old, hence the judges of Luzerne organized and held the courts. By Act of Assembly of March 13, 1879, Lackawanna was made the Forty-fifth Judicial District, and John Handley assigned as president judge, and Alfred Hand as additional law judge thereof.

sioners, H. L. Gaige, H. F. Barrett, Dennis Tierney; County Auditors, W. J. Lewis, Robert Reeves, E. J. Lynett; Jury Commissioners, Eugene Snyder, J. J. Lynch; Coroner, Edward Travers, M.D.

Scranton was naturally selected as the county-seat. On the 2d day of September, 1878, Hon. B. F. Bentley, of Williamsport, who had been appointed president judge, proceeded to organize the several courts of Lackawanna County in Tripp's building, situated on the southeast corner of Wyoming Avenue and Linden Street. On the 17th of the following September the court made an order designating Washington Hall, or the provost-marshal's drafting place, on the corner of Lackawanna and Penn Avenues, as a court-house.

Soon after the "Bentley Court" was instituted, A. A. Chase, of Scranton, applied to the Supreme Court for a mandamus to compel the judges of Luzerne County to meet and organize the courts of the new county, basing his application on the ground that, by the provisions of the New-County Act, Lackawanna was not a separate judicial district, and, therefore, the only court authorized by law was that to be established by the judges of Luzerne County, the Eleventh Judicial District. The application was sustained, and notwithstanding the large number of judgments, mortgages, and deeds recorded, and suits begun, involving hundreds of thousands of dollars, the Supreme Court, on the 18th of October, 1878, issued a peremptory mandamus to Garrick M. Harding, president judge, and John Handley and William H. Stanton, additional law judges of Luzerne County, to forthwith organize the courts of Lackawanna County. And thereby the "Bentley Court" and all proceedings thereunder were annulled.

Pursuant to this mandamus, the judges of Luzerne County proceeded, on the 24th of October, 1878, to organize the courts of Lackawanna County, and the county machinery was started in due form of law.

The constant and increasing demands for space for officers, books, records, etc., upon the county, which the Second National Bank rooms could not furnish, made a new court-house quite as imperative as had been the demands for a new county.

In the early part of 1879 the matter of erecting county buildings began to be agitated. Nothing positive as to a location was determined until the 15th of December, 1879, when the County of Lackawanna, by the county commissioners, accepted as a gift a deed from the Lackawanna Iron and Coal Company and Edward F. Hodges, John B. Newman, and Isaac C. Price, trustees of the Susquehanna and Wyoming Valley Railroad and Coal Company, for the block bounded by Washington Avenue, Linden Street, Adams Avenue, and Spruce Street.

Notwithstanding the many doubts expressed as to the possibility of securing a substantial foundation on this property, which had recently been an impassable swamp, yet the commissioners determined to take the initiatory steps towards erecting a court-house. And on May 15, 1880, they issued a circular inviting competition from architects in presenting plans for a court-house, in size to be not less than 100 feet by 140 feet, and in cost not to exceed $100,000.

Plans were submitted and proposals made in August, 1880, for the erection of the court-house; but it was not until March, 1881, that the contract was awarded to John Snaith, of Ithaca, N. Y., whose bid was $139,927 for superstructure and foundation to a depth of twenty-four feet below water-table, and $5.00 per perch for stone-masonry, and 60 cents per cubic yard for excavation; the building to be made of native sandstone, the same as that in the Library Building, on Wyoming Avenue, and to be trimmed with Onondaga gray limestone. The contract calls for the completion of the building on the 1st day of April, 1883.

Ground was broken by the contractor on the 14th day of April, 1881.

In excavating for the foundation, the greatest depth of excavation is thirty-four feet eight inches below the grade of Washington Avenue; the average depth of foundation is twenty-nine feet six inches. The additional cost for excavation and foundation was $30,932.55; original contract, $139,927.00; total, $170,859.55.

Mr. Snaith gave approved bonds in the sum of $75,000 for the faithful fulfilment of his contract.

In order that the work might be prosecuted as speedily as possible, the commissioners decided, April 23, 1881, to issue bonds for $150,000, pledging in payment therefor the taxable property of the county, which amounts to more than $30,000,000, on full valuation. These bonds bear five per cent. interest, and $100,000 of them have already been delivered, many at a premium.

On the morning of May 25 a heavy, cold rain disappointed the thousands that had assembled to witness and assist in the laying of the corner-stone. The Catholic clergymen of the city very opportunely tendered the use of their large tent for the occasion.

The corner-stone, containing many interesting and valuable contributions, literary and otherwise, was laid with true Masonic ceremony by the Masons of Lackawanna County and Knights Templar as escort of the acting officers of the Grand Lodge of F. and A. M. of the State of Pennsylvania. Messrs. Stevens, Buck, Kingsbury, Jacobs, Van Schoick, Alexander, Lewis, Van Buskirk, Roesler, Williamson, Davis, and Jacobs took part in the ceremony.

We copy largely from Robert McKune's admirable Lackawanna County Memorial.

At this point the Hon. Alfred Hand was introduced, and proceeded to deliver the following oration :

My Fellow-Citizens,—It would have been appropriate to prepare for this important occasion a history and some of the characteristics of our laws, but in the ten minutes allotted me by your Committee of Arrangements I can only give briefly a Tribute to the Jurisprudence of Pennsylvania.

The Commonwealth of Pennsylvania has to-day a system of laws as wise, as just, and as finished as the world has ever seen. Her civil jurisprudence is linked to the wisdom and experience of the ages. It has gathered into its folds principles from Sinai, Rome, Runnymede, and Bunker Hill. Righteousness, philosophy, personal rights, and independence are stones in its foundation-walls. Political equality rests upon all her citizens. Her criminal code is as perfect as human ingenuity and research have been able to formulate. Her principles of equity are applied to the smallest as well as the largest transactions of life in which human interests are at stake. Her administration of justice is comparatively inexpensive, free from intricacy, and, with exceptional and unavoidable cases, speedy. "Right and justice are administered without sale, denial, or delay."

APPENDIX.

We meet here to-day to dedicate this building to Law and Justice, solely and exclusively. In honoring these this great concourse of all classes and divers organizations does honor to itself. Religion is interested in this structure, but we do not rear it to religion. Science is interested, but we raise it not to science; art, but we build it not to art; social and civic life, but we erect it not to these. Business is interested, but we place no tribute to business on its walls. The fireside is interested in these corridors, from the infant drawing life from its mother's breast to the old man tottering on his staff, but they are not dedicated to the family. But to that which regulates human conduct in all departments—Law—and that which judges thereof—Justice—we build a temple, grand in proportions and beautiful in design.

Next to that science which treats of the relations of God to man, is that which comprehends and considers the relations of man to man. Yonder church-spires point man to Almighty God for eternal life; the spire which shall surmount this stone points man to God for the regulation of this mortal life. Next to the church is the temple of Justice—next in dignity, next in usefulness, next in honor. Does the Almighty appear at the altar or sanctuary, so does he appear at the place of judgment; for it is written, " Ye judge not for man, but for Jehovah, who is with you in the judgment." To law and justice we elevate these monumental walls and towers. Law is inseparable from motion or existence. It is written on the universe. There is no speech nor language where its voice is not heard. On the stars of heaven, on the comets whirling through space, on the rocks of the mountains, on the dew-drop flashing in the sunbeam, on the sunbeam coloring the dew-drop, we read the testimony to law. All living creatures are under law. Man alone, in his relation to man, seems without law, until he begins to govern himself. The Creator appears to have decreed that man shall make and enforce his own law for his own conduct, responsible to the Almighty for the mandate and the obedience. In this effort to enact " the rule commanding what is right and prohibiting what is wrong," our own Commonwealth stands high among the States of the world. Our law preserves the good of the past; retains the old, not because it is old, but because it is good. We glory in our common law. Christianity is a part of it. We do equity under the forms of law. We sacrifice not justice to form, protect the officer and citizen, place high responsibility on executive, judge, and legislator, hold them responsible for their trust, and in the administration of that trust make them secure. While we give large liberty to the people and make much of personal rights, we at the same time protect them from their own folly in times of excitement. It has always been the aim of our law-makers and judges to bring law and justice together in theoretical and practical harmony. Our civil law attests success in this direction. Our criminal law is profound and philosophical. It meets, as might be expected, greater obstacles in the investigation and punishment of crimes. To protect the innocent we, at times, screen the guilty. It needs always a just, discriminating, and upright people. Would that I had the power to impress upon the mind of every citizen of this county a proper view of the noble attribute of Justice. Justice springs from the bosom of the Almighty, is strong for good, terrible to evil, full of blessing, security, and health to the State and society. Justice sweeps away all subterfuges, disregards all false apologies, knows no passion or prejudice, entrenches herself in exact truth, honesty, and intelligence. Justice has no maudlin sympathy for evil-doers, falsely called mercy; no disgusting sentiment of licentiousness, falsely called liberty. Justice stands erect in fair proportions, honorably clad, with no blush of shame for her acts. She comes forth to-day and says, in clear and truthful tones, that sympathy for crimes is cruelty to the State. The ancients represented Justice as blind, holding the scales even. She is blind to parties, blind to passion and everything except truth. She begs us never to pluck the bandage from her eyes nor disturb the even balance of her scales.

As we stand here to-day, holding in our minds the picture of this edifice as it will be, imagination brings to view the relation it will sustain to the people of this county. Before this single tribunal, which, under our economy, embraces all legal questions, what scenes of human welfare and human woe will be enacted; what fortunes saved and fortunes destroyed; what hopes elevated and blasted! Homes will be cheered and made desolate, truth maintained and falsehood exposed, reputations vindicated and lost; peace will come to some and unrest to others; the sacred relation of marriage will be protected and also sundered. Here will be brought, as from a rough and troubled sea, the conflicts, passions, and selfishness of the political arena; here the quiet, stern mandate of the law shall say, "Peace, be still," when the people, mindful of the respect due to their own tribunals, with serene dignity, will submit and return to the calm of ordinary life. Here will come up for adjudication the rights of persons and the rights of things; all those interests that relate to personal security, personal liberty, and private property; to magistrates, the Legislature, to the people at large in their organized capacity; matters civil and military; all the relations of master and servant, husband and wife, parent and child, guardian and ward, the rights and duties of artificial persons, bodies politic and corporate. Here will be resolved the intricacies of real-estate, their tenures, the law of their descent and alienation. Here will be redressed private wrongs, calling into action all the machinery of courts of justice in their different divisions of Common Pleas, Orphans' Court, and Equity, with all the multiplicity of suits and pleadings which once made men immortal, but which are now so simplified that it is quite as hard to blunder successfully as to plead scientifically. Here will be investigated and punished public wrongs which test the frame-work of society; offences against God and religion, officers and government, public justice, peace, trade, health, and economy, with the long catalogue of crimes from homicide to misdemeanors. Here will be pronounced that sentence which is heaven's estimate of human life, and tells a man that he is not fit to live, because he has despised God-given life in another—that sentence which no just law will ever repeal or reverse, "Whoso sheddeth man's blood, by man shall his blood be shed."

What power for good in its silent influence has such a building as this? Well may it call together such an expression from the people as we witness here to-day. Not alone in the active judgments rendered within these walls do we find the people's estimate of right and abhorrence of evil, but in that greater, more sublime, more eloquent tribute to justice which comes from the voluntary obedience of the people. Law is best honored in silent, unresisting obedience to her behests. As this corner-stone holds secure for centuries yet to come the evidence of to-day's progress, so our jurisprudence, unique in its combinations, holds the wisdom and principles of to-day, gathered in all the past, to be handed down unimpaired and venerable to the generations yet unborn. This corner-stone, placed at the seat of justice for this newest county of the Commonwealth, allies us to the wisdom of the past, and gives hope in the onward progress of civilization. This is akin to those historical events which in their significance have themselves been termed corner-stones of liberty and truth. Here and there in the great conflict between right and wrong, truth and error, we find sacred spots wet with human blood and tears, where some great principle was maintained and right secured. We here, in harmony and gladness, make sacred this spot on which this stone rests, assuring ourselves and the world that within the lines which comprise this county justice shall be upheld and private and public rights protected. This building, completed as designed, from foundation-stone to turret-pinnacle, is a fit emblem of our jurisprudence. In the long years that are passed in the history of our own and our mother-county, we have dug deep through the muck and mire and tangled roots of human pride, prejudice, and ignorance to lay a foundation for our judicial system upon the primal rocks and stable support of truth and justice; we have builded course after course until our progress has lifted us into the sunlight of a pure atmosphere. On this we have raised a fair structure of equal rights and balanced powers that has called forth admiration and honor, and at the same time points to a higher and nobler state of perfection. We have our institutions preserved to us in wonderful purity and power. On no part of this globe are human rights more accurately adjusted with less friction or cause of complaint than on Pennsylvania soil. On no soil are wicked combinations against the peace of society more surely broken up, nor the judgments of courts and juries more universally just and unimpeachable. Our laws and their administration are as nearly perfect as human nature has yet been able to attain unto. Our machinery is well constructed, ready for perfect action and proper results, and as intelligence, temperance, and integrity pervade the people, so will the dishonoring criticisms which are occasionally made wholly vanish and disappear. On the true instincts of the people, enlightened by experience and strengthened by knowledge and integrity, all security and peace of society rest. We hold the titles to our homes, protection to life, property, and reputation at the disposal of the twelve historic jurymen drawn from the people. When they are wise, educated, and upright, we are safe; when prejudice, passion, ignorance, or recklessness characterize the trial by jury, it loses its honored place in our jurisprudence, and individual rights and safety are gone. May the honored progress of our citizens in all that is noble and lofty, and their respect for the institutions of law and justice that have been handed down to us from our forefathers, preserve this county among those noted for order, thrift, and happiness.

At the close of Judge Hand's address, Grand Chaplain R. W. Van Schoick pronounced the benediction, thus concluding the ceremonies of the fraternity, and, after music by Bauer's Band, the spectators dispersed. The ceremonies were very impressive throughout, and attracted earnest attention.

The following is the history prepared by E. Merrifield, Esq., at the request of the county commissioners, and deposited in the corner-stone:

The County of Lackawanna is the outgrowth of an agitation that continued for nearly forty years. It is the fourth county that has been taken from territory originally embraced in Luzerne. In 1839, Joseph Griffin, of Providence Township, was elected to the House of Representatives, being the first to occupy that position from the Lackawanna District. At that time the question of dividing Luzerne and creating a county out of the northeastern portion began to assume a serious aspect, and became a disturbing element in local politics. The opponents of the measure dealt a serious blow, when, in 1842, they consented to the creation of the new county of Wyoming. But this did not serve to quell the agitation, as in 1843 it was made an issue, and William Merrifield, of Hyde Park, was elected to the Legislature, and continued for three successive terms. At the session of 1844 he succeeded in passing through the House of Representatives the first bill for the creation of Lackawanna County. William S. Ross, of Wilkes Barre, then senator from the district, made a fierce and desperate opposition, which resulted in its defeat by a tie vote. In 1852, A. B. Dunning was sent to the Legislature upon the same issue, and continued the two following years. Several times, by a very flattering vote, he passed the bill through the House, but Charles R. Buckalew, then senator from the district, occupied a very prominent and influential position, and defeated it by a bare majority. In 1857, through the influence of Buckalew, and directly as the result of the agitation of the Lackawanna County project, came the amendment to the Constitution prohibiting the erection of new counties without being first submitted to the vote of the entire county. This was intended as a fatal blow to the project,—in fact, proved such for the time being,—yet it did not stop the clamor of the new-county advocates. In 1863, Jacob Robinson and Peter Walsh, then members of the House of Representatives, passed a bill submitting to the voters of Luzerne the question of the erection of a new county to be called Lackawanna. The election was duly held, and resulted in its defeat by about 3000 majority. This proved a quietus to new-county talk for more than five years. In 1870, however, our people were again actively interesting themselves in behalf of the project, and a bill was before the Legislature for most of the sessions down to the final passage of the enabling act of 1878. The beginning of dawn in the great fight was in 1873, when, in the Constitutional Convention, Lewis Pughe and A. B. Dunning, members thereof, labored so zealously in its interest.

Under the provisions of the new Constitution, all special legislation being prohibited, it became necessary to pass a bill that would not only be operative for one, but for all sections of the State, and during the sessions of 1875, 1876, and 1877 our people were co-operating with other interests to secure the enactment of such a law; especially during 1876, F. W. Gunster then being a member of the House from Scranton, and occupying a prominent and influential position, there was a spirited and determined effort made. The fact, however, that it antagonized so many of the different counties provoked a fight that was not only formidable, but irresistible. Our thoughts and energies were then directed to the question as to whether or not a bill could be framed that would meet the exigencies of the case, and escape such general opposition. At a meeting of the Scranton Bar during the winter of 1878 the matter was duly considered, and the writer deputed to draft an act in accordance therewith. This was forwarded and read in place by James O. Kiersted, member of the House of Representatives from Scranton. On the 17th of April, 1878, it became a law, and under which the new County of Lackawanna was ushered into being.

The fight for the passage of the bill was interesting and exciting. With Mr. Kiersted was D. M. Jones, his colleague, who were ably assisted by A. I. Ackerly and John B. Smith, representing other sections of Luzerne, and George B. Seamans, senator from the district. Among those who devoted a large portion of their time at Harrisburg in behalf of the project were E. N. Willard, R. H. McKune, F. W. Gunster, F. L. Hitchcock, J. E. Barrett, and E. Merrifield, aided from time to time by B. H. Throop, George Sanderson, A. H. Winton, Lewis Pughe, H. S. Pierce, J. A. Scranton, U. G. Schoonmaker, Corydon H. Wells, and John H. Powell. *The Scranton Republican*, very able in the advocacy, was for weeks placed upon the desks of the members, and had much to do in creating a favorable sentiment. After the contest had progressed for quite a length of time, with varying prospects, but without substantial progress, a meeting was held in the city of Scranton, which was the pivotal point, and the result of which finally led to triumph. The soldiers upon the battle-ground had been continually hampered for want of necessary means. Aside from the liberal action taken by the Scranton Board of Trade, the subscriptions had been comparatively small, and now had come a time when princely contributions were a necessity. It must either be a plethoric treasury or a graceful retirement from the field. The major part of the opulent citizens of Scranton were singularly apathetic and indifferent to the necessities of the case. At this juncture Edward N. Willard, Aretus H. Winton, and myself were so fortunate as to call in council Benjamin H. Throop, George Sanderson, William W. Winton, and Horatio S. Pierce, who succeeded in talking each other into such a commendable spirit of liberality as led to an adequate supply of the sinews of war, and without which there would not have been a new county.

On the 17th of April, 1878, in accordance with the requirements of the act, there was filed in the office of the Secretary of Internal Affairs at Harrisburg a petition, it being the initiatory step under the terms of the law for the erection of the county of Lackawanna; whereupon William Griffis, of Bradford County, David Summers, of Susquehanna, and R. H. Saunders, of Philadelphia, were appointed commissioners, who, after the requisite investigation, on the 25th of June, 1878, made report recommending the erection of said county. On the 8th of July following, Governor John F. Hartranft issued a proclamation ordering that an election be held in the proposed district August 13, 1878. There were cast 9615 votes in favor, and 1986 against the new county, being a majority of 7629 votes in favor thereof. A proclamation by the governor, dated August 21, 1878, declared the said county established.

The result, so one-sided in its final showing, was brought about after a most thorough and exciting canvass. The friends of the measure vied with each other in working heartily and faithfully for success, hence it would be impossible, in a brief historical sketch, to give all the names. Besides the gentlemen heretofore named as friends of the cause, William N. Monies, I. H. Burns, Mayor T. V. Powderly, Cornelius Smith, R. W. Archbald, J. R. Thomas, John F. Connolly, J. B. Collings, F. Johnson, and George Allen were particularly active and influential in contributing to the result. In the evening the victory was celebrated in a brilliant and never-to-be-forgotten manner. Lackawanna Avenue was illuminated from one end to the other. Bells were ringing, bonfires roared, the cannon thundered, and thousands of people going from house to house, singing and shouting their glad notes of triumph, formed a pageant that would have done honor to any cause that ever claimed the prowess of knight or hero.

By virtue of the power conferred under the law, the governor commissioned the following-named gentlemen as officers of the county: F. L. Hitchcock, Prothonotary; A. B. Stevens, Sheriff; J. R. Thomas, Clerk of the Courts; A. Miner Renshaw, Recorder; J. L. Lee, Register of Wills; F. W. Gunster, District Attorney; E. J. Lynott, Auditor; James Lynch, Eugene Snyder, Jury Commissioners; William N. Monies, Treasurer; Horace F. Barrett, Henry L. Gaige, Dennis Tierney, County Commissioners.

At the same time Benjamin F. Bentley was commissioned as president judge, but by a writ of mandamus issued by the Supreme Court at the instance of A. A. Chase, the said appointment was declared illegal, and on the 24th day of October, 1878, the several courts of the county were organized by Hon. Garrick M. Harding, President Judge, Hon. John Handley and Hon. W. H. Stanton, Additional Law Judges. At the fall election of 1878 W. J. Lewis and P. M. Moffitt were elected associate judges of the county. There was elected at the same time a full set of county officers, but by a decision of the Supreme Court it was held that the same was premature; hence the first election of county officials by the people took place on the 4th day of November, 1879.

THE BANQUET.

Pursuant to a call, a meeting of the members of the bar of Lackawanna County and the citizens who were active in the new-county movement was held on the evening of May 16. E. Merrifield, Esq., was chosen president, and A. H. Winton secretary. After a free exchange of opinions in regard to the advisability of having further proceedings than those designated by the commissioners, on motion of Hon. F. W. Gunster, seconded by Dr. B. H. Throop, it was resolved that on the evening of May 25 a banquet should be held. It was further resolved that a committee of ten be appointed, with the president as *ex-officio* chairman, to make the necessary arrangements for said banquet. The following persons were chosen as such committee: Dr. B. H. Throop, E. N. Willard, Esq., Hon. R. H. McKune, Hon. F. W. Gunster, Hon. F. D. Collins, John F. Connolly, Esq., I. H. Burns, Esq., Hon. Lewis Pughe, and Hon. D. M. Jones.

At a subsequent meeting the following persons were chosen to act on the several committees:

Committee of Arrangements.—R. H. McKune, J. H. Campbell, R. W. Archbald, W. T. Smith, George Fisher.

Committee on Organization.—Dr. B. H. Throop, E. N. Willard, H. A. Knapp.

Committee on Toasts.—F. W. Gunster, Dr. B. H. Throop, A. H. Winton, F. D. Collins, U. G. Schoonmaker.

Committee on Invitations.—Lewis Pughe, H. M. Edwards, J. F. Connolly, T. V. Powderly, C. Smith.

Committee on Reception.—H. S. Pierce, W. W. Winton, D. W. Connolly, E. B. Sturges, J. B. Collings.

Committee on Tickets.—E. C. Fuller, Thomas Barrowman, G. S. Horn, J. Alton Davis, Victor Koch, Thomas F. Wells, John F. Scragg.

The following invitation was issued to persons residing out of the city:

You are respectfully invited to a
Grand Banquet,
given under the auspices of the
Scranton Bar Association, and Citizens,
in honor of the erection of the County of Lackawanna, and the Laying of the Corner-Stone of the New Court-House,
to be held on the evening of May 25th, at the Wyoming House.

Scranton, Pa., May 18, 1882.

The following is the programme of toasts:

President of the evening, Dr. B. H. Throop; Toast-Master, A. H. Winton.

1. "LACKAWANNA COUNTY—Labor Omnia Vincit." Edward Merrifield, Esq.
2. "OUR INVITED FRIENDS AND GUESTS—We Welcome Them." Hon. G. M. Harding.
3. "OUR COUNTRY—One and Indivisible." Hon. J. A. Scranton.
4. "OUR COMMONWEALTH—The Keystone of the Arch." His Excellency Henry M. Hoyt.
5. "THE PULPIT—The Light of the World." Rev. Dr. J. E. Smith.
6. "OUR MILITARY—The Pride of Our State. May we Never Need their Prowess." Col. H. M. Boies.
7. "THE JUDICIARY—The Purer the Better." Hon. F. D. Collins.

APPENDIX. 513

8. "THE SENIOR BAR—Old Men for Counsel." Hon. George Sanderson.

9. "THE JUNIOR BAR—Lis Sub Judice." John F. Connolly, Esq.

10. "OUR CONSTITUTION—The Stepping-Stone to Our New County." Hon. A. B. Dunning.

11. "OUR MANUFACTURING INTERESTS — By Industry We Thrive." W. W. Scranton.

12. "THE PRESS—The Lever that Moves the World." Hon. J. E. Barrett.

13. "OUR CITY—The Third in the Commonwealth." E. P. Kingsbury.

14. "OUR COMMERCIAL INTERESTS—Made Prosperous by Energy." Thomas H. Dale.

15. "OUR FIRE DEPARTMENT—Nunquam Non Paratus." Hon. Robert H. McKune.

16. "OLD COUNTIES, FAREWELL—The Transplanted Oak." John Beaumont Collings.

17. "OUR ABSENT FRIENDS—Though Absent, to Memory Dear." Col. J. A. Price.

18. "THE LADIES—Omnia Vincit Amor." F. J. Fitzsimmons.

The following gentlemen were present, and partook of the festivities of the occasion:

W. W. Winton,	Scranton.	Thomas Barrowman,	Scranton.
Hon. C. E. Rice,	Wilkes Barre.	H. S. Pierce,	"
Hon. William H. Jessup,	Montrose.	George Fisher,	"
Hon. P. M. Moffitt,	Carbondale.	W. T. Smith,	"
Hon. A. I. Ackerley,	Abington.	Henry Belin, Jr.,	"
Isaac Price,	Philadelphia.	George Jessup,	"
J. J. Williams,	Archbald.	H. H. Coston,	"
I. G. Perry,	Binghamton.	E. P. Kingsbury,	"
John Snaith,	Ithaca, N. Y.	J. E. Carmault,	"
John Jermyn,	Jermyn.	C. H. Welles,	"
Thomas R. Lathrope,	Carbondale.	I. H. Burns,	"
Thomas Johnson,	Milwaukee.	F. J. Fitzsimmons,	"
Hon. F. W. Gunster,	Scranton.	Thomas H. Dale,	"
Hon. D. M. Jones,	"	E. B. Sturges,	"
Hon. A. B. Dunning,	"	Dr. R. A. Squire,	"
Hon. L. Amerman,	"	B. E. Leonard,	"
Col. Ira Tripp,	"	P. J. Horan,	"
Col. George Sanderson, Jr.,	"	Dr. L. Wehlau,	"
Col. U. G. Schoonmaker,	"	H. Webrum,	"
W. W. Scranton,	"	John Tomlinson,	"
E. C. Fuller,	"	Dr. Thomas Stewart,	"

C. R. Pitcher,	Scranton.	Patrick Coar,	Scranton.
R. T. McCabe,	"	Elhanan Smith,	"
J. J. Flanigan,	"	L. A. Watres,	"
John F. Scragg,	"	Joseph Godfrey,	"
John Benore,	"	H. A. Kingsbury,	"
J. D. Knight,	"	R. W. Archbald,	"
D. F. Kearney,	"	H. M. Edwards,	"
H. D. Moses,	"	H. A. Knapp,	"
Henry Morton,	"	Henry Sommers,	"
B. A. Hill,	"	Henry Battin,	"
J. H. Campbell,	"	Dr. W. H. Pier,	"
Dr. H. B. Throop,	"	M. H. Dale,	"
Selden T. Scranton,	Oxford, N. J.	H. D. Hinsdell,	"
Col. Charles Scranton,	"	Victor Koch,	"
Hon. Stanley Woodward,	Wilkes Barre.	Reese G. Brooks,	"
Hon. J. B. Van Bergen,	Carbondale.	William Keiser,	"
Hon. D. R. Grant,	Binghamton.	F. J. Johnson,	"
T. N. Eldridge,	Owego, N. Y.	Dr. A. E. Burr,	"
J. C. Delaney,	Harrisburg.	S. Samter,	"
H. C. Jessup,	Montrose.	C. W. McKinney,	"
H. L. Gaige,	Moscow.	L. L. Eaton,	"
Horace F. Barrett,	Schultzville.	A. McNulty,	"
Hon. Alfred Hand,	Scranton.	John B. Collings,	"
Hon. Lewis Pughe,	"	Robert Reese,	"
Edward Merrifield,	"	J. M. Everhart,	"
A. H. Winton,	"	W. McDaniels,	"
Hon. J. E. Barrett,	"	John Morris,	"
Col. H. M. Boies,	"	Thomas Stewart, Jr.,	"
John F. Connolly,	"	C. E. Pryor,	"
Henry Jacobs,	"	George Throop,	"
W. W. Williams,	"	H. H. Yeager,	"
Dr. H. I. Jones,	"	Robert H. McKune,	"

At eight o'clock the guests began to assemble at the Wyoming House, filling the corridors and parlors. The Committee of Reception was active in receiving and welcoming all, while from Bauer's orchestra came strains of pleasant melodies, filling the house with the sweetest music. The dining-hall was tastefully adorned with flags of all nations. At the side of each plate was laid a copy of the programme, the *menu*, and a buttonhole bouquet. After full justice had been done to the *menu*, prepared by Mr. John McCabe, and which, with one accord, all pronounced most excellent, Dr. B. H. Throop, the president of the evening, announced that, as the inner man had been satisfied, the time had arrived for the commencement of festivities, and requested A. H. Winton, Esq., to proceed with the programme.

A. H. Winton, toast-master, said,—

GENTLEMEN OF THE BAR, FELLOW-CITIZENS, AND INVITED

Guests,—On the night of our great voting contest among ourselves, when immense majorities came pouring in from all directions, and assuring us that the proposed new county of Lackawanna was carried almost unanimously, the roaring artillery, the clanging bells, and the glad shouts of a long-suffering but then delighted multitude, only feebly expressed our joy at the consummation of our most darling wishes.

We will drink our first toast,

LACKAWANNA COUNTY,

and call upon Edward Merrifield to respond. Mr. Merrifield responded in excellent taste, but as much of his speech is embodied in his history of the county we omit it.

Mr. Winton.—We call upon Judge Stanley Woodward to respond to the toast,

OUR INVITED GUESTS.

(*Prolonged applause.*)

Mr. Woodward:

Mr. CHAIRMAN AND GENTLEMEN,—This is a day for congratulation, and I have thought while sitting here that I would begin at the beginning, and would congratulate the people and bar of Lackawanna County, not only upon the present condition and prospect of the county, but also upon the happy auspices under which it first saw the light. Fortunately for me, my duty in that respect has been anticipated by my learned friend, Mr. Merrifield. But it must be evident to all from his remarks that the birth of Lackawanna County was virtuous and pure. (*Applause.*) It came in wedlock, and was not born out of wedlock. No dishonesty was used to produce Lackawanna County, but, on the contrary, it was the outgrowth of public sentiment, yet stimulated by public and private means. Therefore, I congratulate you upon the glory of your beginning. (*Applause.*)

When I received from the commissioners of the county my first invitation to be present to-day at the laying of the cornerstone of your new court-house, something was said about Luzerne County being the mother-county. And the use of this term suggested to my mind several ideas, and one of these ideas was this: that it was rather strange that the people of Lackawanna County should call upon Luzerne as their mother to rejoice with them to-day or to-night. Why? You call upon us to congratulate not only you, but ourselves, upon the breaking-up of the family. You left the family and went out to seek your own fortunes. We were not in favor of peaceable secession, but were thorough Union men. You were opposed to union, and you have succeeded. I can't say it was an elopement. In the first place you did not go off and join yourself to somebody else; you didn't hitch yourself upon some other county. It was a peaceable secession—an independent one. In the second place, as I understand it, you didn't go off suddenly or by night, or without notice (*applause*), and it was not an elopement, therefore, in any sense. We received from time to time notice of your going before you went (*applause and laughter*), and from time to time we put sprags in the progress of your departure, until we ran out of sprags. (*Laughter and applause.*)

But as the mother-county, if I may be so bold as to represent to any extent her sentiments to-night, I say to you that we *do* congratulate you. (*Applause.*) We feel as proud of you as a natural mother feels when the boys and the girls do well.

A new court-house, such as you are going to build, is an emblem and a type of your perseverance and your pluck. I understand it is built on a swamp, a sort of swamp-angel, but I hear, also, it is founded upon a rock, and is going to rise above the mists and miasma, with healing upon its wings. And perhaps a court-house, more than any other structure, does represent the civilization and morals of a community. It speaks for law, and order, and justice, and is a fair expression and exponent of the culture and thrift of the people who build it.

The goddess who holds the scales of justice should have a shrine worthy of her purity and suitable for her purposes. If she is to keep the balances and hold any equipoise, her eyes must be kept clear of dust, her lungs well fed with pure air, and her sense of smell unoffended by the incense of unclean odors.

There can be no rivalry and nothing but friendship between Lackawanna County and Luzerne County. (*Applause.*) Our great veins of anthracite run more nearly north and south than east or west, and therefore we may always work in our great source of wealth on the same line. If it were otherwise, if our veins lay east and west, across instead of along our pathway, we should always be blasting at the same breasts, and should finally blow ourselves up. As it is, we can work in harmony. Your Lackawanna River flows peacefully and quietly into our Susquehanna, and notwithstanding the fact that they have different sources and different names, they flow at last to the one great ocean. And so Lackawanna County and Luzerne County, divided in name, different in origin, bounded by different lines, are still moving onward with one purpose and to one destiny, the proudest territorial portion of the Keystone State. (*Prolonged applause.*)

Mr. Winton.—Now, gentlemen, there is one man, the Hon. J. A. Scranton, our member of Congress, we would like to hear, but he is away. I have no letter. He is trying to make the Susquehanna River navigable. When he gets through with that, I hope he will tackle the Lackawanna, so we can easily steam up to Carbondale and see those men who voted with us on the new county; and in his absence the next toast,

OUR SISTER-COUNTIES AND OUR COUNTRY,

will be responded to by the Hon. W. H. Jessup.

Judge Jessup:

Mr. President,—If my friend, Judge Rice, thinks that "The Commonwealth" is a very broad subject to engage your attention, what must be my feelings when called to respond, not only to all the counties, but to our common country? (*Laughter.*)

Why, I feel, Mr. Chairman, very much as that good lady who removed to the West expressed herself when, at the first broody clucking of her hen in the spring, she surrounded her with three or four dozen eggs and said to her, "Now, old hen, you came West, and this is a growing community, and you must spread yourself." (*Applause and laughter.*)

But what is a country? It is not the inanimate rock, it is not the black diamonds that lie buried in your valleys; it is not the ore in your hills, the precious metals in your mountains, nor the gold in their sands. Your country and my country are the men and women that adorn it. (*Applause.*) Look upon yon uninhabited island, and it is no country. It is mind, it is intellect, brain-power, that make a country; and to make that country one and indivisible, that intellect, that brain-power must be fully developed in the right direction, and it is to that point I desire for a moment to call your attention. The development of the men and women of the country makes the country. This, our beloved country, created on the principle of freedom of conscience, baptized in the blood of martyrs, growing strong in its very infancy and almost springing into mature manhood, increasing beyond the nations in former ages, and coming, in its first century, into a second baptism of fire and blood, because forgetful of the principles upon which it was founded, has come forth now pure, now tried in the furnace, and purified as by fire. (*Applause.*) And as our country is composed of men, so, my fellow-citizens, the future of our country depends upon you and upon me. It will be what we and others like us, its citizens, make it. Do we wish a country lasting? Let us remember the foundation-stones. Let us build upon the triple base of Purity, Patriotism, and Virtue, and we may build a tower which shall grow, and grow, and grow, until the ages grow gray and hoary, and it shall still grow onward and upward. No storms shall uproot it, and no tempests shall cause it to totter. (*Applause.*) But when we forget the foundation-stones, when political impurity and corruption shall be gnawing like a canker-worm at the basis of our institutions, when fraud and corruption shall stalk abroad in high places, when impurity shall pervade our private and social circles, when justice shall lie prostrate in our streets, then look to see the glorious tower of our liberty totter and fall, and we be numbered with the nations of the distant past, whose monuments are warnings to us of their ruin, and among whose sepulchres we are to-day excavating and bringing to light the foundations whereupon they builded, and seeing by what means they fell.

Let us learn the lessons of the past. Let us have a strong desire to preserve our institutions; let us be men of purity, men of justice, men of virtue, and we may hope to see our country a pure, and a happy, and a lasting one. (*Applause.*)

The president moved three cheers, which were given.

Music—"Star-Spangled Banner."

Mr. Winton.—The next toast is,

OUR MILITARY,

"The pride of our State—may we never need their prowess."
I presume that refers to the old song,

> "We'll have no fighting men abroad,
> No weeping maids at home."

Colonel H. M. Boies:

MR. CHAIRMAN AND GENTLEMEN,—I never was called upon to respond to so warlike a toast in so solemn a frame of mind as I am after listening to this anthem. Nor was I ever called up before in the presence of so many judges, and I sincerely trust I never may be again. I don't propose to spread myself all over the military question of the country to-night. I suppose, perhaps, it was intended I should limit myself to the National Guard of the State of Pennsylvania (*applause*), which has become in these later years renowned, not only in our own State, but all over the country, for the perfection of its organization, for the completeness of its equipment, and for the excellence of its drill. And perhaps, to narrow the subject down a little more, I might confine myself more particularly to that part of it which stands, we are all proud to feel, in the very front of the National Guard of Pennsylvania; that part of it which is comprehended within the limits of our own county. (*Applause.*) I say this with all deference to our Wilkes Barre friends, who are present as our guests. In listening to what has been said in regard to the tremendous struggle which preceded the organization and birth of Lackawanna County, a struggle which lasted through forty years, the length of time the children of Israel wandered in the desert, during which a whole generation of men wasted themselves away in the painful effort to achieve success in vain, my mind reverted to the time of the organization of the Scranton City Guard. And there is a very significant fact in this connection. After all this vain struggle and this waste of resources which has been referred to, it was not until the city of Scranton, by her courageous mayor and those historic forty men, quenched the incipient fires of communism in our streets; it was not until Scranton had demonstrated to the State that she was able to take care of herself, and, moreover, had proved conclusively by the formation of the Scranton City Guard that she intended to take care of herself in the future; it was not until this time that the Legislature of our State was influenced to grant our petition. (*Applause.*)

As soon as our organization had been formed—and I want to call your attention to this fact—gentlemen began to come up here from Luzerne to look over the Scranton City Guard,—Major Espy, Major-General Osborne, at that time the chief military dignitary of this section, and our honorable friend, Judge Woodward, who was then nothing but a colonel, I believe (*applause*); and it is a remarkable fact that after they had been here the opposition to the new-county project began to weaken. What report they took back, unless it was that of the emissaries that Moses sent out to view the promised land, that they had seen the sons of Anak there, and verily we were as grasshoppers in their eyes, and so we were in our own eyes. (*Laughter.*) Whether they took back this report or not, I cannot say, but it is certain when the project next came before the Legislature our opponents appeared to have become suddenly very weak-kneed and inefficient, and Lackawanna County sprang into existence perfect, complete, and full-armed, like Minerva from the head of Jove.

Now, this leads me back to the original thought with which I started, and that is, that the object, and aim, and scope of the National Guard is towards the triumphs of peace, and not of war. The influences which the Scranton City Guard had upon the formation of the new county were silent and unobserved, but they were powerful and irresistible as those magic influences of nature which are now bursting the seed and swelling the branch, but with a force sufficient for rending the eternal rocks asunder. We have listened to-day with delight to the grand and eloquent panegyric which our honored Judge Hand has delivered upon the majesty and dignity of the law. But the wisest law, the ablest administration of the law is vain, and weak, and powerless as the wind, unless there stands behind the law an ever-present, palpable, and sufficient power to execute it. And it is this that is the sphere of the National Guard. It is not only its sphere, its scope, and its plan, but it is at the same time its weakness, for as it exists to maintain peace and order, its very success destroys the apparent necessity for its existence. When war's alarm is shaking the land, when our country's government is trembling against the advance of the foe, there is scarcely "a man with soul so dead" who does not feel the fire of patriotism burning in his breast, and is not inspired to deeds of valor; but in time of peace, when there is no apparent necessity for military organization, it is a difficult thing to bring men up and keep them up to that point of patriotism which is necessary to sustain the National Guard, and I wish to impress this upon your minds, because there are many here to-night who are largely employers of men of my command. Now, if we can get these men into the National Guard and induce them, by inspiring their patriotic motives, to devote the time and labor that is necessary to sustain it, we should by all means do so. Because at the present time there seems no necessity for this service, encourage them in every way to devote the time that is necessary to discharge their duty rather than restrain them from devoting this time to it.

The greatest benefit the National Guard can bestow upon this community, and upon the State, and upon the country is the prevention of the evils which we dread. Therefore, it should be sustained, and therefore I appeal to you to sustain it in the future as you have in the past. (*Applause.*)

The president called for three cheers for the National Guard, which were lustily given.

Mr. Winton.—I call upon one of our most promising young attorneys, whose clarion tones are heard daily in our courts, Mr. John F. Connolly. (*Applause.*)

Mr. Connolly:

Mr. Chairman and Gentlemen,—I hardly consider it proper that a member of the bar should be called upon to respond to this toast. You all know, if there is any failing in the world that lawyers have, particularly the younger ones, it is to be egotistical. And I am afraid that the member of the bar called upon to respond to this toast is liable to fall into this error, hence I think the person who responds to it should be very guarded in his remarks. I would say, as far as the junior bar of Lackawanna

County is concerned, that it is second to none in the State—in size. (*Laughter and applause.*) Many of the young gentlemen who are classed among the junior members of the bar are men of great learning and ability. I am touching upon the egotistical part now. If any of the rising towns out West are short of lawyers, all they have to do is to call upon the bar of Lackawanna County, and we will honor their draft with either young or old.

It is true, as has been remarked by Judge Hand, that sometimes the junior members of the bar are somewhat impulsive. It is also very annoying for the Court to listen to the simplest principles and propositions of law they learned in their early days advanced by the juniors with eloquence and vehemence. But the argus-eye of the watchful client is on the budding counsellor, and he must do his duty—his whole duty. But, you must understand, the young members of the bar are eager to earn a fee. They are anxious to make a reputation and satisfy their clients, and in nine cases out of ten the class of clients who employ young attorneys are satisfied if they only "spread themselves." (*Applause.*)

It reminds me of a little anecdote I once heard. A young man, who was about to let the mantle of his father, who was an old lawyer, fall upon him, began to ask his sire what he should do in case certain things occurred. He says, "For instance, if *law* is on my side and *justice* is against me, what shall I do?" "Why," said his father, "advocate the majesty and maintenance of the *law*, though the heavens fall." "But," says he, "father, suppose *justice* is upon my side and the *law* against me, what shall I do?" "Why," he says, "argue in favor of justice, though it cause a revolution." "But," he says, "suppose neither *law* nor *justice* is upon my side, what shall I do?" "Well," he says, "paw the air and talk around it."

That, gentlemen, is the unfortunate condition the junior members of the bar are placed in. They are generally given the cases in which they must do the "pawing" and "talking around," while the cunning old seniors look on and laugh, and never for an instant think of the time when they were juniors. Just where the "line of demarkation"—as the lawyers put it—is drawn between the junior and the senior members of the bar is more than I can tell.

Now, considerable has been said here, and said with truth, about the bar of old Luzerne. That it stood foremost among the bars of the State of Pennsylvania is, as I understand it, a conceded fact. Some of the ablest jurists that Pennsylvania ever boasted of were members of the Luzerne bar, and I am proud to say that all the senior members of the Scranton bar, and a great many of the juniors, once belonged to, and yet, at times, grace that bar with their presence. (*Applause.*)

I regret that some member of the senior bar who is not a comparative stranger among us did not respond to the preceding toast. The gentleman who eloquently responded has been here but a short time, and the task of answering for the seniors should not have been imposed upon him. Yet he did it so well, I feel that I must thank him in their name.

It is no easy matter to become a lawyer. It may be an easy matter for a young man with an ordinary education and ordinary ability, to be admitted to the bar. But there is a good deal of difference between being admitted to the bar and becoming a lawyer. The young man who starts out in life with the idea of getting admitted to the bar and stopping there, falls very far short of reaching the mark. The young lawyer who proposes to succeed in his profession must be incessant in his labors, and he must be a man of ability. His work may be compared to that of the clock. It must be work without *haste*, work without *rest*. Unless he does that—unless he works without *haste* and works without *rest*—he will never attain to that pinnacle of fame to which many of the senior members of the old Luzerne bar have attained. (*Applause.*)

On behalf of the bar of Lackawanna County, although they are quite numerous, I will say we have among them men of ability, men of energy, and, above all, men of integrity. (*Applause.*)

A man who has not integrity, his ability amounts to nothing as a lawyer, because if a man is not truthful and honest—honest to himself, honest to his clients, honest to the Court—he never *can*, he never *will*, succeed as a lawyer. (*Applause.*) I may say for the young men of the bar that they must generally bear all the rebukes and rebuffs of the Court, and when there is any "sitting-down-upon" to be done by the Court, it generally falls to the unhappy lot of the unfortunate junior, whose client is waiting and listening in some prominent part of the court-room, ready to seal his doom unless he comes up to said client's fancied standard. And all the while the young man is quoting "hornbook" law, and the Court is incensed.

I say it with pardonable pride, that the junior—and I might include a majority of the senior—bar of Lackawanna County are straightforward, honest, honorable men. Their escutcheon is as yet unblemished and untarnished, and I trust it will remain so, and in that temple of Justice, the corner-stone of which was laid to-day, may they carve their way to fame and fortune. And in a few years I trust that the bar of Lackawanna County may not only be the first in Pennsylvania, but the first in the Union.

Mr. Winton.—Nearly nine years ago I stood in the city of Philadelphia, in the hall of that convention composed of constitutional tinkers, and sitting there I heard two men advocate Lackawanna County. It was the day when Lewis Pughe and A. B. Dunning made their famous speeches in our behalf. (*Applause.*) Looking with eyes toward the future, I was satisfied that that was the stepping-stone, and I said, "Oh! my prophetic soul, mine uncle!" (*Laughter and applause.*)

And now, to respond to the toast of

OUR CONSTITUTION,

I call upon a man who has held the laboring-oar for thirty years, A. B. Dunning. (*Applause.*)

Mr. Dunning:

MR. CHAIRMAN AND GENTLEMEN,—I feel a pride to-night in meeting my old associates in this new-county fight that I am sure I will be unable to express. After the many speeches we have heard, and the manner in which this whole question has been discussed, I feel as though there was no ground for me to stand upon. In fact, my friend Merrifield carried the fortress in the outset. (*Applause.*) But, gentlemen, I never saw the hour during the last thirty-five years that I was not a new-county man. Now, that is a good ways back. Thirty years ago I was elected to the Legislature, a young man, and the only reason I consented to be a candidate, leaving my business and going to the Legislature for $3 a day—that was the sum-total paid, and if you stayed over 100 days you got $1.50, and no more—was because of the interest I felt in Lackawanna County. I had been familiar with the fight from its inception. I remember well when it was raised, and William Merrifield, the father of the gentleman who introduced the topic here to-night, was elected to the Legislature, and nearly gave us a county. I don't propose to say much about what was done by our friends in the lower end at that time, but the defeat of the measure was one of the smart things they did. But taking the thing all the way along, step by step, I look around me to-night and see gentlemen who stood shoulder to shoulder with me in the Legislature and elsewhere giving material aid. Dr. Throop spent two entire winters there, giving most valuable assistance. I was fortunate enough always to pass the bill in the House, and recollect, the second time it was passed, we had so strong an assurance that it was going through the Senate that my friend Throop, in the full confidence that the thing was accomplished, gave what you may call a little blow-out. He gave a banquet to the friends of the bill that cost him two or three hundred dollars, thus showing the interest he felt on the subject. But I cannot enumerate the many who have given years of service and means to this long-continued struggle. None among them all, however, were more liberal than Dr. Throop, and Col. Ira Tripp, both of whom have kept open house at Harrisburg entire sessions, and their well-known liberality tells the story, so far as expense goes. "All is well that ends well." The struggle is over, and we meet here to-night to shake hands over the bloodless chasm, old and new-county friends to rejoice together. I have the most kindly recollections of old mother Luzerne, and many of her worthy sons are bidding us God-speed in our departure from the old hearthstone.

The lateness of the hour admonishes me to be brief. I will therefore come at once to the toast—"The Constitution, the stepping-stone to the new county." I need not tell you, gentlemen, that constitutions are the fundamental principles or rules for the government of states or nations, dating back many centuries, finding especial voice in *Magna Charta*, when the English Barons in the thirteenth century forced from King John the great charter restraining monarchy and enlarging the rights of the people against kingly tyranny; that *Magna Charta* found its way across the mighty deep in the "Mayflower," its principles taking root in the virgin soil on this side of the Atlantic, growing and spreading until it culminated in the sanguinary struggle of the Revolution, which gave to us the Constitution of 1788, being the first charter of human liberty ever given to an absolutely free people; nor how in the progress of events, like the rapidly-growing boy, the people became too large for their clothes, and Uncle Samuel's pants were found so short that in 1837–38 it required material for a larger pattern.

Good Uncle Samuel, finding himself and family so well dressed in the new suit, felt an inspiration for greater deeds and broader enterprise. A forward movement is ordered along the line. Coal is mined, canals were dug, railroads constructed, factories were built, forges and furnaces, from their thousand stacks, sent their leaping flames toward the heavens, and the busy hum of industry filled the land with joyful sounds.

But history repeats itself. In 1873 the fashions were found so changed that the garment must be revised, and, "Eureka!" in one of the pockets, safely tucked away, is found our *Magna Charta*, inscribed "Lackawanna County," the corner-stone of whose temple of Justice was laid to-day, or, possibly, it may be the "stepping-stone" referred to in the toast to which I am attempting to respond.

Now, gentlemen, I fear I have already wearied you, and, knowing you are anxious to listen to the gentlemen who are to follow me, without dwelling upon our long-continued struggle before success crowned our efforts, our hopes, our fears, or speaking of the treason of pretended friends, or after, how the heart was made sick by hope deferred, the object of our efforts so near at times, and, ah! so far, I will close by returning my sincere thanks for your kindness in recognizing me as one of the humble workers in the cause we all had so much at heart.

Music—Overture, "Aurora."

Mr. Winton.—There is one man here among us who seems to like Wilkes Barre, and has some cases down there. I will now ask him to speak to the toast,

OUR MANUFACTURING INTERESTS.

Mr. W. W. Scranton:

Mr. Chairman and Gentlemen,—When the new county was first talked about, they came to me and said it was a great thing for manufacturing interests. They said law was going to be cheap. I have tried it a good deal since then, but I think they made a mistake in that.

Now, I don't hold myself as a great many do about the town, but it seems to me that this community is based principally upon the mining of coal—half of it depends upon it. Now these mines are being worked out more and more, and, in my mind, it is not going to be forever. It will not be one hundred years before these are all worked out. To me it seems that a great many of us here are going to live to see the time when the growth of this town, so far as it depends upon mining, is not going to increase. When that time comes, we have got to fall back upon something else. It seems to me that we ought to provide for that beforehand, and provide, as far as possible, for our manufacturing interests. For that, we want good government; we want law and order; we want moderate taxation. If you will give us these things, we will prosper and foster these little industries, and in our time we will take care of you. (*Applause.*)

Mr. Winton.—Now we come to a mighty power,

THE PRESS,

and, to respond, we have one of its brightest ornaments—a man who was ever ready at Harrisburg to send therefrom at midnight the breeziest news in our behalf, making the long fingers of the telegraph click out our successes; always ready here at home, also, to assist us. I call upon the Hon. J. E. Barrett.

Mr. Barrett:

Mr. Chairman and Gentlemen,—I have been admonished by our worthy chairman that, as the hour is well advanced, those who have long speeches to make would do well to cut them short. I am further admonished by the frequent visits of the "printer's devil," who has been flitting in and out during the evening for copy, that the paper will go to press very soon; therefore, I must be brief. Besides, it is rather dangerous for the press, in the presence of so many judges and lawyers, to be too free with its utterances and opinions, as every careful editor must always keep in mind the fact that caution is quite as essential as courage, since we have such a thing as a stringent libel law in Pennsylvania. I am pleased to know, however, that in case I should be arraigned in a temple of Justice for anything uttered in this presence, I could bring up my case in banc, as I believe we have a full bench here this evening, in which I have full confidence. Gentlemen, it has been said frequently that the press is the great lever in the world's progress; such I hope it will continue, playing its part in the world's history side by side with law and justice. In returning from the ceremony of laying the corner-stone of our new court-house this afternoon, after standing in the rain, unconscious of the discomfort of the weather because of the great pleasure afforded in listening to Judge Hand's admirable address, I fell in with a friend who told me that he had often skated over the site selected for our temple of Justice, and that he had also, on many occasions, caught bull-heads there. This suggested to my mind a pleasant possibility. We all know that most lawyers and many judges are fond of the good old sport with which the name of Izaak Walton is inseparably connected, and it occurred to my mind just then that for a trifling outlay the county commissioners might provide for excellent fishing on the bench. It would be a most agreeable way to vary the monotony if the judges could drop a line into the basement and enjoy themselves piscatorially in capturing an occasional bull-head, while the intelligent jury, under the somnolent effect of some great advocate's plea, went in quest of pastoral pleasures to the land of Nod.

But, as the press plays its part in the domain of progress, I don't propose that one of its humble representatives will bore you this evening with a tedious dissertation. The press, whatever else may be its shortcomings, is never at a loss to give advice to judges, lawyers, governors, presidents, and emperors. It can dictate a policy for the Peruvians that would discount all the efforts of Blaine or Shipherd, and although the North Pole has never been discovered, it can tell exactly how it can be done. And need you wonder at this, when the electricity of the world is the servant of the press, and through the still hours of night becomes the subtle courier that carries information from the uttermost ends of the earth, to add to our stock of knowledge at the breakfast-table? With the electric telegraph and the press, those twin-ministers of light and liberty, error is impossible, and tyranny becomes a monster of such hideous mien " as to be hated needs but to be seen." The press needs no praise; it is its own best eulogist, and I trust that in the future of Lackawanna County it will be found aiding the right. It was my pleasure to see at Harrisburg, during the progress of our new-county bill, several of the faces that grace this festive board. They were always zealous and energetic in the interest of the people of this section. In those days we all realized, more fully than at any other time, the value of a friendly press, and it was always a pleasure to me to meet a newspaper editor or correspondent whom I could convince of the justice of our side. As the press of Lackawanna has stood by the new county at its birth, and as it stands by it now, so, I trust, it will be found advocating its interests in all time to come; advocating an upright judiciary and the fearless administration of the law, and always raising its voice

> " 'Gainst the wrong that needs resistance,
> For the cause that lacks assistance,
> For the future in the distance,
> And the good that it can do."

(*Applause.*)

Mr. Winton.—I now call upon Mr. E. P. Kingsbury for

OUR CITY.

Mr. Kingsbury:

MR. CHAIRMAN AND GENTLEMEN,—I appreciate the honor conferred upon me in being requested to respond to the toast, "The City of Scranton, the third in this Commonwealth," but it is hard for me to understand why I should have been selected for this response, unless because it is customary to go to the "oldest inhabitants" for information, always being ready to make due allowance for their old age, general debility, and the consequent loss of a portion of their mental faculties. (*Applause.*) This may explain it, and, explaining it, will at the same time account for the feebleness of my effort.

Scranton is properly named, perpetuating as it does the names and memories of the gentlemen who planted here the seeds of industry, watering the soil with their wealth, practical knowledge, and personal zeal, causing to spring forth from the wilderness of a few years ago this city, now the third in population in the great Commonwealth of Pennsylvania.

But is it the third in population only? I think not. Could good Uncle Joseph Albright whisper in your ears the total shipments of coal during the past year in his department; could Brother Storrs, from the stores of his memory, tell you his story for the year 1881; and, following him, the genial gentleman from the old town of Gibsonburg, who thinks well enough of our city to invest largely here in real-estate, relate to you in the "Jermyn" dialect " what he knows about coal-mining," to say nothing of what could be added by the almost endless number of smaller operators who are " Connellizing" here (*applause*), I have a notion that Scranton would rank well as the third city of Pennsylvania in this particular. We might go on and speak of our iron-mills and steel-works, our blast-furnaces, machine-shops, and silk-mills, and many other branches of mechanical industry, and thus show that we can, with much reason, lay claim to being the third city of our State in this particular also. There are some things we may well be proud of as a city. We are well governed, and good order, peace, and quietness prevail to a greater extent than in any other city of its size I know of. I doubt whether there is a city, in or out of our State, with so large a population, where crime and lawlessness exists to a lesser degree than here, and where so small a police force is necessary to maintain good order. (*Applause.*) When we consider the rapidity of our growth, this is truly remarkable. Why, so late as 1852, and even later, I think, the voters of what was then called Harrison (now Scranton) had to go to Hyde Park to vote, and the whole of them put together could be crowded into one of our street cars. Yet at the last charter election, in February last, when our excellent mayor was re-elected, nearly seven thousand votes were polled.

Again, we should congratulate ourselves upon the state of our finances, our city debt, after deducting assets, being but about $260,000. This, certainly, as compared with cities of like population, is not formidable—certainly not formidable enough to forbid its reasonable increase for the purpose of properly paving Lackawanna Avenue.

Again, Scranton, as a city, may be proud of its banks and banking institutions; for there is to-day on deposit in them, subject to check, over $3,500,000, and not one of these institutions but that can easily and promptly meet every one of its obligations. How well I remember when yon First National commenced business in a little frame building (half the dimensions of this room) on Lackawanna Avenue, and the cashier daily placing all the valuables of the bank in a tin box 7 x 9, and depositing it for safe-keeping in the vault of Mason, Meylert & Co. It would take a pretty good-sized vault to hold them now.

But, Mr. Chairman, time will not permit me to say more as to the present proud position that our city occupies, or to give more than a passing allusion to the splendid future which seems opening up before her, and I will conclude with the sentiment, "The City of Scranton, now the third in the Commonwealth: may the rapidity of her growth, and her successes in the past, be an earnest of her glory in the future," only adding that, while in many things she is the third in our Commonwealth, in others she is *first*, for no other city can boast of as big and irregular paving-stones as Lackawanna Avenue can show, nor of mud as deep and thick as can be found on Wyoming. (*Applause.*)

Music.—Plantation Medley.

Mr. Winton.—Out in Covington Township there lives a family so highly respectable, so esteemed, that we delight to honor the very name. I call upon Mr. T. H. Dale to respond to the toast,

OUR COMMERCIAL INTERESTS.

Mr. Dale:

Mr. Chairman and Gentlemen,—I rather suspect that a shrewd man, one who was engaged in commercial interests, could take the self-congratulations and self-praise we have indulged in to-night and discount it fifty per cent., and then have a very reasonable capital to start the new county. (*Applause.*)

When the author Hawthorne was requested to respond to a toast at a banquet given by the Lord Mayor of London, he was greatly agitated, and sought the counsel of a friend as to what he should do. The friend's advice was this, that when he was called upon he must certainly rise to his feet, or else the assembled guests would think he was a fool and did not know enough to say anything, but after he had risen to his feet he must say just as little as possible, or else the same guests would think he was a fool, and did not know when he had said enough. I was reminded of this incident by the fact that when your genial Toast-Master notified me that, as President of the Board of Trade, I would be expected to respond to the toast " Our Commercial Interests," he was particularly emphatic that I should be very brief and not say very much, just as though our commercial interests were a sort of pigmy affair, and could be readily handled in a speech of two or three minutes.

Now, if I may be allowed to use a paradox, commercial interests first made Scranton, and then Scranton made its commercial interests. For before Scranton was, before it had assumed its present stately proportions and "magnificent distances," as so graphically described by Mr. Kingsbury in responding to the toast " Our City," and long before any lawyers were here to give a banquet, " commercial interests" in the persons of the Messrs. Scrantons had sought it out; and the company they organized turned out to be the foundation for that which has since become Scranton City, with all its varied industries, and all its extended business interests. I know, sir, that in the flight of time many things we ought to remember sink out of sight, and the years close over them, but there are some things that remain visible across the years; and so it is that to-night I desire to pay tribute to the indomitable perseverance, to the will, the pluck, and the energy of these pioneers in our commercial interests, and to assert that their methods have been adopted, and have become characteristic of those who have since developed our commercial industries. And it is worthy of mention that if our town is noted for any one thing above another, it is for the push, and the vim, and the energy of those having in charge our commercial interests, and out of this vim and this push has sprung that of which we are so justly proud, the present flattering condition and position of our business interests. (*Applause.*) I feel, too, that credit should not be withheld from others who have aided

in building up our industries and our business enterprises—
manufacturers, bankers, merchants, even lawyers; all have done
their share, and all deserve credit. I shall not even omit a
somewhat noted character, residing on our side of the river,
who some time since started a store in one of the back streets
of our city, and who was inclined to boast a great deal about
the wonderful stock of goods he was carrying, and the large
business he was doing, and who, on one occasion, after expati-
ating largely upon his great purchases, declared he had "everything in the *hardware* line except *molasses.*" (*Laughter.*)

Well, sir, out of these efforts has grown a commercial interest
that to-day is represented by over 850 firms doing business here,
by $7,000,000 invested in iron- and steel-works, by over $6,000,000
invested in merchandise, and over $4,000,000 invested in other
industries and other enterprises, making in all over $17,000,000
invested in business, exclusive of the great railroad and coal
corporations centring here.

I ought not to omit to mention something of the wonderful
growth of these corporate interests, but I am admonished that
one cannot treat this subject in a five minutes' speech, and so I
will simply take the Delaware, Lackawanna and Western Railroad Company, and let that company illustrate what all these
companies are doing in the way of developing our commercial
interests. There was shipped from this region by the Delaware,
Lackawanna and Western Railroad in 1852 (the first full year
of coal shipments by this road) 67,487 tons of anthracite coal,
and this amount has gone on increasing year by year until in
1881 this road shipped the enormous amount of 4,511,636 tons
of coal. To accomplish this result, there has been added to its
property coal-mine after coal-mine, and to its system of roads
railroad after railroad, until to-day it is one of the largest and
strongest corporate interests in our country. And the progress
of the coal industry as shown by this company can also be
applied to a greater or lesser extent to other companies doing
business in this region. The marvellous development of the coal
industry has naturally and rapidly developed our general commercial interests; and in the words of Mr. Storrs, the general
coal-agent of the Delaware, Lackawanna and Western Company,
"if the time ever comes (as I believe it must soon come) when

the consumption of coal overtakes and equals the production, so that there shall be full work for those engaged in the mining and shipping of coal, we shall see a degree of prosperity for these regions heretofore unsurpassed." (*Applause.*)

And now, Mr. Chairman, since this is an occasion for merriment, and inasmuch as self-congratulations and spread-eagleism seem to be the fashion rather than dry figures and statistics, I declare to you that while I am neither a prophet nor the son of a prophet, I yet indulge the hope that in that future which geologists assure us is coming, when the sands of Jersey shall have been covered by the waters of the Atlantic, when great New York shall have been engulfed, when the huckleberry heights of Pocono shall have been submerged, then, sir, will come our glory; then our own classic Lackawanna will have been made navigable, through an appropriation secured by our Congressman, and Scranton will be the metropolis, the beat of whose trade-pulsations will be felt to the utmost limits of the great Republic. (*Laughter and applause.*)

Mr. Winton.—Now I come to one of the California pioneers. I had prepared some remarks, but the best thing I can say is to say he was the man in the gap—the Hon. R. H. McKune.

Mr. McKune:

Mr. Chairman and Gentlemen,—I feel somewhat out of place to-night in responding to the toast, "Our Fire Department." All the other gentlemen that have spoken here this evening have spoken upon subjects they are perfectly familiar with, but the Toast Committee have placed me upon a different ground. I must say this—that this day and this night have been among the happy days and nights of my life. (*Applause.*) The day of the laying of the corner-stone of the new court-house for the County of Lackawanna brings to my mind an incident of which I was a participant in 1850, when, standing upon Telegraph Hill, looking down the straits, as the steamer "Oregon" entered the gates, and upon her fore-sail was printed in large letters, "California—she has been admitted to the Union." We, as pioneers in '49, had in convention met and given birth to a State, which went forth in her full completeness, clothed about her loins with the leaves of the vine and fig. Upon her breasts she bore the sheaves of her bounteous land with sandals of silver,

Upon her brow she wore a crown of the purest gold. In her hands were the products of her vineyards and the fruits of her orchards. As she went forth her path was strewn with flowers such as no queen of the earth had ever trodden upon in their native beauty. As she approached the capitol of our country, where sat in council the sages of the Union, her strength, beauty, and wealth entranced them all. But, alas for the cupidity of man. Some of those sages soon raised against her their opposition. For she was commissioned to bear to the capitol the voice of her people, who, through her constitution, had bade her say that they had decreed that all men who stood upon her soil should be freemen; that no blot of slavery should blacken her escutcheon. She was the first to enunciate the grand principle of "Popular Sovereignty"—that principle that was to bring the minds of the sages in conflict. In the council chamber stood, pleading her cause, Webster, Dickinson, Benton, Seward, and others, while Calhoun and Berrien led on the forces in opposition. There she stood for long and weary months, awaiting permission to enter into union with her sister States. She was not ashamed of her representatives, for among them was Fremont, to the world known as a hardy and successful explorer, who had been the first to place the flag of our country upon the peaks of the Rocky Mountains, who had secured the friendship of Kit Carson and others of those adventurous men who had passed beyond the pale of civilization, and had joined their lives and fortunes with the red men, who then held almost undisputed possession of the vast plains beyond the great rivers. He, better than any other man in the country, realized the value to the Union of the acquisition of California. He plead with the senators to go forth with him and stand upon Mount Diablo, and look away to the West, across to the Pacific, and behold, whitening her bosom, the great fleet of merchantmen who were bringing as their lading the products of the lands of China, Japan, and the islands of the sea; and behold, as they enter the portals of the Golden Gate, they salute the flag which would represent the great country that lay stretched along its thousands of miles, until it meets its boundary in the Atlantic Ocean. At the east lie the valleys of the Sacramento and San Joaquin, while beyond, in the forests, were to be seen the great trees—the wonder and admiration of the world. Still beyond lay the valley of the Yosemite, where the travellers of all nations who are permitted to enter within its portals stand in astonishment and awe as they look around on every side and behold the effect of nature's great forces, which has piled cliff on cliff until their lofty peaks pierce the clouds, telling to man there is a God, while the mountain brooks, leaping along their way and plunging over mighty precipices, forming those beautiful cataracts which waft forth songs of praise to the bounteous Giver of all good and perfect gifts. So great a heritage as this great State, without money and without price, was never before offered to a nation.

I thank you, sir, for introducing me as an old Californian amid these pioneers of Scranton gathered here this evening, as it has revived the memories of those days when I, too, was a pioneer. I said that day, when the news arrived that we had been admitted to the Union, was a happy day to me.

And so when we stood there in the Chamber, tallying as we did when the vote was carried to 101 on the third reading of the new-county bill, that was a happy moment. But there was something in the future,—there was an election,—and to-night we have no question at all in regard to the future. Thanks to the first commissioners of the county of Lackawanna, they have laid their ground well, and the noble edifice to be erected is now in the hands of their successors, which, I have no doubt, under the contractor and the architect, and the vigilant supervision of the commissioners, will rise in all its beauty and majesty, so it will be an honor not only to our city, but to the Commonwealth and to the country. (*Applause.*)

Permit me, Mr. President, in behalf of the fire department of this city, to thank you for remembering them at this banquet and at this time. You citizens of Scranton have as fine an organization as there is in the United States, and are you aware, fellow-taxpayers of the city of Scranton, that your whole fire department of this city costs less money than one-half of the cost of a single company in Philadelphia or New York? (*Applause.*) This city is run under the system of cheap government which Mr. Scranton referred to, and the fire department has had but $5000 yearly appropriation for the last six or seven years, out of which they run their steamers and hose-carts, and supply the hose, and do the work free for you. I speak to you, gentlemen, as representatives of the city of Scranton. Look well to your interests; instruct your law-makers of the city to care well for the firemen, for the day is fast approaching when the volunteer department, if not well cared for, will demand from your hands a paid fire department, which will cost you much more than the present department costs you now. I speak with some pride as a fireman. In 1842 I was elected as a fireman in the village of Newburg. It has been my privilege to be a fireman from that day until one year ago. Thirty-six years of my life have I not laid down at night on my bed, or undressed myself, without knowing where every piece of clothing I wore, or would be compelled to wear if the fire-bell should call me out, was to be found.

I look back over the labors thus performed with feelings of deep satisfaction, and, while life is given unto me, expect to do all in my humble power for the interests of the volunteer firemen. I feel highly delighted with the banquet, for it has gathered together some of the pioneers of Scranton, and many of the workers in the new-county cause, and all has gone as merry as a marriage-bell.

Mr. Winton.—I call upon Mr. F. J. Fitzsimmons to respond to the toast,

WOMAN.

Mr. Fitzsimmons :

Mr. Chairman and Gentlemen,—I will say but a word, as I feel much embarrassed in speaking before this audience. I am inexperienced and young, yet not so young but that I can remember when the Democratic party were successful, and I don't think I will have to live much longer to find it successful again. (*Applause*.)

* * * * * * * * *

The locomotive, with gleaming eye and thunderous voice, as with lightning-speed it annihilates distances, is the grandest of objects, but when it jumps the track and is stuck in the mud it becomes one of the most despicable and helpless objects that can be seen; yet a woman out of her place—"out of her sphere," if you please—is a still more despicable object. In some of the Western States, I learn with alarm, she is being admitted into legal ranks. (*Laughter.*) While the immortal Greeley advised young men to do otherwise, yet my advice to lawyers is, "Don't go West." (*Laughter and applause.*)

What chance would a most ingenious or eloquent advocate have in winning a case before a jury that would be appealed to, implored, and their appearances complimented by some fair Venus? (*Laughter and applause.*)

If it were within the range of possibility that the Court, too, would lend a willing ear to her gentle requests, and lean towards her in its rulings, it requires no prophetic gift to say, with some degree of certainty, that the lawyers of the present may be the farmers of the future. It certainly is within the compass of possibility that the judiciary might become influenced by her wooings. This would be made possible only by the death of our present judges. Some judges die, but few resign. They will in all probability hold court till the Great Judge sends after them to give their proceedings here below a final review.

Woman has been in all ages the kindling inspiration of patriotism, eloquence, poesy, and song. She watched over our infancy, and would not permit the winds of winter to visit us too roughly. She is found by the bedside of the sick, administering every comfort that the fever-heated brain suggests. She places the last wreath of affection on the coffin-lid and decorates the grave with floral offerings. Her tribute of friendship, her mementoes of kindness, her deeds of charity, are too numerous to be further mentioned at this time. Let us hope that at all times to come her virtues may receive from a generous manhood the reward they so richly deserve, and that the bar of Lackawanna, though young in years, yet great in promise, may not only acquire a laudable standing, from a professional standpoint, but that its members may always willingly render their services in defending the fortunes and reputations of the sex, on behalf of whom I have so poorly responded on this highly sociable and memorable occasion. (*Applause.*)

Mr. Winton.—I call upon Mr. S. T. Scranton, who now resides in the foreign land of Jersey, but who was one of the pioneers of Scranton, and who helped to lay well and deep our sure footing whereon we have built so well.

Mr. Selden T. Scranton:

Mr. Chairman,—It gives me great pleasure to see so many citizens of Scranton, a great many of whom I esteem as friends. At this late hour I cannot expect to detain you, but only rise to express my great pleasure in having been here with you on this joyous occasion. I can but feel the liveliest interest in the prosperity of this new county of Lackawanna and of this city of Scranton. I remember it when there were only seventeen souls in this place. I have watched its progress, growth, and prosperity for forty-one years, from the 20th of last August, and shall, while life lasts, look upon it with the liveliest interest. I wish you all the prosperity and success you are worthy of. (*Applause.*)

The chairman then called on Colonel Charles Scranton for a speech.

Mr. Charles Scranton:

Mr. Chairman, and Gentlemen of the Lackawanna County Bar, the Luzerne County Bar, and all the other "Bars" here present (*laughter*), and Fellow-Citizens,—I am very unexpectedly with you on this joyous occasion. When I left my home in New Jersey this afternoon, I did not even know that anything unusual was in progress in your city. I find myself your guest, and now you have called on me for a speech. At this late, or early, hour, after so many good things have been said, by so many good speakers, what shall I say? Shall I go back to the early days of your town's history, and call to mind some of the pleasant incidents of my early recollections of Slocum Hollow? As this part has been somewhat overlooked, I will, in my brief remarks, refer to the glory and work of the early days of your city's history; for, from its foundation to the present time, I have watched with deepest interest every step in your rapid rise and progress, your wealth and prosperity. Then you were a feeble folk. Now you have risen to rank and station, and you are here to-night to celebrate a great event in your history,—the laying of the corner-stone of a new court-house of a county second to none for its real wealth and enterprise in this great Commonwealth. But we must not despise the day of small things. Forty years ago I believe there was but one lawyer (the late Charles H. Silkman) between Carbondale and Pittston, and only the small church-building in the same territory, and very few (and they were very small) school-houses in this same valley. Now your lawyers are numerous, as I notice by the number here present, and your churches and school-houses are numerous, and noted for their style of architecture, and the moral and educational influences going out therefrom. (*Applause.*) I will give you one or two items that can hardly fail to interest those living at that time, and those who have been born since. At that time our worthy chairman was about the only doctor in this section. The families were far apart and generally very healthy. The whole vote of Providence Township, if my memory serves me, was about 147. The doctor, *though exceedingly conscientious,* had pretty hard work to keep his patients at that early day sick long enough to make a fair living. (*Laughter.*) He had to go into the lumber and drug business and trade a horse occasionally to make a decent living. I remember having been called up from New Jersey to help in place of one of the book-keepers who was sick, or nearly so, by the loneliness here after coming from the large town of Oxford. It was then that, in order to relieve the monotony of the situation, I proposed getting up a debating school. The thing took quickly, and I was appointed to draw up the constitution and by-laws, and our worthy chairman was appointed to give the opening lecture. I need not tell you it was a grand one. (*Laughter.*) I believe it had to be repeated at numerous villages in the county. The late Hon. W. W. Ketcham and others began in this little thing to show their brain-power. For the generous part which I bore in the premises I was, with Mr. Charles F. Mattes, excused from taking part in the debates, and we were made "gentlemen judges" for the whole winter. Martin L. Newman, the chief of police of the town, and the only constable for miles around, was also on hand as a debater. Another great event transpired. It was resolved, at a public meeting held at the house of N. D. Green, Hyde Park, that the coming national anniversary ought to be and should be celebrated with imposing ceremony, and the citizens of Razorville, Bucktown, and Slocum Hollow were invited to co-operate to make it a grand success, and show the folks down the valley what could be done up this way. There are a few yet living who well remember the day,—

how the delegations came in from the places named; how proudly old Captain Feltz, the grand marshal, led the procession, with "sword and buckler" by his side, and his numerous Masonic emblems dangling by his coat-collar (*laughter*); how the delegation from Slocum Hollow, in single file, fell in line with Colonel George W. Scranton at the head, Dr. Throop second, with fiddle and bow, Charles F. Mattes next with clarionet, some other one with bass-drum, Esquire Grant, R. W. Olmstead, William Sands, William Manness, and some twenty others, all marching to the tune of "Auld Lang Syne" down the old stump-fence road, over the teetering bridge, up the steep side-hill (*laughter*), and solemnly into the little church, well packed with eager listeners to the oration that was to follow, and the martial music, and to hear the rendering by the vocal and instrumental powers present of the ode prepared for the occasion by one of the *literati* of the valley, which was all played and sung to the principal tune, "Auld Lang Syne." (*Laughter.*) I wish I had time to recite it, and could remember it. (*Cries of* "Give us a verse!") Well, it ran about this way:

> "The land whereon our village stands,
> Where once the savage trod,
> Is mostly cleared, you'll understand,
> And covered o'er with sod."

(*Loud calls were here given for more of it.*) Well, another verse ran about thus:

> "Brave Washington, now dead and gone,
> No more of him you'll see;
> America, her greatest son,
> He gained her liberty."

Now, to be more serious. I have heard from the gentlemen who preceded me of the great struggle you have gone through with in finally obtaining your object,—a new county. How that, as you always need, you have had the good offices and friendship of your worthy chairman, the doctor, all the way through, in having the birth of this new daughter of old Mother Luzerne more than a still-birth. But, as the legal gentlemen present have stated it, no more new counties can be made under your present Constitution. I therefore have to congratulate the friends from old Luzerne on the fact that no more counties are to be cut from her territory; that she will be spared all these birth-pains in the future; and now, side by side, these two great counties, Luzerne and Lackawanna, one in interest and origin, are to go on hand-in-hand in all the great work before them. And, in conclusion, let me here say that the broad, deep, and solid foundations laid here by the late William Henry, Colonel George W. Scranton, Philip H. Mattes, Sanford Grant (who still lives, and ought to be here to-night), and Selden T. Scranton, at the beginning, and later aided by Joseph H. Scranton and others, with the good will and fellowship of your chairman and the other citizens then in this vicinity, have made it possible to have this new county, this corner-stone laid, this banquet, this city—the third in size in this Commonwealth—so well governed and orderly, that its police force is said to be the smallest, for the same-sized population, in the Union; and for my friend, Mr. John Jermyn, who sits there, and who did his first day's work in the garden of Mr. S. T. Scranton for seventy-five cents, to be a millionaire; for your honored chairman to be another; for my good friend on my right, Mr. J. J. Albright, to come back from old Virginia shorn of his fortune, and now rich beyond measure; for my young friend Connolly, whose father did good work for the pioneers at the first old furnace, to be the respondent to-night for the junior members of the bar of Lackawanna County; and so I might go on, did time and your patience permit, and call out by name hundreds of others who have made a name and fame, and money, and homes, here in this city and valley, because of the solid foundations laid, of the privations, hard work, and struggles of the pioneers, which were overcome by their indomitable pluck, and aided by your churches, and schools, and good-fellowship. All these combinations, with those before alluded to, form, in history, a part of the enjoyment of this festive occasion. May God bless you all in all the proper aims and objects of life, and "Justice, with her even scales," be deeply fixed in your hearts, in your business transactions for yourselves and others.

Gentlemen, I thank you for your patience, and your kind attention to my remarks, which have been too long extended. (*Cries*, " Go on! Go on!") No, it is already too late. (*Applause*.)

APPENDIX.   545

The President called upon Mr. J. J. Albright.

Mr. Albright:

MR. CHAIRMAN AND GENTLEMEN,—You all know I am no speaker. I can only say I was here among the first pioneers. When I came I was offered this whole plot of ground, about 500 acres, for $10 an acre. (*A voice:* "Why did you not buy it?") I had not the five thousand dollars. (*Laughter.*) At that time I did not remain here, but went to Virginia and returned in 1851. The outgrowth of Scranton has been much greater than any of us, even in what our friends call our fancy flights, ever conceived; and as we have listened this evening to the recitals of the pluck and energy that have been for forty years with the citizens of this section on the subject of a new county, so I may say the same spirit has been manifested in her coal, her manufacturing, and commercial interests. (*Applause.*) Dark clouds have settled, and storms at times have swept over us, and many have been shipwrecked, but dismay came not so strong as to entirely dishearten all. There are those here to-night, and in our cemeteries lie others, who were always ready when the least glimmer of light appeared above the horizon to push forward to victory. (*Applause.*)

Mr. Chairman and gentlemen, I am thankful that I have been permitted to see this day. It has been to me one of great joy, and as I have listened this evening to the many most excellent speeches of congratulation, I desire to say that, while I wish to see prosperity and success on every hand, yet I more rejoice in the success of every effort that tends to add prosperity to this city. I trust that no person who was active in the formation of this new county will ever have cause to regret the labor performed, and that the temple of Justice, whose corner-stone has this day been laid, will always be the house wherein *equal and exact justice to all* shall be administered by pure and upright judges. (*Applause.*)

Calls for Mr. John Jermyn.

Mr. Jermyn:

MR. PRESIDENT AND GENTLEMEN,—I do not know as I would have been here with you to enjoy this most pleasant occasion if I had had the least intimation that I should be called upon for a speech, and I beg to assure you, gentlemen, that, with the exception of this call, I am free to say that this has been one of the most agreeable evenings, and I may say mornings, I have ever been permitted to enjoy. The reminiscences of many incidents that have transpired during my residence here, some of which I was permitted to be a participant in, has brought to my mind the period when I came first to Scranton. The world has dealt generously with me since then, and for that success I feel under great obligations to one who at all times and under all circumstances was my friend, and who, as his brother has told you, I did my first day's work for in this locality. I have desired for some years to give a public recognition of the esteem in which I hold his memory. This, to me, seems my opportunity, and, as no monument marks the spot where he now lies, I would suggest that a subscription for the erection of a monument to Colonel George W. Scranton be now started, and you may put me down for one, two, or three hundred dollars. (*Applause.*)

Dr. B. H. Throop seconded the suggestion, and H. M. Edwards, Esq., moved the appointment of a committee of five to act with the chairman in carrying it into effect. The committee was appointed, and consists of Dr. Throop and Messrs. John Jermyn, R. W. Archbald, H. M. Edwards, J. J. Albright, and Henry A. Kingsbury.

Three cheers for the Toast-Master were lustily given.

Calls for F. W. Gunster.

Mr. Gunster:

MR. CHAIRMAN AND GENTLEMEN,—When I consented to act on the Committee on Toasts, it was with the distinct understanding that I would not be called upon to speak to-night. I tried to do my work well on that committee, and the fact that we have been so well entertained this evening is proof that the work of that committee has been done well.

I am sorry that the gentleman who was on the programme to-night, and who would have done the subject justice, is not here to respond to the toast, "Our Absent Friends."

Many men have been interested in this new-county question who are not with us to-night, and whom we shall never see again in this life,—men like William Merrifield and Captain Robinson. And there is another man whom I shall always think of with the feeling that when I met him, I met a *man*. He wasn't born in this country; he was a Scotchman, and, like all good Scotchmen, he loved the land of his birth, but because he preferred a country where it wasn't necessary to have a standing army to keep the crown upon the royal head, he came to this country. A man of keen perception, of strict integrity, of great energy; a man of unusual ability; a man who was devoted to his country, and when his country called, he was ready; a man who was devoted to the interests of this community; a man who may have had his faults, but a man who had his virtues and his friends. I know that man is with us in spirit to-night. I propose the name of William N. Monies. (*Applause.*)

The guests then rose and drank to the memory of William N. Monies.

The President called upon Mr. Isaac C. Price.

Mr. Price:

Mr. Chairman and Gentlemen,—By a mere chance I am here with you this morning. I heard yesterday that during the evening of that day you were going to have the laying of the corner-stone, and I took a great deal of pleasure in attending yesterday and hearing the eloquent remarks of Judge Hand upon that occasion. I came here on my first visit some nineteen years ago, when certain gentlemen who had control of my movements thought you could not take care of yourselves. I was sent up here and remained four or five months at that time. I have listened to-night with pleasure to the remarks that have been made, and I am fully confident that if one tithe of what has been said about Lackawanna County and about Scranton City is true, you are amply sufficient to attend to your own wants at this time.

I have heard this evening that this is one of the greatest counties, the third largest city in the Commonwealth, with the best judiciary, a most numerous and most distinguished bar. Some of that is news to me. I did think that the little settlement wherein I live down on the Delaware and Schuylkill Rivers had something of a bar, and some legal talent, but it is now somewhat of a question in my mind whether it amounts to as much as I thought it did. I have about made up my mind, while sitting here, that if in my lifetime the period shall come that Mr. Dale has spoken of, and my city shall be submerged, why I'll come up here and live (*Laughter*)—that is, if you will let me ("Yes, yes, come"); for I am really glad to say that I believe that Scranton is a live place. When I first visited here nineteen years ago all of the opposite side of the street was bare. Now on every hand I see good, substantial improvements, and as year by year I visit you, these improvements stand out in bold relief before me. I am glad to see them. I have some interests here. I have had confidence in the future of Scranton, and I am pleased to fully realize that my confidence has not been misplaced. If time would permit, I should be pleased to speak of some incidents that I have witnessed here, but the morning hour warns me 'tis time to stop. I thank the President, Dr. Throop, for his invitation that permitted me to be with you and enjoy this pleasant occasion. (*Cheers.*)

The band then played a medley of "Old Lang Syne" and "Home, Sweet Home," and amid universal congratulations, all retired, each to his home as best he could to enjoy his dreams.

THE SCRANTON POOR-HOUSE.

From the first settlement of the valley in 1769 up to 1835 there is no record of a single pauper being in Providence township. This included all the territory between Blakely and Pittston. But a single "crazy person" or idiot was found in 1845 within a radius of five miles. For years afterwards foolish people were confined in a wooden cage in some remote corner of the house, without medical treatment or care, and thus they passed away their lives without murmur or complaint.

With the development of Scranton, more especially, how changed the condition of things. On the cold uplands of Newton township, seven miles from Scranton, a large tract of land was purchased some years ago by the late Henry Griffin and others for a poor farm, upon which buildings for the insane and poor were erected for the township of Providence.

A visit to this place less than a dozen years ago by Hon. John E. Barrett, then the able local of the *Scranton Daily Republican*, with the writer, led his versatile pen to portray in such a true and graphic manner the character, the number, and the treatment of the unfortunate inmates which led to a general change in every department.

People ignorant of even the existence of the poor farm began to visit and interest themselves in the place, and the taxpayers erected large and substantial buildings for the destitute and for the insane.

The institution is now in a healthy condition, and is managed by a board of directors, of which Hon. Lewis Pughe is president. Every department is looked after so carefully by Superintendent Beemer that the labor is thoroughly utilized from the pauper quarters, and the poor tax is comparatively light.

INDEX

ABBOT, John 191
ABBOTT, James 198 213 214 308 314 318 Philip 198 213 215
ACKERLEY, A I 513
ACKERLY, A I 509
ADAMS, Daniel 123 124 J B 258 259
AILSWORTH, David 295 Franklin 295 Ruth 295
ALBERT, G 447
ALBRIGHT, J J 229 544 545 546 Joseph 532 Joseph J 224 461
ALBRO, John P 478 Zeno 229
ALDEN, Fitch 127 John 128 Prime 112
ALDREN, 189 John 188
ALESWORTH, Wm 198
ALEXANDER, J M 489 J Marion 268 James 76 Mr 502
ALLEGER, Thomas J 258 Thos J 259
ALLEN, Col 184 Ethan 183 188 George 510 Horatio 355 356 385 Isaac 112 William E 267
ALLSWORTH, 275 Mr 207 208 Mrs 207 William 206 Wm 208
ALSWORTH, 322 Widow 307 William 321 Wm 318
AMERMAN, L 513
AMHERST, Governor 96
ANDERSON, 64 John 33 98 99
ANDREWS, M J 478
ANGUISH, Jacob 112
ANSLEY, Joseph 484
ARCHBALD, 452 James 299 491 499 Mr 230 R W 510 511 514 546 Robert W 457
ARCHIBALD, James 354 396
ARMSTRONG, Brigadier-Gen 180 Edward 228 Mr 76 229 386
ASBURY, Bishop 321 323 325

ASTER, John Jacob 317
ATHERTON, 195 Corn's 198 Cornelius 302 Elezer 198 Henry F 461 John 198
ATKINSON, Asher M 461
ATWATER, 307 Benj 198
AVERY, 143 177 Christopher 188
BABCOCK, 111
BACHUS, Ebenezer 113
BACKSINOSA, 70 83 84
BACON, Lord 368
BAGGLEY, 196
BAGLEY, Asher 198 James 188 198 305 Jesse 198
BAILY, 189 Benj 188 Benjamin 135
BAKEHORN, Job 33
BAKER, John F 234 Mr 494
BALDWIN, Gideon 123 188 191 Waterman 146 148 181 318
BANCROFT, G C 233
BANK, Elizabeth 385
BARBER, Mr 493
BARD, James 94
BARKER, Abel 493
BARNARD, George F 478
BARNES, William 267
BARRETT, H F 500 Horace F 510 514 J E 452 509 513 514 529 John E 466 548
BARROWMAN, Thomas 512 513
BARTHOLOMEW, D 477 478
BATES, Caleb 112 116 Capt 113 138 Solomon 195 198
BATTIN, Henry 514
BEACH, Ephraim 381 Maj 227
BEAMISH, F A 456
BEAUMONT, 498 Andrew 400
BECK, Professor 45
BEDFORD, Andrew 383 387 Deborah 165

BEEBER, T R 447 451
BEEMER, Superintendent 549
BELIN, Henry Jr 450 513
BENEDICT, 121 Mr 259 Silas 198
BENJAMIN, J 489 R S 491
BENNETT, 121 Ishmael 301
  Thomas 111 Thos 108
BENORE, John 514
BENTLEY, 457 B F 500 Benjamin F 511 Benjamin S 499
BENTON, 537 J B 267
BERRIEN, 537
BERTRONG, Jas 113
BESECKER, John 288
BESSEL, J H 447
BEVAN, Isaac 235
BIDLACK, 498
BIDWELL, David 198
BINGHAM, R 388
BISHOP, William 216 312 314
  Wm 198 304
BLACKMAN, Mr 68
BLAINE, 530
BLAIR, Mrs James 451
BLAKELEY, Johnston 269
BLANCHARD, 121 Capt 121 163
  Jeremiah 113 117 121
BLEWITT, Mine Inspector 462 P 499
BLOIS, Hiram 267
BODEMAN, F 267
BOIES, H M 451 477 482 484 490 512 514 521
BOIS, H M 452
BORTREE, Sheriff 474
BOUTON, B A 458 Bennet A 267
BOWMAN, Ebenezer 285
BOYD, 160 George B 267
BOYLE, John D 207
BRADDOCK, 34 81 397
BRADFORD, A P 478 Mr 102
BRADY, Edward 477
BRANT, 158 161 166 John 376
BRAODHEAD, Mr 34
BRECK, Charles Du Pont 268
BRIGHTMAN, Mrs S A 451
BRINKORKOOF, Garrit 149
BRINTON, Gen 474
BRISBIN, John 264 390 393 472
BRISTOL, 456 Judge 485
BROADBENT, Sidney 484

BROADHEAD, 81 84 Charles 33
  Daniel 71 75 147
BRODERICK, P F 448
BROOKS, Reese G 514
BROWN, 121 A E 380 Benj 198
  David 112 113 307 318 J E 478
  James 191 198 208 301
BRUCE, 27
BRUNDAGE, Asa H 267
BRYDEN, 365 Alexander 364
BRYSON, A Jr 477 499 Capt 477
BUCK, Mr 502 Samuel 288
BUCKALEW, Charles R 508
BUNELL, Lewis M 268
BURGESS, J C 255
BURGOYNE, 157 308
BURK, Wm 106
BURKE, Capt 479
BURNETT, Roger L 478
BURNS, A W 267 I H 510 511 T H 513
BURR, A E 267 514
BURTCH, Mr 260
BUTLAND, Mr 38
BUTLER, 162 164 167 323 498
  Chester 197 Col 165 167 J 172
  John 161 163 166 172 Lord 342
  Major 172 Z 167 168 Zeb'm
  198 Zebulon 114 131 163 166
BYRNE, M J 268 Peter 268
CALDWELL, Capt 162
CALHOUN, 537
CALVERS, Mr 34
CAMERON, Joseph P 444 447
CAMPBELL, J H 511 514 James
  323 Sidney A 267
CANNON, Waite 498
CAPOOSE, 29 30 33 55
CAPWELL, Albert M 267
CAREY, 70 121 Barnabas 117 199
  288 Eleazer 69 John 128 198
  208 307 Mr 138 168
CARL, Mr 260
CARMAULT, J E 513
CARMECKLE, John 33
CARR, David 116
CARSON, Kit 537
CARTER, Mr 318 485 Nathaniel
  288 Pulaski 205
CARY, Barnabas 115 191 Barney
  453 Elezer Jr 115

CHALMERS, 19
CHAMBERLAIN, John 198 Mrs A 451
CHAMBERS, 111 Mr 428
CHAPMAN, 22 36 51 53 105 429
CHARLES II, king of England 72 74 101 177
CHASE, A A 500 511 Aaron A 268 Ezra B 258 268 Mr 260
CHILDS, Archippus 288 Orville W 385
CHITTENDEN, Jared M 461 463
CHRISTIE, Capt 118
CIST, Jacob 342 398 Mr 397
CLAPHAN, William 28
CLARK, Deacon 129 276 278 Dr 267 Judson 135 318 Mrs O P 451 Samuel 111 William 198
CLARKESTON, Mr 491
CLAYTON, Major 95
CLEMSON, Wm F 386
CLINTON, De Witt 462
CLYMER, Mr 288
COAR, Patrick 514
COBB, Asa 198 288 289 321 378 John 50 133 290 Mrs 290 291
COFFEY, T F 448
COGWELL, William 198
COHEN, Isaac 267
COLBERT, William 233
COLEMAN, 485 John J 477
COLLINGS, 456 J B 510 512 John B 514 John Beaumont 513 Samuel P 498
COLLINS, F D 511 512 Francis D 268
COLVILLE, G M 447
CONNELL, A J 478 Mrs Wm 451 William 450
CONNER, James 198
CONNOLLY, 544 D W 512 J F 511 John F 510 511 513 514 523
CONYNGHAM, 457 John N 442 Redmond 297
COOK, Jabez 111 James 175 Mr 176 Valentine 323
COOLBAUGH, John 380 Moses W 388
COOPER, C W 444
COREY, Jenks 112 John 113 Jonathan 113 Phebe 198

CORNELL, Wm 452
CORNSTACK, 111
COSTEN, 485
COSTON, H H 513
COTRILL, Nathaniel 498
COTTRILL, Mrs 204 N 204 273 Nathaniel 203 315 383 387
COURSEN, H A 478
COURSON, A H 478 H A 477
COVEL, Mathew 198
COVEY, Ebenezer 288
COVINGTON, Brig-Gen 287
COXE, Tench 185
CRAMER, Mr 297
CRANDALL, F A 259 Mr 260
CROGAN, George 36
CROKER, Joseph 84 85
CURTIS, Anson H 458 Fred 188 John 79
CUSICK, 17
DADDOW, 463
DALE, David 288 M H 514 Mr 547 Mrs T H 451 T H 533 Thomas H 513
DALSON, Mathew 135 188
DAMAN, Peter 112
DAVID, David 308
DAVIES, Jonathan 148
DAVIS, A 258 458 Augustus 267 Dr 259 J Alton 512 John F 237 Joseph 200 217 267 Mr 502
DEAN, 305 Azariah 111 Ezra 279 James 279 Johnathan 198
DECKERS, Luke 494 Michael 494
DELANEY, J C 514
DELONG, John 111 284
DENISON, Nathan 124 131
DENNISON, Col 167
DEPEIW, John 112
DEPUY, Charles W 478 Levi 208 307 Samuel 208 315
DERBY, 456
DERSHERMER, Lawrence 288
DEWEE, David 308
DEWIT, John 188 191
DEWY, William 385
DICKINSON, 537
DICKSON, A W 452 G L 447 482 George L 480-482 James 298 James P 451 John A 480 481 Mrs George L 451 Mrs James P 451 Mrs Jas P 451

DICKSON (continued)
  Thomas 266 360 461 471 480-482 494
DIMMICK, E J 478
DIMOCK, Asa 147
DINGS, John 315 486
DOLPH, 216 Aaron 198 216
  Alexander 307 Charles 198 208 216 307 Edward 62 271 307 Isaac 208 Johnathan 198 Jonathan 216 Moses 198 216 271 307
DORRANCE, C 442 Col 167
  George 166 John 233
DOW, Lorenzo 327
DRESSER, H H 447
DRINKER, 227 253 284 288 369 382 383 384 387 443 H W 287 383 Henry 185 285 Henry Jr 284 Henry Sr 284 285 Henry W 208 222 223 284 285 380 Mr 223 228 286 381 386 Richard 56 284 285
DUNDAFF, Lord 297
DUNN, Rev Father 473
DUNNELL, H N 477
DUNNING, A B 393 499 508 513 526 Abram B 294
DUPUE, Samuel 33
DURKEE, Capt 159 167
DURKINS, John 138 Mr 138
DUWAIN, James 217 Mr 218
DYSERT, Henry 33
EATON, L L 514
EDWARDS, H M 511 514 546
  Jonathan 447 Richard 288
ELDER, John 95
ELDERKIN, Vine 123
ELDRIDGE, T N 514
ESPY, Maj 522
EVANS, Edward 478
EVENS, E B 267
EVERETT, N W 233
EVERHART, J M 514 James M 484 L F 267
EWEN, John 211
FARIES, F L 499
FAULKNER, Mr 146 Robert 146
FELL, Jesse 339 340 398 Judge 339 340
FELLOWS, Benjamin 199 Esq 456 Joseph 146 147 198 333

FELLOWS (continued)
  Joseph Sr 303 Turvy 303
FELTZ, Capt 543
FERRIS, John 307 Mr 273 493 Samuel 307 William 307
FILLMORE, Mrs B F 451
FILLSBURY, Elizar 112
FIN, James 183 Mr 184
FINCH, A P 260 484 I A 484
FINN, Solomon 149
FISH, J B 479 John 288 Joseph 113
FISHER, 280 C H 267 George 511 513
FITCH, 128 189 Governor 75 76 Maj 188
FITZSIMMONS, F J 513 539
FLANIGAN, J J 514
FLEDGET, James 113
FOLLET, Benjamin 123
FOLLETT, Benj 106 111
FORBES, General 37
FORDHAM, Mrs J R 451
FOSTER, 429
FOX, Geo 288 J M 267 John 288
FRANCIS, Tench 185
FRANKLIN, Benj 152 Benjamin 73 81 Col 184 John 183 189
FRAZIER, John 115 116
FREMONT, 537
FRENCH, Arter 115 Lucius 267
FREUDENTHAL, S 444
FREY, C L 478
FRISBY, Hiram 298
FROTHINGHAM, William 267
FULLER, 498 A C 486 E C 240 449 512 513 Edward C 444 Frederic 268 L S 240
GAIGE, H L 500 514 Henry L 510
GARDNER, A P 267 Abel D 478 Geo 279 John 111 119 192 Stephen 198
GATZMER, Wm H 414
GAY, Lord 101
GAYLOR, 199
GELHAAR, Wm 267
GENTER, Mrs J 451
GENTHU, John 288
GEORGE III, king of England 191
GI-EN-GWAH-TOH, 158
GIBBS, John W 267 Willoughby W 267

GIDDINGS, Nathaniel 200
GIFFORD, John 195 198 304
GILDERSLEEVE, Cyrus 233
GILL, Dr 24
GILLISPIE, Joseph 466
GINTHER, 397 Philip 336
GODFREY, Joseph 255 514
GOFF, James W 298
GOODMAN, M A 487
GOODRICH, 304 Phineas G 320
GOODRIDG, Wm 198
GORAM, B W 233
GORE, 111 Daniel 138 142 167 Danl 138 Obediah 335
GOSS, Mr 138 Phillip 138
GRANT, D R 514 Esquire 543 Mr 232 243 262 263 Sanford 230 231 544
GRATTAN, Thos 388
GREELEY, 540
GREEN, George 385 Job 192 Levi 112 N D 449 542 Paul 192 William 267
GRIFFIN, Alderman 305 Henry 548 Isaac 197 James 197 200 201 Jo 120 Joe 215 303 Joseph 197 507 Josh 135 Joshua 315 486 Stephen 197 Thomas 201 Thos 197 Widow 305
GRIFFIS, William 510
GUILD, George E 447
GUNSTER, Charles W 478 F W 499 508-511 513 546 Fred W 450
GUNSTUR, F E 268
HACKETT, Wm 414
HACKLEY, H 299
HAGGERTY, William 267
HAINS, Daniel 111
HALL, Nathan 198
HALLER, Daniel 113
HALSTEAD, John 198 Jonar 198 Mr 471 472 W F 479 Wm R 452
HAMILTON, Gov 73 75 94-96 113 James 72 Lt-Gov 92 Stone 298
HAMLIN, Orlo 208 267
HANCOCK, Gen 472
HAND, 452 Alfred 268 450 457 502 514 E J 485 Judge 507 524 530 547

HANDLEY, John 268 457 500 511 Judge 452
HANFORD, Nehemiah 267
HANHAM, Thomas 100
HANNAH, Daniel 268
HARDEN, Abram 113 Samuel 121 Stephen 116
HARDING, 157 Elisha 119 179 G M 512 Garrick M 500 511 Judge 457 Samuel 113
HARDY, Wm 198
HARFORD, Edmund 149
HARMAN, George 324
HARRINGTON, David C 268
HARROD, Asher 111
HARTLEY, Col 173
HARTRANFT, Gov 471 John F 510
HAUGAWOUT, George D 268
HAUTO, George F A 398 Mr 399
HAYES, 469
HAYS, John 85
HAZARD, Erskine 398 Mr 399
HEATH, Frederick 34 W H 267
HECKEWELDER, 19
HEERMANS, 456 Alva 224 Philip 216
HENDRICKS, Mrs 451 Mrs A 451
HENRY, 382 387 Mr 227-230 263 386 387 397 413 William 227 231 240 337 380 381 385 404 544
HENWOOD, Charles 487 William B 478
HESDALE, James 112
HEWIT, Capt 164 Dethic 153 160
HIBBERT, Ebenezer 198
HICKMAN, Andrew 120 188 193 Mr 173
HICKOK, M J 234
HILES, Jane 404
HILL, 498 B A 514 E S M 258 259 456 Elliot S M 268 Mr 432
HILLEGAS, Mr 397
HINDS, Samuel 487
HINES, Samuel 478
HINSDELL, H D 514
HITCHCOCK, Elisha 219 F L 477 478 499 509 510 Frederick L 268
HOCKSEY, 128 James 193 Mr 173

HOCKSEY (continued)
  Solomon 187
HOCKSY, Mr 120
HODDS, Simon 141
HODGES, Edward F 501
HODSON, Mathew 288
HOLBERT, Christopher 183
HOLDEN, James 295
HOLLAND, A D 447
HOLLENBACK, 280 Geo M 224
  George M 340 342 Judge 168
  Mathias 305
HOLLISTER, Alanson 378 Alpheus 378 388 Amasa 378 Dr 419 420 422 423 427 428 434 441 442 H 419 423 427 434 441 Horace 267 Mr 442 Wesley 288 378
HOLLSTED, Richard 181
HOLMES, 200 201 Enoch 194 198
  Enock 305
HOPKINS, Ichibod 198 Sarah E 451 Wm 112
HORAN, P J 513
HORN, G S 512
HORTON, L M 478
HOSIE, Mr 366
HOUSE, John 195
HOW, John 198 John Jr 198
HOWARD, James 198 John 187
HOWE, Brother 233 Gen 158 John 215 Seth 215
HOWES, John 217 Lydia 217
HOYT, Henry M 512 Jediah 318 Ransford 198 Stephen 198
HUBBUTS, Mr 147
HUDSON, Henry 60
HUGHES, Benjamin 451
HUGHS, B 452
HULBURT, Rheuben 111
HULL, William 493
HUNT, 192 A P 267 August 191 Augustin 113 Augustine 120 Austin 112 Mrs A E 451 T F 447 Thomas P 233
HUNTER, John 198
HUTCHINS, Mr 305
HUTCHINSON, John N 414
ILSLEY, John P 403
IVES, W W 477
JACOBS, Henry 514 Mr 502
JAMES, Owen 444

JAMES, king of England 100
JAY, 456
JENKINS, 157 420 John 106 111 119 138 183 189 Mr 107 422 442 Sheriff 123 Steuben 58 419 421 422 425 426 430 437 441
JERMYN, John 447 452 454 490 494 513 544 545
JERVIS, John B 385
JESSUP, 457 George 513 H C 514 W H 519 William H 513
JOHN, king (of England?) 527
JOHNSON, 494 Colonel 76 Ebenezer 182 F 510 F J 514 Henry 298 Jacob 310 311 322 Rev Mr 311 Roswell B 296 Solomon 121 188 Thomas 513 William 35 36 72 Wm 367
JOHNSTON, Ebenezer 181 John T 414
JONES, 177 492 D M 509 511 513 Edward 493 H I 514 Lewis 304 Lewis Jr 268 Mr 494 R Faulk 448 R S 448 W Gibson 268
JORDON, John Jr 382
JUDD, Mrs E G 451
KEARNEY, D F 514
KEIFER, F 498
KEISER, William 514
KELLOW, William 478
KENNEDY, Mrs W D 451
KERNAN, Thomas 448
KERR, S G 477
KETCHAM, W W 542
KEYS, 128 173 Timothy 120 123 187 191 193
KIDDER, 498
KIERSTED, James O 509
KING, Henry 414 Thomas 91
KING PHILIP, 18
KINGSBURY, E P 513 531 Edward P 247 H A 514 Henry A 546 Mr 502 534
KINNGSBURRY, H A 477
KLUGE, John P 267
KNAPP, H A 451 478 511 514 Joseph 308 Mr 430 Samuel O 429 Zephaniah 220
KNIGHT, J D 514
KOCH, Victor 512 514
KOLB, Jacob 447
KOON, 456

556

KOONS, John 288
KRAMER, L N 452
KRESLER, Mr 255
LACKEY, Harper B 267
LADD, Horace 267
LAFLIN, 490
LAFRANCE, John 288
LAFRONSE, Mr 303 Phebe 217
LAKE, Lot 448
LAMKINS, John 198
LANGSTAFF, Mrs D 451
LANNING, Mr 266 481
LANSING, J A 486
LATHROP, Charles E 258 F S 471 Salmon 298 Thomas R 513
LAWRENCE, Rufus 141
LEACH, 173 277 278 456 Ebenezer 276 Ephraim 149 276 Mr 278
LEBAR, H M 388
LEDLIE, Dr 113
LEE, J L 510 John 111 John L 499 Joseph 111
LEET, N Y 267
LEGGETT, Gabriel 318 James 134 135 188 Mr 194
LEISENRING, John 403
LEONARD, B E 513 John 111 William 111
LEUCHENS, 271 Nicholas 270 306
LEVERETT, Johnathan 267
LEWIS, 296 G C 447 James 198 199 295 John 279 Mr 502 W J 500 511
LILLIBRIDGE, Levi 498
LINDERMAN, Mr 492
LINEN, J A 478
LODER, Mr 244
LOFTUS, M W 456
LOGAN, H V 478 S C 447
LOGGIT, 135
LONG, John 235
LOOMIS, Francis E 268
LOVELAND, Mrs H A 451
LUCE, Benjamin 181 Mrs R W 451 R W 452
LUDWIG, E A 259
LUNNON, Edward 208
LUTZ, Conrad 307 Coonrad 195 198 Jacob 195 198 John 198 307 Michael 486

LUTZE, 196
LUTZENS, Nicholas 198
LUTZS, Mich 198
LYDIAS, Mr 76
LYNCH, J J 500 James 510
LYNDE, Edward C 247
LYNETT, E J 500
LYNOTT, E J 510
LYONS, 177
MACDANIEL, John 198
MACK, 23
MACLAREN, John 260
MADISON, H R 478
MADOX, G H 477
MAHOMET, 17
MAHON, James 268
MALLORY, Judge 457
MANNESS, W W 232 William 543
MANROW, Charles 181
MANVILLE, R 355 360 461
MARCY, 121 173 Ebenezer 112 113 116 149 301 318 Zebulon 116 162 192
MARPLE, A A 235
MARR, Charles 267
MARSH, N F 267
MARSHALL, Mr 266 481
MARTIN, Capt 329
MARVIN, R E 298 Samuel 111
MASON, 533
MASSASOIT, 18
MASSER, G W 259 George W 267 458 Mrs H A 451
MATHEWS, Peter 112
MATTES, C C 478 Charles F 232 542 543 P H 232 Philip H 231 544
MATTHEWS, Mrs C P 451 R J 450 452
MAY, William A 478
MCANDREWS, R A 448
MCCABE, John 514 R T 514
MCCALPINE, John 299
MCCARTNEY, F A 259
MCCLAY, William 174
MCCLINTOCK, Adw T 442
MCDANIELS, W 514 Wm 306
MCDOWELL, John 111 John Jr 111
MCGINLIE, 267
MCKEAL, Michael 203

MCKINNEY, C W 514 Carl 474 Mr 473
MCKUNE, Mayor 472-474 R H 456 509 511 536 Robert 502 Robert H 471 513 514
MCLAREN, John 484
MCMANUS, Rev Dr 448
MCMICHAEL, 34 John 33
MCNULTY, A 514
MEAD, Selah 305
MEREDITH, 253 369 383 Mr 288 Wm 223
MERRIAN, S C 477
MERRIFIELD, 498 E 507 509 511 Ed 452 Edward 268 512 514 517 Judge 216 William 220 229 315 497 507 527 546 Wm 304
MEYERS, J H 444
MEYLERT, 533
MICKSCH, Christian 337
MILLAR, W S 478
MILLER, 456 485 Christopher 198 Elder 276 281 John 195 276 280 297 300 Samuel 198 318
MILLS, John 199 Stephen 298
MILNER, Charles 19
MINER, 20 33 36 105 117 122 132 160 173 220 Bill 423 Charles 46 118 153 305 309 338 342 398 Mr 34 352 William P 464
MITCHELL, J D 234 Michael 288
MOFFITT, Mrs E S 451 P M 511 513
MOIR, James 478
MONIES, Col 466 William N 456 499 510 547
MOODY, P H 267
MOORE, John W 252 Mrs Thomas 451 Thos 452
MORGAN, B G 450
MORRIS, Gov 29 39 76 77 John 514
MORTON, Henry 514
MOSES, H D 514
MOSS, Joseph 111
MOTT, 493 Barton 230 443 Ithamar 288
MULLER, L C 444
MURRAY, C A 386 Charles Augustus 386
MYERS, Philip 342

NAGEL, P 235
NASH, S M 447
NAYLOR, N E 447
NELSON, Mortin 116
NEWELL, J V 233 447
NEWMAN, John B 501 Jonathan 317 318 Martin L 542
NEWTON, 493
NICHOLS, Andrew 461
NICHOLSON, John 185
NOBLE, Mr 347
NOBLES, 345 David 344 346 Mr 297 345
NORRIS, Isaac 73
NUGENT, Washington G 458
NULTRIP, Ebenezer 111
NYCE, W 388
O'HARA, William 448
OBEDIKE, Lodwick 199
OBER, Mrs Joseph 451
OGDEN, Amos 107 Capt 113 122 123 Mr 107
OJIDIRK, 189 Lodwick 188
OLMSTEAD, R W 543
OLYPHANT, George T 360 President 461 494
OSBORN, John 112
OSBORNE, Col 471 Maj-Gen 522
OSGOOD, Joseph 267
OSPUCK, Henry 288
OVERFIELD, A 388
OWEN, Anning 323 326 Elder 324 326
PACKER, Asa 413 Judge 414 Mr 46 Robert A 417
PANCOST, Mr 306
PARK, Ebenezer 199
PARKER, 278 George 296 Stephen 276
PARKS, N G 234 Silas 112
PARSONS, C 442 Major 37 William 71 Wm 75
PATTERSON, Alex'r 176
PATTISON, Gov 450
PAYNE, Mrs 449
PEARCE, 105
PECK, 105 Dr 220 342 George 325 403 Rev Dr 233 Samuel 493
PECKENS, E R 461
PEDRICK, Ben 199 Benjamin 195
PEIRCE, Ezekiel 124
PENCIL, John 170

PENDERGRAST, P 234
PENDLETON, J Philip B 447
PENN, Governor 30 97-99 107 110
    John 73 99 131 Mr 97 103
    Richd 73 Wm 72 98 102 103
PERKINS, Mrs W H 451 W H 484
    William H 482
PERRY, I G 513
PHELPS, H A 390 John C 482
PHILIP, 18
PHILIPS, Comer 308 John 317
    318
PHILLIPS, 120 Frank 117 John
    117 118 141 301
PHINNEY, Mrs 204
PICKET, Thomas 199
PIER, Dr 240 W H 458 514 William H 267
PIERCE, Ezekiel 141 H S 451 452
    509 512 513 Horatio S 466 509
PIERSON, Benjamin 480 C T 480
    Job 385 Joseph 480
PIKE, 160
PITCHER, C R 514
PITT, Wm 120
PLACE, I 388
PLATT, J C 247 451 452 490 Mr
    243
POCAHONTAS, 20
POOR, John M 298 466
PORTER, James M 413 James N
    380
POST, Christian Frederic 82
    Frederic 85 Isaac J 268 Mr 86
POTTER, 456 David 199 Elisha
    233 Elisha S 203 204 271 383
    455 Mr 289 Squire 324
POWDERLY, T V 456 510 511
POWELL, John H 509 Mrs L B
    451
PRATT, Wm H 268
PRESTON, Paul S 346
PRICE, Col 452 463 Eli K 494 G
    A 452 Isaac 513 Isaac C 501
    547 J A 464 486 513 Mr 306
PRYOR, C E 514
PUGHE, Lewis 452 466 469 493
    499 508 509 511 514 526 549
    Mr 494
PUKITS, Thos 188
QUEEN ESTHER, 162 166 171
    432

RAFERTY, Dr 458
RALPH, Johnathan 199
RANCH, J M C 268
RANDALL, 498 David R 268
RANKIN, 498
RANKINS, Daniel 268
RANSOM, Capt 159
RAYNOLD, William 140
RAYNOR, Samuel 298
READ, Mr 102
REED, Joseph 176 S P 267
REESE, Robert 514
REEVES, Robert 500
REGAN, Jeremiah D 268
REINE, Abel 142 Timothy Jr 116
RENSHAW, A M 499 A Miner 510
REYNOLDS, Dr 267
RICARDO, Dr 267
RICE, C E 513 Judge 519
RICHMOND, Mr 497 W H 452
    William H 466 Wm H 494
RICKETSON, William 229
RIPPLE, Col 452 474 E II 451
    477 478
RIX, George 295
ROBATHAN, John W 267
ROBERTS, Dr 466 Henry 267 465
    N B 267 Nathan 305
ROBINSON, Capt 546 Dr 240 440
    J M 432 Jacob 508 Silas B 55
    201 267 458 W C 235
ROCKWELL, H B 485 W B 479
    Wm B 485
ROESLER, Charles W 449 Mr 502
ROGERS, Professor 331 Stephen
    298 William E 267
ROSS, John 288 Nathan 199
    Timothy 199 William 288
    William S 507 Wm 199
ROWLAND, Mr 38
ROZEL, John 199
RUPERT, Peter 288
RUSH, Benj V 388
RUSSELL, H G 447
SAINT JOHN, 121 173 Dan'l 112
SAMTER, S 514
SANDERSON, George 268 307 486
    509 513 George Jr 513 Thos
    452
SANDS, William 543
SANFORD, David 112 113 Joseph
    David 115

SARGEANT, Mr 102
SAUNDERS, R H 510
SAWYER, 121
SAYRE, Robert H 413
SCARGG, John F 514
SCHARAR, Chris 461 Ed 461
SCHELLE, John 448
SCHOOLCRAFT, 45 436 439 Mr 47
SCHOONMAKER, A H 233 U G 509 511 513
SCHULL, Wm 335
SCHUYLER, Gen 159
SCOT, John 152
SCOTT, Daniel 199 282 David 380 Elias 282 308 John 308 Mr 283 Mrs C B 451 Zephaniah 308
SCRAGG, John F 512 514
SCRANTON, Charles 514 541 Col 239 243 254 255 346 387 404 408-410 E C 238 Geo W 230 388 George W 231 236 247 252 253 341 389 403 407 543 544 546 J A 509 512 Jane 404 John 403 Joseph 243 Joseph A 444 Joseph H 238 243 244 247 255 341 544 Mr 227 260 262 534 538 S T 540 Selden 243 Selden T 230 231 239 240 247 255 514 541 544 W W 471 513
SEAMANS, George B 509
SEAMONS, George B 267
SEARLES, 189 Constant 117 195 199 314 318 Ebenezer 188
SEAVERS, Daniel 267
SECOR, John 307
SELAH, Obediah 199
SEVERANCE, Otis 204
SEWARD, 537
SHAW, Mr 432
SHERRERD, John B 240 267 Samuel 268
SHIPHERD, 530
SHOEMAKER, Benj 106 111 Benj Jr 111
SHOOMAKER, S W 388
SHRAWDER, Capt 118
SIGOURNEY, Mrs 42
SILBEY, 121
SILKMAN, 499 Charles H 268 498 541 Daniel 195 305 H O 486 Henry O 262

SILLS, Shadrick 199
SILSBEE, Jonathan 493
SIMPSON, George 492 Mrs C D 451
SIMRAL, Wm 199
SKINNER, Winley 296
SLAITER, Samuel 199
SLATER, Saml Jr 124 Samuel 113
SLAUGHTER, Sam'l 112
SLIGH, D G 491
SLOAN, President 393 Samuel 390 471 479
SLOCUM, 154 219 221 443 456 Benj 220 Benjamin 147 216-218 220 308 Ebenezer 147 216-218 220 222 308 Ebenezer Sr 216 Frances 220 Johnathan 188 Jonathan 188 220 Joseph 222 342 Mr 221 229 Phebe 217 Samuel 222
SLOUGHER, Samuel 116
SMITH, 20 278 C 511 Charles 298 Cornelius 510 Deodat 275 302 Dr 152 153 E O 478 Elhanan 514 J E 512 Jno B 377 John 18 111 John B 211 371 450 452 509 M D 477 Mr 372 Theodore 259 Thomas 199 275 276 383 387 Thos 302 W T 511 513 William Hooker 151 337 William T 450 Wm Hooker 153 218 302 323
SNAITH, John 501 513
SNYDER, Eugene 500 510 Peter A 494
SNYDERS, Eugine 295
SOMMERS, Henry 514
SPENCER, 456 485 David 444 447 Mr 488
SPRAUGE, Dr 151 Granny 150 Joseph 121 150
SQUIRE, R A 513
SQUIRES, Ralph A 267
STAFFORD, John 215
STAHL, M F 447
STANTON, Abraham 135 Judge 457 W H 456 478 511 William H 500 Wm 199 268
STAPLES, John 135 305 Joseph 140
STARBURD, F 388
STEANS, W I 448

STELLE, Mrs J L 451
STEPHEN, Timothy 199
STERNS, John O 414
STETLER, Mrs S N 451
STEVENS, 128 189 270 A B 499 510 Asa 142 C A 267 Elephat L 149 Elipolet 112 John 121 127 Mr 147 502 Timothy 149 306
STEWART, Charles 110 335 Lazarus 114 Mr 107 Thomas 267 513 Thomas Jr 514 William 138 146
STILES, Horace 296
STILL, Isaac 82 85
STODDARD, John 285
STOKES, S 380
STORRS, Brother 532 Mr 535 W R 471
STOTT, Capt 239
STROND, Jacob 29
STRONG, 321 Seth 320 Solomon 135 149 183 188
STROUD, Daniel 380 Jacob D 380 Jas H 388
STUBBS, Samuel 112
STUDEVANT, S Burton 267
STULL, John 288 Lewis 288
STUMP, Frederic 98
STURDEVANT, Byron D 233 E W 442
STURGES, E B 451 512 513
SULLIVAN, 152 175 Gen 69 174 176 193 337 416
SUMMERS, David 510
SUTTON, James 153 302 323
SWARTS, Daniel 182
SWARTZ, Jacob 288 Philip 208
SWEET, Thomas 298 458
SWIFT, Dr 428 431
TAYLOR, Abraham 199 Brother 325 Daniel 199 233 314 318 John 120 199 Preserved 195 199 233 323 324 342 Reuben 215 303 Samuel 388
TEAL, John 63 Mr 69
TEEDYUSCUNG, 35 36 38 39 41 70 83-87 89 91 92 106 137
TETAMY, Moses 82 85
THAYER, David 135
THOMAS, J R 510 Joshua R 499

THOMPSON, George B 478 John 288
THOMSON, Chas 137
THROOP, B H 447 449 494 498 509 511 512 514 546 Benjamin H 267 509 Dr 60 239 240 247 432 452 458 527 548 George 514 H B 514
TIDD, James 33
TIERNEY, Dennis 500
TIERNY, Dennis 510
TILSTON, Mr 485
TOMLINSON, A B 437 John 513 Joseph 437
TOMPKINS, Ben 199
TOMSON, Charles 82
TORREY, Jason 287
TOTOMY, Moses 30
TOWNSEND, E M 299
TRAVERS, Edward 500
TRAVIS, Levi 201 Mr 493
TRIPP, 129 143 196 500 Amasey 199 Henry D 318 Henry Dow 317 Ira 127 304 452 513 527 Isaac 106 122 123 127 128 139 147 149 173 176 191-193 199 304 318 Isaac 3d 193 Isaac Jr 188 199 Isaac Sr 127 129 197 217 Isaac the elder 128 Isooc 124 Job 192 279 317 318 John 306 Mr 135 188 Sam 253 Stephen 147 149 193 194 199 304 333 374 Wm 304
TRUMBULL, Jonth 131
TRYP, Esq 138 Isaac 146 Isaak 122 Job 140
TRYPP, Isooc 188
TUNSTALL, John 485 Stephen 485
TURNBULL, William 38
UNDERWOOD, Gideon 239 267 458
UTTER, Abraham 113
VANBERGEN, 489 J B 490 514
VANBUSKIRK, Mr 502
VANCLEFT, A J 444
VANDERLIP, Frederick 191
VANDLING, A H 452 461
VANFLEET, Charles G 268
VANSCHOICK, Mr 502 R W 507
VAUDREUIL, Gov 397

VAUGHN, John 147 220 306 323 Moses 149 305
VOLNEY, C F 44
VONSTORCH, 305 342 456 Gregory 485 H C L 200 305 340 Mr 341 Mrs Wm 451 William 485
VOSBURG, 493
WADERMAN, 296 Daniel 195 201 Henry 305 Peter 295 Ruth 295
WAGNER, F 259 267
WALL, Ezra 279
WALLACE, 27
WALLER, Joseph 233
WALSH, P M 499 Peter 508
WALTER, J S 267 Philip 227
WALTON, Izaak 530
WARD, 456 485 Simeon 232 W G 456 Washington G 268 Zebulon M 268
WARDELL, Edward 288
WASHBURN, Elizabeth 199
WASHINGTON, Gen 157 158
WATRES, L A 450-452 478 514 Lewis S 271
WEBSTER, 537
WEHLAU, L 513
WEHRUM, H 513
WEILSON, Martin 112
WEISER, Conrad 23-25 34 39 75 96
WEISS, Col 397 Jacob 336 Mr 397
WEISSKOPFF, Eugene 448
WELCH, Jacob 111 Mr 56
WELLES, C H 513 Charles H 451
WELLS, Corydon H 268 509 Erastus 267 Thomas F 512
WEST, Ebenezer 112 113 John 208 Richard 113 William 192
WESTON, Charles T 479 E W 360 Edward W 461
WEYBURN, Samuel 111
WHALING, Henry 486
WHARBURT, John 111
WHEAT, John 111
WHEELER, 469 Silas M 259 458
WHELAN, J B 448
WHITE, Josiah 398 399 L 485 Mr 492
WHITNEY, 429
WHITTEY, Moses 234
WHITTLESEY, 167 F 385

WHITTY, M 448 Moses 450
WILBUR, Christopher E 296 Mr 297
WILCOX, Mark 185
WILKOX, Stephen 112
WILLARD, E N 452 509 511 Edward N 268 509
WILLIAMS, J 267 J J 513 J W 447 James J 492 P 112 Topez 112 W W 514
WILLIAMSON, Mr 502
WILOHICK, Samuel 288
WILSON, Henry 478 Isaac 301 Jared 385 Julian N 267 Mr 102 Robert G 429
WINTERMOOT, 156 161 163
WINTERS, Peter 267
WINTON, A H 509 511 512 514 Aretus H 268 509 Mr 517 519 520 523 526 528 529 531 533 536 539 540 Mrs W W 451 W W 492 512 513 William W 509
WISE, 493
WOOD, J A 233
WOODWARD, 457 Chief-Justice 469 Frank B 498 Franklin B 258 Judge 522 Richard 112 Stanley 514 517 Warren J 132
WRAGG, John 288
WRIGHT, 111 498 Benjamin 350 Judge 385 Thomas 199
WURTS, 224 253 340 347 354 357 369 390 443 453 488 Charles 370 Charles P 480 494 John 358 Maurice 223 269 297 300 341 343 346 348 349 352 357 358 360 461 464 480 Mr 345 William 269 297 300 341 343 344 348 350 352 358 360 370 461 464 488 Wm 223 493
YARINGTON, D 298
YARRINGTON, D 488
YEAGER, H H 514
YOUNG, C F 360 Coe F 461
YOUNGS, 128 John 121 Mary 121
YOUNGS, Thos 298
YURIK, 490
ZEISBERGER, David 78
ZINZENDORF, 23 Count 22 24 29
ZISBERGER, David 367
ZITZELMANN, P F 448
ZWEIZIG, M L 447

www.ingramcontent.com/pod-product-compliance
Lightning Source LLC
Chambersburg PA
CBHW052136300426
44115CB00011B/1401